Career Counseling

Career Counseling

Theoretical and Practical Perspectives

Edited by

Stephen G. Weinrach
Villanova University

McGraw-Hill Book Company

New York St. Louis San Francisco Auckland Bogotá Düsseldorf
Johannesburg London Madrid Mexico Montreal New Delhi
Panama Paris São Paulo Singapore Sydney Tokyo Toronto

CAREER COUNSELING: Theoretical and Practical Perspectives

1 2 3 4 5 6 7 8 9 0   FGRFGR   7 8 3 2 1 0 9

This book was set in Times Roman by BookTech, Inc. (ECU).
The editors were Eric M. Munson and David Dunham;
the cover was designed by Charles A. Carson;
the production supervisor was Leroy A. Young.
Fairfield Graphics was printer and binder.

Library of Congress Cataloging in Publication Data

Main entry under title:

Career counseling.

 Includes bibliographies and indexes.
 1. Vocational guidance—Addresses, essays,
lectures.   I. Weinrach, Stephen G.
HF5381.C26524   378.1′94′25   78-23447
ISBN 0-07-069017-0

Contents

Section 1
THE COUNSELOR AND SOCIETY: PRESSURE FROM ALL SIDES

Section 2

STRUCTURAL APPROACHES

Section 3
PROCESS APPROACHES

Section 4

SPECIAL TREATMENT GROUPS

Section 5

COUNSELING ACROSS A LIFE SPAN

List of Contributors

STANLEY B. BAKER
Pennsylvania State University

RAY H. BIXLER
University of Minnesota

VIRGINIA H. BIXLER
Vince A. Day Center, Minneapolis
Minnesota

HENRY BOROW
University of Minnesota

DONN E. BROLIN
University of Missouri—Columbia

ROBERT E. CAMPBELL
Ohio State University

LESLIE H. COCHRAN
Central Michigan University

JOSIAH S. DILLEY
University of Wisconsin—Madison

ELI GINZBERG
Columbia University

NORMAN C. GYSBERS
University of Missouri—Columbia

L. SUNNY HANSEN
University of Minnesota

JO ANN HARRIS
Willowbrook High School, Villa Park,
Illinois

SAMUEL T. HELMS
Center for Social Organization of Schools,
Johns Hopkins University

EDWIN L. HERR
Pennsylvania State University

JOHN J. HORAN
Pennsylvania State University

JAMES C. HURST
Colorado State University

DAVID A. JEPSEN
University of Iowa

MARTIN R. KATZ
Educational Testing Service

EARL J. MOORE
University of Missouri—Columbia

JAMES I. MORGAN
University of Florida

WESTON H. MORRILL
Colorado State University

RICHARD J. NOETH
American College Testing Program

EUGENE R. OETTING
Colorado State University

PATRICIA M. OLSSON
Augsburg College

JAMES M. ORR, JR.
University of Florida

ROBERT P. OVERS
Vocational Guidance and Rehabilitation
Service, Cleveland, Ohio

DALE J. PREDIGER
American College Testing Program

ANNE ROE
Harvard University

JOHN D. ROTH
American College Testing Program

DANIEL SINICK
George Washington University

THOMAS M. SKOVHOLT
University of Minnesota

EDWARD D. SMITH
West Chester State College

RICHARD R. STEPHENSON
University of Iowa

DONALD E. SUPER
Columbia University

RICHARD J. THONI
Augsburg College

CHARLES F. WARNATH
Oregon State University

STEPHEN G. WEINRACH
Villanova University

ROBERT H. WOODY
University of Maryland

Preface

Work is a major part of human experience. Many people spend more time at work than at any other activity, except perhaps sleep. Work has a major impact on other aspects of existence. To some extent, work defines our socioeconomic status, where we live, whom we socialize with, how we spend our leisure time, and our hopes and aspirations. Work is so central to most people's daily existence that their entire outlook is affected by it as is, in many cases, their mental health. Problems that people experience at work often manifest themselves in other parts of their lives. In essence, a vocational decision implies a life-style decision. Probably the most important decisions people make deal with their choices of work. *Career Counseling: Theoretical and Practical Perspectives* is designed to provide an even balance between the *theory* and the *practice* of career counseling. This book emphasizes the vocational needs of individuals across their life span and the needs of special populations.

Career Counseling is divided into five sections. Section One, "The Counselor and Society: Pressure from All Sides," presents some of the realities of vocational counseling, including many of its contradictions, limitations, and shortcomings. This section concludes with a list of strategies by which counselors can increase their impact on society. Sections Two and Three deal with various approaches to career counseling. Section Two, "Structural Approaches," which includes the trait-and-factor approach and the theories of Holland and Roe, provides an explicit link between the worker and the world of work. Section Three, "Process Approaches," focuses on how careers develop and includes the theories of Ginzberg and Super, as well as a survey of behavioral-counseling, decision-making, and systems approaches to career counseling.

There are basically two types of articles represented in this collection—those which are theoretical and those which describe how to apply the theories. In selecting the theoretical readings, I have tried as much as possible to include the "classics." However, since some of these were originally published over a quarter of a century ago, there were cases when the classic texts were no longer appropriate. Although there is an abundance of literature dealing with the trait-and-factor approach, there is no single article which describes its current status. Also, Holland's theory has undergone major revisions since its inception in 1959, and no article existed which adequately reflected its more recent changes. Hence, I prepared two articles specifically to fill the void.

At the time when many of the classic articles originally appeared, authors tended to employ the male singular pronoun, *he*, in discussions pertaining to both men and women. More recent articles tend to reflect our greater awareness of the implications of nonsexist language for sex-fair counseling. However, in Chapter 8, I myself make an exception in my discussion of the "nature of man." The discussion obviously applies both to men and women, but I have been unable to come up with a satisfactory substitute for "man" when dealing with certain philosophical issues.

I frankly had the most fun with the articles which describe how to apply the theories. Theorists tend to be highly creative individuals, but their work is often technical, even tedious. But I gained a new respect for members of our profession who have developed imaginative, original ways to apply theory. In selecting the application articles, I made no effort to single out an article which would provide a definitive model for applying any given theory. Rather, I tended to favor those which demonstrated a unique, creative way in which some small part of the theory could be applied. In a few cases, I was able to find pairs of articles which contradicted each other. These pairs were included as reminders that there are many ways to help, and that we do not yet know which way is best.

No existing approach adequately explains the vocational behavior of the wide diversity of populations that counselors are expected to serve. Section Four, "Special Treatment Groups," includes articles on the unique counseling needs of women, men, the disadvantaged, and the disabled. Section Five deals with individuals across their life span. Entitled "Counseling across a Life Span," this section considers the types of interventions appropriate for children, young non-college-bound adults, college students, and those about to make a mid-life career change or about to retire. The book concludes with a proposal for viewing the entire career-counseling enterprise in terms of *life career development*.

This book is designed to elicit the reader's active participation. Counseling is a practitioner's discipline. Learning about theories is an essential prerequisite to *doing* the things counselors do to help people. Considerable time has been devoted to the preparation of exercises and activities which are carefully coordinated with the readings. A complete learning experience must include both a mastery of the concepts and practice in the skills associated with career counseling. Reading books cannot make a full-fledged counselor, but students who satisfactorily complete the exercises will be well on their way to performing many of the central services of career counseling.

At the end of each section, there are two types of follow-up activities. First there is a series of questions which for the most part the student can complete independently. The questions test recall of basic facts and require conceptual analysis and synthesis. Where appropriate, the questions help the student integrate the ideas of several contributors. Second, there is a series of activities called "Learn by Doing," which usually require students to work together, often outside the classroom setting. These activities are designed to give the student the chance to practice what has been learned in the classroom.

Two activities are frequently repeated: *interviewing* and *conducting group guidance lessons.* Interviewing, regardless of philosophical orientation or purpose of intervention, is the common thread that ties all forms of counseling together. Group guidance lessons are an efficient method for providing large groups of individuals with career counseling at a relatively low cost. Complete ordering information for all simulated materials mentioned in these activities is provided in Appendix H.

Each section concludes with a section called *Additional Resources.* These bibliographies include both print and nonprint materials. It is unlikely that a basic text such as this one could fully accommodate the varied and specific interests of all its readers. Students interested in exploring topics in greater depth should find these bibliographies helpful.

The sources and uses of occupational information are an integral part of career counseling. Information is only valuable when it is relevant, accurate, and *integrated* into the counseling experience. The identification of sources relies heavily on basic library-research skills; evaluating and using occupational information calls for counseling-related skills. Increasingly, counselors are expected to make prepurchase decisions about the potential value of certain materials. The emphasis here is on effective selection, evaluation, and use of simulated materials *within the context* of career counseling. Therefore, there is no separate section devoted to the topic. Exercises following each chapter, call upon students to *select*, *evaluate*, and *use* print and nonprint materials within the counseling context. These exercises stress the mastery of skills rather than the recall of sources of information. Appendix F contains a set of guidelines that facilitate this process.

The appendices are extensive because I am committed to providing students with an opportunity to *practice* outside the classroom what they have *learned* inside the classroom. Appended matter includes, among other things, guidelines for interviewing, preparing case studies, evaluating simulated career guidance materials, and abstracting articles. The appendices are coordinated with the follow-up activities so that students can complete the Questions and the Learn-by-Doing activities with a minimal amount of teacher intervention.

Who is this book for? Earlier drafts of it have been used successfully with preservice students enrolled in basic career counseling courses variously known as Career Development Theory and Informational Sevices, Occupational Guidance, Vocational Counseling, and Career Counseling. The contents are not geared to a particular work setting, and will be appropriate for individuals working in schools, agencies, and postsecondary educational institutions. The material will also meet the needs of those interested in the counseling aspects of career and vocational education. The exercises following each chapter are for the most part equally appropriate for teachers and counselors. The book is intended both for preservice and in-service training of individuals who will be helping others deal more effectively with the world of work. Each section should be viewed as a self-contained unit devoted to one particular aspect of career counseling, and portions of the book can be adapted to meet the time constraints of workshops and staff-development programs. When the text is used for these purposes, the follow-up activities in general and the Learn by Doing exercises in particular should be emphasized. Doing is basic to learning.

This text was created with the direct and indirect assistance of many individuals. I am indebted to the contributors, without whose permission this collection would not have been possible. Institutional affiliations as indicated in the list of contributors were current at the time the articles were originally published. The administration of Villanova University has consistently encouraged me to explore and to develop new materials by providing generous support and considerable experimental freedom. The secretaries who typed the final draft from my rough notes deserve a deciphering award. I am indebted to many graduate students who shared with me, whether I wanted to hear or not, their critical comments on the relative merits of the voluminous handouts I have distributed. With the publication of this collection, I promise to be content—at least for a while. Patricia Broderick and Catherine Sullivan, two graduate assistants who helped in various aspects of the preparation of the book, were a pleasure to work with.

Dr. John Holland has influenced my thinking. Probably more than anyone else, he has helped me conceptualize what career counseling is all about. Dr. L. Sunny Hansen has been exceptionally generous with her time and has taught me new ways to apply familiar theories. Dr. Elizabeth Van Dalsem provided invaluable editorial assistance at various critical stages of this project. I consider myself fortunate to have had the opportunity to benefit from the experience and wisdom of those named above.

There are five people who have had a major impact on my life. Each in his own way has reached out and touched me. Rea Alsup, Leo Goldman, Allen Ivey, Jeffrey Messing, and Derald Sue have been excellent teachers, stern critics, superior role models, and, above all else, beloved friends. My life is so much the richer for having the opportunity to spend time with them at work and at play, both.

I would not be writing this preface in the first place if it were not for the encouragement, support, and love which I have consistently received from my best friend, Esther Weinrach. Her generosity in sharing me with my typewriter is only exceeded by her good nature, patience, understanding, and beauty. She has been the best friend a fellow could ever hope for. Thank you all.

Stephen G. Weinrach

Career Counseling

The Counselor and Society: Pressure from All Sides

Work!
Who likes it?
Who controls it?
What role do counselors play?

Regardless of their reasons or their culture, men and women have worked for thousands of years. Many of the values we associate with work today have been transmitted to us from earlier generations. Our ancestors' desire for more personally fulfilling work has not left us. Today's workers want the power to integrate their work into meaningful life-styles. People have become more sophisticated and sensitive to their own need for fulfillment. Client awareness combined with increased economic pressures has placed vocational counselors in a highly sensitive position.

Section One deals with the counselor's interaction with the world of work. The role of the vocational counselor in industrialized society is to assist clients in their career development. Yet, counselors can expect to experience obstacles and barriers. As frustrating as it is for counselors, today's clients can anticipate economic sanctions, various forms of discrimination, and stiff competition for few jobs. The realities of the world of work are not always encouraging, and they place a great responsibility both on the counselor and the client. Counselors need to understand how to effect change within the educational system, and must participate in active, not passive, outreach strategies.

The contributors to this section provide partial solutions to some of the problems discussed above. In "Shifting Postures toward Work: A Tracing," Henry Borow reflects on the cultural and religious influences on the American work ethic and concludes that today's youth want more, not less, from their work experience; but the likelihood of getting more from the work experience may be determined more by economic realities than by client desires. In "The Interaction of Vocational Counseling with the Economic System," Robert Overs discusses basic principles of labor economics and vocational counseling, pointing out that the attainment of client vocational goals and society's attainment of economic stability are often mutually exclusive. For example, vocational counseling insists that individuals should have the right to choose whatever occupation they like; labor economics, however, is simply concerned with the efficient utilization of the work force, when necessary at the expense of individual worker fulfillment.

In "Dimensions of Counselor Functioning," Morrill, Oetting, and Hurst analyze the various ways counselors function. They have provided a model that expands the traditional dyadic model of interviewing that has gained wide acceptance over the past quarter century. According to Morrill et al., counselor intervention can be viewed in terms of *targets, methods*, and *purposes*. Targets include individuals, primary groups, associational groups, and institutions or communities. The purposes of intervening include remediation, prevention, and development. Media, consultation and training, and direct service are the three methods of intervention. The model outlined in this selection is central to the organization of this book and will be referred to in introductions to later sections. An organizational scheme such as this can assist counselors to identify systematically what they are doing, for whom, and how. Such an approach increases the likelihood of counselor effectiveness since it is based upon an evaluation of client needs before counselor intervention begins.

Morrill et al. provide a scheme by which counselors can identify their clients' needs; Campbell articulates several specific needs which vocational counselors are likely to encounter. In "Career Guidance Practices Transcending the Present," he identifies trends for the 1970s, and predicts that targets requiring the most attention will prove to be group career counseling, computer-assisted guidance, practices for special groups, career education, and assessment of career development. Campbell is not alone in calling for closer scrutiny of career development practices.

Eli Ginzberg's critical assessment of the present status of guidance in the United States indicates that counselors do not spend their professional time wisely. In "A Critical Look at Career Guidance," he urges counselors to spend less time dealing with clients' emotional problems and more with the cognitive processes which lead to better career choices. Ginzberg is an economist and approaches his topic systematically. In this article, he integrates the economic realities as presented by Overs with the strategies for client support as recommended by Morrill, Oetting, and Hurst. Ginzberg contends that successful vocational counseling is not the counselor's *exclusive* domain; it requires the coordination of a wide range of society's resources.

This book is concerned primarily with *one* of society's resources—its counselors. It is to society's best interest that vocational counselors function efficiently. In the past, experienced counselors have found that working from a theoretical orientation facilitates effective functioning. Theories serve as road maps. They provide a rationale for counselor and client alike. Vocational counseling consists of assisting clients in exploring a wide range of variables. The theories help organize these variables into a manageable format. Unfortunately, the theories are incomplete, account for precious little vocational behavior, and contradict each other. Charles Warnath's "Vocational Theories: Direction to Nowhere" provides an introduction to the theories presented in later chapters of this book. Warnath's criticism raises valid questions, but the theories presented in this book are pretty much the only ones we have. At the present time we do not have a single integrated theory of career choice. If we did, there would be little need for this book. We would have the knowledge and technology to write prescriptions to relieve the frustrations of helping clients make and implement better career decisions. Warnath wonders if vocational counseling, as we know it today, can make any difference for clients at all.

Daniel Sinick believes that counselors *can* make a difference. In "Can Vocational Counselors Change Society?" he suggests several strategies for intervention geared to several different targets: Clients, their environments, employers of counselors, professional associations, and vocational counselors themselves. Written from an optimistic perspective, Sinick suggests that counselors no longer need to accept automatically the constraints imposed by society, and his article serves as a reply to Warnath's.

The past has taught us that no single approach will work all the time, for every client, in every setting. Professional helpers, such as teachers, administrators, and counselors, need to be flexible. There is much truth in the adage, Different strokes for different folks. The first step toward differential diagnosis and differential treatment is to articulate the issues confronting the vocational counselor. The readings in Section One are intended to assist students to recognize the enormous challenge vocational counselors confront.

1. Shifting Postures toward Work: A Tracing*

Henry Borow

That a society's norms are mirrored in its work values and habits appears beyond dispute. When anthropologists undertake to characterize a culturally distinct people, they are likely to give major attention to the meaning and form of work in that culture. When social psychologists like David McClelland attempt to account for root differences between technologically and economically advanced nations and those less sophisticated, they speak of work-relevant motives and of achieving versus nonachieving societies.

To understand a culture, we must know something of the prevailing work beliefs and practices of its members.

The history of the meanings of work in Western civilization has been chronicled by Adriano Tilgher, Max Weber, Harold Wilensky, and others. While it is possible to identify a variety of contrasting philosophical positions about man the worker from the pre-Christian era to the present, it is tempting to describe the nation states which have embraced these positions in simplistic, monolithic terms.

Thus, the ancient Hebraic tradition is usually represented as placing a severely punitive interpretation upon work. Labor was a divinely imposed sentence pronounced upon man as a consequence of his transgressions. Through work, man performed a continuing act of expiation for spiritual wrongdoing and thus repaired his relationship to God.

In the pagan civilizations of both Athens and Rome work was similarly demeaned. In those societies work was regarded as befitting slaves but not citizens and men of intellect. It is an interesting footnote to Western intellectual history that, while the Greek mathematicians made remarkable contributions to the quantitative sciences, they generally considered their efforts to be *nonwork*, a form of civilized contemplation and mental diversion. By personal preference, they applied their skills to the solution of practical problems in mensuration for architectural purposes only when expressly directed to do so.

CARRIED SEEDS OF CHANGE

Such vignettes of Hebrews, Greeks, and Romans at work are, at best, abstractions of a dominant but not universally shared view of labor as drudgery and as a curse.

In truth, by interpreting work as a rite of atonement, the early Hebrews were assigning it both negative and positive values. On the one hand, work was an unsavory experience, a bane; on the other, it was a divinely conferred means of reclaiming one's lost spiritual dignity. Work, then, while not in itself an act of joy or of intrinsic goodness, became a means of achieving personal worth.

One discovers that in Greece, too, some occupations, farming, for instance,

Source: Reprinted with permission of the author and publisher from the *American Vocational Journal*, 1973, *48*(1), 28–29 and 108. Copyright 1973 The American Vocational Association, Inc.

were exempt from the stigma associated with other forms of work, presumably because they permitted man to attain the economic self-reliance requisite to the cultivation of the amenities.

Some Grecians of high social rank went even further in challenging the view that to labor debases man. Several centuries before the Christian era the poet Hesiod wrote, "Work is no disgrace." Ovid, the Roman, who was a contemporary of Christ, declared, "When I die may I be taken in the midst of work." Emperor Marcus Aurelius employed suasion, advising the listless to think "I am rising to a man's work."

It is likely, then, that philosophies of work did not change abruptly from era to era but that subdued elements imbedded in the value systems of earlier civilizations were absorbed, in adapted and extended form, into the belief structure of succeeding societies.

The religion-dominated Europe of the middle ages, in repudiating the state of idleness as spiritually and practically improper, reflected the ethical principle repeatedly stressed in the Judean tradition and espoused by the early Christian church. Not to be productive was to fail in the fulfillment of one's moral obligation.

The concept of useful labor as an ethical precept assumed a new urgency in the Christian era because of its obvious relation to the notion of charity. In the noblest sense, the harvest of one's work was to be shared with the less fortunate and the needy.

RISE OF CALVINISM

Martin Luther elaborated on the theme of work as a moral obligation and a means to spiritual redemption. It was Luther's conviction, a persuasion shared by writers like Tolstoy and Carlyle, that work was the soul of life. All useful work bestowed dignity and worth, but to each according to his social station. Occupation was a matter of social class inheritance, and to labor at one's calling, that is, at the work for which one was destined, was good.

John Calvin, too, propounded the principle of hard work as a matter of religious piety but, unlike Luther, he condoned freedom of choice in one's occupation and felt it was morally acceptable for one to become wealthy through his work, provided that wealth was put to good social use.

The growth of the European merchant system and the concomitant rise of a strong economic middle class were influential factors in the Protestant Reformation and established a receptive climate for the Calvinist work doctrine. For man to work hard was to do God's will; moreover, to acquire wealth in the course of work was virtuous since, as Gardner Murphy interprets it, "It is through the success of his works that (man) apprehends his status among God's elect."

Thus, work, wealth, and capitalism became concepts which were compatible with one another and harmonious with religious duty.

More than thirty years ago Max Weber brought a fresh interpretation to these historical developments in his classical thesis, *The Protestant Ethic and the Spirit of Capitalism*, and it is principally to Weber that we are indebted for the notion of the Protestant work ethic in modern Western society. In the United States, this expression has been used more particularly in reference to Puritanism, with its emphasis on ascetic living, prodigious labor, and the acquisition of wealth for use in ways that serve God's will.

With the gradual secularization of American society, the religious meanings and motives attached to work have declined in significance. While the work ethic appears to persist today as an important personal-social motive for many individuals, it assumes an essentially nonreligious form and is far more complex than hitherto.

Its origins are not now so readily traceable (for example, the deliberate teaching of the virtue of labor or the modeling of industriousness in the family setting is far less common now) and its former universality has diminished in a pluralistic society whose divergent ethnic and social class groupings attach differential values to institutional roles.

Furthermore, while the meanings imputed to work in Luther's time and before might be said to have been anchored chiefly in two motives, biological survival and sacred duty, contemporary meanings of work form an intricate network. Involved are such varied personal-social needs as the attainment of improved socioeconomic status; heightened self-esteem; preferred life-style; increased leisure time; the acquisition of congenial associates; the extension of one's personal and geographic freedom; and the establishment of a comfortable psychological identity.

It has become less meaningful to speak about the valuing of work in itself and far more relevant to inquire about the worth that individuals assign to specific types of occupations. One asks not only whether John Brown is motivated to work but also in what occupational role; not whether he places a high premium upon work in the abstract but what it is he wishes to derive from the experience of work.

The blurring of traditional work meanings has posed an awesome adjustment problem for many youths in our society who are faced with imminent transition from the comparatively sheltered and dependent roles within the family and at school to the more autonomous role of worker.

For more than a few, it is an existential problem, one of identity diffusion and personal role clarification.

In an earlier age when man's work was predominantly farming, the family functioned rather efficiently as a tightly knit economic unit, each member with his assigned duties to perform as a necessary contribution to the livelihood and safety of the kinship group.

While the advent of the Industrial Revolution in the latter half of the eighteenth century brought changes in the nature of work roles within the family, the work of children remained highly important to the economic survival and comfort of the kinship group, so much so that wholesale numbers of adults exploited their children with little or no thought of wrongdoing.

In the earlier "cottage system" found prominently in the British textile trades, virtually all ablebodied children not born to affluence were expected as a matter of course to spend long hours at daily home labor in the spinning of wool and cotton and the looming of fabrics. But with the establishment of the mills, children were removed from the home setting and placed in factory sites where they were frequently required to work 12-hour days.

Orphans and the children of the poor were collected and bound out to factory owners in both Europe and America, with resultant flagrant abuses that led to vigorous social protests and the ultimate enactment of child labor laws. For youth, the difficulty with work in a rapidly expanding industrial economy whose manufacturing methods were yet relatively primitive and inefficient was that there was too much of it and they were too readily available for exploitation.

LEGACY OF THE GREAT DEPRESSION

It is difficult to locate the point in American social history at which children and adolescents ceased to be accepted as an instrument of the family's economic viability. The devaluing process was clearly manifested, however, during the Great Depression of the 1930s.

At a time when national unemployment crested at almost 25 percent of the labor force the outpouring of high school and college graduates each spring was seen as a severe threat to the job security of adults, particularly to that of older workers with inadequate savings.

It was widely assumed, particularly in the leadership ranks of organized labor, that massive unemployment was the bitter yield of a machine-centered economy and its resultant overproduction of goods. Heightened educational requirements became a means not only of qualifying youth for jobs, but quite oppositely, of delaying their early entry into the work force and of establishing a social control over labor supply-and-demand ratios. At the same time, the long-standing function of the family in readying youth for the work role was being eroded.

These were trends that outlived the depression and whose effects are clearly discernible today. Adolescents are commonly regarded as superfluous commodities in an adult-operated economy. In the minds of many is the question of what to do with our young until the economy can somehow absorb them.

In the decade of the 1960s alone, the unemployment rate among those in the 16-to-19 age range ballooned from 3.5 times to 5.5 times that of the 25-and-over segment of the labor force.

The changing climate of work values and employment opportunities for youth has produced ambivalent attitudes and responses in students. On the debit side, one observes a tendency on the part of youth to denigrate many fields of work. Further, one sees a display of what may only be termed occupational illiteracy in an age in which a grasp of the requirements and conditions of employment is assumed to be prerequisite to realistic vocational choice and effective adjustment to work. And most alarming of all, perhaps, one finds a steadfast resistance to life career planning, a form of virulent avoidance behavior.

Conditions such as these pose serious challenges to the vocational counselor and vocational educator committed to facilitating the complex process of career development in youth.

On the credit side of the ledger, a great many young people appear to sense that it is through work that they must ultimately validate their adult status and acquire a measure of power and self-determination.

Speaking at the 1960 White House Conference on Children and Youth, Marcia Freedman asserted that work remains the chief vehicle for the psychological coming of age in America.

That observation may still hold true. A national poll by the Daniel Yankelovich firm recently revealed that nearly four out of five college students affirmed a commitment to career as an essential way of life. While young Americans frequently disdain preparation for occupations which they consider to be dehumanizing, renounce the work-for-profit value, and scorn the Horatio Alger legend, they have not, common belief notwithstanding, repudiated the secular work ethic per se.

Indeed it may be argued that adolescents and young adults are expecting and demanding more, not less, from the work experience; that they see worth or worthlessness in work in proportion to its capacity to allow them, as Donald Blocher puts it, "to organize life in some meaningful or need-fulfilling way."

Findings from a recent report of the Purdue Opinion Poll show that the work ideals of the majority of American high school students are not radically different from those of adults; that they seek security through work and an opportunity to use and to expand upon their skills and abilities.

It is not the abstract idea of work that remains what it has long been—how to somehow discover a way to provide work that will nourish man's potential for human growth and self-realization.

2. The Interaction of Vocational Counseling with the Economic System*

Robert P. Overs

Sociologists are interested in the structure of a society which encourages, sustains and supports a certain type of economic system. A recent analysis by Talcott Parsons is of significance here.[1] He points out that in an industrial society the economic system either is given or has been given special emphasis. Greater concern has been shown with handling the external environment than with values internal to the society. Western industrial civilization obviously differs widely from other civilizations in this respect. To meet the needs of an industrial economy, labor as a commodity must be emancipated from the demands of other structural areas of society. In order that labor might be sufficiently mobile to meet the rapid changes in an industrial economy, the family structure had to change. The small, mobile family replaced the large kinship group. In a similar manner, the geographical and political limitations of the worker under feudalism gave way to permit a more mobile labor supply.

Parsons emphasizes the importance of a value commitment to exploiting the external environment as essential for the development of an industrial society and traces this to the Judaeo-Christian tradition.[2] The internalization of this high valuing of the conquest of the outside environment provides the motivation for workers to meet the complex work demands of an industrial system. In Parsons' words:

> . . . (1) people must be motivated to serve the goal of *production* beyond the levels previously treated as normal, desirable, or necessary in the society, and (2) they must perform such tasks to a far higher degree than before, in organizations specifically differentiated from other, nonproductive functional contests, *i.e.*, labor must be "alienable."[3]

This fundamental valuing of work within the industrial framework is substantially different from the economic hedonism postulated by the economists.

One of the institutional bases necessary for the development of an industrial society is the substitution of a legal system supporting universalism and specificity for primary group controls. This permits the contractual relationships necessary for industrial enterprise. Characteristic of this legal system is a definition of what could be contracted, what was illegal in securing the other party's agreement to the contract, how unforeseen events should be handled under the contract and the nature of society's interest in the contract.[4]

---

[1] T. Parsons, *Structure and Process in Modern Societies* (Glencoe, Ill.: Free Press, 1960), Chap. IV.

[2] *Ibid.*, p. 138.
[3] *Ibid.*, p. 140.
[4] *Ibid.*, p. 145.

*Source: Reprinted with permission of the author and publisher from the *American Journal of Economics and Sociology*, 1964, *23*, 213–222. Copyright 1964 The American Journal of Economics and Sociology, Inc.

Another institutional base necessary for industrial society is the concept of authority. This is defined as the ability to make decisions within the economic framework. It permits whoever is exercising the leadership to make disposition of material and labor in a rational way to maximize production. This is clearly at odds with nonindustrial civilizations where such authority is weakened by the coexistence of other and frequently nonrational authority systems.

The concept of regulation is different from that of authority. Some occupational activities cannot be successfully carried on under direct authority. That is to say, such professional activities as are carried on in universities, hospitals and industrial research laboratories require some independence from authority in order to maximize production.[5] A system of regulation or setting outer limits of performance is operative here in lieu of direct authority.

In understanding the place of government in industrial society, Parsons notes that "government must be sufficiently stable and also sufficiently *differentiated* from institutionalized structures in the society which are incompatible with industrialization. . . ." Government support of other institutional patterns interfering with the industrialization process must be withdrawn. We turn now to a more detailed consideration of vocational counseling within this structure.

I. INTERRELATION OF THE VOCATIONAL COUNSELING AND LABOR ECONOMICS THEORY SYSTEMS

By definition, any occupation interacts with the economic system. However, vocational counseling has a special relationship because of the significance of vocational choice. Since vocation choice in our democratic society may be generally regarded as free, within the limits of certain determining influences, those who are in a position to influence vocational choice may be said to occupy a special position vis-à-vis the economic system. The more specialized the society, the more important the process. In sacred societies, the assigning of vocation was accomplished through social inheritance of jobs, status and skills. Such a system, aside from other considerations, would not meet the needs of a secular society such as ours. American society is, within limits, an open society. Who enters what occupation is influenced, however, by the social-class position of the parents.[6] This, in turn, is strongly affected by the father's occupation.[7] There is an intervening variable of the educational ladder which children of the middle and upper social-class families find easier to climb.[8] In any event, the individual has considerable latitude in choice of occupation, probably greater than in any other than frontier societies.

One aspect of labor economics is signified by the label "manpower." The study of manpower needs and problems has drawn together an assortment of labor economists, educators, business executives, union representatives, government officials and occasionally vocational counselors (usually as consultants).

[5] *Ibid.*, p. 153.
[6] A. B. Hollingshead, *Elmtown's Youth* (New York: Wiley, 1949).
[7] W. L. Warner, R. J. Havighurst, and M. G. Loeb, *Who Shall Be Educated* (New York: Harper & Bros., 1944).
[8] C. W. Mills, *White Collar* (New York: Oxford University Press, 1951), pp. 266–8.

Most vocational counselors would not quarrel with the following ambitions of manpower organizers:

1   To maintain a high-level employment economy which can provide job opportunities for all those willing and able to work.

2   To build and maintain a stable work force which is, at the same time, sufficiently mobile to adapt to the changing needs of a dynamic economy.

3   To utilize the labor force efficiently through proper matching of jobs with people, effective management, and the appropriate education, training and development of people, and thus to raise the productivity of labor and the general standard of living through the nation.

4   To provide reasonable security against the hazards of illness, unemployment, disability and old age.

5   To preserve and enhance the freedom, dignity and worth of the individual both as a member of the labor force and as a citizen.

6   To provide the proper and necessary distribution of manpower between our armed forces and civilian work forces in order to maintain adequate national defense and a healthy economy.[9]

Vocational counselors are critically interested, however, in how and to what degree these statements are implemented in the lives of individual clients. In a statement such as the following they see the possible neglect of client needs:

Manpower policy, therefore, should be conceived of as one aspect of total public policy in economic affairs and not as a separate or unique problem.[10]

Vocational counseling as a practicing profession has sought a theoretical base for its practice primarily in psychology, to a far lesser extent in sociology. Economics as a possible theoretical base has been strangely neglected. Only occasional concern with the theory of manpower needs has maintained a minimum cross fertilization.[11] While Freud is well known to most counselors, the name of Keynes or Galbraith might not even be recognized. This is not to say that writers in other fields have not been concerned with this problem of cross fertilization. A body of relevant literature is accumulating.[12] There has been marked dissatisfac-

---

[9] W. Haber, *et al.* (eds.), *Manpower in the United States* (New York: Harper, 1954), p. x.

[10] F. H. Harbison and A. Rees, "Manpower Mobilization and Economic Controls," in *ibid.*, p. 213.

[11] R. F. Berdie, "The Counselor and His Manpower Responsibilities," *Personnel and Guidance Journal*, XXXVIII, No. 6 (February, 1960); D. W. Bray, "Vocational Guidance in National Manpower Policy," *Personnel and Guidance Journal*, XXXVI, No. 4, (December, 1955); J. P. Mitchell, "Vocational Guidance and Skills of the Work Force," *Personnel and Guidance Journal*, XXXV, No. 1 (September, 1956); S. S. Olshansky, "Guidance and the Labor Market," *Personnel and Guidance Journal*, XXXIV, No. 9 (May, 1956); W. Reuther, "The Crisis Before Us," *Personnel and Guidance Journal*, XXXVI, No. 1, (September, 1957); D. E. Super, "Guidance: Manpower Utilization or Human Development?", *Personnel and Guidance Journal*, XXXIII, No. 1 (September, 1954); H. Winthrop, "Automation and the Future of Personnel and Industrial Psychology," *Personnel and Guidance Journal*, XXXVII, No. 5 (January, 1959).

[12] J. M. Clark, "Economics and Psychology," *Journal of Political Economy*, XXVI, No. 5; C. A. Hickman and M. H. Kuhn, *Individuals, Groups, and Economic Behavior* (New York: The Dryden Press, 1956); G. Katona, *Psychological Analysis of Economic Behavior* (New York: McGraw-Hill, 1951); A. Lauterbach, *Man, Motives, and Money: Psychological Frontiers of Economics* (Ithaca: Cornell University Press, 1954).

tion among economists themselves with their own concepts pertaining to human motivation.[13] Nevertheless, a textbook published as late as 1952 describes economic incentives in terms of instincts.[14] Since the power elite supports the older assumptions in respect to the motivations of men in the functioning of the economic structure, legislation passed or not passed is generally enacted or defeated within the framework of these traditional assumptions. Therefore, in analyzing the economic concepts which impinge on the practice of vocational counseling we are concerned with the older doctrine which is still dominant in the actual decisions made. Vis-à-vis orthodox economics as a theoretical science, vocational counseling as a practicing profession is still accepting such basic assumptions as "economic man," "competition," "laws of supply and demand" in a naïve fashion. It follows that vocational counseling is operating on a very shallow theoretical base in respect to the institutional arrangements of society in the world of work. To press the matter further, we suggest a series of propositions to place in juxtaposition the separate approaches of vocational counseling and labor economics to the problems of vocational choice and vocational adjustment.

II.   SOME CONNECTING PROPOSITIONS

Proposition 1

Vocational Counseling

Vocational counseling insists on the freedom of individual choice and the fullest development of the capacities of each individual.[15]

Labor Economics

Labor economics is concerned with the utilization of manpower in the most effective way to further the maximum production for the economy as a whole.[16]

Both vocational counseling and labor economics pay lip service to the goals of the other. Labor economists disclaim any authoritarian tinge to their proposals. They believe that if counselees are given the facts about the manpower needs of the country they will elect suitable choices. They want vocational counselors to bring these facts to the attention of the counselees. [15,16]

Proposition 2

Vocational Counseling

As a psychological base, vocational counseling, for the most part, uses the

Labor Economics

As a psychological base, labor economics, for the most part, still uses the

---

[13] J. K. Galbraith, *American Capitalism* (Boston: Houghton Mifflin, 1952); also his *The Affluent Society* (Boston: Houghton Mifflin, 1958); R. A. Dahl and C. E. Lindblom, *Politics, Economics and Welfare* (New York: Harper, 1953), pp. 219–20.

[14] T. Suranyi-Unger, *Comparative Economic Systems* (New York: McGraw-Hill, 1952), p. 176.

[15] R. Hoppock, *Occupational Information* (New York: McGraw-Hill, 1957).

[16] L. Tyler, *The Work of the Counselor* (New York: Appleton-Century-Crofts, 1953), p. 3; L. G. Thomas, *The Occupational Structure and Education* (Englewood Cliffs, N.J.: Prentice-Hall, 1956), pp. 11–2.

phenomenological personality theory as a base.[17]

"economic man" theory as a base.[18]

Schism between the two is perhaps clearest in the concept "competition." The pertinent use of the word in labor economics means competition for work among workers. This is the normal operation of the market mechanism, and presumed to motivate workers to look for jobs and to motivate them to work hard once they have a job. Psychological research indicates that a moderate amount of anxiety may be motivating but that greater amounts of anxiety are incapacitating rather than motivating. Clinical experience suggests that for many people the anxiety involved in competing for a job is so overwhelming as to be incapacitating rather than motivating. If this is true, the economic model breaks down for those individuals who are incapacitated by this amount of anxiety. The concept "competition" (competition among workers for jobs) is not an operational concept until it is restated to exclude the potential job seekers immobilized by anxiety.[17,18]

Proposition 3

Vocational Counseling

As a philosophical base, vocational counseling accepts the inalienable right of the individual to life, liberty and pursuit of happiness. What is good for the normal individual is good for society.

Labor Economics

As a philosophical base, labor economics accepts the inalienable right of the individual to life, liberty and pursuit of business. The individual in this case is defined as the entrepreneur and subsequently the corporation. "What is good for General Motors is good for the country." The discrepancy between the rights of the entrepreneur (corporation) and the rights of the worker is glossed over semantically by considering all workers potential entrepreneurs.

The basic conflict here is that vocational counselors experience the work which people do through the client's perceptual field. The labor economist views the work which people do as a commodity. The commodity construct is divorced of psychological and sociological meaning. Boulding defines it this way:

> The basis of the economists' system is the notion of a commodity. The economist sees the world not as men and things, but as commodities, and it is precisely in this abstraction that his peculiar skills reside. A commodity is anything *scarce*. That is, in order to get more of it a quantity of some other commodity must be relinquished.[19]

[17] D. Snygg and A. W. Combs, *Individual Behavior* (New York: Harper, 1949).

[18] T. Scitovsky, *Welfare and Competition* (Chicago: Richard D. Irwin, Inc., 1951), pp. 94–104, 339–41, 426–7; J. R. Hicks, A. G. Hart, and J. W. Ford, *The Social Framework of the American Economy* (New York: Oxford University Press, 1955), pp. 74–82.

[19] K. E. Boulding, *The Skills of the Economist* (Cleveland: Howard Allen, Inc., 1958), pp. 9–10.

The orthodox economist has assumed that large-scale movements of labor as a commodity could be profitably discussed without recourse to any psychological or sociological referents. It is this gap with which we are primarily concerned.[20],[21]

Proposition 4

Vocational Counseling	*Labor Economics*
Work is considered psychologically desirable for the fulfillment of intrinsic needs for achievement, craftsmanship and to provide earned income with which to satisfy extrinsic desires.[20]	Work is considered economically desirable to maximize productivity. But productivity is defined within the special circumstances of the price-profit system. Work outside this system has no legitimate status:
a. In government as with work within the price-profit system, both intrinsic needs and extrinsic desires may be met. There is some evidence that intrinsic needs may be more fully satisfied and extrinsic desires less fully satisfied, although with some people and some jobs the reverse may be true.	a. In government—a necessary evil and a tax drain on the price-profit system—to be reduced to the minimum.[21]
b. In cooperatives the intrinsic needs are apt to be more fully satisfied than the extrinsic desires.	b. In cooperatives—an unfair (socialistic) threat to the price-profit system.
c. In prisons, the satisfaction of intrinsic needs is the primary concern.	c. Prison Labor—an unfair threat to the price-profit system (unless farmed out through the price-profit system).

Work, in the eyes of the vocational counselor, is meaningful for certain intrinsic satisfactions it brings to the client as well as for its contributions to the productiveness of the country. Thus, work outside the price-profit system is valued equally by the vocational counselor, provided that he is not too strongly influenced by the business ethos. The labor economist experiences difficulty with the concept "productiveness." To group all activities which are measured in the calculation of Gross National Product as productive and exclude all others creates many dilemmas. For instance, under this definition, the man who distributes advertising handbills (most of which blow into the street) is productive; the street cleaner who cleans up the handbills is not.[22],[23],[24]

---

[20] J. G. Darley and T. Hagenah, *Vocational Interest Measurement* (Minneapolis: University of Minnesota Press, 1955), p. 10.

[21] J. K. Galbraith, *The Affluent Society* (Boston: Houghton Mifflin, 1958), p. 133; F. Sutton, S. E. Harris, C. Kaysen, and J. Tobin, *The American Business Creed* (Cambridge: Harvard University Press, 1956), p. 195; for a different view see T. Scitovsky, *Welfare and Competition, op. cit.*, pp. 91, 185-7.

[22] Galbraith, *The Affluent Society, op. cit.*, p. 134.

[23] Galbraith, *American Capitalism, op. cit.*, p. 196.

[24] *Ibid.* J. Shister, *Economics of the Labor Market* (New York: J. B. Lippincott Co., 1949).

Proposition 5

Vocational Counseling	Labor Economics

Vocational Counseling

Unemployment in "normal" times is considered a pathological state against which the entire armamentarium of counseling techniques will be deployed. Three separate views are held of un-employment:

a. It is dysfunctional to *family organization.* Failing to fulfill the bread-winning role, the head of the household loses status and friction develops.

b. It is dysfunctional to the social security of the wage earner and his de-pendents. For lack of funds they are unable to fulfill their usual social roles.

c. *Morale* of the wage earner and significant others is threatened. This in turn is dysfunctional to mental health, and support of primary, associational and community activities.

Labor Economics

Unemployment is considered a market mechanism, essentially normal at certain stages of the business cycle. Three separate views are held of unemployment:

a. The *practical-administrative view.* Being unemployed is a temporary status, and besides, the needs of the unemployed are met by unemployment insurance and public welfare.[23]

b. The *"bird dog"* (and guilt-relieving) *view.* They need not be unemployed if they had the initiative to become entrepreneurs (mow lawns, shovel snow, wash windows) at prices people would be willing to pay.

c. *Labor as a commodity view.* The price-profit system requires a surplus labor pool to prevent inflation. This is based on the concept "competition" (for jobs).[24]

The vocational counseling concept of unemployment as a pathological state is at odds with the practical-administrative view of unemployment. Clinical experience suggests that for a substantial group of the unemployed, being unemployed is not a temporary status. It also affirms that for few workers is the status of receiving unemployment insurance a satisfactory way of life.[25] Finally, existence on public welfare is so unsatisfactory that it creates secondary problems of social disorganization highly costly in the long run to the price-profit system.

In contrast to the "bird dog" view, the clinical experience of vocational counselors gives evidence that the unemployed do a great many odd jobs (primarily the repair and painting of homes of relatives and friends). A secondary pattern is for the husband to stay home and baby-sit while the wife secures a part-time job as clerical worker, waitress or nurse's aide. The unemployed as a group lack the capital, initiative and know-how required to become successful entrepreneurs.

The concept of unemployment held by vocational counselors is diametrically opposed to the labor-as-a-commodity view. Should it be true that the price-

---

[23] Galbraith, *American Capitalism, op. cit.,* p. 196.

[24] *Ibid.* J. Shister, *Economics of the Labor Market* (New York: J. B. Lippincott Co., 1949).

[25] G. Miller, "The Effect of Social Security on Manpower Resources," in Haber *et al.* (eds.), *op. cit.,* pp. 59–64.

profit system requires a surplus labor pool to prevent inflation, then the efforts of vocational counselors to help the unemployed reenter employment are either:

    a. futile: for every worker employed, another must be laid off;

or

    b. dysfunctional: to the operation of the price-profit system.

Proposition 6

Vocational Counseling	*Labor Economics*
Vocational counselors accept the forecasts of economic activity and manpower requirements promulgated by the labor economists and reformulate them for use in counseling individuals.	These forecasts are rarely geared to the problem of producing the exact number of workers required. Implicit in most of them is the assumption that a surplus of skilled manpower is desirable.

From the point of view of the vocational counselor's client, the situation of being trained for an occupation and unable to secure placement in it is as frustrating as not being trained for an occupation in which there are openings.[26] Economists speak frequently of the high cost to industry of a "tight" labor market; little or no attention is paid to the economic waste of producing more workers with particular skills than are required. The employer is interested in a reservoir of skilled labor sufficient so that he need neither incur any costs for recruitment nor make any concessions to nonrational standards in respect to age, color, religion, etc. There is a strong suspicion that the forecasters of manpower needs adhere rather closely to the employer's point of view. Were the concept of labor as a commodity to be followed in all its implications, this utilization of trained manpower would be in sharp contrast to current operations of large corporations in respect to materials inventories. Here, to reduce inventories means cutting costs (within the framework of the accounting system of the individual corporation), and materials are scheduled to arrive to supply assembly lines in the nick of time. The formula seems to be that it is no longer desirable to stockpile inanimate commodities but it is desirable to stockpile animate commodities, since the latter cost the employer nothing.

A quotation from Professor Hathway applied to social work may be equally applicable to vocational counseling.

> Either we accept professional responsibility in relation to the environment and follow the road to the control of forces which threaten to destroy human personality or we admit that the problems are insoluble and become, in the oft-quoted words of Roger Baldwin, "merely stretcher bearers of industry."[27]

[26] S. E. Harris, *The Market for College Graduates* (Cambridge: Harvard University Press, 1949); W. Kotschnig, *Unemployed in the Learned Professions* (London: Oxford University Press, 1937).

[27] Hathway, "Social Action or Inaction: The Challenge," in *Training for Social Work in the Department of Social Science* (University of Toronto, 1894–1940), p. 35, as quoted in E. L. Brown, *Social Work as a Profession* (New York: Russell Sage Foundation, 1942), p. 186.

The vocational counselor is ideally situated to appraise the exact manner in which the economic structure is functional or dysfunctional in the case of the individual worker or would-be worker. He is able to supply the worm's eye view of the human situations in which the meaning of broad economic concepts are spelled out in the lives of individuals. He is able to bring to this analysis relatively keen tools from psychology with which to appraise in clinical situations the meaning of broad concepts in microeconomics. A similar orientation is expressed in the introduction to *Manpower in the United States*.

> The editors can hope that the reader will bring to the sixteen essays comprising the volume what might be termed the humanist approach to manpower. Simply stated, that is the realization that the proper study of manpower is man. To assist in achieving this recognition of manpower as a collection of individual, sentient human beings in a social milieu of economic activity and to dispel the concept of a mobile mass statistic, it is sometimes helpful to contemplate the obvious in a sharper focus.[28]

Proposition 7

Vocational Counseling

Vocational counseling makes no value judgment as to the inherent usefulness of respective vocations. Counseling philosophy explicitly precludes the counselor from favoring one choice over another in terms other than that of client self-fulfillment.

Labor Economics

For his part, the orthodox labor economist makes no value judgment as to the social desirability of one set of goods or services over another.

Vocational counselors and labor economists merge on this point: neither makes any value judgment as to the social desirability of the goods or services involved. For the counselor, as an ideal type, the predatory occupations and the social service occupations are of equal worth. To what extent in actual counseling a sense of valuing is communicated implicitly to the client is unknown. The labor economist makes no honorific distinctions among the various goods and services produced so long as they are produced within the price-profit system.

In summary, it has been the attempt of this article to compare and contrast the conceptual bases on which the science of labor economics and the practice of vocational counseling are founded, with the hope that eventually solutions may be found to the current ambiguous conflicting positions.

---

[28] W. Haber, *et al.* (eds.), *Manpower in the United States, op. cit.*, p. vii.

3. Dimensions of Counselor Functioning*

Weston H. Morrill, Eugene R. Oetting, and James C. Hurst

Over the years many counselors have written about a wide variety of approaches or orientations to counseling. Such intervention concepts as prevention, remediation, outreach, normal development, use of paraprofessionals, and consultation have been discussed. To date, however, there has been no effort to tie these concepts together systematically to describe the dimensions of counselor functioning in a meaningful fashion. A descriptive model of the dimensions of counseling intervention is needed.

Counseling interventions comprise all counselor functions designed to produce changes in clients, groups, or institutions. This article introduces a model that provides for the description and categorization of a very broad range of possible counseling interventions. Figure 1 presents a model of the three dimensions to be discussed. This model permits the identification and classification of a variety of counseling programs or counseling approaches and thereby serves as a means of categorizing and describing the potential activities of the counselor in a variety of settings. The three dimensions described are the intervention target, purpose, and method.

- *The Target of the Intervention.* Interventions may be aimed at (a) the individual, (b) the individual's primary groups, (c) the individual's associational groups, or (d) the institutions or communities that influence the individual's behavior.
- *The Purpose of the Intervention.* The purpose may be (a) remediation, (b) prevention, or (c) development.
- *The Method of Intervention.* The method of reaching the target population may be through (a) direct service, which involves direct professional involvement with the target; (b) consultation with and training of other helping professionals

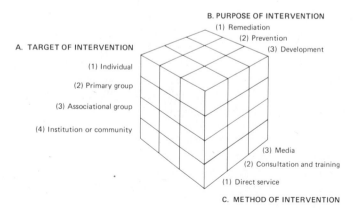

Figure 1

Source: Reprinted with permission of the authors and publisher from the *Personnel and Guidance Journal*, 1974, *52*, 354–359. Copyright 1974 The American Personnel and Guidance Association.

or paraprofessionals; or (c) indirect interventions utilizing media, i.e., computers, programmed exercises, books, television, and other media.

Any intervention has these three dimensions: who or what the intervention is aimed at, why the intervention is attempted, and how the intervention is made.

TARGET OF THE INTERVENTION

The question of who should be the target of counseling intervention has not been asked very often in the counseling profession, because the target has generally been assumed to be the individual. In other words, it is assumed that the objective of counseling is to produce positive changes in the individual client. The move to group counseling usually does not reflect an effort to change the group as a functional unit but rather to influence individuals by means of group methods. This first dimension introduces the possibility that interventions aimed at the groups, institutions, and communities that influence individuals may be direct goals in and of themselves. Ultimately, of course, such interventions effectively influence the quality of life of the individual, but the primary goal of an intervention may be the group structure or the organizational characteristics of an institution or community. The counselor can choose to intervene at any one of four levels.

1. *Individual.* The target of the intervention can be the individual, usually on either a one-to-one or small group basis. The attempt is to influence the individual through altering his or her knowledge, attitudes, perceptions, responses, etc.

2. *Primary Group.* In many cases the target of the intervention should be the primary groups that affect the individual. The *primary group* is the basic unit of social organization—that group (or groups) most influencing the individual. Primary groups are described as intimate, continuing personal associations on a face-to-face basis, determined by the degree of intimacy rather than by proximity. Primary groups such as the family, couples, or close friends strongly influence the individual's self-concept and behavior. The behavior of individuals in the group and their presence or absence from the group can profoundly influence the other individuals in the group as well as the group itself. Intervention at this level would include attempts to alter communication and interaction patterns, perceptions, structure, relationships in the individual's primary groups, etc.

3. *Associational Group.* The target of the intervention may also be the associational groups to which individuals belong. Bierstedt (1970) uses the term *associational groups* to describe more organized groups. These are groups based on choice or chance associations. Group members share a consciousness of similar interests or needs and band or join together in some organizational way to pursue those interests. The distinction between this and the next category, the institution or community, is that members of associational groups meet together with other members of the group. Examples of associational groups are classes, clubs, student government groups, the students on a floor in the dorm, and all the students in a dorm. Interventions at this level would include attempts to alter goals, communication patterns, interactions, organization, methods of achieving goals, and so forth.

4. *Institution or Community*. The target of the intervention can be an institution and/or a community. These groups differ from associational groups in that they do not necessarily involve any meeting of the members of the group. Members are aware of their membership as parts of an institution or community. Examples include an individual school, a school system, a town or city, a neighborhood, a religious organization, a state, or a nation. Interventions at this level would include attempts to alter goals, communications, system linkages, power distribution, information flow, sanctions, and so on.

PURPOSE OF THE INTERVENTION

The second dimension deals with what the counselor function is designed to accomplish. The purpose of a counseling intervention may be the remediation of an existing problem, the prevention of a potential problem, or the development of skills leading to positive and creative growth.

The definition of this dimension suggests both a reactive and a proactive role for the counselor. Until recently, many counselors have seen their role as totally reactive. That is, they were available to see a client after he or she had recognized a problem and had come to the counselor seeking help. The counselor then reacted with remedial efforts. This dimension embodies the recognition of alternate roles: preventing problems and promoting positive development.

1. *Remediation*. Interventions at the remedial level generally involve some pain for individuals or a failure of a group, and this has made it obvious that remedial action is needed. A discrepancy has existed between the skill and the environmental demands. Examples would include the usual counseling problems of lack of social and interpersonal skills, failure to make valid vocational development decisions, and failures of groups because of organizational or structural deficiencies.

2. *Prevention*. Prevention is concerned with identifying those skills which are needed now or which may be needed in the future and with providing a means for acquiring them. The intent is to anticipate future problems and move to prevent them by providing individuals or groups with needed skills or by creating changes in the environment so as to prevent the development of problems. This definition encompasses both primary and secondary prevention as described in the public health model. An example of preventive intervention might begin with the recognition that transition from high school to college is a traumatic experience for many students. Programs designed to lessen the casualties of this period could include such things as group programs to create primary group support for individual students, precollege counseling to prepare students for the transition, and attempts to modify institutional rules and procedures or classroom environments that contribute to the problem. The objective is to provide the skills that will be needed to adequately meet the environmental demands and/or modify unnecessary and debilitating environmental demands.

3. *Development*. Developmental interventions include those programs designed to enhance the functioning and developmental potential of healthy individuals and groups. Such programs are often proactive, promoting the devel-

opment of potential. While related to prevention, development has the primary focus of promoting positive growth for all, not only for those identified as having or about to have problems.

METHOD OF INTERVENTION

The method of working with or reaching the target of the intervention can vary, depending on the intent or stage of the program. The limited number of professionals available in most settings has made it essential that some means of increasing their range of influence be developed. The method dimension is in this respect related to the target dimension in that efforts to work with associational groups or institutions are also means of extending the range of influence of the professional. However, this dimension poses the question of how the actual intervention is presented to the target population. Professional counselors can be directly involved with target populations, can consult with or train other individuals to improve their ability to deal with target populations (i.e., consult with and train allied professionals and paraprofessionals, etc.), or can utilize media as the vehicle for the intervention (newspapers, computers, programmed materials, books, TV, etc.).

1. *Direct Service.* Most traditional counseling programs have utilized direct professional involvement with the target. There are situations in which professional skills and experience can be critical. The person involved in critical stress frequently needs the highest level of help available. There are problems that require the experienced judgment or skills that only fully qualified professionals can provide. There are other situations in which the status of the professional is important, when such status provides a reassurance or charisma that is necessary for a particular program. Some of the disadvantages of direct professional involvement with all targets are: (a) the cost, both in money and in scarce professional time; (b) the limitation of being unable to deal with large numbers of clients; and (c) the resultant inability to reach some groups of clients or provide some kinds of programs.

2. *Consultation and Training.* Through consultation with and training of allied professionals and paraprofessionals, the counselor can affect the target population not by direct interaction but through other individuals. The underlying concept of consultation is that with limited resources and almost unlimited mental health problems the professionals can have greater impact if they work with people who work with the client.

An important resource resides in the selection and training of paraprofessionals to work in a variety of settings. The professional is involved in conceptualizing a program and in selecting and training the paraprofessionals, who provide the service. The use of paraprofessionals has two distinct advantages: First, it increases the mental health work force; second, paraprofessionals often are able to work with certain groups more effectively than are professionals.

3. *Media.* There are numerous examples of the use of various communications media to extend and enhance the influence of counseling. These include such things as computer-assisted counseling (Super 1970), programmed human

relations training materials (Human Development Institute, Inc. 1969), television (Higgins, Ivey & Uhlemann 1970), and other media approaches such as newspaper articles and radio programs. These are efforts and attempts to reach and influence individuals and groups through means other than direct intervention by a professional. The body of research and literature about computer-assisted counseling indicates that this may be a major future thrust.

ASSESSMENT AND EVALUATION

One overriding set of counselor functions that relates to all of the above dimensions is that of assessment and evaluation. A recognition of the range of potential counselor functions highlights some critical needs. Counselors are forced to make important decisions about the nature of the services they offer. They are faced with decisions of priority concerning the target to select for their interventions, the purpose of these interventions, and the most efficient and effective method for these interventions. These questions clearly underline the critical need for a systematic assessment of institutional and individual needs in order to plan appropriate and effective interventions, and this must be followed by systematic evaluation of the effects of whatever programs are developed. There is evidence that many programs are not effective in achieving their goals, yet counselors are often guilty of offering programs year after year with no evidence concerning program impact.

CONCLUSION

The model for counselor functioning presented here not only provides a framework within which alternate modes of intervention can be both classified and understood; it also implicitly carries with it the stimulation to consider various targets, purposes, and methods so that the best all-around intervention procedures will be developed. The process of planning intervention strategies should begin with an assessment of needs and of the personal, environmental, and institutional conditions that limit potential. The model then provides a point of departure—a stimulus for creative thinking about alternative interventions. Evaluative research is the feedback mechanism that leads to further implementation or change. Counseling as a profession simply cannot afford to function in the comparatively ineffective ways of the past. Utilizing a comprehensive intervention model can lead to new and meaningful programs that really meet the human needs of our society.

REFERENCES

Bierstedt, R. *The social order.* (3rd ed.) New York: McGraw-Hill, 1970.

Higgins, W. H.; Ivey, A. E.; & Uhlemann, M. R. Media therapy: A programmed approach to teaching behavioral skills. *Journal of Counseling Psychology*, 1970, *17*, 20–26.

Human Development Institute, Inc. *Basic interpersonal relations: A course for small groups.* Atlanta, Ga.: Bell & Howell, 1969.

Super, D. E. *Computer-assisted counseling.* New York: Teachers College Press, 1970.

4. Career Guidance Practices Transcending the Present*

Robert E. Campbell

The selection and implementation of practices are vital events which represent the backbone of daily guidance. Too often guidance as with other professions can fall victim to routine, obsolete practices which stagnate the profession. Only through self-criticism, questioning conventional wisdom, intelligent inquiry, and subsequent research and development do we advance our professional effectiveness.

The purpose of this article is to alert readers to emerging practices for the seventies. It is hoped that knowledge of future horizons will stimulate an assessment of present practices and encourage positive change.

Since a discussion of emerging practices spans a wide spectrum, it is necessary to set parameters. First, what are practices? A *practice (or method)* is any technique or approach the counselor employs to achieve a specific career guidance objective (or goal) with a client. It can be as broad as a career information library or as specific as an interest inventory. The critical element of the definition is that the practice is goal-directed, intended to achieve a specific objective with a client—in this instance to facilitate career development.

Second, consistent with the theme of NVGA, the emphasis will be on career guidance practices not guidance in general. Very little attention will be given to the counseling process per se.

CURRENT STATUS OF CAREER GUIDANCE PRACTICES

Hansen and Borow [18] in their recent comprehensive review concluded that present-day guidance is markedly inadequate. They listed 11 deficiencies such as limited counselor time to work with students; overemphasis on the single-job-for-life assumption; overconcern with testing; inadequate linkages among counseling, education, placement, job adjustment, and follow-up; disproportionate attention to the college-bound and not enough to the work-bound; few students reporting that counselors have an important influence upon their career planning; gross neglect of program evaluation studies; and too much stress on job content at the sacrifice of occupational life style. They added that although the present is gloomy, the future is encouraging by virtue of the many innovations under development.

Campbell, Walz, Miller, and Kriger [9] initiated a project several years ago to encourage innovative practices. Through a joint effort of their ERIC Clearinghouses (Counseling and Personnel Services at the University of Michigan and Vocational and Technical Education at Ohio State University), they compiled a handbook of career guidance methods K-14, based on a national survey of 2,000 innovative practices since 1965 and intended as a sourcebook for improving guid-

*Source: Reprinted with permission of the author and publisher from the *Vocational Guidance Quarterly*, 1974, *22*, 292–300. Copyright 1974 The American Personnel and Guidance Association.

ance programs. Although the survey identified many promising new methods, it also uncovered deficiencies. Most notable among these was the paucity of practices for special groups, such as blacks, women, American Indians, and Mexican-Americans, and for assisting students in their transition from school to work (job placement and adjustment).

TRENDS FOR THE SEVENTIES

Forecasting career guidance practices for the seventies requires the identification and assessment of many variables. Since history often repeats itself, a historical analysis of the determinants that have shaped past and current practice often provides clues for identifying predictor variables [22]. Past history suggests the following list of variables: societal needs and values, the availability of funds, professional fadism, the status of research and theory, the content of counselor education programs, the research-to-practice lag, and practices under experimental development. From a less scientific but perhaps more realistic perspective, a school counselor would probably advise you to forget all of these and put your money on the administrative preferences of the building principal as the most critical predictor.

In consideration of the foregoing variables, what practice trends can be expected for the seventies? Fourteen probable trends are briefly described here.

1. *Group career counseling*. There are many arguments for the continued popularity of group counseling—i.e., the current momentum of the group movement, new techniques, vicarious learning, and problem sharing. Perhaps the greatest advantage might be economic, since group counseling allows the counselor to have direct personal contact with a larger proportion of students than in one-to-one counseling. Group counseling could very likely increase in popularity if minimal budgets prevent lower counselor-student ratios [see 6, 40, 48].

2. *Computer-assisted guidance*. The first computer-based guidance prototype was developed in 1965. In the interim, great strides have occurred in both software and hardware technology [41]. Initial computer models provided only minimal information such as test results, lists of occupations, and course schedules. Current models have extended their information banks to give the student and counselor a much wider range of assistance—e.g., job opportunities, assistance in the selection of post-high school institutions, taxonomies of occupations, job requirements, and simulated job sampling. Some models have even gone beyond the mere transmission of information to teaching career planning skills such as identifying personal values and decision making [20, 25, 32]. In addition, hardware improvements have resulted in reducing the cost per student as well as providing better services, such as synchronized visual displays and personalized printouts.

3. *Facilitating the transition from school to work*. Helping students select their occupational goal only partially completes the mission of career guidance. In many ways the more difficult task involves assisting students with their next step which for many is work entry. Work entry problems and training strategies have been reviewed by Haccoun and Campbell [16, 17]. Historically guidance has been

weak in facilitating this transition, but the seventies might show considerable improvement. Several promising projects are under way which could serve as practice models such as high school job placement programs and vocational adjustment instructional units [7, 30, 47].

4. *Overlooked Americans: Practices for special groups.* Little progress has been achieved in developing unique practices for special groups such as women, blacks, and Mexican-Americans. Part of the reason for the lack of progress has been a deficient research base for analyzing career development. Much of career development theory is based on white middle-class males and overlooks special groups. Picou and Campbell [35] are partially attempting to remedy this through an interdisciplinary volume on the career behavior of special groups. Another positive sign is the increasing number of professional committees focused on these groups such as those appointed by the American Psychological Association and the American Personnel and Guidance Association. [See also 39, 46, 51, 54.]

5. *Career development resource centers.* With the advent of career education, there is the continual emergence of resource centers to assist students in their career development. These vary in size and scope, ranging from state-wide dissemination units to school district laboratories and mobile vans. Typically they are intended to supply up-to-date career information services to the student as well as innovative guidance techniques for school staff. [See 21, 33, 37, 50.]

6. *Behavior modification approaches.* The behavior modification movement will probably continue to grow. Career guidance applications thus far have been limited but could expand to include vocational behaviors such as job seeking, decision making, job interviewing, career exploration, and on-the-job adjustment [26, 43, 55].

7. *Life style counseling.* Teaching students to examine the mode of living and roles associated with occupational membership as a method of exploring alternative careers has long been advocated by vocational experts [5]. The idea has considerable face validity since one's occupational identity governs a significant proportion of one's life style, e.g., peer patterns, social status, neighborhood, and standard of living. The progress of life style counseling may be influenced by books such as Packard's *A Nation of Strangers* [34] and Toffler's *Future Shock* [44]. [See also 1, 4, 14, 19.]

8. *Systems methodology.* Growing public pressure to upgrade obsolete guidance programs, demonstrate accountability, and improve the delivery of services has caused researchers to examine the application of systems methodology to the design of guidance programs. Systems methodology advocates the systematic design of programs in terms of needs and resources, the specification of program goals and student behavioral objectives, the generation of methods for achieving the objectives, and process and product evaluation. Systems models for guidance have been rapidly gaining national appeal, and several prototypes have been developed [8, 23].

9. *Assessment of career development.* Within the past decade the parameters of career guidance in public schools have changed. Historically, it focused on senior high school, but now has expanded to include K-14. A number of events have stimulated this change such as the concept of career education, the desire for

orderly career development, and a need for accurate information about the world of work at an earlier age.

Concurrent with this change has been the realization that to effectively design and evaluate practices that span K-14, adequate assessment techniques are needed for diagnostic evaluation of career development, evaluation of practices and programs, identification of deficiencies in education, and crosscultural comparative information. In response to this need, the concepts of vocational maturity and developmental tasks have been proposed as a framework for assessing career development. Additionally, several new instruments are under construction which should impact during the seventies [3, 5, 11, 12, 42, 49].

10. *Career guidance curriculums.* In 1966 a national conference was devoted to implementing career development theory and research through the curriculum [2]. Despite great expectations, little impact has been achieved on a national scale. Guidance leaders continue to stress the need for more curricular breakthroughs since they would represent a giant step in student services. At present, guidance curriculum units such as those for career exploration, decision making, and learning work concepts have to be inserted through the backdoor, tagged on to traditional courses such as English and social studies. Although in some instances it is desirable to integrate career guidance units with subject matter courses to achieve a vocational objective, a void still exists for the systematic delivery of guidance services. Much of the problem stems from the resistance of schools to squeeze more into an already crowded curriculum. The seventies might prove more favorable for a guidance curriculum in view of the career education movement and the many innovative career development curriculum units undergoing field testing [13, 27, 28, 52].

11. *Emphasis on transferable skills.* Traditionally, guidance has relied primarily on conveying vocational facts and concepts to students, such as information about jobs, careers, and training opportunities. But future practice will have to go a step further and equip students with vocational skills which have transferable value beyond the school setting. Since students eventually spend the bulk of their lives outside the formal classroom coping with vocational problems, they need durable skills, such as occupational decision making, job hunting, job interviewing, and on-the-job adjustment, which can be applied as these problems arise. Several current projects are geared to this task [7, 29, 31].

12. *Roles of "significant others."* In assessing the current status of career guidance practice, Campbell and others [9, p. 204] concluded that "the roles of 'significant others' in career guidance planning and decision making and the means to include them in career guidance equations have been treated only minimally." In addition to the counselor, many others play a prominent role in influencing the student's vocational behavior—teachers, parents, peers, celebrities, relatives, and job incumbents. The magnitude of "significant other" influence may be great, as is being suggested by Woelfel and Haller [53] and Picou and Curry [36]. The latter point out that although it is methodologically feasible to identify and assess the influence of significant others, it is far more challenging to construct guidance mechanisms to capture their contributions to career development. Several approaches are being considered, such as educating both signifi-

cant others and students to their interactive roles and the value of their influence.

13. *Career education.* Although the concept of career education is still emerging, Goldhammer and Taylor [15, p. 6] have defined it as

> A systematic attempt to *increase* the career options available to individuals and to facilitate more rational and valid career planning and preparation. Through a wide range of school- and community-based resources, young people's career horizons should be broadened. Their self-awareness should be enhanced. The framework for accomplishing these goals are the phases in the career education program: career awareness, career exploration, career preparation.

> The educational program should be sequenced and postured to optimize career development and should provide as broad a base of understanding of self and the world of work as possible. It should be designed so youngsters will, in fact, have two options at several levels: continuing education or employment.

The implications and challenges for career guidance are far reaching. Although it is clear that guidance has a central role in career education, it is not clear how this role should be achieved. Traditional organizational structure and personnel will not be adequate. Major modifications will have to be conceptualized such as hiring a career specialist who is responsible for program coordination. The coordinator would spend little time with students and most of his time ensuring that the program has continuity, viability, resources, and credibility. Personnel might also include career development specialists, placement officers, job development specialists, and career guidance librarians. Guidance staffing for career education programs will have to reach beyond traditional guidance. An optimal combination of staff should include representatives from industry, the classroom, and the community. [See 10, 13, 15.]

The career education concept is gaining national prominence. Almost every state and hundreds of school districts are initiating programs. Career education provides an excellent opportunity for guidance, and the seventies could become an exciting decade if guidance optimally mobilizes its forces to meet the challenge.

14. *Adult counseling.* How many times have you heard the story about the man who reported "I am 45 years old and I still don't know what I want to do when I grow up!" It is very likely that the largest and fastest growing segment of our society has been the one least served by guidance. The youth generation of the sixties which caught guidance unprepared will become the heart of the over-30 group in the seventies. Will guidance be prepared? [See 24, 38, 45.]

One university president in his recent commencement address warned the graduating class that they will have to be flexible to cope with the job market. Changes in the economy or in individual values often result in career redirection, for example, the PhD glut, funding reductions in the aerospace industry, and the oversupply of teachers. Britain is currently suffering a more dramatic example due to the fuel shortage. British workers are facing a two- or three-day work week if they keep their jobs, and it is predicted that 10 million will be unemployed eventually (40 percent of the total work force). In addition to economic forces, there are many who need career guidance for reasons such as late initial entry into the labor force (working mothers) and changes in their life circumstances or state of health. There are also frequent instances of individuals who desire career redirection as a result of reassessing their personal values. It is not uncommon for a business executive to retrain for a service occupation, consequently starting a second career in the middle years.

CONCLUSION

The seventies could become a golden age or a dismal flop for guidance. If guidance takes advantage of the many promising innovations such as career education, it could become a historic decade. With the ever increasing public pressure for accountability and credibility, guidance will be closely scrutinized for its effectiveness to deliver. Meeting the challenge will require aggressive local, state, and national leadership. Lip service and abstract promises are not enough. Failure to deliver could be disastrous and would serve to reinforce the ubiquitous critics who have frequently reminded us of our ineffectiveness and need for improvement. Let's hope guidance is ready for the challenge.

REFERENCES

1   Adkins, W. R. Life skills: Structured counseling for the disadvantaged. *Personnel and Guidance Journal*, 1970, *49*, 108–117.

2   Ashcraft, K. B. (Ed.) *Implementing career development theory and research through the curriculum*. Report of a conference sponsored by the National Vocational Guidance Association, Warrenton, Virginia, August 1966. (Monograph, available through ERIC ED 010 182.)

3   *Assessment of career development*. Iowa City: American College Testing Program, 1973.

4   Birney, D.; Thomas, L. E.; & Hinkle, J. E. Life planning workshops: Discussion and evaluation. *Student Development Report* (Colorado State University), 1970, *8*(2).

5   Blocher, D. H. Social change and the future of vocational guidance. In H. Borow (Ed.), *Career guidance for a new age*. Boston: Houghton Mifflin, 1973. Pp. 41–83.

6   Boocock, S. S. The life career game. *Personnel and Guidance Journal*, 1967, *46*, 328–335.

7   Campbell, R. E. *An intervention strategy to improve the vocational coping of students in their transition from school to work*. Columbus, Ohio: Ohio State University, Center for Vocational and Technical Education, 1975 in press.

8   Campbell, R. E.; Dworkin, E. P.; Jackson, D. P.; Hoeltzel, K. E.; Parsons, G. E.; & Lacey, D. W. *The systems approach: An emerging behavioral model for vocational guidance. A summary report*. Research and development series no. 45. Columbus, Ohio: Ohio State University, Center for Vocational and Technical Education, 1971.

9   Campbell, R. E.; Walz, G. R.; Miller, J. V.; & Kriger, S. F. *Career guidance: A handbook of methods*. Columbus, Ohio: Charles E. Merrill, 1973.

10 *Career education curriculum materials, Preliminary products list*. Columbus, Ohio: Ohio State University, Center for Vocational and Technical Education, 1973.

11 Crites, J. O. *Vocational psychology*. New York: McGraw-Hill, 1969.

12 Crites, J. O. Career maturity. *Measurement in Education*, 1973, *4*, 1–8.

13 Drier, H. N. (Ed.) *Career development resources: A guide to audiovisual and printed materials for grades K-12*. Worthington, Ohio: Charles A. Jones, 1973.

14 Eason, J. Life style counseling for a reluctant leisure class. *Personnel and Guidance Journal*, 1972, *51*, 127–133.

15 Goldhammer, K., and Taylor, R. E. *Career education: Perspective and promise*. Columbus, Ohio: Charles E. Merrill, 1972.

16 Haccoun, R. R., & Campbell, R. E. *Work entry problems of youth—A literature review*. Columbus, Ohio: Ohio State University, Center for Vocational and Technical Education, 1972. (a)

17 Haccoun, R. R., & Campbell, R. E. *Training methods and intervention strategies relevant for work entry problems of youth*. Columbus, Ohio: Ohio State University, Center for Vocational and Technical Education, 1972. (b)

18 Hansen, L. S., & Borow, H. Toward effective practice: Emerging models and programs. In H. Borow (Ed.), *Career guidance for a new age*. Boston: Houghton Mifflin, 1973. Pp. 177–235.

19 Hansen, L. A. *A learning opportunities package*. Minneapolis: University of Minnesota, Department of Counseling and Student Personnel Psychology, 1970.

20 Harris, J. *Computerized vocational information system project*. Villa Park, Ill.: Willowbrook High School, 1973.

21 Indiana Career Resource Center, 1205 S. Greenlawn Avenue, South Bend, Indiana 46615, 1973.

22 Jantsch, E. *Technical forecasting in perspective*. Paris: Organization of Economic Corporation and Development, 1967.

23 Jones, G. B.; Nelson, D. E.; Ganschow, L. H.; & Hamilton, J. A. *Development and evaluation of a comprehensive career guidance system*. Palo Alto, Calif.: American Institutes for Research, 1971.

24 Karr, K. Models in adult guidance services: Proactive community-based counseling. Symposium presented at the American Personnel and Guidance Association Convention in San Diego, February 1973.

25 Katz, M. R. *System of interactive guidance and information*. Princeton, N.J.: Educational Testing Service, 1973.

26 Krumboltz, J. D.; Baker, R. D.; & Johnson, R. G. *Vocational problem-solving experiences for stimulating career exploration and interest: Phase II. Final report*. Stanford, Calif.: Stanford University, School of Education, 1968. (Available through ERIC ED 029 101.)

27 Lux, D. G., & Ray, W. *World of manufacturing: Industrial arts curriculum project, 4th edition*. Bloomington, Ill.: McKnight & McKnight, 1970.

28 Lux, D. G., & Ray, W. *World of construction: Industrial arts curriculum project*. Bloomington, Ill.; McKnight & McKnight, 1971.

29 Mallory, A. E.; Campbell, R. E.; & Drake, J. W. Report of the proceedings of the Tenth Annual Conference for Systems under Development for Career Guidance, Genesee Intermediate School District, Flint, Michigan, October 11 and 12, 1973.

30 McBride, C. A. The Cleveland job development service. Quincy-Woodhill Center, 10600 Quincy Avenue, Cleveland, Ohio. Bureau of National Affairs, Inc., Case Study, Public Schools. *Manpower Information Service* (Washington, D.C.), 1972, *3*(17).

31 Mihalka, J. A. Job hunting course. Columbus, Ohio: College of Education, 1972. (To be published by NVGA as part of their "How to . . ." series)

32 Myers, R. A.; Thompson, A. S.; Lindeman, R. H.; Super, D. E.; Patrick, T. A.; & Friel, T. W. *Educational and career exploration system: Report of a two-year field trial*. New York: Teachers College, Columbia University, 1972.

33 National Center for Career Information Services. Bloomington: NCCIS, Indiana University.

34 Packard, V. *A nation of strangers*. New York: McKay, 1972.
35 Picou, J. S., & Campbell, R. E. (Eds.) *The career behavior of special groups*. Columbus, Ohio: Charles E. Merrill, 1975 in press.
36 Picou, J. S., & Curry, E. W. *Interpersonal determinants of the vocational and educational decision-making process of male black and white adolescents*. Columbus, Ohio: Ohio State University, Center for Vocational and Technical Education, 1974 in press.
37 Ritter, R. *Project VISION: An approach to a model system of occupational employment information*. Indianapolis: Indiana Manpower Research Association, 1967.
38 Second careers as a way of life: A symposium. *Vocational Guidance Quarterly*, 1971, *20*, 89–119.
39 Stilwell, W. E., & Thoreson, C. E. Social modeling and vocational behaviors of Mexican-American and non-Mexican-American adolescents. *Vocational Guidance Quarterly*, 1972, *20*, 279–287.
40 Stogdill, R. M., & Bailey, W. R. *Changing response of vocational students to supervision: The use of motion pictures and group discussion*. Columbus, Ohio: Ohio State University, Center for Vocational and Technical Education, 1969.
41 Super, D. E. Computers in support of vocational development and counseling. In H. Borow (Ed.), *Career guidance for a new age*. Boston: Houghton Mifflin, 1973. Pp. 285–317.
42 Super, D. E., & Forrest, D. J. Career Development Inventory, Form 1, Preliminary manual for *Research and Field Trial*. New York: Teachers College, Columbia University, 1972.
43 Thoresen, C. E. (Ed.) Behavior modification in education. *The seventy-second yearbook of the National Society for the Study of Education*. Part 1. Chicago: University of Chicago Press, 1973.
44 Toffler, A. *Future shock*. New York: Random House, 1970.
45 U. S. Department of Labor, Wage and Labor Standards Administration, Women's Bureau. *Continuing education programs for women*. Washington, D.C.: Author, revised 1971.
46 Vetter, L., & Sethney, B. J. *Planning ahead for the world of work: Research report abstract, teacher manual, student materials*. Columbus, Ohio: Ohio State University, 1971.
47 Wasil, R. A. *Akron-Summit County Placement Project*. Akron, Ohio: Akron and Summit County Public Schools, 1974.
48 Weals, R., & Johnson, E. Doubled and vulnerable: A sociodrama on vocational decision making. *Vocational Guidance Quarterly*, 1969, *17*, 198–205.
49 Westbrook, B. W., & Parry-Hill, J. W. The measurement of cognitive vocational maturity. *Journal of Vocational Behavior*, 1973, *3*, 239–253.
50 Whitfield, E. A., & Glaeser, G. A. *Project VIEW. History and development*. San Diego, Calif.: San Diego County Department of Education, 1968.
51 Winborn, R., & Martinson, W. Innovation in guidance: A mobile counseling center. *Personnel and Guidance Journal*, 1976, *45*, 818–820.
52 Winefordner, D. W. *Career decision making program*. Charleston, W. Va.: Appalachia Educational Laboratory, 1974.
53 Woelfel, J., & Haller, A. O. Significant others, The self-reflexive act and the attitude formation process. *American Sociological Review*, 1971, *36*, 74–87.
54 Women and counselors, Special Issue. *Personnel and Guidance Journal*, 1972, *51*(2).
55 Woody, R. H. Vocational counseling with behavioral techniques. *Vocational Guidance Quarterly*, 1968, *17*, 97–103.

5. A Critical Look at Career Guidance*

Eli Ginzberg

Guidance is a young profession, only a little more than 60 years old. During its brief existence it has undergone several major changes in orientation. It began by helping low-income youngsters—most of them were no more than 14 years old—to find jobs after they left school. That was in 1908. In the thirties, guidance attempted "to match men and jobs" by assessing the aptitudes of unemployed people in the light of skill requirements for specific jobs.

In the fifties, the profession adopted a psychological development approach. The whole person—his attitudes, feelings, and aspirations—became the center of concern. The guidance counselor, in effect, became a kind of therapist. No longer was his chief concern primarily a vocational one. The net effect of this change has been that today guidance has an exaggerated and unrealizable ambition: To add significantly to human happiness in what, for most clients, amounts to only a few hours of counseling.

A study of career guidance is a complex undertaking. Guidance is provided at thousands of sites and in many different kinds of settings. Its practitioners have widely varying educational backgrounds. The potential clientele is in all races and ethnic groups, income levels, parts of the country, age brackets, and stages of career development.

MOST COUNSELING DONE IN SCHOOLS

In the recently completed 3-year study of guidance by the Conservation of Human Resources Project at Columbia University we set out to learn how guidance functions and how well it meets society's needs. The study covered the practitioners, the institutional frameworks in which they work, and the role of guidance in career decision making. The researchers also made recommendations—to the profession and to the public—on ways to strengthen guidance and to expand its use by those whose needs for it are critical.

Today most guidance counseling takes place in junior and senior high schools. At these sites, counseling centers primarily on helping students make "life adjustments" and achieving emotional maturity. High school counselors, of course, also spend time helping seniors decide on a suitable college and fill out the necessary applications.

The great preoccupation of counselors with adolescents' emotional development is based on the assumption that what youth need most is help in clearing away some of the psychological underbrush which litters their pathways into the world. Do this, so the professional thinking goes, and youth will be freer to make their own choices.

Unfortunately, the paths of many youth have been narrowed or closed, starting at birth, by family and neighborhood poverty, minority status, poor schooling, and the like. Often the prime need of such persons is for substantive advice

*Source: Reprinted with permission of the author and publisher from *Manpower*, 1972, 4, 3–6.

on jobs, skill training, 2-year-college programs with direct links to occupations, and other information and services with strong vocational input that will help them find ways to make a living. Guidance counselors might broaden the options of these young people if counseling were better oriented to their needs.

Those who can best afford self exploration—the middle class and the rich— already have the largest number of options. Even so, the assumption that guidance significantly enhances their prospects for a satisfying life is open to challenge. A suburban high school student, who generally has the greatest access to guidance services, sees a counselor on the average of two to four times a year for less than 20 minutes at each session in his 6 years of junior and senior high school. At the beginning of the 1970's the national ratio of counselors to students was in the neighborhood of 1 to 550. It would be astonishing if the amount of counseling available to each student could significantly change his life.

What seems to occur is that persons with higher incomes have more opportunity than the poor to make mistakes and recover from them in their career planning. Youth in higher income families, for example, can stay in school for longer periods and can achieve a satisfactory resolution of their career problems by revising their plans—several times, if necessary—if they become dissatisfied with their initial choices. They learn about themselves, their strengths, interests, values, potentialities, and limitations as related to the world of work in a dynamic process which starts at birth and stretches over a long period and has inputs from family, friends, peers, the communications media, and society at large. Obviously, this process of exploration is foreshortened among the disadvantaged youth who must settle early on a way to support themselves and their families.

But even if school counselors did try to offer more vocational information than they now do, they are poorly prepared for this role by training and experience. Most are former teachers because entrance into school counseling requires a teaching license in most States. This pattern has no counterpart in any other professional field, with the possible exception of public health, where the leadership—but only the leadership—is drawn from among medical school graduates. In addition, most high school counselors acquire a certificate or master's degree through part-time graduate programs which have a heavy dose of didactic instruction in psychology and very little instruction on occupations and skills.

To be sure, even if counselors were able to offer extensive vocational assistance, there would still be little they could do for large numbers of young people passing through an educational system which fails to teach them essential skills and prepare them for work. Correcting this situation requires basic institutional realignments of priorities and resources. Counseling alone—either in or out of the school system—cannot make up for educational skill deficiencies.

NEEDED INFORMATION ON JOBS LACKING

Nevertheless, the profession should be doing a better job than it is doing of helping young people make the important and often difficult school-to-work transition. What is now often perfunctorily done in this area is to distribute printed information on various careers, most of which has not been prepared specifically for students—and often is not read by them. These materials seldom tell the student what he wants or needs to know about jobs in his neighborhood—how to get them, how much they pay, or what the future looks like.

Other occupational information counselors use also is seriously deficient. Materials such as the OCCUPATIONAL OUTLOOK HANDBOOK, for example, are unsuited to the needs of high school dropouts or high school graduates who are ready to enter the labor force. The materials also have limited use for students continuing their education or training. Among their shortcomings are that they tend to be too general in describing the nature of specific jobs, the alternative paths into jobs, the probable limits of advancement in each field, and linkages between occupations. Moreover, the employment and wage data are given in national aggregates rather than in detail on regional and local labor markets.

Generally, the guidance profession also places disproportionate stress on tests and other instruments such as interest inventories in helping individuals learn about their aptitudes, interests, and values, and the relationships of these factors to different occupational fields.

Recently, there have been experimental efforts in schools to computerize information for career decision making. At best, these efforts are premature and of questionable value. The cost of computer installations can be justified only if they are in constant use and are fed data which are being updated constantly, as in the employment service job banks. At worst, the computerization of information for career decision making focuses attention on gadgetry and deflects the attention of the guidance profession away from recognizing a task which needs badly to be done—deepening understanding of the process of making choices and improving the overall quality of information on which career judgments are based.

There are an estimated 60,000 persons in the United States who work as guidance counselors. Perhaps as many as two-thirds of them are employed in secondary schools. Next in importance are vocational rehabilitation agencies and the Federal-State employment service. A small number of counselors work in elementary schools, colleges and universities, community service or profit-making organizations, or are self-employed.

These logistics of the profession reflect an inadequate allocation of guidance resources available to serve large numbers of persons who have serious career problems, including members of minority groups; young, out-of-school adults; returning veterans; mature women reentering the labor force; mature men seeking to change jobs or careers; and older persons who face hard choices as they approach retirement.

Guidance counselors located in vocational rehabilitation agencies and the employment service come from a wider variety of occupational backgrounds than school counselors. Some began their careers in industry, social work, or teaching, while others took a counseling job immediately after college. A significant number worked first in some other capacity for their employer before taking training and a job as a guidance counselor.

The educational backgrounds of these rehabilitation agency and employment service counselors range from doctorates in clinical psychology followed by a year's internship to less than the college degree.

According to a 1968 Manpower Administration survey, nearly a quarter of some 4,400 employment service counselors who were spending at least half their time in counseling activities had a master's degree or its equivalent, and nearly 2,600 were more than halfway toward earning this degree. Only 9 percent were not college graduates.

Of course, not all counselor training takes place while the candidate studies for a degree. In every occupation, skills grow on the job. As the old saw has it, experience is a great teacher. Counselors can grow in expertise and understanding as they work with the complex problems of their clients. An important consideration in this growth is the quality of professional supervision counselors get. Is the counselor also able to learn from highly trained and experienced colleagues in his own field? This learning environment is probably more characteristic of guidance and professional counseling in the Veterans Administration and in well-run community agencies which have strong supervision than it is in the typical school or employment service setting where counselors often are supervised by nonguidance personnel.

LOW EMPLOYMENT SERVICE PAY CITED

Of the three major guidance groups—school, vocational rehabilitation, and the employment service—the last group is the lowest paid. Few employment service counselors earn more than $10,000—most earn $6,000-$8,000.

Looking at guidance generally, Conservation of Human Resources Project researchers concluded that it is deficient in standards which mark other professions. Usually the hallmarks of a profession are: Strong educational and training institutions which both instruct and indoctrinate future practitioners with values and goals; professional responsibility for determining the shape and direction of work, subject to peer judgments and control; and career opportunities which attract and hold able people in the profession. In the guidance profession these hallmarks are the exception, not the rule.

In higher education, most guidance departments are located in schools of education or are closely allied with them. Faculty and courses are frequently borrowed from other departments and adjusted, often with some difficulty, to guidance department interests. Many students attend classes part time and earn a living the rest of the time, which makes it difficult for them to become fully engaged in their studies. In training, there is over-reliance on classroom work to the neglect of field work. These are only a few of the problems at the education and training level.

On the job, most guidance personnel have their work cut out for them not by themselves but by others. They are far more subject to the administrative exigencies of the school or agency for which they work than they are to professional goals and guidelines. As for career opportunities, there are few rungs on the guidance ladder above counselor. For most persons in guidance there is no place to advance unless they leave the field.

But although the guidance profession has some inherent weaknesses, it also has the potentiality for providing important services which are sorely needed by many persons. The Conservation of Human Resources Project has made a number of proposals based upon its study directed at helping the profession realize its full potential for service. These recommendations are in two categories—some to the profession itself and some to the public which, after all, controls by its attitudes and actions the kinds of demands made and support given to the guidance field.

The profession should take the following steps:

● Abandon psychotherapeutic focus and concentrate, as in the beginning, on educational and career guidance. In the employment service and at other sites where practical career guidance is emphasized, it is clear that the profession can perform a vital function for the unemployed, minorities, veterans, and others whose patterns of employment have been erratic or nonexistent.

● Firmly link counseling services to other kinds of client support. Unless the counselor can deliver concrete help to students with inferior educational preparation, for example, he might as well forgo counseling. Students who need remedial education, help in entering a training program, and help in getting a job are likely to look upon general advice as worthless.

Among the many lessons learned in the administration of the Manpower Development and Training Act is the fact that some clients, particularly among the disadvantaged, may need intensive, wide-ranging supportive services. These may include orientation to work, day care, transportation, skill training, job development, referral to jobs, and even some assistance with medical and other problems in the initial stages of employment. The counselor can be an effective link between these services in the community and his client.

● Make major reforms in the education and training of guidance counselors. These should include emphasis on the world of work and pathways into it, stress on mobilizing and using all available community resources for helping clients, and supervised field work to improve student-counselors' ability to listen to and interact with their future clients.

● Work to change the almost universal regulation that only teachers can become certified school counselors and thereby widen the funnel through which recruits into counseling must pass.

● Expand guidance resources for both young and mature adults, who are at a critical period in their lives, and retard the slow but steady trend toward bringing guidance services into the elementary school. Properly trained guidance counselors primarily concerned with career development have little to contribute to young children. Moreover, school psychologists and other pupil personnel specialists are increasingly available and they are better able than guidance counselors to deal with the needs of elementary pupils.

To improve career guidance, the public should take these steps:

● Recognize that guidance can make a contribution to improved career decision making and work adjustment for many persons, but that it cannot compensate for basic inadequacies which often exist in our educational or other preparatory and employing institutions.

● Take the initiative—as businessmen, union members, and the like—in forming relationships with schools which will provide youth with broadened opportunities for work exposure and experience and the school system with advisory services.

● Become involved, through such organizations as parent-teachers' associations, in the direction, scope, and emphasis of school guidance services.

There is a third sector Federal, State, and local governments—which must also become more concerned with career guidance. Governments' budgetary functions give them extensive control over the directions and scale of guidance services as well as the quality of information which is available to guidance counselors.

Better occupational information, for example, is needed to help counselors provide guidance which is realistic and work oriented. Governments should give increased attention to coordinating occupational data gathered by various agencies, to presenting this data in more usable forms, and to the ways and means of adapting such information to local and regional situations.

Another body of information which should be gathered and kept up to date covers all financial aid available for study or training and the conditions governing its allocation. This information is particularly important for young people outside the main academic stream.

LINKS URGED WITH OTHER AGENCIES

Government at all levels and private foundations should make more research funds available for studies of the world of work and of career development so that we better understand the various factors, both institutional and personal, that contribute to career decisions and career success.

The Conservation of Human Resources Project also recommended that:

● The employment service, working in closer liaison with the schools, provide improved transitional services for terminal high school students.

● Better linkages be formed at State and local levels between the employment service and other manpower-related agencies in the interests of clients.

● Foundation support be given to setting up a model for guidance services for older workers approaching retirement.

More than ever before, our society needs strong career guidance services. We are concerned that there be equal opportunity in employment and open pathways to employment, and we are no longer willing to leave such matters only to the vagaries of birth and chance. At the same time, there are changing requirements in industrial jobs, altered market conditions for professional manpower, the development of paraprofessional occupations, and many other labor market trends which make occupational selection more difficult than ever. Clearly, we greatly need quality career guidance.

We are now at a crossroads with much experience behind us and a good view of the alternatives ahead. With the cooperative efforts of the profession, a concerned public, and government agencies, we can use what we have learned to strengthen career guidance so that it can provide more and better services to a public that needs and wants them.

6. Vocational Theories: Direction to Nowhere*

Charles F. Warnath

The perceptions of the world of work presented by a variety of writers who appear infrequently in the vocational psychology literature confront those in counseling with the possible unreality of current vocational theories—theories based on propositions and assumptions relevant for an ever-decreasing proportion of the American work force. These perceptions also confront some fundamental issues raised by those inside and outside the profession who view counselors in their social context as primary supporters of the status quo (Bond 1972; Halleck 1971; Stubbins 1970; Torrey 1974).

One basic assumption underlying the current vocational theories is populist in nature: that each individual, with adequate motivation, information, and guidance, can move through the educational process to satisfying job goals that allow him or her to express personality characteristics or implement self-concept. This assumption cannot be made unless one holds a prior assumption that every job is capable of engaging the human qualities of an individual and that, in the Protestant tradition, each job has the potential of being a "calling." The vocational theorists have reinforced the concept that the job is the primary focus of a person's life. This may have been true during the years of the small farmer and the independent entrepreneur; but under present conditions, where almost all people work for organizations whose survival is dependent on generating profit and operating efficiently, the needs of the individual are subordinated to the goals of the organization.

WORKING CONDITIONS: IMPLICATIONS FOR SELF-FULFILLMENT

The implementation of automation throughout the American work world raises questions about the logic of continuing to encourage people to believe that their jobs should be the central focus of their lives. The arguments over whether automation increases or decreases the number of jobs do not address themselves to the critical issue of whether the jobs created can carry the weight of importance consigned to work by vocational psychologists. A recent HEW report (U.S. Department of Health, Education, and Welfare 1973) has stated unequivocally: "It is illusory to believe that technology is opening new high-level jobs that are replacing low-level jobs. Most new jobs offer little in the way of 'career' mobility—lab technicians do not advance along a path and become doctors" (p. 20). And earlier in the report: "Many workers at all occupational levels feel locked-in, their job mobility blocked, the opportunity to grow lacking in their jobs, chal-

*Source: Reprinted with permission of the author and publisher from the *Personnel and Guidance Journal*, 1975, *53*, 422–428. Copyright 1975 the American Personnel and Guidance Association.

lenge missing from their tasks. . . . For some workers, their jobs can never be made satisfying, but only bearable at best" (pp. xvi–xvii). The findings of the HEW Special Task Force have been given added weight through interviews conducted by Terkel (1972) and Lasson (1972) with workers in a wide range of jobs.

Career development is an abstract construct. It permits vocational theorists to hypothesize about factors that appear to affect vocational decision making without regard for the quality of jobs in which people eventually find themselves. Although career development research may result in more efficient means of sorting people into vocational slots, the assumptions about personality expression and self-concept implementation in work on which this research is based may encourage workers to expect self-fulfillment in jobs that the modern industrial-bureaucratic work structure is not designed to meet. As Green (1968) has indicated: "Under the conditions of a society in which automation is fully exploited . . . such an understanding of work would constitute a cruel hoax" (p. 85).

Trends toward a reduced work week and part-time work also pose serious questions regarding the assumption that jobs can serve as a major focus of personal fulfillment, as do the pressure toward early retirement and the shifting of middle-aged people out of jobs with which they have identified to jobs in which age is considered less damaging to the efficiency or public image of the organization. Older workers are becoming victims of the youth image and economic demands of a work system that has little sympathy for the needs of the individual.

THE CHANGING NATURE OF WORK

The world of work in America has changed significantly over the past few decades. The proportion of people working on small, privately owned farms, working in rural areas, and working in small businesses is now relatively small in comparison to those working for administrators and managers in the bureaucracies of the large metropolitan centers. Job activities have been reduced to ever-smaller units of specialization. White-collar and professional workers have been organized into pools or teams, decisions about their work being made at some higher level of management. Academic credentials have been given added importance for entrance into jobs, while the complexity of those jobs has remained the same or actually been reduced. As Berg (1971) has stated: "The use of educational credentials as a screening device effectively consigns large numbers of people, especially young people, to a social limbo defined by low-skill, no-opportunity jobs in the 'peripheral labor market' " (p. 186). Berg's evaluation is echoed by the HEW report, which notes: "While new industries have appeared in recent decades that need a well-educated work force, most employers simply raised educational requirements without changing the nature of the jobs. . . . For a large number of jobs, education and job performance appear to be inversely related" (p. 135).

Holland (1973), in a recent book, has indicated: "The goal of vocational guidance—matching men and jobs—remains the same despite much talk, research, and speculation. Our devices, techniques, classifications and theories are more comprehensive than in the days of Parsons, the founder of vocational guidance, but the goal is still one of helping people find jobs that they can do well and that are fulfilling" (p. 85). There is no doubt that vocational guidance has remained steadfast in its goal of matching people and jobs, but it is problematic whether vocational counselors can claim that their matches have resulted in placing people in jobs that are "fulfilling." Observations from the field seem to indicate that personal fulfillment in jobs is more mythical than real for the great mass of workers. One would have to assume that Holland's reference to "fulfillment" is connected to the fact that counselors administer and interpret tests that presumably permit some "fit" with the characteristics of persons already on the job. This appears to be a rather flimsy rack on which to hang a person's self-fulfillment.

Neither vocational theorists nor counselors have confronted the issue raised by writers such as Jenkins (1973), who has stated: "There is no question that work, and the image of work, has sunk badly—for blue-collar workers, for organization men, for contemptuous young people, for almost everyone. . . . One can almost conclude that the only force keeping anyone at it is the mythology of the nobility of the thing, however distasteful it may be" (p. 16). The vocational theorists have ignored the growing number of writers who seriously question the myth of the meaningfulness of work in our industrial society. Those who write for a readership of counselors, as a matter of fact, appear to be the principal supporters of the myth, speaking for the status quo no matter how oppressive the working world may be to most individuals. "Even as adults, only a small percentage of Americans have the privilege of feeling that their work is essential or important" (Benet 1971 cited in Jenkins 1973, p. 54). That is the central issue, which vocational theorists and counselors have avoided. The world of work as they view it no longer exists.

DECISION MAKING FOR WHAT?

Although holding a liberal attitude toward the development of human potential, vocational counselors and theorists have been conservative in their assumptions about the world of work. Their perspective has been fixed within a nineteenth-century model. Their efforts are devoted primarily to increasing the efficiency of matching people and jobs, which they humanistically translate as improving vocational decision making. Few ask the question, "Decision making for what?" despite the fact that, for an increasing number of workers, "Work comes to be less and less defined as a personal contribution and more and more as a role within a system of communication and social relations" (Touraine 1974, p. 185). The counseling literature, seemingly unrelated to the new realities of work for the great majority, reflects obsolete assumptions about work as a "calling," stripped of its religious connotations but nevertheless related to the internal imperatives of self-concept fulfillment, personality expression, and the like.

RESPONSIBILITY AND POWERLESSNESS

Our society has become characterized by individuals' struggle for personal meaning and by their feelings of increasing powerlessness. If those who have studied the world of work are to be believed, the sense of meaninglessness and powerlessness is probably most intense on the job. As Green (1968) has put it: "We have learned to view work as the way in which a man defines for himself who he is and what he shall do with his life. The difficulty is, however, that today men must do this increasingly in a society that lists among its primary purposes the efficient production of goods and services rather than the celebration of human dignity. They have to undertake their self-definition in an environment that has purposes of its own and for that reason does not necessarily have room for individuals to express their own purposes" (p. 35).

Vocational psychologists have centered their theories of vocational decision making on the individual. They have assumed an open market, the dignity of all work, and, as Stubbins (1973) has put it, the person's "ability to operate free of environmental constraints. . . . The vocational psychologist operates in a world that economics and political science have long since discarded—a perspective that ignores the fact that the [person's] world has already taught him that socioeconomic status, racial origin, and power are more determinative than aptitude or interests" (p. 24). As leading advocates of populism and romantic individualism, vocational theorists have concentrated their attention almost exclusively on those characteristics of the individual that can be exploited in the individual's search for self-realization. This perspective has blinded them to the realities of the social forces swirling through the society in general and the world of work in particular. Vocational theorists and counselors ignore the fact that, in the American work world, "What is wanted is not the person but the fulfillment of a function, not the human capacity for work but the human potential for labor" (Green, 1968, p. 39).

With their attention focused on improving the efficiency of input to the work force, counselors appear to those outside the profession as not only the major supporters of the status quo but also the key to the entire educational credentialing system, which depends for its effectiveness on the counselor's assigned functions of guiding, selecting, and sorting. "In short, the role of the guidance counselor is strategic because of its importance in reinforcing the tendency to couch the language of teaching, schools and schooling increasingly in terms of output and product. . . . The fundamental work metaphor is strong: the school is a productive institution, its productive work is in the hands of teachers, its quality control in the hands of the guidance staff" (Green 1968, p. 164).

PERSONAL NEEDS VS. ORGANIZATIONAL NEEDS

Vocational theories are almost uniformly grounded on the proposition that jobs are intrinsically satisfying. The person need only find that job which offers an outlet for personal abilities, interests, values, and personality traits (Holland 1973; Super et al. 1957; Tiedeman & Schmidt 1970). That jobs within the American economy are designed to meet the needs of production and profit or bureaucratic relationships and not to meet the personal needs of the people who fill those jobs has not been included as a contingency factor in the theoretical structures. Little attention has been paid to the fact that over the past few decades the power of individual workers in their work situations and their control over their work activities have been significantly diminished, although these are critical factors in the worker's ability to express personal characteristics.

This reduction of human expression in work is not restricted to the poorly trained or poorly educated; Denitch (1974) has commented, in regard to college graduates: "Whole generations trained to think in terms of societal issues are offered roles as powerless, if well-paid employees. Those with specific skills find their work compartmentalized and routinized. The shift in the authority of engineers and skilled scientists in industry also reduces them to a *new* highly-trained working class" (p. 176). But nowhere in the vocational theories is there even an allusion to the steady reduction of power and control in jobs at all levels of the American economy. "What dominates our type of society is not the internal contradictions of the various social systems but the contradictions between the needs of these social systems and the needs of individuals. This can be interpreted in moral terms, which has aroused scant sociological interest because there is nothing more confused than the defense of individualism against the social machinery" (Touraine 1974, p. 185).

Vocational theorists too have avoided the moral issues related to the individual's struggle with the social system of work. "There is considerable interest among the theorists in classifying, stratifying, compartmentalizing and, more recently, computerizing. While purporting to have as its major purpose the facilitation of a person's educational-vocational planning, its effect is to stabilize the economic system by offering hope that there are reasonable logical paths through the maze of the occupational structure to the one best job that can make each individual happy and satisfied" (Warnath 1973, p. 16). Ostensibly, vocational counseling is a humanistic enterprise. Its theories, however, are designed to explain principles concerning the process of occupational decision making and vocational adjustment to the end that the individual's behavior might be predicted and controlled (Super 1957). These goals are softened by the humanistic affirmation of human potentials, which the theories—through their application by counselors—will presumably assist individuals to discover and exploit. Counselors have defined themselves as humanists on the basis of their stated purpose of helping clients make maximum use of their potentials through a process in which the counselor expresses personal qualities of warmth, empathy, and authenticity.

But neither theorists nor counselors come to grips with the conflict between the needs of the people who are the objects of their attention and the needs of the economic system—which are the needs that determine the operations of the world of work. On the contrary, the romantic individualism inherent in both theory and practice leaves the individual isolated and exposed by its proposition that the person alone is responsible for his or her fate, that only an unwillingness to be sufficiently motivated or to discover and use some unique talent stands in the way of the individual's finding a self-fulfilling work situation. Neither theorists nor counselors address themselves to the world of work as experienced by most workers—or, for that matter, to the contradiction pointed out by Aronowitz (1974) between the rising level of education of larger numbers of workers and the increasingly restricted scope of their labor.

Both vocational theorists and counselors are engaged in a basically amoral activity, operating on the premise that the working world is just and is guided by rational principles in regard to those employed in work—despite the fact that the system within which those workers are engaged responds to factors quite unrelated to the welfare of the individual worker and can fulfill the needs of individuals only insofar as those needs support the needs of the organization.

NEEDED: A NEW PERSPECTIVE

Touraine (1974) has pointed out that a new kind of society is being born; it can be called the programmed, or technocratic, society. This new society is served by vocational theorists and counselors whose perspectives of work are drawn from the past, causing their efforts at increasing the effectiveness of moving people into jobs to negate their professed humanistic concern for people.

The counselor continues to assume that vocational counseling can result in a match of the person with a satisfying job, but as Ferkiss (1970) has noted: "The myth of 'the happy worker' is still just that. Where the old centralized rigid processes have been automated with machines taking over routine tasks, working conditions, especially psychological ones, have not improved. Such evidence as exists indicates that the watchers of dials—the checkers and maintainers—are likely to be lonely, bored, and alienated, often feeling less the machine's master than its servant" (p. 123). And these feelings are not restricted to specific job categories or classifications. They are pervasive throughout the working world, not only among the lower level of jobs but extending up through the white-collar and managerial ranks. Their effects generalize, leading workers "to become 'stupid and ignorant' not only on the job, but off as well" (Jenkins 1973, p. 40).

Braginsky and Braginsky (1974) have argued convincingly that psychologists, either unwittingly or as a means of self-preservation, operate within a framework of generally accepted cultural values that are encouraged and supported by those in power to ensure societal stability and their own dominant positions. In accordance with this concept, the prediction and control models used by psychologists are more for the benefit of those with power than for the benefit of the individual whose behavior is being predicted.

Counselors are positioned at the service delivery end of a chain of information, data, and how-to-do-it prescriptions generated by vocational psychologists. They have a direct involvement with the clients who come to them for assistance, and they carry the burden of responsibility for ensuring that their promises about the improvement of human welfare through counseling can be kept. With the values of society in flux, counselors must not only evaluate their own attitudes toward the concept of work as the major source of self-fulfillment; they must also test their attitudes against the experiences of workers in a variety of occupations. They need not be passive consumers of the products of academia. They can, through direct communication with the writers and theorists and through discussions within their professional groups, begin to raise questions about the assumptions on which vocational theorizing is based as well as about the perspectives through which conclusions and interpretations of research data are filtered.

Six years ago, Osipow (1969) suggested that perhaps vocational psychologists were not asking the "right" questions, that concern with vocational preference and selection might be of relevance for only a minority of the population, and that we should be placing more emphasis on questions related to those factors in the work situation which encourage satisfaction and permit feelings of worth and human dignity. But beyond these considerations, counselors might begin considering a theoretical model or framework broader than the vocational choice or vocational development models, a theoretical model that is based on general human effectiveness and that does not require a fulfilling job as its core concept.

The connection between work and the confirmation of one's worth as a human being has been severed for the great majority of our population. Other disciplines are already engaging in a search for alternative means by which people can express their individuality and gain a sense of control over some significant parts of their lives. Counselors should be no less involved in this search. Because they are central to the life planning of millions of people, their responsibility for assisting in the search for means other than paid employment through which people can gain meaning from life is all the greater.

REFERENCES

Aronowitz, S. Does the United States have a new working class? In B. Silverman & M. Yanowitch (Eds.), *The worker in "post-industrial" capitalism*. New York: The Free Press, 1974.

Benet, S. Why they live to be 100 or even older in Abkhasia. *New York Times Magazine*, December 26, 1971. (Cited in D. Jenkins, *Job Power*. Garden City, N.Y.; Doubleday, 1973).

Berg, I. *Education and jobs: The great training robbery*. Boston: Beacon Press, 1971.

Bond, J. Address to the Annual Conference of University and College Counseling Center Directors, Vail, Colorado, November 1972. *Proceedings*, Colorado State University, 1972.

Braginsky, B., & Braginsky, D. *Mainstream psychology*. New York: Holt, Rinehart and Winston, 1974.

Denitch, B. Is there a new "working class"? In B. Silverman & M. Yanowitch (Eds.), *The worker in "post-industrial" capitalism*. New York: The Free Press, 1974.

Ferkiss, V. C. *Technological man*. New York: Mentor Books, 1970.

Green, T. *Work, leisure and the American schools*. New York: Random House, 1968.

Halleck, S. *The politics of therapy*. New York: Science House, 1971.

Holland, J. *Making vocational choices: A theory of careers*. Englewood Cliffs, N.J.: Prentice-Hall, 1973.

Jenkins, D. *Job power*. Garden City, N.Y.: Doubleday, 1973.

Lasson, K. *The workers: Portraits of nine American jobholders*. New York: Bantam Books, 1972.

Osipow, S. H. Some revised questions for vocational psychology. *Counseling Psychologist*, 1969, *1*, 17–19.

Stubbins, J. The politics of counseling. *Personnel and Guidance Journal*, 1970 *48*, 611–618.

Stubbins, J. Social context of college counseling. In C. Warnath (Ed.), *New directions for college counselors*. San Francisco: Jossey-Bass, 1973.

Super, D. E.; Crites, J.; Hummel, R.; Moser, H.; Overstreet, P.; & Warnath, C. F. *Vocational development: A framework for research*. New York: Teachers College, Columbia University, 1957.

Terkel, S. *Working*. New York: Pantheon Books, 1972.

Tiedeman, D. V., & Schmidt, L. D. Technology and guidance: A balance. *Personnel and Guidance Journal*, 1970, *49*, 234–241.

Torrey, E. *The death of psychiatry*. Radnor, Pa.: Chilton, 1974.

Touraine, A. New classes, new conflicts. In B. Silverman & M. Yanowitch (Eds.), *The worker in "post-industrial" capitalism*. New York: The Free Press, 1974.

U.S. Department of Health, Education, and Welfare, Special Task Force. *Work in America*. Cambridge, Mass.: MIT Press, 1973.

Warnath, C. F. *New myths and old realities: College counseling in transition*. San Francisco: Jossey-Bass, 1971.

Warnath, C. F. Whom does the college counselor serve? In C. Warnath (Ed.), *New directions for college counselors*. San Francisco, Jossey-Bass, 1973.

7. Can Vocational Counselors Change Society?*

Daniel Sinick

It is not revolutionary to recognize that society must be changed if client self-actualization is to be maximized. Vocational counseling is limited in its assistance to clients by various social constraints. Vocational counselors must therefore do the best they can within status quo constraints, but can they not at the same time work toward changes that will enhance the lives of their clients?

Some would answer "No" to this question, as well as to the question raised in the title. As Hansen [6] has pointed out, two divergent views of the counselor's role have long existed; one emphasizes society as the entity to be served, the other stresses the client. Those who favor society are not likely to work toward changing it. Nor do all who favor the client feel that counselors can effectively change society. Blocher [2], for example, held that a counselor who tried to be an agent of change might no longer be perceived as a helping person and might get into trouble on the job.

It is held here that counselors can be effective helping persons and retain their jobs while they change society. The picture of a passive counselor that emerged from Carl Rogers's early impact was apparently generalized by some to passivity in relation to social change. The more recent view of vocational counselors as actively assisting clients is readily generalizable to activity in changing society. As Ben Franklin urged: "We constantly change the world, even by our inaction. Therefore, let us change it responsibly."

How can vocational counselors responsibly change society? In carrying out what may indeed be regarded as a responsibility of counselors, at least five possible approaches are available. Not mutually exclusive, all or any of them can be used by the same counselor. Five approaches involve clients, client environments, counselors' employing institutions, professional associations, and counselors as citizens. Each of these approaches requires some explication.

CLIENTS AS THE FOCUS OF CHANGE

Note that the heading is not "Clients as the Vehicle of Change," for there is no intent to use clients to reach counselors' goals. This approach cannot be employed without the greatest concern for ethical considerations. Fenlason [4] in her classic text on interviewing emphasized (p. 237) "a basic concept in the client-worker relationships: To treat a client as an end, never as a means."

Nor is the intent to change clients, but rather to keep them open to being themselves or changing themselves as appropriate to a society in need of change. The intent is to counteract the traditional approach in which counselors are—in Shoben's colorful term [8, p. 433]—"smugglers of values" who socialize clients

*Source: Reprinted with permission of the author and publisher from *The Vocational Guidance Quarterly*, 1977, *25*, 245–251. Copyright 1977 The American Personnel and Guidance Association.

into the status quo. Gordon [5] placed explicit emphasis on counselors' responsibility to help clients (p. 113)

> to learn not only what is expected of them by the social order—the traditional concern of socialization—but how they can effectively use themselves in relation to other people to cope with the systems which in large measure control their lives.

With so much external control of clients' lives, counselors are well advised to avoid added control and instead to maximize the control clients themselves can exercise. In carrying out this further basic concept of vocational counseling, counselors orient clients to the potential of an internal locus of control, to the power that resides in themselves as determiners—in part at least—of their own destinies. While clients may not thus become irresistible forces, society may cease to appear an immovable object.

Ethical concern suggests caution in efforts to orient clients to social change. Clients are not to be used, as already indicated, as vehicles of social change desired by counselors. Pushing socially disfavored clients, for example, into occupations constituting a frontier not previously breached may seem like commendable counselor risk taking, but the clients are the ones exposed to such risks. They must be ready, willing, and able to pursue a course of action they have chosen. Other ethical dilemmas may arise from value conflicts involving clients, counselors, counselors' employing institutions, and society.

Vocational counselors confront additional situations calling for circumspection and possible restraint. Raising clients' aspirations without an accompanying rise in appropriate occupational opportunities can simply raise anxieties and sometimes create emotional disturbance. The general emphasis on psychic income as an important consideration for clients can paradoxically cause added frustration among clients who learn of subtle job satisfactions they cannot attain.

Counselors aware of the limitations and dangers in helping clients to cope with social constraints rather than succumb to them can better serve client interests and—ultimately—a changed society. In this approach clients are not used as instruments of change or instructed in how to change society. They are assisted in using themselves in a maximally self-actualizing manner that may, in turn, actuate change in society.

CHANGING CLIENT ENVIRONMENTS

A second approach whereby counselors can responsibly change society involves various client environments. The plural *environments* represents an important emphasis that requires constant recognition in vocational counseling. This plural parallels the equally important emphasis on client potentials or potentialities rather than on a single facet of a multidimensional person. Together with client multipotentiality, counselors must help clients consider their multiple environments.

Since efforts to effect change are naturally oriented toward the future, client environments include not only present ones but possible future ones as well. Among the environments affecting clients are their current and future families, educational institutions or training situations, and present and prospective employers. In each instance counselors proceeding with caution may have an opportunity to effect change of benefit to their clients.

Current families of clients have increasingly been recognized as sources of influential impact on vocational counseling. Parents, spouses, and significant others commonly exercise influence—whether conscious or unconscious, whether blatant or subtle—on client values, goals, and expressed vocational preferences. Before inadequately considered preferences become fixed vocational choices, members of the family can be brought into the counseling arena.

More complex interactions within the present family that have vocational implications might call for family counseling. Although mounting knowledgeability about family counseling marks this multiperson procedure, it is not to be used indiscriminately or by counselors lacking pertinent expertise. The same caution applies to vocational planning as it relates to family planning, but clients and counselors do need to be alert to interactions of working lives and nonwork living. Changing one's work role can change one's role within the family.

Educational or training environments are subject to modification by alert clients and counselors who perceive needed change. Such alertness, perceptiveness, and consequent action are only normal aspects of the accepted emphasis on individual differences. If a school program or a training schedule is not responsive to the needs of a particular client, it can often be individually tailored. Even physical environments on numerous campuses have been changed through the efforts of counselors and students. Once these sometimes awesome environments cease to be taken as givens, changes can be accomplished.

In regard to employers, clients presently employed or planning for employment need to be aware of variables in the work situation and in the hiring process that might be changed. Clients frequently quit jobs otherwise satisfying because of factors they regard as fixed. Flexibility is often possible, however, in such matters as work hours, job duties, fringe benefits, and even promotion. Hiring restrictions, already modified by affirmative action legislation, can be further reduced through job development and job placement that open up employer attitudes.

CHANGING COUNSELORS' EMPLOYERS

Institutions employing counselors are no less in need of change than other institutions. There is indeed a recurrent theme in the professional literature that not only recognizes the need for change in employing institutions but also emphasizes the need for counselors to effect change. Waiting for change to occur so that clients may be better served may be regarded as an error of omission.

Among writers who have stressed change in employing institutions are Shoben [8], McCully [7], and Stubbins [10]. Schools were the focus for Shoben and McCully, while Stubbins considered institutional settings more generally. Shoben saw a role for counselors in changing the schools and McCully specified the counselor's effecting change within the educational system to enhance the uniqueness of individuals and their freedom of choice. Stubbins, in his article on "The Politics of Counseling," viewed institutional settings as an obstacle to the accomplishment of the goals of counseling.

Unfortunately, institutional goals and counseling goals differ dramatically in their view of individuals. Employing institutions measure accomplishment of their goals mainly in quantitative terms and display their achievements through charts and graphs. Individuals are at best represented by pins stuck into paper, a depersonalized process that is tantamount to hangings in effigy. Counselors' efforts to treat each individual as a person and to evaluate their effectiveness qualitatively require parallel efforts to create a conductive institutional environment.

Vocational counselors in private practice may feel no necessity on their part to change institutions that employ counselors. Unless they practice in a vacuum, however, their work with clients interacts with related work in institutions employing counselors. Private practitioners also have an indirect stake in improving the world of counseling.

CHANGE THROUGH PROFESSIONAL ASSOCIATIONS

Employed counselors and private practitioners alike have their professional associations available as facilitators of change in society. The strength of counselors banded together is greater than the sum of their single efforts. Professional associations can supplement counselors' change efforts involving clients, client environments, and counselors' employing institutions.

The American Personnel and Guidance Association and its component divisions and branches have become increasingly active and effective on the legislative front. Laws at the federal and state levels can constitute concrete contributions to change related to vocational counseling. The National Vocational Guidance Association has a major role to perform in this regard; as Stephens [9] pointed out, vocational guidance originated as a vehicle for social reform.

The role of professional associations as facilitators of change must itself be facilitated by the active participation of change-oriented counselors. It would be fatuous of counselors to expect their associations to accomplish needed change without inputs, first of all, regarding change needed. Committee work, convention attendance, relevant writing, and other individual means can be employed to further the ends of professional associations and their members.

In addition to exerting influence on pertinent legislation, professional associations can have an impact on federal, state, and local agencies toward increased visibility and added funding for vocational counseling. Faddish funding for career education and failure to distinguish vocational counseling from vocational education obscure the specific contribution of vocational counselors. Agencies such as the U.S. Bureau of Labor Statistics, which is responsible for the *Occupational Outlook Handbook* and other material important in vocational counseling, could be persuaded to augment their staffs with professionally prepared vocational guidance personnel.

VOCATIONAL COUNSELORS AS CITIZENS

In the four approaches previously delineated for effecting change in society, counselors functioned in their conseling role, whether through clients, client environments, counselors' employing institutions, or professional associations. In a fifth approach, counselors function outside their counseling role, simply as citizens. By so doing, they avoid some possible ethical dilemmas and add a whole dimension to their change efforts.

As citizens as well as in their counseling role, counselors can endeavor to influence legislation and social policy. One way of doing this parallels the use of professional associations. A number of nonprofit associations are now available composed of public citizens who have joined hands in a common cause. Such associations are freer than professional associations to engage in lobbying activities. They tend to be larger than professional associations and better staffed for legislative and related campaigns.

Another way counselors can try to influence legislation and social policy is by functioning as individual citizens. They can keep their congressmen, state legislators, and other holders of public office apprised of the need for specific changes that will ultimately benefit the clients of vocational counselors. They can do the same with candidates for public office. These efforts can be made through personal contact or by writing letters.

Letter writing can also be employed by counselors as citizens to reach far more readers. Letters to the editor of a newspaper or of a magazine may stimulate other citizens to become interested and perhaps take positive action with respect to relevant legislation. Some readers are in strategic positions to influence the development of social policy and the course of legislation. Similar outcomes are possible through appearances on radio or television, if these can be arranged by counselors functioning as citizens.

CONCLUSION

It has been proposed that vocational counselors can responsibly change society through five approaches involving: Clients, client environments, counselors' employing institutions, professional associations, and counselors as citizens. Societal change sought is not necessarily radical, abruptly uprooting traditional practices, as desirable as that might be in many instances. Although sweeping change is achievable through broad legislative enactments, efforts to achieve such dramatic change must be accompanied by a constant chipping away of policies and practices that limit the efficacy of vocational counseling.

Counselors who engage in large or small efforts to effect change depart sharply from the passive model that many now regard as passé. Dworkin and Dworkin [3] expressed an expectation that the "passive, cloistered counselor is about to disappear" (p. 753), thus echoing Wrenn's earlier dissatisfaction [11] with "the culturally encapsulated counselor, . . . seeing that which is as though it would always be" (pp. 444–445). A sound professional basis has developed for counselors to be more active both in counseling clients and in changing society.

Since counselors who assume the professional responsibility of endeavoring to change society may run some risk to themselves in the established order of things, they deserve the backing of their professional associations, both to support their efforts and to protect them. Baker and Cramer [1], citing status quo pressures that hamper the "change agent" role of counselors, called for concerted support from the profession to prevent professionally responsible counselors from becoming sacrificial offerings. Change-oriented counselors and their professional associations must be mutually supportive in their common endeavor to create a better world for clients.

REFERENCES

1 Baker, S. B., & Cramer, S. H. Counselor or change agent: Support from the profession. *Personnel and Guidance Journal*, 1972, *50*, 661–665.
2 Blocher, D. H. Can the counselor function as an effective agent of change? *The School Counselor*, 1966, *13*, 202–206.
3 Dworkin, E. P., & Dworkin, A. L. The activist counselor. *Personnel and Guidance Journal*, 1971, *49*, 748–753.
4 Fenlason, A. F. *Essentials in interviewing*. New York: Harper & Row, 1962.
5 Gordon, E. W. Perspectives on counseling and other approaches to guided behavior change. *The Counseling Psychologist*, 1970, *2*, 105–114.
6 Hansen, D. A. Social change and humanistic confusion: Considerations for a politics of counseling. In E. L. Herr (Ed.), *Vocational guidance and human development*. Boston: Houghton-Mifflin, 1974. Pp. 130–155.
7 McCully, C. H. The counselor: Instrument of change. *Teachers College Record*, 1965, *66*, 405–412.
8 Shoben, E. J., Jr. Guidance: Remedial function or social reconstruction? *Harvard Educational Review*, 1962, *32*, 430–443.
9 Stephens, W. R. *Social reform and the origins of vocational guidance*. Washington, D. C.: National Vocational Guidance Association, 1970.
10 Stubbins, J. The politics of counseling. *Personnel and Guidance Journal*, 1970, *48*, 611–618.
11 Wrenn, C. G. The culturally encapsulated counselor. *Harvard Educational Review*, 1962, *32*, 444–449.

FOLLOW-UP FOR SECTION ONE

Questions

1 The following pertain to Borow's "Shifting Postures toward Work: A Tracing" and your reactions to it.

    a What is the Protestant ethic?

    b What effect does the Protestant ethic have on your work behavior? If your answer is "none," describe the work ethic to which you do subscribe.

    c What are your personal attitudes toward work?

    d What effect does your socioeconomic status (SES) have on your attitudes toward work?

    e What effect has your upbringing had on your attitudes and your work behavior?

    f What effect do your personal attitudes and work behavior have on your capacity to provide vocational counseling?

2 On the basis of Overs's article "The Interaction of Vocational Counseling with the Economic System," what should counselors *do* differently?

3 Morrill, Oetting, and Hurst identify three dimensions of counselor functioning. Describe and give an example of each. Then divide the fourteen practices which Campbell suggests in "Career Guidance Practices Transcending the Present" into their appropriate categories according to the Morrill, Oetting, and Hurst model.

4 According to Ginzberg in "A Critical Look at Career Guidance," the profession must take several steps if it wants to improve the delivery of vocational guidance services. Select one of his recommendations and prepare a 500-word argument either agreeing or disagreeing with the premise.

5 Compare and contrast the views about the potential for providing quality vocational guidance as expressed by Warnath in "Vocational Theories: Direction to Nowhere" and Sincik in "Can Vocational Counselors Change Society?" in terms of (a) the economy; (b) the adequacy of our present theories; and (c) society's needs.

Learn by Doing

1 What's important? Some occupations are seen as making a greater contribution to society than others. Present the "Fallout Shelter" exercise to a group of students. It may be found on page 281 of *Values Clarification* (Hart Publishing Co., Inc.).*

2 Why work? The purpose of this exercise is to provide counselor-trainees with insight into how others feel about the world of work. Present a group guidance lesson on one of the following topics or a similar one of your own:

    The Changing Work Ethic (Guidance Associates)*

    Conflict in American Values: Life-Style vs. Standard of Living (The Center for Humanities)*

    The Work Ethic: A Victim of Progress (Current Affairs)*

    Job Attitudes (Guidance Associates)*

3 What makes you tick? Complete the assignment of the same name in Appendix B.

4 How do others feel? The purpose of this assignment is to provide the counselor-trainee with information about how others feel about the world of work. Select an individual and use the appropriate set of guidelines for interviewing which will be found in the Taped Interview Format in Appendix A.

*See Appendix H for additional information.

5 Does simulated poverty hurt? Play the popular game Monopoly* with several class-mates. Compare and contrast the feelings of the winner and the loser. To what extent did the experience represent a microcosm of the class struggle in our country today?

6 To learn more: Prepare an abstract based on one of the articles listed below under Additional Resources. Consult Appendix G for format suggestions.

Additional Resources

Ciavarella, M. A. Toward an integrated theory of educational and vocational choice. *Vocational Guidance Quarterly*, 1972, *20*, 251–258.

Crites, J. O. Career counseling: A review of major approaches. *Counseling Psychologist*, 1974, *10*, 3–23.

Darcy, R. L. A classroom introduction to work. *Occupational Outlook Quarterly*, 1971, *15*, 23–26.

Dolliver, R. H., & Nelson, R. E. Assumptions regarding vocational counseling. *Vocational Guidance Quarterly*, 1975, *24*, 12–19.

Gartner, A., & Riessman, F. Is there a new work ethic? *American Journal of Orthopsychia-try*, 1974, *44*, 563–567.

Ginzberg, E. *Career guidance*. New York: McGraw-Hill, 1971.

Heilbroner, E. L. Middle-class myths: Middle-class realities. *The Atlantic*, October 1976, pp. 37–42.

Hoffman, S. D., & Rollin, S. A. Implications of future shock for vocational guidance. *Vocational Guidance Quarterly*, 1972, *21*, 92–96.

The job blahs: Who wants to work? *Newsweek*, Mar. 26, 1973, pp. 79–90.

Lasson, K. *The workers: Portraits of nine American jobholders*. New York: Bantam Books, 1972.

Noeth, R. J. Student career development: Where do we stand? *Vocational Guidance Quar-terly*, 1975, *23*, 210–218.

Osipow, S. H. *Theories of career development*. New York: Appleton-Century-Crofts, 1973.

Samler, J. *The vocational counselor and social action*. Washington, D. C.: American Person-nel and Guidance Association, 1970.

Stefflre, B. Vocational development: Ten propositions in search of a theory. *Personnel and Guidance Journal*, 1966, *44*, 611–616.

Stephen, W. R. *Social reform and the origins of vocational guidance*. Washington, D.C.: American Personnel and Guidance Association, 1970.

Terkel, S. *Working*. New York: Pantheon Books, 1972.

Walton, L. E. The scope and function of vocational guidance. *Educational Outlook*, 1957, *31*, 119–128.

Walz, G., Smith, R., & Benjamin, L. (Eds.) *A comprehensive view of career development*. Washington, D.C.: American Personnel and Guidance Association, 1974.

Weiss, R., & Kahn, R. Definitions of work. *Journal of Social Problems*, 1960, *8*, 142–150.

Whiteley, J. M., & Resnikoff, A. (Eds.) *Perspectives on vocational development*. Washington, D.C.: American Personnel and Guidance Association, 1972.

Winters, A. R. Another view of the American work ethic. *The Vocational Guidance Quar-terly*, 1972, *21*, 31–34.

Wool, H. What's wrong with work in America. *Vocational Guidance Quarterly*, 1975, *24*, 155–164.

*See Appendix H for additional information.

Section Two

Structural Approaches

The study of theory serves as a link between researchers and practitioners. But for the practitioner, the study of theory alone is not sufficient. Without an appreciation for practical implications of theories, practitioners would be left to their own devices—some of which might work and some of which might not. Therefore, each article on theory in this and the next section is followed by readings that describe how the theories can be applied.

There are several ways that the various approaches can be organized. Any scheme is to some extent arbitrary, especially since the theories are more similar than dissimilar. Yet the theories appear to differ on one basic issue. Some of the theories provide an explicit link between people and the world of work and others do not. Approaches which do provide this link are called *structural* approaches and are discussed in this section. Those that do not are called *process* approaches; they will be discussed in Section Three.

The link between the individual and the world of work is crucial. Structural approaches provide an organization of both the individual *and* the environment. Since the ultimate outcome of vocational counseling for most clients is the choice of a vocation, the interaction between the individual and the environment is of the utmost significance. Studying the *link* between them permits the counselor and client to explore systematically not only the client's characteristics but also the characteristics of the marketplace. To learn about the marketplace, structural approaches rely heavily on the use of occupational information. Counselors are called upon to provide clients with a vast array of facts about the world of work.

The link between the client and the environment is established by means of psychometric instruments and matrices that integrate client personality, needs, or interests with job titles or occupational groups. The greatest strength of structural approaches is the ease with which counselors can help clients coordinate their characteristics with concrete job titles or occupational groups; and this may also be its greatest weakness. Some critics view the structural approach as simplistic and static: It is seen as simplistic because it is so very easy to apply and tends to *describe* vocational behavior rather than *explain* it. It is static in that it does not emphasize the processes associated with making a choice but rather assumes that individuals make one choice at one point in their lives and tends to suggest that they never get a second or third chance. Those who endorse the structural approach would respond that their emphasis is on the immediate choice, and that there is nothing to prevent clients from choosing anew throughout their lives as needed.

The structural theories are the oldest in the field, and the trait-and-factor approach dates back to the early 1900s. The trait-and-factor approach has been associated variously with Frank Parsons, one of the founders of the guidance movement, and later with E. G. Williamson of the University of Minnesota, where much of the pioneering work on interest measurement has taken place over the past half century. The trait-and-factor approach has played such a prominent part in the development of guidance that any discussion of today demands an overview of its historical antecedents. My article, "Trait-and-Factor Counseling: Yesterday and Today," describes the basic three-step trait-and-factor approach as originally established by Parsons over fifty years ago. Probably the greatest continuing contribution of this approach has been the development of interest inventories and other psychometric devices by Edward K. Strong, Jr., G. Frederick Kuder, and others.

Devices such as inventories and tests are popular with counselors because they make their job easier. A skilled interviewer can of course determine a client's interests without the use of psychometric devices, but using them takes considerably less time and may be more reliable. Trait-and-factor counselors are characterized as relying too heavily on tests and inventories, and it is true that in the past some counselors relied on them almost to the exclusion of developing a working relationship with their clients. Premature testing (administering a test before rapport has been established) is too often a function of the counselor's low frustration tolerance, and counselors would be wise to postpone the use of psychometric instruments until they have some assurance that they have developed a solid working relationship with their clients. Typically, this takes several sessions. Once the basis for an open and honest relationship has been established, the counselor is in a better position to help the client deal with test results. There are several approaches to interpreting test results.

Ray Bixler and Virginia Bixler describe two basic approaches: In the first the counselor shares with the client his or her opinion about what the client should do, and in the second the counselor does not. In "Test Interpretation in Vocational Counseling," Bixler and Bixler conclude that the best approach, for them, is a straightforward five-step model which stresses the need for a simple statistical prediction based on the test data. First published in 1946, this article is still applicable today.

Richard R. Stephenson does not agree with the Bixler and Bixler approach. He takes issue with the counselor's interpretive role. In "Client Interpretation of Tests," he argues that clients benefit most when they interpret test results themselves. His position is consistent with nondirective therapy. The two basic approaches to test interpretation are very different. The former places a great deal of responsibility on the counselor, the latter places chief responsibility on the client. Just as no single theory is best, there is no best way to interpret test results. Counselors need to decide which approaches work best with which clients.

John Holland's work represents a digression from the trait-and-factor approach. He identifies six types of environments, commonly referred to by the acronym RIASEC. The environments are Realistic, Investigative, Artistic, Social, Enterprising, and Conventional. Corresponding to these six environments are six personality types (also referred to by RIASEC). To a greater or lesser degree, each client's personality resembles one or more of the six personality types. The counselor's job is to help clients identify their personality type and explore occupations in the corresponding work environment. Holland's theory might be summed up by the saying, Birds of a feather flock together. I describe the theory and its application in my article, "The Holland Model: What It Is and How It Works."

Holland's work qualifies as a structural approach because it organizes both people (six personality types) and the world of work (six environments); it provides a convenient model for classifying occupations and those who work in them. Samuel Helms discusses various uses of the system in his article "Practical Applications of the Holland Occupational Classification in Counseling."

Holland has developed two inventories: the Vocational Preference Inventory (VPI) and the Self-Directed Search (SDS). The SDS is a self-scored simulated guidance experience. It is popular because it is efficient and easy to use. Counselors find it practical because SDS output and results are coordinated with the input for the Holland Occupational Classification. A client's personality type can easily be translated into a series of corresponding job titles. Clients enjoy the informal format of the SDS and its immediate feedback. Like the trait-and-factor approach, it tends rather to describe vocational behavior than to explain it. Holland does not go into how people develop the types of personality they exhibit. Nor does he provide much assistance for individuals who are dissatisfied with their personality types and the corresponding occupational titles.

Anne Roe's theory is based upon Maslow's needs theory of personality. Her approach, unlike the others mentioned above, is not as yet associated with any instrumentation. Roe postulates that a client's childhood upbringing influences what type of occupation the client will seek out and the probable level of attainment in the chosen field. Her theory qualifies as structural in that it posits a link between an individual's personality and the world of work. Roe's six-by-eight classification scheme is the basis for Jo Ann Harris's article, "The Computerization of Vocational Information." Harris demonstrates how Roe's approach can be successfully integrated into high-school vocational-guidance programs.

In summary, all of the approaches in this section are structural: They organize both individuals *and* the world of work. They permit the client to translate information on certain psychological characteristics into information on corresponding occupations. They are popular because they are efficient and easy to implement. Critics claim that the trait-and-factor and Holland approaches do not sufficiently explain how people become the way they are. None of these approaches emphasizes the processes by which people develop their careers; the articles in Section Three address those matters more directly.

8. Trait-and-Factor Counseling: Yesterday and Today*

Stephen G. Weinrach

To understand the present and make reasonable predictions about the future, we must look to the past. Vocational guidance did not come about overnight, but as the result of experimentation and various social and environmental conditions. Most of the experimentation and research was conducted by industrial and differential psychologists. Educators, social reformers, and political leaders reacted to the social and environmental conditions of their times. After a survey of the antecedents of vocational guidance, we will proceed to discuss the use of the trait-and-factor model today.

THE ANTECEDENTS OF VOCATIONAL GUIDANCE

A thorough investigation of the historical background of vocational guidance reveals no clear-cut beginnings. Borow (1964) attributes the slow evolution of the vocational guidance movement to the following four conditions: "*economic* (e.g., the rise of industrialism and the growing division of labor); *social* (e.g., urbanization, child labor, immigration, and transmigration); *ideological* (e.g., a restless spirit of freedom and a spreading belief in the improvability of man and his status); and *scientific* (e.g., the emergence of the human sciences—psychophysiology in the first half of the nineteenth century and, subsequently, the psychophysics and experimental psychology of Fechner, Helmholtz, and Wundt, and the mental testing of Cattell, Binet and others" (p. 48). This article outlines the contributions of Frank Parsons, D. G. Paterson, E. G. Williamson, Elton Mayo, and Frederick Taylor, and looks at the impact of World War II. What we know as the trait-and-factor approach bears the stamp of these individuals and that decisive historic event.

The Contributions of Frank Parsons and Donald G. Paterson

The work of Parsons (1854–1908), who is credited with being the father of the guidance movement, and that of D. G. Paterson (1892–1961) are closely related. Parsons is generally credited with initiating systematic vocational guidance in the United States. His contribution is one of the many spontaneous developments that marked the onset of the movement. Parsons' posthumously published *Choosing a Vocation* (1909) elaborates his conceptions of vocational guidance and is one of the earliest and most influential statements about the nature of the enterprise. He brought to the field not only a zeal for reform in accordance with the social and economic movements of his time, but a conception of vocational guidance which was to become known in later years, as it is today, as the trait-and-factor approach. According to Parsons (1909):

*I wish to acknowledge the assistance of Jayne Fonash and Patricia Broderick in the preparation of earlier drafts of this article.

In a wise choice there are three broad factors: (1) a clear understanding of yourself, your attitudes, abilities, interests, ambitions, resources limitations, and their causes; (2) a knowledge of the requirements and conditions of success, advantages and the disadvantages, compensation, opportunities, and the prospects in different lines of work; (3) true reasoning of the relations of these two groups of facts (p. 5).

He further asserts that there were three basic components to vocational guidance: (1) Testing; (2) information giving; and (3) decision making through "true reasoning." He envisioned appraising the individual through the use of psychometric methods which would measure abilities, interests, and various other characteristics. Since there were few psychometric instruments for the assessment of the individual at that time, Parsons was forced to rely on case studies.

Parsons also had a keen interest in collecting and disseminating occupational information. He felt that his students needed to be aware of the differences in occupational and educational requirements (including aptitudes, interests, and personality factors) which were necessary for success in particular job settings. He developed the concept of "true reasoning," which is concerned with matching an individual to a job on the basis of rational decision making. Unfortunately, this approach has tended to emphasize matching, disseminating occupational information, and giving advice—at the expense of encouraging self-realization through occupational choice.

Psychometrician D. G. Paterson feared that counselors had become overwhelmed with the second of Parsons' principles—dissemination of occupational information to clients—and were neglecting them as individuals. To correct this condition, Paterson studied individual differences and test development during the 1930s in association with the Minnesota Employment Stabilization Research Institute, and his work resulted in a series of published bulletins.

Paterson and his colleagues provided an objective and scientific basis for Parsons' early formulations. Their development of such instruments as the Minnesota Mechanical Abilities Tests (Paterson, Elliot, Anderson, Toops & Heidbreder, 1930) and the Minnesota Occupational Rating Scales and Counseling Profile (Paterson, Gerkin & Hahn, 1941) has proven invaluable to psychologists and counselors.

Role of Industrial Psychology

While Parsons was approaching the problem from the vantage point of an educator, industrial psychologists like Hugo Munsterberg were pursuing their own aims by testing job applicants to identify their suitability for given jobs. "One may observe that Munsterberg and later industrial psychologists understood Parsons' reasoning and strategy better than did vocational educators and some psychologists who were content with job observations and second-hand descriptions as well as with self-analysis" (Williamson, 1965, p. 8). Interest continued outside the educational community for many years and continues today.

In 1912, Munsterberg published the original German edition of *Psychology and Industrial Efficiency*, which remains one of the seminal contributions to the study of occupational choice and industrial performance. An American edition appeared in 1913, and Munsterberg immigrated to America to continue his study of occupational psychology at Harvard University.

Elton Mayo (1880–1949) and his colleagues, also at Harvard, experimented with worker behavior at the Hawthorne plant of the Western Electric Company in Chicago. Their most famous investigation, designed to study the relationship between environmental conditions of work, monotony, and employee fatigue developed into "an extended series of precedent-setting researches revealing the complex nature of worker performance" (Borow, 1964, p. 53). The results of this study are referred to today as the "Hawthorne effect." It states, in brief, that production will increase or decrease in direct proportion to the amount of attention the workers receive from management, and makes clear the importance of interpersonal relations, employee morale, and leadership in the performance and productivity of industrial workers.

In a similar vein, Frederick Taylor (1856–1915), who investigated the nature of production, "standardized work units by means of objective observation and studies of time and motion of workers" (Williamson, 1964, p. 855). A standardized work unit provides a basis of comparison of productivity from worker to worker, and is thus an objective external criterion.

> For the first time we had available an *objective external criterion* against which to check and to correlate the emerging psychometric tests of aptitudes. This use of an external criterion in validating aptitude tests proved to be not only significant for the emerging psychology of work and of human capabilities, but it also made possible the diagnosis of capabilities required for various tasks *before training or employment was undertaken.* This invention was as significant for western industrial civilization as was the invention of the wheel in earlier centuries (p. 855).

Concurrently with these developments in the United States, researchers were busy in other parts of the world. Lahy and Clarapede began using psychological tests for industrial and vocational purposes in France. Both applied psychological testing "to the identification of workers in various industries who were either accident prone . . . or unsatisfactory in meeting the requirements of the employer" (Williamson, 1964, p. 855). As history would have it, educators and industrial psychologists were working on similar aspects of the same problem simultaneously, but independently. Only later did they begin to benefit from each others' efforts.

The Role of World War II

The national emergency leading up to and during the participation of the United States in World War II pushed work-force problems to a crisis. Our nation needed increased productivity at the very time when thousands of workers were serving in the armed forces overseas. The efforts of counselors, personnel psychologists, and placement workers were greatly stepped up. The U.S. Employment Service and War Manpower Commission constantly worked together to broaden and intensify their research, testing, and placement programs. War Department classifications and assignments were developed into tests and allied selection tools by the Personnel Research Section of the Adjutant General's Office. Similar research and procedures evolved in each of the armed services. For example, the Army developed the Army General Classification Test (U.S. Army, 1948). All these new instruments set new standards for the validation and standardization of psychometric testing. Stanine scores, which convert raw scores to standard scores on a scale of 1 to 9 were also introduced at this time.

Contributions of the armed forces and government agencies continued throughout the war and continue to the present day. Millions of dollars have been appropriated by Congress and federal agencies for research, training programs, and the dissemination of vocational information. Vocational guidance received a tremendous boost from nationwide work-force studies and the establishment of vocational counseling services for the veterans of several wars.

As can be seen, there have been various contributing factors to the development of what we know today as vocational guidance. The attention of social reformers and educators, like Parsons, was largely limited to the assessment of individuals and matching them to suitable jobs. On the other hand, industrial psychologists were more concerned with identifying the characteristics associated with job performance. World War II to a certain extent caused the integration of these two approaches. To help meet the complex industrial needs of a nation at war, highly sophisticated psychometric instruments and procedures were developed. Many of the instruments and procedures used at that time are still in use today. And thus, vocational guidance had its beginnings as a result of experimentation and various social and environmental conditions. The model which evolved is known as trait-and-factor counseling; it has also been referred to as the Minnesota Point of View and Actuarial Counseling.

TRAIT-AND-FACTOR COUNSELING TODAY

Trait-and-factor counseling, as we know it today, is predicated on the assessment of occupational attitudes and abilities and requirements for jobs. The name "Minnesota Point of View" came about because of the pioneering work of Edmund G. Williamson (born 1900) and his colleagues at the University of Minnesota. Williamson, who was Dean of Students between 1941 and his retirement in 1969, spent considerable time counseling students for educational and vocational choices. Others, including Paterson, have contributed to the Minnesota Point of View, but it has come to be identified primarily with Williamson. "The combination of the vocational-occupational background and the educational setting distinguishes this approach from all the other points of view in counseling" (Patterson, 1973, p. 8).

Counseling as a Rational Experience

While this approach is essentially rational and logical, it is still associated with what Williamson calls "personalism"—a concern for the whole individual. Williamson views "man" as a largely rational individual, capable of wise choices so long as he has adequate information on which to base them. Williamson concedes that a major objective of education is knowledge of the world, but contends that another kind of knowledge, useful to the student in achieving and maintaining personal adjustments, should also be made available in the educational framework.

Trait-and-factor is a cognitive approach and falls in line with other learning approaches to counseling theory. In brief:

> . . . the individual is organized in terms of a unique pattern of capabilities and potentialities (traits). These traits, in turn, are correlated with the requirements of different jobs. Thus, there is a rather homogeneous set of qualities (factors) which are both needed for success in each job and possessed by workers within any given job category. Testing, i.e., the objective measurement of traits, is the best means for predicting future job success. Each individual attempts to identify his own traits and to find a way of working and living which will enable him to use his capabilities effectively (Zaccaria, 1970, p. 26).

Here counseling joins with teaching in "a comprehensive program geared to the strategic objective of helping each individual to select and grow toward personal goals, of which one is the full development of each individual member of our democratic society" (Williamson, 1950, p. 4). Williamson views the goals of education and counseling as the same—"the optimum development of the individual as a whole person and not solely with respect to his intellectual training" (p. 25). Therefore, "counseling is as fundamental a technique of assisting the individual to achieve a style of living satisfying to him and congruent with his status as a citizen in a democracy as are the instructional techniques used by the teacher in classroom and laboratory, to achieve stipulated academic or educational goals in the field of knowledge" (p. 3).

WILLIAMSON'S VIEW OF MAN

Like other counseling approaches, the trait-and-factor model is predicated upon the belief in certain philosophical principles. According to Williamson (1965), people are rational and capable of solving their own problems. "Counselors must believe that man is capable of learning to solve his own problems, especially if he learns to utilize his own abilities . . . I wish to be counted among those who have very strong prejudices in favor of man's rational processes, in contrast with any intuitive capacity he might possess" (pp. 181–183).

Williamson (1950) expresses his view of the nature of man in terms of five basic questions for which he has only provisional answers himself. He suggests that counselors need to address themselves regularly to these questions in relation to their counseling. They are (Patterson, 1973):

1 What is the nature of human nature, the nature of man?
2 What is the nature of human development?
3 What is the nature of the "good life" and "the good"?
4 What is the nature of the determination of the "good life"?
5 What is the nature of the universe, and what is man's relationship to that universe? (pp. 10–11)

Williamson's approach is thus concerned with the total development of individuals so that they may grow and develop to their optimum potential.

THE THREE-STEP PROCESS

The trait-and-factor model for vocational counseling consists of the following three-step model:

Step 1. Discovering individual traits or characteristics. It is assumed that each individual is made up of a unique set of traits or characteristics, which can be identified through a systematic use of psychometric instruments. The instruments attempt to uncover the individual's interests, values, experiences, and wishes. The student's abilities, both academic and manual, are assessed through a formal assessment program as well as through the use of cumulative records. Although the purist trait-and-factor counselor may rely exclusively on surveys and tests to obtain the data this process requires, it is possible to interview a client and gather much of the information through self-report. Once the data-collection phase is completed, certain inferences and predictions are made about the type of work, work setting, and working conditions under which the individual is likely to perform satisfactorily.

Step 2. Analyzing occupational requirements. This requires counselors to have at their disposal information about employment trends, entry-level requirements, and the personal characteristics and skills suitable to given occupations. Some of this information is "common sense," while some is based on statistical evaluation of individuals employed in given occupations.

Step 3. Matching individual to the job. This aspect of the process is largely dependent on the economy and availability of employment at the time when the client is seeking help. Because the trait-and-factor approach views human beings as rational, it assumes that the choice a client makes will be based on true reasoning and will not be affected by irrational factors. The matching phase is highly pragmatic. In essence, it is the fitting of round pegs into round holes and square pegs into square holes.

BUT OFTEN IS.

Using Tests in Counseling

Despite the increasing sophistication of psychometric instruments, critical issues remain regarding their appropriate use. Super (1958) suggests the following rationale:

> Tests for use in counseling should describe a person so that we can see him as he is at the time of testing; they should predict what he will be like and what he will do at some future date; they should be relatively timeless and they should, like the people they test, be multipotential. . . . They should tell what curricular and occupational groups he resembles, and how closely he resembles them. One of the purposes of testing is to get a picture of the person with whom he is dealing, to see to what degree he has a variety of psychological characteristics, where his relative strengths and weaknesses are, and how he compares in each of these characteristics with others who have had comparable experiences and have reached a comparable state of development, or who are engaged in activities in which he might engage (p. 3).

In addition, counselors are well advised to consider the following questions carefully before administering any instruments, and thus to ensure more conscientious and reliable vocational guidance.

1 Will this instrument help this particular client answer his or her questions?
2 What type of population was used in establishing norms for this instrument?
3 What ways are there, besides testing, to obtain the same information?
4 Will I be able to interpret the results in a meaningful way to the client?

The effective and appropriate use of tests requires a good deal of information and skill. Counselors often rely on three different kinds of instruments: (1) aptitude tests; (2) interest inventories or surveys; and (3) performance tests. Tests, by definition, have preferred responses; there are right and wrong answers or desirable performance levels. Surveys and inventories which measure interests, however, do not have preferred responses. There are no right or wrong answers when interests are being measured. It is especially important to make this distinction clear when communicating results to clients. The following is a brief description of three types of instruments mentioned above.

Aptitude Tests
An aptitude test is often defined as measuring "readiness for learning," in terms of genetic characteristics, life history, physical surroundings, and previous learnings. Aptitude tests are thus ability tests "designed to appraise what the individual *can learn to do* if he receives appropriate education or job training" (Thorndike & Hagen, 1969, p. 644). Two examples are: The General Aptitude Test Battery (GATB) (U.S. Department of Labor, 1973) and the Differential Aptitude Test Battery (DAT) (Bennett, Seashore, & Wesman, 1974).

Interest Inventories or Surveys
Interests are tendencies to prefer particular types of vocational and avocational activity. They should not be confused with readiness or abilities. Interest surveys "tend to focus on occupational and educational interests" (Thorndike & Hagen, 1969, p. 649) through the choice of preferred activities. Since there is no preferred response per se, such instruments should be referred to as surveys or inventories; not tests. Two examples are the Kuder Form DD Occupational Interest Survey (Kuder, 1976) and the Strong-Campbell Interest Inventory (SCII) (Campbell, 1977).

Performance Tests
"A [performance] test [is] most often an intelligence test, in which ability is evaluated in terms of something the individual *does*, rather than something he *says*. Tasks included are such things as mazes, form-boards, block-building, etc." (Thorndike & Hagen, 1969, p. 651). A typing test is a measure of performance. Two other examples are the Wechsler Adult Intelligence Scale (WAIS) (Wech-

sler, 1955), and the Stanford-Binet Intelligence Scale—Form LM (Terman, Merrill, & Thorndike, 1972).

Beyond the role of tests in counseling and their proper selection and use, there are still other issues on which there is not unanimous agreement among the experts. Many of these unresolved issues revolve around the questions which Williamson raised about counseling theory and philosophy. It is also important to consider the decline in popularity of the trait-and-factor approach.

Underlying Assumptions: Some Second Thoughts

The process of the three-step model can be stated simply, but there are certain philosophical assumptions that warrant further discussion. Counselors subscribing to the trait-and-factor approach need to address themselves to the following issues.

1 *Is the current state of the art of testing (diagnosis) sufficient?* The trait-and-factor approach is dependent on testing and on certain research models. The entire matching procedure assumes that the collection of data through tests is accurate since, according to Williamson (1968), without proper diagnosis effective counseling cannot take place. One must seriously question whether our assessment techniques are sufficiently sophisticated for us to place so much emphasis on them.

2 *Are tested interests necessarily primary vocational interests?* Let us consider the individual who indicates a high interest in manual work, for example a welder, who also scores high on tests of academic achievement. The counselor may interpret the interest in manual dexterity as a primary interest related to vocational choice rather than as an avocational interest. In reality, the individual might succeed and find greater job satisfaction as a teacher whose hobby is sculpture than as a full-time welder or mechanic.

3 *Will tested interests remain constant throughout a person's life?* To assume that they will is based on a static view. The interests and values one expresses at age 20 may be quite different from one's interests and values at age 45. To view the process of choice as a single, unrepeatable event is to deny the likelihood that interests and values are subject to the fluctuations of circumstance and experience.

Jones (1970) identifies the following four assumptions underlying the trait-and-factor approach:

4 *The opportunity for occupational choice occurs once during a client's life span.* The trait-and-factor point of view, tending to view the client in a static manner, does not rely on the knowledge we now have about human development. It seems more likely that vocational choice is a lifelong process that reaches from early childhood to death. Counselors working from a trait-and-factor point of view may spend a good deal of time with clients at one particular stage of development, e.g., between ages 17 and 22, and not address their clients' initial explorations during elementary school or their continuing needs at middle age.

5 *Vocational development is essentially a cognitive process rather than an affective one—or possibly a combination of the two—and the use of reasoning alone is sufficient to come to a wise choice.* In fact, decision making is a function of both thought and emotion.

6 *There is an occupational choice open to each individual.* This directly conflicts with the economic realities of the world of work. In most industrialized societies, like the United States, 100-percent employment seems unlikely. There will always be some unemployed; complete freedom of choice does not exist for all.

7 *There is a single right choice for each individual.* Not only is the chance of a single right choice remote, but it is virtually impossible to determine. Occupational choice is frequently a function of circumstance rather than of so-called true reasoning. It would be unrealistic to view the matching process as a one-shot chance for a perfect match.

Dolliver and Nelson (1975) identify two further untenable assumptions:

8 *Work can be inherently satisfying for everyone.* This is unrealistic. Large numbers of workers receive neither gratification nor adequate compensation for what they do. For many people work is only the means by which they support themselves. Their pleasures and satisfactions come from their non-work-related activities.

9 *Vocational counseling is a simple process requiring little effort, commitment or time on behalf of the client.* Clients often expect the process to take less than one hour. In reality, helping individuals make wise choices takes a considerable amount of time. Client discomfort is not unusual.

THE DECLINE OF THE TRAIT-AND-FACTOR APPROACH

The rigidity of matching individuals with occupations and the popularity of the client-centered approach of Carl Rogers (1951) have both contributed to the decline of the trait-and-factor approach. According to Aubrey (1977):

> Unfortunately most of the tools adopted by vocational guidance did not fulfill the hopes and aspirations of its early founders. If anything, these tools worked against the very individuals it sought to help by rigidly labeling, classifying, categorizing, and sorting individuals instead of aiding them in arriving at greater self-determination and human dignity (p. 291).

Critics of the trait-and-factor approach disapproved of its *directive* methods. They claimed that the teacher-pupil relationship on which the Minnesota Point of View was based fostered client dependence upon the counselor. The *nondirective*, client-centered therapy of Carl Rogers stood out in sharp contrast to the directive approach and was quickly embraced by the counseling profession. Emphasis thus shifted from vocational guidance through testing to counseling for personal development (Aubrey, 1977, p. 292). Counselors rejected the trait-and-factor approach with its emphasis on assisting clients in their cognitive development and began helping clients explore their feelings. Unfortunately, this shift does not coincide with the needs perceived by the clients. In a nationwide survey of students in grades 8 and 11 (Prediger, Roth & Noeth, 1974, pp. 209–210), results indicated that students expressed concern twice as often in the area of "making career plans" than in the area of "discussing personal concerns." Fortunately, we are currently experiencing a rebirth of interest in career education and vocational guidance.

SUMMARY

Skilled trait-and-factor counselors attempt to help their clients assess their strengths and weaknesses and interests and values in relation to the characteristics and skills required for employment in various occupations. This assistance is offered in one or more interviews in which test results are reviewed and interpreted and rational decisions are attempted.

The trait-and-factor approach to vocational counseling is a highly pragmatic three-step cognitive process. The first step consists of assessing the client's interests and abilities (traits). The second step consists of determining which characteristics (factors) are required for each occupation. The third step is one of matching the individual with an occupation. One reason that trait-and-factor counseling remains popular is that it can be implemented with great ease by means of commercial and government-prepared materials. These give the counselor access to information on the characteristics thought to be prerequisites for entry into various occupations. In a short series of interviews during the latter years of high school or college, the counselor can assist clients in making rational choices on the basis of the already collected data.

Clients' interests may change over the years, but choices must be made at specific points in life. Decisions are not made in abstraction but somewhere along the continuum of a client's life. The first phase of the model, collecting data, provides clients with some useful, reality-based information about themselves at the time when decisions must be made.

In a review of the contributions of the trait-and-factor model over the past half-century, Williamson (1964) applauded Super's innovative approach to the integration of life stages within a theory of career development. He concluded that Super's process model "promises to make vocational guidance a lifelong process for many individuals at various stages of emerging need for reconsideration and rediagnosis of capabilities and then rematching them with opportunities" (p. 858). A more integrative view of trait-and-factor counseling would necessitate ongoing contact with clients at various stages of their development in an attempt to provide them with opportunities to learn more about their interests and abilities, and to use their knowledge in terms of course selection and similar types of ongoing decision-making situations.

REFERENCES

Aubrey, R. F. Historical development of guidance and counseling and implications for the future. *Personnel and Guidance Journal*, 1977, *55*, 288–295.

Bennett, G. K., Seashore, H. G., & Wesman, A. G. *Differential Aptitude Test Battery*. New York: Psychological Corporation, 1974.

Borow, H. (Ed.) *Man in a world at work*. Boston: Houghton Mifflin, 1964.

Campbell, D. P. *Strong-Campbell Interest Inventory Manual*. Stanford: Stanford University Press, 1977.

Dolliver, R. H., & Nelson, R. E. Assumptions regarding vocational counseling. *Vocational Guidance Quarterly*, 1975, *24*, 12–19.

Jones, A. *Principles of guidance* (Rev. 6th ed.), New York: McGraw-Hill, 1970.

Kuder, F. *Kuder Form DD Occupational Interest Survey*. Chicago: Science Research Associates, 1976.

Munsterberg, H. *Psychology and industrial efficiency*. Boston: Houghton Mifflin, 1913.

Parsons, F. *Choosing a vocation*. Boston: Houghton Mifflin, 1909.

Paterson, D. G., Elliott, R. M., Anderson, L. D., Toops, H. A., & Heidbreder, E. *Minnesota Mechanical Abilities Tests*. Minneapolis. University of Minnesota Press, 1930.

Paterson, D. G., Gerkin, C. d'A., & Hahn, M. E. *Minnesota Occupational Rating Scales and Counseling Profile*. Chicago: Science Research Associates, Inc., 1941.

Patterson, C. H. *Theories of counseling and psychotherapy*. New York: Harper & Row, 1973.

Prediger, D. J., Roth, J. D., & Noeth, R. J. Career development of youth: A nationwide study. *Personnel and Guidance Journal*, 1974, *55*, 97–104.

Rogers, C. R. *Client-centered therapy*. Boston: Houghton Mifflin, 1951.

Super, D. E. *Use of multifactor test batteries in counseling*. Washington, D.C.: American Personnel & Guidance Association Press, 1958.

Terman, L. M., Merrill, M. A., & Thorndike, R. L. *Stanford-Binet Intelligence Scale—Form LM*. Boston: Houghton Mifflin Co., 1972.

Thorndike, R. L. & Hagen, E. *Measurement and evaluation in psychology and education*. New York: John Wiley & Sons, 1969.

U.S. Army. *Army General Classification Test*. Chicago: Science Research Associates, 1948.

U.S. Department of Labor. *General Aptitude Test Battery*. Washington, D.C.: U.S. Government Printing Office, 1973.

Wechsler, D. *Wechsler Adult Intelligence Scale*. New York: Psychological Corp., 1955.

Williamson, E. G. Counseling and the Minnesota point of view. *Educational and Psychological Measurement*, 1968, *7*, 147–157.

Williamson, E. G. *Counseling of adolescents*. New York: McGraw-Hill, 1950.

Williamson, E. G. An historical perspective of the vocational guidance movement. *Personnel and Guidance Journal*, 1964, *42*, 854–859.

Williamson, E. G. *Vocational counseling*. New York: McGraw-Hill, 1965.

Zaccaria, J. *Theories of occupational choice and vocational development*. Boston: Houghton Mifflin Co., 1970.

9. Test Interpretation in Vocational Counseling*

Ray H. Bixler and Virginia H. Bixler

There are two aspects to the problems of test interpretation: (1) the presentation of test results and their predictive possibilities in a manner which is understandable to the client, and (2) methodology of dealing with the client in order to facilitate his use of this information. The ultimate goal of vocational guidance is not only accurate prediction but also optimal use of the prediction by the client. It is in this respect that vocational guidance differs most from personnel selection.

Vocational counseling as a process has not received a great deal of attention in the literature. Neither formal discussions nor case records provide the counselor with an understanding of how the counseling process develops. The usual case record merely states "Tests were interpreted." There has been no scientific study of various counseling procedures and their effectiveness when tests are introduced into the process. However, it is only through the evaluation of counseling processes that we shall be able to improve the more subjective skills involved in dealing with client motivation—the factor which facilitates or handicaps his use of job information, test data, and academic planning.

Test interpretation seems to fall into two broad categories: one involves the opinion of the counselor as well as the data; the other deals with the prediction alone. Examples have been taken from case records to illustrate each approach.

INTERPRETATIONS INVOLVING OPINIONS OF THE COUNSELOR

1. Clinical Interpretations   (as opposed to scientific). George verbalized an interest in medicine. Measures of established predictive value indicated that the vast majority of students at his level of academic aptitude and achievement would succeed. However, he earned a low score on the *Cooperative Natural Science Achievement Test* which has little or no predictive value for medicine (at the University of Minnesota). The counselor *felt* this was evidence that George would be handicapped in the pre-medical curriculum. On this basis, he urged George to go into business or law, his secondary interests.

2. Interpretation Involving Persuasion   Robert's test results indicated that success was more likely for the majority of students with scores like his in fields other than engineering, his preference. In interpreting the tests the counselor explained that he had a better chance of success in business and urged him to enter this field because he would be happier in a field where he was successful.

3. All or None Interpretation.   A graduate student who received a percentile

*Source: Reprinted with permission from the authors and publisher from *Educational and Psychological Measurement*, 1946, *6*, 145–155. Copyright 1946 Educational and Psychological Measurement.

rank of 19 on *Miller's Analogies* as compared to graduate students, came to one of the writers in tears saying, "Dr. X. told me that graduate work was the last thing in the world I should be doing. He said I had no business even attempting it."

INTERPRETATION INVOLVING LITTLE OR NO OPINION

1. Statistical Prediction Applied to the Individual Client   "You have an 80% chance of succeeding in agriculture and a 60% chance of succeeding in business."

2. Straight Statistical Prediction   "Eighty out of one hundred students with scores like yours succeed in agriculture while sixty out of one hundred succeed in business."

The above interpretations need not be mutually exclusive and seldom are. In order to evaluate these approaches, one must consider them in relation to difficulties which may hinder the client's acceptance of information which is offered.

Distortion of information on the part of the client is a frequent obstacle. The client's desires and fears interfere with the use he may make of information and may color his interpretations.

Even in the traditional information-giving situation of the classroom, instructors are aware of the fact that distortion does operate. The grading of examinations at the end of the quarter verifies the ineffectiveness of books and lectures in giving information to students. Vocational test interpretation is much more personalized and there is greater opportunity and reason for the student to distort or disregard information given to him.

It is not difficult to find examples of the distortion of data by the client. One young man who had been tested and counseled reported to the speech clinician who was responsible for the referral, that he was in the upper 20% of the general population in intelligence. In response to a question about the rest of the tests he replied that that was all the counselor had told him. In reality, this client had been given information concerning the complete battery of tests he had taken. He had chosen to remember only that aspect which was important to him. An emotionally immature adult, he was the rejected member of a family of three sons. He didn't go to college as had his brothers because his father decided he was "too dumb." One would expect him to cling to his intelligence test results which seemed to vindicate him. All other results were quite extraneous to his needs.

Another client, after being told his results on the *Kuder Preference Record*, and their significance, decided that they meant he should go into engineering despite the fact that his computational interest score was at the twentieth percentile and his only high percentile was persuasive. As he said himself, he "had never thought of anything but engineering."

Reports often filter back to a counselor about the "things recommended and discouraged" which have no basis in fact. The distortion of information is usually more in keeping with the desires of the client than the actual test results. Distortion seems to occur more frequently with interest and personality tests.

Another obstacle to optimal use of test interpretation by the client is the occasional traumatic effect of the predictions. Failing students frequently turn to vocational tests in the hope of determining another field in which they can be successful. When test results indicate that they are not suitable college material they are brought face-to-face with a terrifying fact. Their defenses are stripped from them by the concreteness of the data. Here test results operate in much the same manner as an interpretation of emotional behavior to a disturbed client who is not ready to accept it. Intellectual recognition of limitations can be traumatic when it is not also accompanied by an emotional acceptance.

Therefore, in choosing a method of test interpretation and guidance, the counselor must remember that the client may find it necessary to distort or disregard information or that he may become disturbed by its significance.

The method of test interpretation and vocational counseling described in the remainder of this paper has been employed with college students and in the rehabilitation of the tuberculous. Any evaluation of it must be empirical at present.

In accepting any philosophy of counseling, one's answers to the following questions are pertinent.

1   Shall the counselor's goal be to avoid failure on the part of the client?
2   Shall the counselor pave the way for the client?
3   Shall the counselor contribute his opinion as well as information? (There are many who feel that the counselor's opinion is his major contribution because there are now areas in which there is relatively little scientific certainty.)
4   Shall the counselor adhere to the concept that the client is fundamentally responsible for the decisions made and the manner in which they are carried out?

In other words, how much can the counselor respect the integrity of the client? The method of vocational counseling which will be presented is based upon this faith in the fundamental integrity of those we assist. The counselor does not urge a plan of action nor does he set goals. The counselor's responsibility is to give the client information, clarify his attitudes toward that information and towards his limitations, and finally to assist him in implementing his plans.

How the process of vocational guidance is structured to the client will affect his reaction to this method of test interpretation. The preliminary interview has been described elsewhere.

After taking the battery of tests the client is given an interpretation of the results without the counselor's opinions. The results are presented in general terms and illustrated with examples. A student in the upper 10% of his high-school class and in the upper 25% on a college aptitude test might be told, "We have found that the best indication of success in most college courses is how well you do in high school and how you rate on a learning ability test. You were in the upper 10% of your high-school class and exceeded seven or eight out of ten college students on the learning ability test. Most people with scores like that learn complex things relatively easily and quickly. For example, most students with scores like yours would succeed in college and get better than average grades." The counselor should use actual prediction tables when they are available. The last sentence of the interpretation then might be "Eighty out of one hundred students with scores like yours would succeed in college and sixty would get better than average grades."

The counselor does not personalize the prediction for the client nor does he imply in any fashion what he thinks the client's course of action should be. This responsibility is assumed by the client. This tends to free the client to discuss his reaction to the test results and to clarify the application he may make of them to his problems. The counselor who states, "You ought to do excellent work in college," will probably find the client less responsive, and as a result will be of less service in helping him to integrate the data with his personal desires.

Even the interpretation of low academic aptitude should be handled in the same factual manner. Some counselors cannot bring themselves to be frank with such clients, while others avoid the issue by pushing the client towards an occupation requiring little academic aptitude. It would seem that the interpretation of low scores in the same way as high scores is also a matter of ethics. Clients in a neutral setting can and frequently do make a real growth in self-acceptance if they are free to give vent to their anxieties and disappointments.

Personality and interest tests are difficult to interpret since they are demonstrated to have little or no predictive value, and the question of what they actually measure remains unanswered. In spite of this inadequacy some vocational counselors still base their decisions about which field the client should enter largely upon the way a client classifies himself on an interest test. Sometimes other tests such as the Minnesota Clerical and achievement tests are used to encourage clients to enter fields for which they have no predictive value. Perhaps this is due to the need felt by the counselor to give more than he can in terms of vocational advice.

The following procedure is suggested as an alternative. "This test gives us an indication of what you may enjoy doing. So far as we can tell it has nothing to do with how successful a person will be in a field. The majority of people with scores like yours enjoy helping people. (High social service—artistic and musical, secondary.) Fields like social work, clinical psychology, nursing and teaching appeal to them. People with scores like yours are also somewhat interested in art and music. There are areas which combine both of these interests, like occupational therapy and nursery school work." This interpretation is impersonal; it enables the client to relate it to himself, or to reject it, and it frees him to clarify his own motivation. Interpretation of personality tests is even more challenging. Because they deal with the most personal qualities of the individual, their interpretation is often traumatic. Neither of the writers feels he has found a satisfactory method of interpreting these tests to clients, and for the most part does not attempt to do so. Of the *Bell Adjustment Inventory*, for example, one could say, "You seem to feel that you have more difficulties at home than you do at work, or in your social living."

A client categorized as maladjusted is usually unable to use it in a constructive sense. On one hand such a person finds it necessary to rationalize his test results, or otherwise defend himself, making it difficult for the counselor to serve him in a therapeutic sense while, on the other hand, his problems are intensified by this seemingly undeniable objective measure of his weakness.

The frequency with which clients come to counselors quite disturbed about personality test interpretations given by others, is, when combined with our own experience, mounting evidence that when such interpretations are given at all, they must be adroitly handled.

Personality tests do not seem to contribute to the psychotherapist since they yield symptomatic diagnosis rather than any picture of causal relationships. Their use in personnel selection seems justifiable even in their present stage of development, but it is difficult to know what they can contribute to counseling.

Actual statements of prediction are only the beginning phase of vocational counseling. When the client begins to apply these predictions to his own plan, deciding what they mean to him, and what he wishes to do as a result of them, the more crucial phases of counseling have begun. The client either integrates the test predictions into his thinking and thus makes use of them, or he distorts or rejects them. The more he feels free to discuss his reactions with the counselor, the more likely it is that he will come to a logical acceptance of their significance. The following case excerpts illustrate this phase of vocational counseling:

C: There are studies which demonstrate that students' ranks in high school along with the way in which they compare with other entering students in mathematics, are the best indication of how well they will succeed in engineering. Sixty out of one hundred students with scores like yours succeed in engineering. About eighty out of one hundreed succeed in the social sciences (names several). The difference is due to the fact that study shows the college aptitude test to be important in social sciences, along with high school work, instead of mathematics.

S: But I want to go into engineering. I think I'd be happier there. Isn't that important too?

C: You are disappointed with the way the test came out, but you wonder if your liking engineering better isn't pretty important?

S: Yes, but the test say I would do better in sociology or something like that. (Disgusted.)

C: That disappoints you, because it's the sort of thing you don't like.

S: Yes, I took an interest test, didn't I? (C nods.) What about it?

C: You wonder if it doesn't agree with the way you feel. The test shows that most people with your interests enjoy engineering and are not likely to enjoy social sciences.—

S: (Interrupts.) But the chances are against me in engineering, aren't they?

C: It seems pretty hopeless to be interested in engineering under these conditions, and yet you're quite sure.

S: No, that's right. I wonder if I might not do better in the thing I like— Maybe my chances are best in engineering anyway. I've been told how tough college is, and I've been afraid of it. The tests are encouraging. There isn't much difference after all—Being scared makes me overdo the difference.

He decides to go into engineering and seems quite at ease with his decision.

The next excerpt portrays a different problem. The student has been in pre-medicine for two quarters and is beginning to fail. His scores on all tests are very low. Some explanation of prediction has already been given:

C: About two or three students out of one hundred with scores like yours succeed in pre-med.

S: I knew they'd turn out like that. (Disappointed.)

C: Even though you expected this, it's pretty hard to take.

S: Yes sir, but I got off to a bad start this year. It's the same story. My advisor discouraged me, so did Mr. R. in Dean X's office, and now the test discourages me. I want to try another quarter next fall with a fresh start. I think starting new with a good rest I can do it. If I fail then, I'll know I can't be a doctor, but I'm not satisfied with that yet.

C: You feel everything discourages you, but you haven't given yourself a fair trial. You think next fall will tell the story.

S: Yes, I do, even though they didn't agree with me, and the tests are on their side.

The third illustration deals primarily with distortion of data. The client's interest scores were typically persuasive (99th percentile). Other scores mechanical (72nd percentile) computational (20th percentile) science (70th percentile). C. has already interpreted results.

S: That means I'm best suited for engineering, doesn't it?

C: That's the way it seems to stack up to you.

S: Yes. (Turns the discussion to persuasive fields and merits of various phases of them then.) I really ought to be much more interested in mathematics to go into engineering, shouldn't I?

The trauma of low scores is illustrated in the next excerpt. The counselor has indicated that about fifteen to twenty students out of one hundred succeed in college:

S: (Looks stunned, then confused.)

C: This is awfully disappointing.

S: Yes, it is. I had hoped I'd find something I could succeed in.

C: It seems to leave you without anything to go into.

S: Yes, but I can do the work. I have trouble concentrating, my study habits are poor, I never studied in high school and I don't know how.

C: You feel the reason for your trouble is your poor study habits, not a lack of ability.

S: Yes, I didn't get good grades in high school, but I didn't study either. Now when I want to study I worry and get tense. My mind goes blank when I take tests.

C: You're pretty worried about your school work and that seems to make it harder to succeed. (Pause.)

S. It's my last hope. (Head sinks on chest, lips quiver.)

C: You're so upset about this you feel like crying.

S: (Does) I feel so silly. (C recognizes her embarrassment, and she continues to cry and discuss various elements of her anxiety about school.) I've got to make good. I'm not as smart as most kids, that's true. There are some subjects that go over me, but I think I can make it. I don't know what to do.

C: You have to make good and yet you're afraid you can't. It leaves you pretty badly mixed up.

S. decides to continue seeing C. until she can work out a solution. She leaves interview accepting her limited ability, but is not sure which of several courses to take.

The counselor has made no attempt to correct distortion or encourage a plan of action, or to comfort the client through reassurance. If the counselor has given the client an adequate interpretation, further explanation at that point is of less value than an opportunity for the client to come to grips with his motivation for distortion. In the first illustration the prospective engineer not only arrives at an excellent application of a test to his own problems, but is capable of minimizing the anxiety he has held for college work when he has insight. In the second and third illustrations the counselor could have stepped in to correct the client's application of test data to himself, but it is questionable whether this would have achieved anything. The counselor's acceptance and clarification of the client's attitude did seem to bring each to a better understanding.

The pre-medical student brings into focus the ineffectiveness of authoritative advice when the client is not in agreement. Discouragement on the part of this student's advisor, the dean's assistants and the test data was ignored. Perhaps it is necessary for some students to be faced with the reality of failure in order to change their goals. This client's goal probably never could be changed by counselors. The persuasion of counselors only motivated him to strengthen his defenses and postpone acceptance of the inevitable. This client may return for further help if he feels a need for it because the counselor has not made eventual failure an issue between them.

In the last illustration the client is able to express her anxiety, to obtain a better acceptance of her limitations, and to come to a realization that there is a solution. She was deeply disturbed by her college experiences to date, and the test results intensified this. The counselor's recognition and clarification of feelings has been instrumental in her expression of these anxieties and her subsequent modification of them.

When the counselor allows the client to make his own personal interpretation, he is free to express these attitudes which so frequently interfere with his use of test data. As he expresses them to an accepting counselor, there is a greater opportunity for them to dissipate and the client will gain better insight into his motivation. It is only as the client can understand and accept himself that he can make actual use of tests or other data.

Recognition of elements in vocational guidance which are emotional rather than intellectual in nature allows the counselor to become more effective in helping clients.

SUMMARY

Vocational counselors should utilize not only test interpretation and vocational information but also techniques to facilitate the client's utilization of this data. Counselors should:

1   Give the client simple statistical predictions based upon the test data.
2   Allow the client to evaluate the prediction as it applies to himself.
3   Remain neutral towards test data and the client's reaction.
4   Facilitate the client's self-evaluation and subsequent decisions by the use of therapeutic procedures.
5   Avoid persuasive methods. Test data should provide motivation—not the counselor.

REFERENCES

Bixler, R. H. and Bixler, V. H. "Clinical Counseling in Vocational Guidance." *J. clin. Psychol.*, I (1945), 186–192.

Rogers, Carl R. *Counseling and Psychotherapy*. New York: Houghton-Mifflin Company, 1942.

10. Client Interpretation of Tests*

Richard R. Stephenson

Basic to all educational-vocational counseling is the clinical use of psychological tests. All counselor training curricula require that an intern counselor become proficient in the areas of test construction, validation, administration, and interpretation. There are many good textbooks in these areas. Unfortunately, however, in the important area of communicating the results of these tests to clients, there are few published references.

Indeed, the didactic need for explication in this area is conspicuous. The research need for such explication was clearly stated by Williamson and Bordin, in their critique of methodology in counseling investigations, as follows: "The scant knowledge of specific counseling techniques has forced us to study the total process. . . . As specific techniques are isolated and described, then new types of evaluation studies may replace the present gross experiments. Such studies, however, would not appear to be possible until more adequate descriptions of techniques are made available by those who actually counsel students" [15, p. 459]. One wonders why 20 years have seen so little satisfaction of these needs?

In 1955, Strong [11, p. 195] observed that: "It is most likely that every expert counselor has several 'pet' interpretations of the different tests that he employs which would amaze everyone else and probably amaze him if he ever stopped to scrutinize them." Perhaps this applies also to techniques of test interpretation to clients, and perhaps this is the reason why the needs in this area have not been met. Notwithstanding, the purpose of the present paper is to present for scrutiny a somewhat different method of test interpretation for use in educational-vocational counseling. The difference is that, in the proposed method, the *client* plays the role of test interpreter.

While the proposed method was developed independently by the writer, there is, of course, no claim that the writer is the only person to have developed this particular method, nor is it claimed that this is the best of all possible methods. Usage verifies that the proposed method is an adequate method, while common-sense questions that there is one "best" method. (It seems likely that client, counselor, or situational differences make different methods "best" under different circumstances.)

The proposed method has been used with good results with college and precollege students, with non-college persons who come to a university counseling center, and with state vocational rehabilitation clients. It is not for use with clients who are emotionally disturbed.

TRADITIONAL APPROACHES

By way of contrast and introduction, it seems best to begin with a brief survey of basic approaches to the prevailing and traditional philosophy of "counselor-in-

*Source: Reprinted with permission of the author and publisher from *The Vocational Guidance Quarterly*, 1963, *12*, 51–56. Copyright 1963 The American Personnel and Guidance Association.

terprets" test interpretation. With this in mind, the writer was able to locate three, explicit, published sources of "what to say" in test interpretation to clients. These three seem to fairly represent clear-cut points on the traditional interpretive continuum [2, 3, 14].

It should be noted that there are other published references, of which a representative eight are included in the references for this report [1, 4–7, 10, 11, 13]. However, these add little to the basic three to be cited. It should be further noted that an even 50 books and journal references, not here cited, whose titles indicated that they might cover this aspect of educational-vocational counseling, were consulted. These 50 contributed nothing on didactics and are the reason for the opening statement about the absence of published materials on specific techniques.

Thus, we return to the basic three references, of which representative excerpts from each are included in the present paper.

In the Bixlers' method [2] the interpretive technique is oriented along a bipolar dimension involving, at one pole, the opinion of the counselor as well as the data and, at the other pole, interpretation involving the data only. The Bixlers argue for the latter method, stated to the client in the following manner:

> We have found that the best indication of success in most college courses is how well you do in high school and how you rate on a learning ability test. You were in the upper 10 per cent of your high school class and exceeded seven or eight out of 10 college students on the learning ability test. Most people with scores like that learn complex things relatively easily and quickly. For example, 80 out of 100 students with scores like yours would succeed in college and 60 would get better than average grades.

While the Bixlers do present test data in objective terms, it must be noted that they then, though again objectively, *interpret* the data to the client; which is, of course, their intent. For present purposes, then, the Bixlers stand as a clear example of one possible type (non-personalized, counselor-objective, statistical prediction) of counselor interpreted test interpretation to clients.

In the Williamson method [14, p. 140], on the other hand, the approach is personalized, subjective, and nonstatistical, as in the following excerpt:

> (The counselor) . . . phrases his explanation in this manner: As far as I can tell from this evidence of aptitude, your chances of getting into the medical school are poor; but your possibilities in business seem to be much more promising. These are the reasons for my conclusions: You have done consistently failing work in zoology and chemistry. You do not have the pattern of interests characteristic of successful doctors which probably indicates that you would not find the practice of medicine congenial. On the other hand, you do have an excellent grasp of mathematics, good general ability, and the interests of an accountant. These facts seem to me to argue for your selection of accountancy as an occupation. . . .

Williamson characterizes the above method as the "explanatory" approach, which he distinguishes from both the "persuasive" method and the method of giving "direct advice," these latter methods being even more forceful than the example cited. Thus, again we find counselor interpretation, coupled now with subjective, nonstatistical, personalized prediction.

The third example, from the Callis, Polmantier, and Roeber *"Casebook"* [3, pp. 134–135] is cited as an example of an interpretive method that is perhaps midway between the Bixlers and Williamson. The client (S) has just asked about "that intelligence test" he took, and the counselor (C) responds:

> C5—On this test, this is the Wechsler, half of the people will score between 90 and 110, one-fourth of the people below 90 and a fourth of the people above 110. This is the normal curve. *(Counselor sketches a simple curve to illustrate his point.)* I suppose you have been graded on the curve, where most of the people make average grades, a few people make high grades and a few people make low grades. Your score would be right here *(pointing)* 92 indicating as far as average intelligence is concerned you are right here in the average range. You have what we usually call average intelligence. However, there are a number of people who will, on a test such as this, score higher than you will. A number of people will score lower than you will, so you are in this general range in the middle. . . .

> C12—Yes. In other words, this (interpretation) would apparently agree somewhat with your own experience?

> S12—Yes. That came out pretty accurate. I was surprised they could tell that well.

> C13—Mm-huh. Well, if the test is a good test it shouldn't tell you anything that you didn't suspect in the first place. . . . (pause) well, what implications does that have for you?

In the preceding typescript, the data are being presented personally and non-personally, the counselor is being alternately objective and subjective, and the client *is* playing a greater role in the interpretation interview. However, the client is still in the position of receiving the *counselor's* interpretation of the results.

In contrast, let us now consider the proposed alternative technique.

ALTERNATIVE TECHNIQUE

In essence, the proposed technique requires that *the client* interpret *his own* test results! The counselor's role in this situation is to prepare the client for this task and to give guidance and support during the client's interpretation. The client's role is to learn the information necessary for interpreting his test results, to make the interpretation, to explore the ramifications of this interpretation, and to follow through in the sense of making decisions or adjusting plans, or otherwise implementing his modified thinking about himself.

Let us consider the technique in two specific areas, interpreting vocational interest test results and interpreting the results of scholastic aptitude. To keep the discussion of vocational interest test interpretation concrete, we will consider an interpretation involving the Strong Vocational Interest Blank for Men (SVIB). The principles involved are equally applicable, however, to any test or vocational guidance instrument. Scholastic aptitude tests may be considered as general cases.

The counselor begins the interpretation by defining what is meant by the term "vocational interest" or "scholastic aptitude." This general definition leads naturally into a discussion of what the test at hand is measuring. It is at this point that the counselor ensures that no fears or stereotypes are going to distort later reception of test results.

The discussion is then focused on errors of measurement which the writer lumps together under the single rubric "guessing." Next, there is a brief discussion of what the test concerned is *not* measuring. Finally, a word or two is said about stability and faking. This introductory section is then concluded with a summary.

While the introductory section is essentially a teaching situation, the teaching is only partially by "lecture." The remainder is Socratic. Judicious use of the lecture saves time and insures that the client is receiving accurate information. Further, since the information is presented in a conversational style, the client does not perceive that this is an instructional period, nor does he feel that he is being "talked down to." There are frequent summaries. *Any comments of the client may be explored by the counselor.*

Thus, in spite of the information giving role that he is playing, the counselor is counseling all of the time, and may shift out of the test interpretation role at any time. (If he does, however, and only returns to it much later, he will start again with the summary of what and how well the test measures.)

The second phase of the interpretation procedure covers the manner in which the test profile presents the information. In SVIB interpretation this involves discussing letter grade ratings on individual occupational scales and interest family groups. On instruments where this is relevant, there is a discussion of the implications involved in making forced-choice comparisons. Where the test results are to be presented as percentile ranks, the discussion centers on the meaning of a percentile rank, illustrated on scratch paper with an ogive. Norm groups are very carefully examined.

The approach in this second phase is again more active than non-directive, and, again, Socratic. (The intent, again, being both to involve the client in the learning and to "begin the learning from where the student is.") Again, there are frequent summaries and single question "quizzes." Correct learning and client insights are verbally reinforced. At no time during this entire introductory phase does the client see his test profile.

By now, however, the counselor can be fairly sure that the client has no emotional problems that must be worked through and that the client has assimilated the basic knowledge necessary for interpretation. It is at this point, then, that the client is shown his profile form. This is introduced with a comment that he (the client) is to study it awhile, and then tell (the counselor) what it means, with the counselor's role now shifting to clarification and exploration of interpretations. It is at this point that the test interpretation begins. Thus, all interpretations, evaluations, or biases, are the client's.

Generally, the client's first reaction to the SVIB is his high and/or low scores on individual occupational scales. This is, then, the first test of the effectiveness of the counselor's teaching. If, for example, the client says, "It looks like I'd be a good _____," then the teaching was not as effective as when the client says, "It looks like my interests are like those of _____."

In this latter case, by simple reflection or restatement, the counselor can get the client to clarify and elaborate upon the *meanings* of these scores to him, the client. In the former case, it seems that the counselor is faced with a problem of incorrect learning. In this situation it seems incumbent upon the counselor to represent the correct introductory material. Information that is incorrectly given or incorrectly received is worse than no information in educational-vocational counseling.

Assume, however, that the interpretive problem is a problem in distortion. A better example here would be the situation where the client has a number of high scores in, say, social welfare areas, and low scores in biological science areas, but comments, "Gee, I do have interests like doctors, don't I?" While this comment gives the counselor more information in less time than is perhaps possible with any other method of test interpretation, still the problem remains of how to treat the distortion.

The writer feels that more harm than good may result from apparent agreement with a distortion (while waiting to work it through). Especially is this true in the brief contacts that characterize educational-vocational counseling. Thus, the writer does not hesitate to immediately correct the inaccuracy (this doesn't *have to be* done in a rapport destroying manner). Following this, if the client desires, the distortion can be worked through.

Most typically, the client perceives the test results, vocational interest test profile or scholastic aptitude percentile, exactly as they are, though he may not be happy with the reality. If he is unhappy, it cannot be because of something that the counselor has said to him or forced upon him. Thus, the counselor can begin immediately to help the client work through the unhappiness.

However, since most clients are not surprised by their test results, it is most typical of the client at this time to move forward into the areas of decision making, planning, and implementation of this planning. If he does not, the counselor may nudge him just a bit with a general lead, such as, "Well, how does this information affect your plans?" Note that while the test profile is left open face on the desk from this time following, it is the rare client who will refer back to it, which is some indication that the *meaning* of the results has been integrated into the client's thinking.

The above procedure may take from 30 to 50 minutes. This variability is a direct function of the client, both the speed with which he learns and the number of uncovered problem areas that must be worked through. However, there is generally time left over to interpret yet another test, to discuss educational or vocational plans, to discuss occupational information, or to engage in more clinically oriented therapy, if the test results were disturbing to the client.

On the other hand, since the client *may* approach his task slowly, and since interpretation is a process and not a pronouncement, the interpretation of a complex instrument, for example, the SVIB, is never begun except at the start of a counseling hour, nor is the interpretation of a single score test, for example, a test of scholastic aptitude, begun with less than 20 to 25 minutes remaining.

CLIENTS ARE CAPABLE

In a recent paper [9] the writer attempted to delimit objectively all possible techniques of test interpretation to clients. One of these techniques was called "Client Interprets." This technique was included both to make the paradigm complete and also because the writer is, at present, an advocate of this interpretive method.

However, both counselor training experience and professional discussion experiences indicate that it is difficult to gain acceptance for the notion that the client himself is capable of interpreting his own psychometrics, assuming, as ethically we must, that the counselor is present. For example, in his recent text on the use of tests in counseling, Goldman [6, pp. 378–382] summarizes the degree to which the client may be involved in the interpretive process with three examples. These examples parallel closely two of the examples used in the present paper with the third, and preferred, example closely approaching the specific method presented here. The essential difference between the present method and Goldman's third example is that the Goldman technique does not go all the way. That is, the client is involved in the mechanics of interpretation without being given the final interpretive task; the method is not *client* interprets.

SOME ADVANTAGES APPARENT

We may close by citing some of the advantages of a client interpretive approach over the traditional approaches to the problem of communicating test results to clients.

- The counselor makes fullest use of his professional training and status in his teaching role, which is the strength of the Williamson stereotype, but exerts little (ideally, no) pressure on the client through this status.
- The chances of the client misinterpreting what the test actually measured are, if not eliminated, then, at least, greatly reduced.
- All interpretations are insights of the client, and they are all correct or corrected.
- The client is more ready, in the sense of being adequately prepared, to understand and assimilate the test results following this type of interpretation.
- The client has assumed the role of major responsibility for movement and direction from the moment of interpretation, through decision making, to planning for implementation of decisions made, which is the strength of the Rogerian stereotype of client-centeredness.

REFERENCES

1 Bingham. W. Van D. *Aptitudes and Aptitude Testing*. New York: Harper & Brothers, 1937.

2   Bixler, R. H. and Bixler, V. H. Test Interpretation in Vocational Counseling. *Educational and Psychological Measurement*, 1946, *6*, 145–155, and reprinted in Brayfield, A. H. (ed.) *Readings in Modern Methods of Counseling*. New York: Appleton-Century-Crofts, 1950, pp. 184–193.

3   Callis, R., Polmantier, P. C., and Roeber, E. C. *A Casebook of Counseling*. New York: Appleton-Century-Crofts, 1955.

4   Combs, A. W. "Non-directive Techniques and Vocational Counseling." *Personnel and Guidance Journal*, 1947, *25*, 261–268.

5   Darley, J. G. *Clinical Aspects And Interpretation of the Strong Vocational Interest Blank*. New York: Psychological Corporation, 1941.

6   Goldman, L. *Using Tests in Counseling*. New York: Appleton-Century-Crofts, 1961.

7   Gysbers, N. C. "Test Profiles are for Counselees." *Vocational Guidance Quarterly*, 1960, *9*, 9–12.

8   Hadley, J. M. *Clinical and Counseling Psychology*. New York: Knopf, 1958.

9   Stephenson, R. R. Dimensions of Educational-Vocational Test Interpretation Technique. *American Psychologist*, 1962, *17*, 337–338 (abstract).

10 Strang, Ruth M. *Counseling Technics in College and Secondary School* (rev. ed.). New York: Harper & Brothers, 1949.

11 Strong, E. K., Jr. *Vocational Interests 18 Years After College*. Minneapolis: University of Minnesota Press, 1955.

12 Traxler, A. E. *Techniques of Guidance*. New York: Harper & Brothers, 1945.

13 Tyler, Leona E. *The Work of the Counselor* (2nd ed.). New York: Appleton-Century-Crofts, 1961.

14 Williamson, E. G. *How to Counsel Students*. New York: McGraw-Hill, 1939.

15 Williamson, E. G. and Bordin, E. S. "The Evaluation of Vocational and Educational Counseling: A Critique of the Methodology of Experiments. *Educational and Psychological Measurement* 1941, *1*, 5–24, and reprinted in Brayfield, A. H. (ed.) *Readings in Modern Methods of Counseling*. New York: Appleton-Century-Crofts, 1950, pp. 456–473.

11. The Holland Model: What It Is and How It Works

Stephen G. Weinrach*

John L. Holland first published a description of his theory of vocational choice in 1959. Since then, he has developed two psychometric instruments: The Vocational Preference Inventory (VPI) and the Self-Directed Search (SDS). His model for the delivery of vocational guidance services and the Holland Occupational Classification represent other recent extensions of his theory. Holland's theory of vocational choice (1973a) is based on the assumption that vocational interests are one aspect of what is commonly called personality, and that the description of an individual's vocational interests also describes the individual's personality.

Data obtained from interest inventories have traditionally been used in research in the area of interest measurement and vocational counseling, and they have been viewed as rather restricted in application. But they tell us much about an individual's self-concept (Bordin, 1943; Super, 1972), life goals (Biard, 1970), and originality (Holland, 1963). Personality traits are identified by preferences for school subjects, recreational activities, hobbies, and work; vocational interests can be viewed as an expression of personality.

THE THEORY: A TYPOLOGY

Holland's work on personality focuses on the study of types (typology). He contends that each individual to some extent resembles one of six basic personality types. The more one resembles any given type, the more likely one is to manifest some of the behaviors and traits associated with that type. Just as there are six types of personalities, there are six types of environments, which, like personalities, can be described according to certain attributes or characteristics. *Environments are characterized by the people who occupy them.* The personality type of those who work in a school environment (such as teachers) differs from that of office workers (such as typists or file clerks). Environmental type is assessed by surveying its occupants.

Six Types

Holland (1966) originally believed that people could be characterized as belonging to a single one of the six types. His revised theory (Holland, 1973a) suggests that while one type usually predominates, individuals use a wide range of strategies for coping with their environment, and that many coping strategies fall within the boundaries of two or even more types. Heredity and a variety of cultural and personal forces contribute to developing one of the six personality types, which in turn represents preferred ways of coping. Individuals, he argues, should be viewed as belonging primarily to one type, with apparent influences of a second or third type contributing to their overall approach to coping with their environment.

* I wish to express my appreciation to John L. Holland and John H. Hollifield for their comments on earlier drafts of this article. Complete responsibility for its accuracy rests with the author.

The personal characteristics associated with each type include both likes and dislikes. Individuals in each group tend to *approach* certain kinds of activities and *avoid* others. Depending on one's values, the characteristics used to define each type may or may not seem flattering. Some examples are: Conforming vs. nonconforming, rational vs. emotional, practical vs. impractical, attention-getting vs. shy. A complete description and explanation of the types may be found in *Making Vocational Choices: A Theory of Careers* (Holland, 1973a).

The *realistic* individual prefers activities involving the systematic manipulation of machinery, tools, or animals. Such an individual may lack social skills. A typical realistic occupation is that of a machinist.

Investigative people tend to be analytical, curious, methodical, and precise. A typical investigative occupation is that of a biologist. Investigative individuals often lack leadership skills.

Artistic individuals tend to be expressive, nonconforming, original, and introspective. Decorators and musicians are artistic types. Artistic individuals may lack clerical skills.

Social individuals enjoy working with and helping others but avoid ordered, systematic activities involving tools and machinery. Bartenders, funeral directors, and counselors are all social types. Social types tend to lack mechanical and scientific ability.

Enterprising individuals enjoy activities that entail manipulating others to attain organizational goals or economic gain, but they tend to avoid symbolic and systematic activities. Salespeople, office managers, and lawyers are enterprising types. Enterprising individuals often lack scientific ability.

Conventional types enjoy the systematic manipulation of data, filing records, or reproducing materials. They tend to avoid artistic activities. Secretaries, file clerks, and financial experts are conventional types.

Holland's Assumptions

There are four basic assumptions underlying Holland's theory:*

(1) *"In our culture, most persons can be categorized as one of six types: realistic, investigative, artistic, social, enterprising or conventional"* (p. 2). The acronym RIASEC is helpful for remembering the names and order of the six types. The use of types represents an ideal against which each individual can be compared. The manner in which an individual chooses to relate to the environment indicates type.

(2) *"There are six types of environments: realistic, investigative, artistic, social, enterprising or conventional"* (p. 3). For the most part, each environment is populated by individuals of the corresponding personality type. For example, more realistic-type individuals are found in realistic environments than social-type individuals. As people congregate, they create an environment in which individuals of a certain type dominate, and the environment thus created can be identified in the same manner as the individuals dominating it.

*Source: John L. Holland, *Making Vocational Choices*, 1973 (c), pp. 2–5. Adapted by permission of Prentice-Hall, Inc., Englewood Cliffs, N.J.

(3) *"People search for environments that will let them exercise their skills and abilities, express their attitudes and values, and take on agreeable problems and roles"* (p. 4). This assumption is well expressed in the saying, Birds of a feather flock together.

(4) *"A person's behavior is determined by an interaction between his personality and the characteristics of his environment"* (p. 4). The identification of a person's personality type and environment can provide information about the quality of fit or the nature of the pairing.

In addition to the four basic assumptions, Holland (1973a) introduces four key concepts:

1. *Consistency:* This applies both to personality and environmental types. Some types have more in common with other types. For example, artistic and social types have more in common than investigative and enterprising types. One

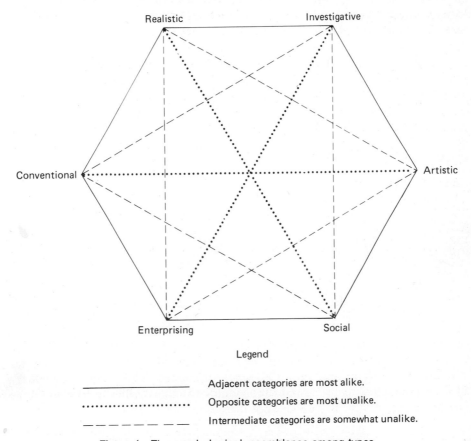

Legend

————————————— Adjacent categories are most alike.

····················· Opposite categories are most unalike.

— — — — — — Intermediate categories are somewhat unalike.

Figure 1 The psychological resemblance among types.

of the main functions of the hexagon is to define the degree of consistency of one's personality. The closer on the hexagon the types that figure in an individual's personality, the more consistent the individual is said to be. For example, the realistic individual who also expresses interest in investigative and conventional activities (RIC) is considered to be more consistent than the realistic individual who expresses a preference for enterprising and social activities (RES).

2. *Differentiation:* Some persons or environments are more pure, which is to say that they show a higher resemblance to a single type and a minimal resemblance to other types; while other persons or environments show an equally relative resemblance to several types. An individual or environment showing an equal resemblance to all six types would be considered undifferentiated or poorly defined. Differentiation can easily be determined by inspecting Total Scores on page 10 of a completed *SDS* booklet.

3. *Congruence:* "Different types require different environments" (p. 4). Congruence occurs when individuals work or live in environments of a type identical or similar to their own. Incongruence occurs, for example, when a realistic individual works or lives in a social environment. Individuals tend to flourish in environments which provide the kinds of rewards which are important to them. Social types prefer the rewards social environments have to offer. The hexagon can be used to determine the degree of congruence between an individual's type and environment. For example, a perfect fit would occur in the case of a realistic type in a realistic environment. The next best fit, or the next highest degree of congruence, would be represented by a personality type which is adjacent to an environment type, e.g., a realistic person working in an investigative environment. The least degree of congruence between person and environment occurs when a person's type and environment appear at opposite points of the hexagon.

4. *Calculus:* According to Holland, "The relationships within and between types or environments can be ordered according to a hexagonal model in which the distances between the types or environments are inversely proportional to the theoretical relationships between them" (p. 5). The hexagon provides a graphic representation of the degree of consistency (within a person or an environment); it also explains the internal relationships of the theory. It has several practical uses. Besides helping counselors understand the theory, it can also be used with clients. *Understanding Yourself and Your Career* (Holland, 1977a) contains a succinct description of the hexagon in language most clients with a seventh-grade reading level or above should be able to comprehend.

Assessing Types

Holland developed two instruments to assess types. The Vocational Preference Inventory (VPI) (Holland, 1975, 1977b) first appeared in 1953 and subsequently has been revised twice. It requires individuals to indicate their vocational interests by selecting job titles which appeal to them. The Self-Directed Search was first published in 1970 and revised in 1977. The SDS was designed to provide vocational guidance by helping individuals expand the number of occupational alternatives they might consider when making an initial occupational choice, changing jobs, or considering additional training. The VPI and SDS may be used at any time in a person's life when vocational decisions must be made. The SDS consists of a consumable assessment workbook to be scored by the client, and a reusable booklet entitled *The Occupations Finder* (Holland, 1977d). The workbook begins with a section on occupational daydreams. Sections follow dealing with competencies, attitudes toward specific occupations, and self-estimates of abilities. The raw scores are converted into a three-letter summary code which reflects a preferred style. The order of the three letters in the summary code is hierarchical, the first letter representing the strongest preference for a particular type.

According to Holland (1972), when counselors interpret the summary code, they should remember that "the first letter in the summary code is the most important because it is the product of a person's most outstanding characteristics. The remaining two letters are by definition less important. However, this interpretation should be moderated according to the actual scores that form the summary code. For example, a code of RIE with scores of 12, 6 and 2 is different than the same code with scores of 12, 11 and 10" (p. 11). The first example, which represents a well-differentiated pattern, has both high (12) and low (2) scores, whereas the second example is flat, or not well differentiated, since the three highest scores differ less than 0 to 4 points.

If the occupations under the categories identified by the client's summary code do not interest the client, then the code can be easily expanded to other permutations of the letters. For example, ESC can be expanded to include SEC, ESC, SE, and SC. This is particularly appropriate where the code is undifferentiated. Where the code is clearly differentiated, exploring the various permutations would negate the strongest characteristic.

The summary code provides the link with the *Occupations Finder,* (Holland, 1977d) which was intentionally organized according to the three letter summary codes, and not alphabetically, so as to force the client to browse through the booklet and thereby explore, at least momentarily, a full range of occupations. The *Occupations Finder* includes a list of the 500 most common occupations in the United States. Each entry includes a six-digit *Dictionary of Occupational Titles* (DOT) number, which facilitates further exploration, and a separate single-digit number that gives a general index of the educational level the occupation requires.

The VPI and the SDS are not the only instruments for assessing types. The Kuder DD (Kuder, 1976) provides individuals with a computer printout of their interests according to job titles; job titles can be converted into Holland codes. The *Professional Manual* for the SDS (Holland, 1972) includes an alphabetical listing of occupations and their corresponding summary codes. The Strong-Campbell Interest Inventory (SCII) (Campbell, 1977) gives scores on the Holland scale.

THE HOLLAND OCCUPATIONAL CLASSIFICATION

Holland's theory loosely organizes people and environments. A logical outgrowth of this approach is the development of a classification system. Holland's Occupational Classification organizes occupations according to the psychological similarities of its workers. Holland's theory is structural, and thus by its very nature provides a link between the individual and the world of work. The Occupational Classification *is* that link.

Organizing occupational information around the coding system used in the theory and the assessment instruments has the advantage of providing an integrated, coordinated, and systematic approach to the delivery of vocational counseling. Furthermore, it affords counselors and clients an opportunity to work together from a common frame of reference.[1]

THE DELIVERY MODEL

There is no single best way to help all clients. Differential treatment and differential diagnosis are basic to good counseling regardless of a counselor's theoretical orientation. Holland and Gottfredson (1975) speculate that a client's code may help indicate the kinds of attention that might be useful. "Still unexplored is the possibility of using the typology to assign or suggest treatment according to type. For instance, I's may profit more from reading, S's from group activities, C's from structured workbooks" (p. 29). In the final analysis, the strategies used for intervening should be adjusted to the needs and expectations of the client.

The Self-Directed Career Program (SDC) (Holland, Hollifield, Nafziger, & Helms, 1972) is a model for delivering vocational guidance services to groups of individuals ranging in age from 15 to 50. This model requires a minimum of *initial* professional intervention. The following materials are required: The SDS Booklet (1977c); *The Occupations Finder* (1977d); and a current edition of the *Occupational Outlook Handbook* (OOH) (U.S. Department of Labor, 1976–1977). *Understanding Yourself and Your Career* (Holland, 1977a) explains the typology to clients in a simple and straightforward manner.

The system consists of a set of simple directions and a checklist. Participants are instructed to take the SDS, calculate the summary code, and read about several appropriate occupations in the *Occupational Outlook Handbook*. The concept of consistent summary codes is explained, and clients whose codes suggest virtually no options in the *Occupations Finder* are instructed to notify their counselors. The SDC is not intended to replace counselors; it does permit one professional to assist many students simultaneously in their *initial* exploration into the world of work. As is often the case, some students will respond well, complete the various steps, and feel comfortable with what they have learned about themselves and the world of work. In these cases, minimal professional intervention seems indicated. The SDC is open-ended, with possibilities limited

---

[1] The various uses of the Holland Occupational Classification are explained in the following article by Samuel T. Helms.

only by the creativity and resources of the counselor. There are several commercially prepared sets of materials which lend themselves to incorporation in the Self-Directed Career Program.

SRA's Job Experience Kits (Krumboltz, 1970) are work-simulation activities. The SRA *Occupational Briefs* (Science Research Associates, 1971) are another source of occupational information for client use. The briefs are particularly useful when time is limited. Both are coded according to the Holland Occupational Classification. Field trips and group guidance activities can be integrated into the Holland model as well.

There will always be students who have trouble with the process described above. Difficulties may take the form of reading problems, indecisiveness, lack of interest, and frustration. The solution in such cases is much the same for counselors working from Holland's perspective as for those working from other perspectives. Individuals with problems need specific types of intervention. Flat profiles are not uncommon. When they appear, counselors need to determine some of the contributing factors. Reading problems or errors in computation of the summary code should be checked first. Often individuals with flat profiles are as indecisive about vocational questions as about matters dealing with life in general. Vocationally related problems frequently have their counterparts in situations outside of work. *Vocational counseling cannot take place apart from educational and personal counseling.* Vocational theories, and Holland's is no exception, apply best to individuals who demonstrate "normal" general development. Individuals experiencing severe personal or educational problems generally need to deal with these concerns before vocational counseling can successfully commence.

RESEARCH

Probably no theory of career development or vocational choice has been researched so extensively as has Holland's. The theorist himself and his associates, as well as the profession at large, have substantiated various aspects of the theory (ranging from the legitimacy of using a typology in the first place to unique applications of the SDS) in over 100 studies. Since 1959, when Holland first published his theory, it has undergone refinement, research, and reformulation (Holland, 1966, 1973a; Holland & Gottfredson, 1974; 1975; Holland, Gottfredson & Gottfredson, 1975). His latest efforts in this direction have yielded an occupational classification system (Holland, 1973c; Holland, Whitney, Cole & Richards, 1969; Nafziger & Helms, 1972; 1974; Nafziger, Holland, Helms & McPartland, 1974) and a self-administered simulated guidance experience, both of which assess personality types (Holland, 1977c). His theory has generated considerable research in the area of bias-free vocational counseling (Holland, 1973a; Holland, 1973d; Zener & Schnuelle, 1972). His model for the delivery of vocational guidance services integrates his theory, classification system and instrumentation (Holland, 1973b; 1977a; Holland, Hollifield, Nafziger & Helms, 1972).

EVALUATION

The foregoing discussion of Holland's model has been essentially free of any of the criticisms leveled against it. Below are some of the more common limitations ascribed to it. A review of Holland's work indicates that over the years many refinements of his theory have come about in response to objections by his critics. As one would expect, his theory is far more refined today than it was at its inception in 1959. Holland is a prolific researcher and writer, and he can be relied on to refine the theory even more in the future. The following list represents frequently expressed objections.

1. *The SDS in particular and Holland's model in general is sexist.* Critics use Holland's own data, which indicate that women score higher than men on the SDS Conventional scale and men score higher than women on the SDS Realistic scale, as proof that the instrument is sexist. They argue that it discourages women from entering the skilled trades and men from entering office occupations. Holland (1973d) contends that: "If one asserts that the SDS does discourage women from entering the skilled trades, then they should demonstrate that there are women, who, if they never encounter the SDS, will choose occupations in the skilled trades" (p. 6). There seems to be little evidence that this in fact is the case. At this time, it appears that whether or not they have been exposed to the SDS, more women choose to enter office occupations than the skilled trades.

Furthermore, women who have spent most of their time raising children, as opposed to working outside of the home, invariably tend to have a summary code of SAE (homemaker) or a code very similar to SAE. Holland (1973d) contends that "it is important to remember that at the time of any vocational assessment of fitness for an occupation, everyone's performance (women, men, blacks, psychiatric or physically handicapped) depends upon one's past experience as well as one's innate potential. And no matter what, everyone has to live for a while with his current level of proficiency. The SDS is one example of a device to help a person make decisions in terms of current assets or liabilities" (p. 5).

Reliable interest inventories accurately reflect the interests of the individual at the time the inventory is administered. That many women and men respond in traditional ways is not so much an indictment of the instruments but rather a reflection of the cultural influences on their development. Good vocational counseling requires counselors to assist their clients in expanding their vocational options (Holland, 1974a).

2. *The theory does not sufficiently explain how people become the types they are.* According to Osipow (1973, p. 77), Holland is vague on this topic. This is probably a fair objection to Holland's earlier work. Recently, however, Holland has made some effort in this direction. He states (1973d):

> According to the theory that led to the SDS, a person becomes oriented toward some occupations as opposed to others because of a special life history of activities, competencies, self-perceptions, values, etc. Consequently, if we desire to change the vocational aspirations of a person or a special group, we must change the experience of people before they arrive at the age when they must go to work. The SDS works as

well as it does because it relies upon the special socialization that leads to a person resembling one personality type more than another (pp. 5–6).

The fact remains that although Holland's theory of vocational choice is predicated on the assumption that vocational choices are a function of one's personality, it does not provide a full account of how personalities develop or can be changed.

3. *Counseling needs to be a personalized experience for everyone.* Counseling, in a traditional sense, has been a dyadic relationship between a highly skilled counselor and a client in need of assistance. Even with the emergence of group counseling, the emphasis has been on establishing a close relationship. Counseling as a discipline tends to attract individuals who themselves prefer personal, close, intimate relationships, as opposed to detached, impersonal ones. (Counselors are social types.) Consequently many counselors believe that all of their clients *need* that same kind of intense and personal relationship. According to Holland (1973b), "These beliefs have prevented any major revision of the delivery system for vocational services. Some experience and recent experiments strongly imply that most people want help not love" (p. 5). This is Holland's defense against criticism that his Self-Directed Career Program (Holland, et al., 1972) and The Paper Guidance System (Holland, 1974b) ought to be more humanistically oriented.

4. *Matching models are static and outdated.* Holland's model is far removed from Parsons' strict approach to traits and factors circa 1909. Furthermore, there is nothing to prevent counselors from repeating the matching process whenever clients need vocational counseling. Only the structural theories provide an explicit link between the individual and the world of work. This permits the client to translate personal characteristics, interests, and abilities into an appropriate occupational title. It is pragmatic.

Some critics believe that Holland's system is simplistic and that, by definition, career counseling must be a highly complex procedure in every case. Holland disagrees. There appears to be ample evidence of the legitimacy of using a typology like his. However, Holland would agree with his critics that the process of assessing type is not always easy. It often requires a skilled counselor to assist a client who has an inconsistent or undifferentiated profile. Professionals are often needed to help students explore various permutations of their code and to help them locate appropriate occupational information.

SUMMARY

Holland's theory of vocational choice is based on the study of personality types. It has been nicknamed "Birds of a feather" because that saying sums up its basic assumptions about social behavior. Holland's (1973a) most recent revision of the theory includes a number of important refinements. The most important is the recognition that people and environments are not of a single type, but rather belong primarily to one type with apparent influences from a second and frequently a third. Holland has developed two instruments for the purpose of assessing types. The Vocational Preference Inventory was developed in the fifties.

More recently he developed the Self-Directed Search, which is a simulated guidance activity. Its *Occupations Finder* facilitates the exploration of a wide range of occupational alternatives. Holland's model is structural, and his typology of persons and environments represents an explicit link between the individual and the world of work. His model is a pragmatic method for the systematic delivery of vocational guidance services.

REFERENCES

Baird, L. I. The relation of vocational interests to life goals, self-ratings of ability and personality traits, and potential for achievement. *Journal of Counseling Psychology,* 1970, *17,* 233–239.

Bordin, E. S. A theory of interests as dynamic phenomena. *Educational and Psychological Measurement,* 1943, *3,* 49–66.

Campbell, D. P. *Strong-Campbell Interest Inventory Manual.* Stanford: Stanford University Press, 1977.

Helms, S. T. Practical applications of the Holland Occupational Classification in counseling. *Communique,* 1973, *2,* 69–71.

Holland, J. L. A theory of vocational choice. *Journal of Counseling Psychology,* 1959, *6,* 35–45.

Holland, J. L. Explorations of a theory of vocational choice and achievement: II. A four year prediction study. *Psychological Reports,* 1963, *12,* 537–594.

Holland, J. L. *The psychology of vocational choice.* Waltham, Mass.: Blaisdell Publishing Co., 1966.

Holland, J. L. *Professional manual—the self-directed search.* Palo Alto: Consulting Psychologists Press, 1972.

Holland, J. L. *Making vocational choices: A theory of careers.* Englewood Cliffs, N.J.: Prentice-Hall, 1973. (a)

Holland, J. L. *Some practical remedies for providing vocational guidance for everyone.* (Center for Social Organization of Schools Report No. 160). Baltimore: Johns Hopkins University, October, 1973. (b)

Holland, J. L. *The development and current status of an occupational classification.* Presentation at the American Personnel and Guidance Association Convention, San Diego, February, 1973. (c)

Holland, J. L. Sexism, personal development and the self-directed search. Baltimore: Johns Hopkins University, Center for Social Organization of Schools. Unpublished manuscript, 1973. (d)

Holland, J. L. Some guidelines for reducing systematic biases in the delivery of vocational services. *Measurement and Evaluation in Guidance,* 1974, *6*(4), 210–218. (a)

Holland, J. L. The paper guidance system. Baltimore: Johns Hopkins University, Center for the Social Organization of Schools. Mimeographed paper, 1974.

Holland, J. L. *Manual for the Vocational Preference Inventory.* Palo Alto: Consulting Psychologists Press, 1975.

Holland, J. L. *Understanding yourself and your career.* Palo Alto: Consulting Psychologists Press, 1977. (a)

Holland, J. L. *The Vocational Preference Inventory.* Palo Alto: Consulting Psychologists Press, 1977. (b)

Holland, J. L. *The self-directed search.* Palo Alto: Consulting Psychologists Press, 1977. (c)

Holland, J. L. *The occupations finder.* Palo Alto: Consulting Psychologists Press, 1977. (d)

Holland, J. L., & Gottfredson, G. D. *Applying a typology to vocational aspirations.* (Center for Social Organization of Schools Report No. 176). Baltimore: Johns Hopkins University, June, 1974.

Holland, J. L., & Gottfredson, G. D. *Using a typology of persons and environments to explain careers: Some extensions and clarifications.* (Center for Social Organization of Schools Report No. 204). Baltimore: Johns Hopkins University, October, 1975.

Holland, J. L., Gottfredson, G. D., & Gottfredson, L. S. Read our reports and examine the data—A response to Prediger and Cole. *Journal of Vocational Behavior,* 1975, *7,* 253–259.

Holland, J. L., Hollifield, J. H., Nafziger, D. H., & Helms, S. T. *A guide to the self-directed career program: A practical and inexpensive vocational guidance system.* (Center for Social Organization of Schools Report No. 126). Baltimore: Johns Hopkins University, 1972. (ERIC Document Reproduction Service No. 064-516).

Holland, J. L., Whitney, D. R., Cole, N. S., & Richards, J. M., Jr. *An empirical occupational classification derived from a theory of personality and intended for practice and research.* (ACT Research Report No. 29). Iowa City, Iowa: The American College Testing Program, 1969.

Krumboltz, J. D. Job experience kits. Chicago: Science Research Associates, 1970.

Kuder, F. Kuder Form DD Occupational Interest Survey. Chicago: Science Research Associates, 1976.

Nafziger, D. H., & Helms, S. T. *Cluster analyses of the SVIB, MVII, and Kuder OIS as tests of an occupational classification.* (Center for Social Organization of Schools Report No. 138). Baltimore: Johns Hopkins University, September, 1972.

Nafziger, D. H., & Helms, S. T. Cluster analyses of interest inventory scales as tests of Holland's occupational classification. *Journal of Applied Psychology,* 1974, *59,* 344–453.

Nafziger, D. H., Holland, J. L., Helms, S. T., & McPartland, J. M. Applying an occupational classification to the work histories of young men and women. *Journal of Vocational Behavior,* 1974, *5,* 331–345.

Osipow, S. H. *The theories of career development.* New York: Appleton-Century-Crofts, 1973.

Science Research Associates. *Occupational briefs.* Chicago: Science Research Associates, 1971.

Super, D. E. Vocational development theory: Persons, positions, processes. In J. M. Whiteley & A. Resnikoff (Eds.), *Perspectives on vocational guidance.* Washington, D.C.: American Personnel and Guidance Association, 1972.

U.S. Department of Labor, Bureau of Labor Statistics. *Occupational outlook handbook.* Washington, D.C.: Government Printing Office, 1976–1977.

Zener, T. B., & Schnuelle, L. *An evaluation of the self-directed search.* (Center for Social Organization of Schools Report No. 124). Baltimore: Johns Hopkins University, 1972.

12. Practical Applications of the Holland Occupational Classification in Counseling*

Samuel T. Helms

Every year reams of occupational literature are written, published, and disseminated. It arrives in the counselor's office in various forms—booklets, pamphlets, leaflets, brieflets, and so on. How, then, can all this literature be organized so that counselors, clients, and students can use it productively?

Holland's classification demonstrates that occupations may be organized into homogeneous groups based on their psychological similarities. Furthermore, these homogeneous groups are interrelated. It makes sense, then, to consider organizing this mass of occupational information in the same manner—that is, grouping the *literature* about occupations in the same way that the occupations themselves have been grouped.

To implement this idea, the first step is to obtain an alphabetized listing of the occupations in Holland's classification, complete with assigned codes. (This listing is available in the Counselor's Manual for the Self-Directed Search.) Using the list, the proper code may be assigned to each piece of information. Next, some bookcases can be placed in a high traffic area. One shelf may be assigned to each of the six major occupational categories—RIASEC. Each shelf could contain file boxes for the literature. The boxes could be labeled with two-letter codes indicating the primary and secondary characteristics of the occupations within that category. For example, the "Investigative" shelf would hold separate boxes labeled **IR, IA, IS, IE & IC.** An additional box, simply labeled **I,** could accommodate publications that discuss several different **I** occupations or that discuss broad **I** topics, such as "Careers in Science."

In high schools and colleges, financial aid and scholarship information, which is career-specific, may be similarly coded and filed. Likewise, directories of accredited institutions offering career programs may be included in the boxes. For instance, lists of schools offering nursing degrees and information about them would be found in the **SI** box. In employment and rehabilitation agencies, information on approved training facilities, MDTA programs, apprenticeships and on-the-job training opportunities would be coded and filed with the occupational literature.

The alphabetical list of occupations and corresponding codes should be available to all students, thereby accommodating those who are seeking information about specific occupations. For these people, there are two added advantages: first, exposure to literature describing occupations that are psychologically related to the original one of interest; and second, possible discovery of jobs not previously considered.

The complexity of organizing occupational information according to the Holland classification will, of course, depend on the amount of space available;

*Source: Reprinted with permission of the author and publisher from *Communique*, 1973, 2, 69–76.

the number of filing cabinets, bookcases, or shelves on hand; the size of one's collection of literature, and the time that may be devoted to the task. The use of two-letter codes on file boxes will save space, because a greater number of occupations may be grouped together. However it would seem reasonable to employ three-letter coding for certain large categories; for example, the **RI** group may be too cumbersome and better organized into **RIA, RIS, RIE, & RIC**.

Some commercially available vocational guidance materials are quite easily organized according to the classification—namely, the Science Research Associate's 400 Occupational Briefs and the Krumboltz Job Experience Kits. Both of these have already been assigned appropriate codes, which can be found in the publication, *A Guide to the Self-Directed Career Program.* The Career Summaries, published by Career, Inc., also lend themselves to easy classification. This organizational system allows easy access and use of occupational information for counselors, clients, and students.

Another practical use of the classification is that it helps the counselor interpret adult work-histories. Each letter of an occupational code provides a clue to understanding the nature of a work environment. For instance, let's look at the group of occupations coded **SEC. S** represents environments that primarily require, stimulate, and reinforce interpersonal contacts and relationships—cooperation, social skills, and helping and understanding others. The second letter, **E,** represents an environment that stimulates the person to engage in activities such as selling, or leading others; rewards the person for displaying enterprising values and goods such as money, power and status; and encourages the person to see himself as aggressive, popular, self-confident, responsible. The **C** component of the environment is third in importance. The environmental demands and rewards are for systematic manipulation of data such as records and files; operating business and data processing machines; conforming and orderly behavior; and practicability.

The *code,* then, conveys much more information about the prominent characteristics of work environments than occupational titles alone. From an occupation's code one can better understand what it would be like to work in the occupation. For example, if a counselor sees that a person has worked as a dormitory director, a job analyst, and a bartender, this list of titles reveals little. Noting from the classification that these are all **SEC** jobs, however, the counselor gets a more complete understanding of the occupational environments the person has experienced.

Elaborating on this idea, a counselor could take a work history composed of three or four occupational titles, find the three-letter codes for each, combine them, and obtain one three-letter summary code for the work history. The procedure for summarizing codes is this. Each time a letter appears in the first position, it receives a score of three; each time it appears in the second position, it receives a score of two; and each time it appears in the third position, it receives a score of one. By simple addition, the totals for each letter can be calculated and rank ordered with the three highest letters constituting the three-letter summary code for those occupations. The work-history summary code could provide some clues to the nature of the overall occupational environment represented by the three or four titles. This puts the counselor in a position to provide appropriate vocational guidance in accordance with whether the person's work-history has been a satisfactory one or a dissatisfactory one.

First, let's assume that the person is dissatisfied with his previous jobs—he did not like any of them. His work-history summary code, then, represents components of work environments that are incongruent and incompatible for that individual. The counselor can evaluate new career alternatives for this person in terms of the absence or presence of these incongruent environmental components. That is, occupations whose codes do *not* contain *any* of the letters appearing in the dissatisfactory work-history summary code might be considered first. Examining the separate codes for the job changes might show that the person has been moving from one incongruent environment to another.

As an example of how useful the work-history summary code can be, take the individual who has worked as a mechanic, plumber, electronics technician, and instrument repairman. These occupations are coded **RIE, RIE, IRE,** and **IRC.** If this person is dissatisfied with his work history, the counselor can suggest that he explore occupations that have no **R, I,** or **E** components—that is, he should explore the **S, A** and **C** occupational categories.

If the person feels that his work history has been *satisfactory*, then the work-history code represents *congruent* work environments for him. The summary code could then be used to identify other jobs where the work environment is similar to those experienced in the past. This may be important if a person incurs a disability which precludes returning to his former job. The summary code obtained from his prior satisfactory work-history would provide a tool for the rehabilitation counselor to identify groups of occupations with similar work-environment characteristics. Each occupation thus identified would then be evaluated in terms of the limitations imposed by the disability. The basic idea is to *minimize* the stress of adjusting to a new job by identifying new work environments similar to pre-disability occupational environments, thereby allowing more time, effort, and psychic energy for adjusting to the disability itself.

The satisfactory work-history code may also be useful in counseling the person who, in spite of general satisfaction with his previous work, feels that he is, perhaps, not advancing quickly enough or not utilizing the full range of his talents. The occupational classification would point to similarly-coded occupations, some of which may provide greater opportunity for advancement.

The third practical application of the Holland classification system is that counselors may use it simultaneously as a tool *and* a framework for developing an occupational exploration plan with a student or client. Exploration might begin by identifying those occupations that are most congruent with the client's personality type; that is, ones closely in line with his competencies, self-estimates, and preferences for selected activities. Groups of congruent occupations may be identified by summarizing the codes obtained from various sources including interest inventories, vocational aspirations, college majors, avocational activities, and actual satisfactory work experiences. The technique for summarizing these codes is the same as for summarizing work-history codes, as explained previously.

Let us assume that a three-letter summary code of **ESC** has been derived from the above sources. Obviously, all occupations listed under **ESC** in the classification would constitute a first-priority list of exploration, along with all other occupations having **ES** and **EC** as their first two letters. This list would provide a person with some tangible direction in searching the career literature. It would give him a "handle" to begin his exploration and would make this activity more efficient and productive.

If, for various reasons, this first list of occupations is not productive or the person is interested in expanding his career alternatives, a second list may be generated by reversing the first and second letters of the code—in other words, **SEC** instead of **ESC.** All occupations coded **SEC,** along with those having **SE** and **SC** as their first two letters, would constitute the second list. Finally, to develop additional alternatives, a third list could be generated by placing the third letter first and reversing the first and second letters.

Taken together, the three lists will provide a large number of occupations to explore, but it is unlikely that many clients would require or use all three. Theoretically, at least, a person with a consistent and well-differentiated code may expect to find, from his first list, a cluster of congruent and appealing occupations that will provide reasonable outlets for expression of his personality.

At the other extreme, however, is the person whose code is undifferentiated and inconsistent. Undifferentiated means the person has a relatively flat personality profile; inconsistent means he resembles personality types which are themselves quite different, such as Conventional and Artistic or Enterprising and Investigative. In this case, it may be advisable to generate and use all three lists. Perhaps other interventions such as therapeutic counseling may be indicated.

One approach for clients with undifferentiated codes might be to provide them with literature or expose them to simulated or real-life experiences that are *contrasting* in nature—that is, representative of opposed occupational categories. The contrasting pairs would be Realistic with Social, Artistic with Conventional, and Investigative with Enterprising. Exposure to these contrasting experiences might help the person to determine his main competencies and interests. For example, if a client is exposed to a Realistic experience (such as running a drill press), then exposed to a Social experience (such as helping a child with a homework assignment), he should be able to determine which experience he enjoys most and does best. By also offering contrasting experiences for **I** vs. **E** and **A** vs. **C,** three occupational categories can be eliminated and the remaining three used to form a three-letter code from which the three occupational lists can be generated. Exploration of these lists can then proceed. In this case, then, the occupational classification first provides a way to help the person differentiate his interests and abilities, then provides the framework for his occupational explorations.

In conclusion, three ideas for using the classification have been set forth:

first, organizing career information; *second,* interpreting work histories; and *third,* conducting occupational explorations. As these three applications are comprehended, other applications of the system may become evident, such as clustering career education programs and experiences, conducting vocational evaluations based on work samples in rehabilitation centers, and facilitating the relationship of course-content of academic subjects to career alternatives.

13. Early Determinants of Vocational Choice*

Anne Roe

This paper suggests some hypotheses about the relationships between early experience and attitudes, abilities, interests, and other personality factors which affect the ultimate vocational selection of the individual. Although the writer has drawn heavily upon the general literature, as well as some of the psychoanalytical studies, upon studies of early interest patterns, of parent-child relations, and of personality differences related to parent attitudes and to birth order, data from individual studies are not quoted. This is a speculative paper, and there is little *direct* evidence for the hypotheses which are suggested. However, the writer does not know of any contradictory evidence and believes most of these hypotheses would be relatively easy to check. In a paper of this length only an outline can be given.

These hypotheses have been developed with reference to the present United States culture, including the major variations due to gross socioeconomic subdivisions, but the author has not tried to consider alterations which might be introduced by minority positions of one sort or another. Differences between gross cultural subdivisions are primarily differences in percentages of incidence of types of behavior, rather than absolute differences in kind of behavior, and are analogous to the differences in incidence of different bloodgroups in different races. It is to be understood that these hypotheses are intended to indicate major trends, and that other variables not mentioned here can be expected to introduce modifications in specific instances.

Let us first consider some general hypotheses with regard to personality variables as these are expressed in behavior, and particularly in behavior of the sorts that psychologists concern themselves with, for example, intelligence, interests, and special abilities. Some of the individual variation in all of these is undoubtedly due to inheritance, to differences in genetic endowment, but of the extent and precise nature of these genetic differences we know almost nothing certainly. We not only know nothing about probable genetic differences in the strengths of basic needs or drives, but we have not even begun to consider this problem. Gross hereditary differences in such things as specific sensory capacities and the plasticity and complexity of the central nervous system must greatly affect behavior, but beyond these it is uncertain how far specifically genetic elements are primary factors.

In this connection the author offers five hypotheses.

HYPOTHESES ON RELATION OF EARLY EXPERIENCE TO VOCATIONAL CHOICE

1. *The hereditary bases for intelligence, special abilities, interests, attitudes, and other personality variables seem usually to be nonspecific.* There may be a genetic basis

*Source: Reprinted with permission of the author and publisher from the *Journal of Counseling Psychology*, 1957, 4, 212–217. Copyright 1957 The American Psychological Association.

for some "factors" of intelligence or aptitudes, but on this there is no clear evidence. Sex, as genetically determined, also involves some differentiation of abilities. It is, nevertheless, probable that in most instances genetic elements limit the degree of development rather than directly determine the type of expression.

2. *The pattern of development of special abilities is primarily determined by the directions in which psychic energy comes to be expended involuntarily.* The statement applies also to interests, attitudes, and other personality variables. Please note the word *involuntarily.* It is intended to emphasize the fact that the things to which the individual gives automatic attention are keys to his total behavior. The point will not be expanded here, but the relevance of these hypotheses to the relations between personality and perception is clear.

3. *These directions are determined in the first place by the patterning of early satisfactions and frustrations.* This is the developing pattern of need primacies or relative strengths. In the earliest years these are essentially unconscious, and they probably always retain a large unconscious element. As noted before, we know nothing at all about genetic variability in basic needs, but it can be fairly assumed that it exists.

Maslow's hierarchical classification of needs is the most useful for focussing the present discussion (Table 1).

The hierarchical arrangement is important. Maslow's theory states that higher order needs cannot appear until lower order needs are at least relatively well satisfied. It seems reasonable to assume that higher order needs are of later evolutionary development in man and some of them may not be well established in terms of species evolution. If this is so, it would follow that they would show greater variability within the species. Lower order needs, on the other hand, are essential for the maintenance of life, and this permits much less variability in their strength. Differences in the degree of variability of these needs are of significance for us, and it is particularly the higher needs with which we are concerned. It would also appear that there is some difference in the age at which these needs or drives may begin to function. By the time the healthy child is a few months old the first five are probably affecting his behavior, although in widely varying degree.

Table 1   Basic Needs (Maslow)

1. Physiological needs
2. Safety needs
3. Need for belongingness and love
4. Need for importance, respect, self-esteem, independence
5. Need for information
6. Need for understanding
7. Need for beauty
8. Need for self-actualization*

* The author would place this lower in the hierarchy or handle it as a more generalized need.

4. *The eventual pattern of psychic energies, in terms of attention directedness, is the major determinant of the field or fields to which the person will apply himself.* This is relevant not only to vocation, of course, but to the total life pattern of the individual. It determines what sort of special abilities and interests will be predominant.

5. *The intensity of these (primarily) unconscious needs, as well as their organization, is the major determinant of the degree of motivation as expressed in accomplishment.* This implies that all accomplishment is based on unconscious as well as on conscious needs, but it does not imply that these needs are necessarily neurotic. There is accomplishment which is a free expression of capacity, although this may be relatively rare. Accomplishment on this basis can generally be distinguished from accomplishment on other bases. The relevance of this hypothesis to eventual vocational performance is evident.

It may not be so evident how the patterns and intensities of these basic needs are affected in the first place by the early experiences of the child. The following three hypotheses are concerned with this problem.

6. *Needs satisfied routinely as they appear do not develop into unconscious motivators.* Intensity of the need is not a variable, since it is stated that the need is "satisfied." The fact that the satisfaction is gained routinely is important, and it implies the need to distinguish sharply between simple, direct, matter-of-fact need gratification and gratification with fuss and fanfare.

7. *Needs for which even minimum satisfaction is rarely achieved will, if higher order, become in effect expunged, or will, if lower order, prevent the appearance of higher order needs, and will become dominant and restricting motivators.* Lower order needs, of course, require some degree of satisfaction for the maintenance of life. The hypothesis would mean, e.g. that a child whose expressions of natural curiosity were thoroughly blocked, would cease to be curious. On the other hand, with less effective blocking, hypothesis 8 would apply.

8. *Needs, the satisfaction of which is delayed but eventually accomplished, will become unconscious motivators, depending largely upon the degree of satisfaction felt. This will depend, among other things, upon the strength of the basic need in the given individual, the length of time elapsing between arousal and satisfaction, and the values ascribed to the satisfaction of this need in the immediate environment.*

The last hypothesis is the most significant for this study. It must be understood that the forms in which need satisfaction will be ultimately sought, in adult life, may not be obviously related to the basic needs referred to in the hypothesis. All of the well-known mechanisms of displacement, projection, etc. may function here. The problem of tolerance of deferred gratification is linked to such experiences as are implied in this hypothesis.

PATTERNS OF EARLY EXPERIENCE WITH PARENTS

Let us turn now to variations in the early experiences of children, and in particular to differences in parental handling of children. We can consider only major variations here, and it must be understood that the classification used is an arbitrary one, intended to delimit, as usefully as possible, nodal areas in a series of essentially continuous distributions. Several levels of classification are suggested, overlapping variously. Major behavioral variations are presented in outline form below, and a figure shows these, together with their relation to basically warm and cold attitudes of parents, and their relation to the outcome in the child in terms of his orientation with regard to persons.

The specific behaviors of the parents are of less importance than their attitudes towards the child. It is impossible here to discuss the relative effect of maternal and paternal attitudes, of similarities or differences in them. The classification used here refers to the dominant pattern in the home, whether shown by one or both parents. The major subdivisions refer to the child's position in the family emotional structure: as the center of attention, as avoided, or as accepted.

A. Emotional Concentration on the Child

This ranges between the extreme of overprotection to that of overdemandingness. Perhaps a sort of mean between these two is the quite typical anxiety of parents over a first child, anxiety which, in the same parents, may be much alleviated for the second child, with resulting considerable differences in the personality pictures of the two children.

1. *Overprotection.* The parent babies the child, encourages its dependence and restricts exploratory behavior. There is often concentration upon physical characteristics and real or fancied "talents" of the child. The parents maintain primary emotional ties with the child.

2. *Overdemanding.* The parents make heavy demands upon the child in terms of perfection of performance and usually institute quite severe training. In later years they may push the child to high achievement in school and work. In somewhat milder forms we may have the sort of family status "noblesse oblige" pattern, in which development of skills is encouraged but the pattern of skills is a prescribed one. This is very typical of upper class families, with emphasis upon development of conceptual as opposed to motor skills. Severer forms may blend into rejection or may be cover for this.

B. Avoidance of the Child

Here, too, two extremes are suggested—rejection and neglect. Care below the minimum adequate amount has well-documented effects, as studies of orphans have shown. Most other studies have few, if any, children in this group. Parents providing this sort of home do not cooperate in psychological studies. (The author would not suggest that non-cooperation is evidence of this type of care!) Minimal need gratification is provided.

1. *Emotional rejection of the child,* not necessarily accompanied by overt physical neglect. Lack of gratification is intentional.

2. *Neglect of the child.* This may, in fact, be less harmful psychologically than emotional rejection accompanied by physical care. It shades into the next classification. Gratification lacks are generally not intentional.

C. Acceptance of the Child

Children in this group are full-fledged members of the family circle, neither concentrated upon, nor overlooked. Parents are noncoercive, nonrestrictive, and, actively or by default, encourage independence. The minimum amount of social interaction is supplied at one extreme (this may be very low) and at the other extreme the group approaches the overprotecting one. The major breakdown in this group is on the basis of the warmth or coldness of the family climate.

1. *Casual acceptance of the child.* Noninterference here is largely by default.

2. *Loving acceptance.* Noninterference and encouragement of the child's own resources and his independence may be intentional, even planned, or a natural reflection of parental attitudes towards others generally.

RELATION OF PARENTAL ATTITUDES AND NEED SATISFACTION

Homes in which children are the center of attention provide pretty full satisfaction, of physiological and safety needs, and attention to needs for love and esteem, but gratification is usually not entirely routine. The overprotecting home places great emphasis upon gratification, and generally upon immediacy of gratification, which keeps lower level need satisfaction in the foreground. Belongingness, love, and esteem are often made conditional upon dependency and conformity, and genuine self-actualization may be discouraged. There is likely to be encouragement of any sort of any special or supposedly special capacities, however. The overdemanding parent may make satisfaction of needs for love and esteem conditional upon conformity and achievement, which is frequently oriented to status. Needs for information and understanding may be encouraged, but within prescribed areas, and the same is true for self-actualization needs.

By definition, the next group has major lacks in need gratification. Rejecting parents may provide adequate gratification of physiological and safety needs, but refrain from love and esteem gratification, and frequently seem deliberately to withhold the latter or even to denigrate the child. Neglect of physiological and safety needs, but not beyond necessary minimal gratification is much more tolerable than personal depreciation and deliberate withholding of love. If there is no contrast with attitudes towards others in the immediate group there will be stultification of the child's development in some respects but not distortion of it.

Accepting parents offer reasonable gratification of all needs. This is unlikely to be emphasized in the way in which the first group do it, although the extremes of the loving subgroup may tend in this direction. Gratifications will not be deliberately delayed, but neither will delay be made disturbing. The major difference in the subgroups is probably in the way in which gratifications are supplied, and in the degree of deliberate encouragement and gratification of needs.

PARENTAL HANDLING AND ADULT BEHAVIOR PATTERNS

It has been suggested before that perhaps the earliest subdivision of direction of attention, and one which has significance for the whole life pattern of the individual, is that referring to persons, and that this may be towards persons or towards nonpersons. The author does not say towards persons or away from persons, since away from persons may imply defensiveness; the term *object* is avoided since attention may go to animate or inanimate nonpersons, and because object, in psychoanalytic terminology usually comes out to mean other person. Perhaps primary attention to self should be a separate division, or a subdivision of attention to persons. (The exclusiveness with which one of these attitudes dominates the attention of any individual is, of course, another variable, not taken into account here.)

Possible relationships between these orientations and parent-child interaction are suggested in Figure 1. The next to the outer segment of the circle indicates the probable orientation of the child in terms of persons or nonpersons. The division is suggested by jagged lines, since it is uncertain. The other subdivisions were set arbitrarily.

This basic orientation with respect to persons later ramifies into patterns of special interests and abilities. The degree of social interests is clearly related, and it is likely that verbal abilities are associated with this, since personal interactions are so largely mediated through words. Scientific and mechanical interests reach their fullest development in those who are concerned with nonpersons.

GROUPS I, II, III, VII, VIII

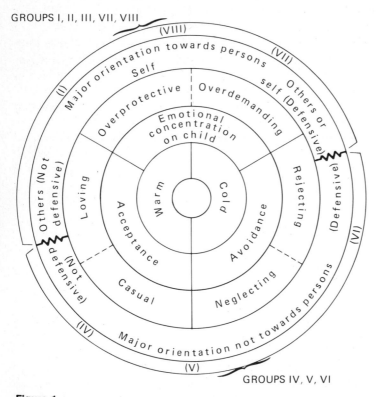

Figure 1

REFLECTION OF EARLY EXPERIENCE IN VOCATIONAL CHOICE

Depending upon which of the above situations are experienced, there will be developed basic attitudes, interests and capacities which will be given expression in the general pattern of the adult's life, in his personal relations, in his emotional reactions, in his activities, and in his vocational choice. More than any other aspect of life, the occupation usually reflects most clearly the coalescence of the genetic and experiential variables discussed above.[1]

Persons from child-centered families who do not develop primary self-concentration will still be quite constantly aware of the opinions and attitudes of other persons towards themselves and of the need to maintain self-position in relation to others.

Persons brought up in rejecting homes may develop intense defensive awareness of others; if so they will probably have aggressive tendencies which may most readily find socially acceptable expression in occupational terms. On the other hand, they may strongly reject persons and turn defensively to nonpersons, or they may be unaware of other persons as different from objects in the environment, so far as their own relation to them goes.

Those from accepting homes may have primary interests in persons or in nonpersons; it will not be defensive in either case, and it will not carry the sort of uncertainty that many in the first group show.

It is possible to relate these attitudes quite directly to occupational choice (Roe, 1). The major occupational groups discussed below can, however, be thought of as indicating general patterns rather than specific occupational groups. This strengthens the general theory, but makes its relevance to this symposium less exact.

This classification has two dimensions: focus of activity and level at which the activity is pursued. The categories are shown in Table 2.

Relationships between group categorization and early experience are suggested in the outer section of Figure 1.

Table 2   Categories in Roe Classification of Occupations

Groups	Levels
I. Service	1. Professional and managerial 1.
II. Business contact	2. Professional and managerial 2.
III. Organizations	3. Semiprofessional, small business
IV. Technology	4. Skilled
V. Outdoor	5. Semiskilled
VI. Science	6. Unskilled
VII. General cultural	
VIII. Arts and entertainment	

[1] There are clearly exceptions to the usual role of the occupation as a focus of attitudes, capacities, and interests. In these instances, an avocation, or some other aspect of life, serves the same purpose.

Although most of this discussion refers to Group rather than Level, Hypothesis 5 has relevance to the latter category. This concerns the degree of motivation. Need intensity may affect, within limits due chiefly to socioeconomic background and intelligence, the level at which the mature occupational life is set; it must definitely affect the relative position within that level which the individual attains, and even more specifically the position attained within his own occupational group. Most of those selecting occupations in Groups I, II, VII, and VIII have major orientation towards persons as do many, if not most, in Group III. Groups IV, V, and VI, are chiefly comprised of persons whose major orientation is towards nonpersons. More exact relations cannot be generally indicated. There are, however, some relations which are strongly suggested; these are shown in parentheses in the figure. Indeed, there is some indication that an ordered, counterclockwise arrangement of these groups is not untenable.

REFERENCE

Roe, Anne, *Psychology of occupations.* New York: Wiley and Sons, 1956.

14. The Computerization of Vocational Information*

Jo Ann Harris

Willowbrook High School is a large, comprehensive high school of approximately 3200 students, located fifteen miles west of metropolitan Chicago. Approximately 60 per cent of its graduates attend two- and four-year colleges, and the remainder enter the local job market. The school, therefore, places a strong emphasis on trade, technical, and business courses as well as on its college preparatory curriculum.

The Guidance staff consists of twelve full-time counselors, including the Director. One of the staff serves as a Vocational Counselor. An increasing effort is being made to get vocational information to the students in a variety of ways and to acquaint both the counseling staff and students with the excellent local job opportunities.

In spite of this kind of setting, the staff still faces the problem of getting students interested in reading vocational material, and knowing how to relate it to their own abilities and interests. Keeping vocational information current and updated and keeping the counseling staff informed are equally difficult problems.

While discussing these problems informally in the spring of 1966, members of the Guidance staff began to think of ways in which modern computer technology could be applied to these problems. A proposal was written and submitted to the Research Coordinating Unit of the Illinois Board of Vocational Education and Rehabilitation in the fall of 1966. The proposal was approved for funding, and in January of 1967, the first phase of the development of Willowbrook's Computerized Vocational Information System began. Members of the working team were Miss Jo Ann Harris—Project Director, Director of Guidance; Miss Lorraine Foster, Vocational Counselor; Mr. Willis Farnham, Counselor; Mr. Robert Austin, Psychologist; and Mr. James Boyd, Chairman of the Mathematics Department, programmer.

A SYSTEM OF CLASSIFICATION

After having gathered materials from other projects of a similar nature, the Committee began to build the framework for its own system. Various methods of job classification were studied and a decision was made to use a two-dimensional system developed by Anne Roe and explained in her book *Psychology of Occupations.* Roe's classification system divides occupations into six levels by amount of training required and degree of responsibility assumed by the worker. The six levels are as follows:

1. *Professional and Managerial 1.* Independent Responsibility. This level includes not only the innovators and creators, but also the top managerial and administrative people, as well as those professional persons who have indepen-

*Source: Reprinted with permission of the author and publisher from the The Vocational Guidance Quarterly, 1968, 17, 12–20. Copyright 1968 The American Personnel and Guidance Association.

dent responsibility in important respects. For occupations at this level there is generally no higher authority, except the social group. Several criteria are suggested:

a. Important, independent, and varied responsibilities.
b. Policy-making.
c. Education: When high-level education is relevant (it is not required in the creative arts, for example, or a necessity for dictators, or even for our own high government officials) it is at the doctoral level or equivalent.

2. *Professional and Managerial 2.* The distinction between this level and level 1 is primarily one of degree. Genuine autonomy may be present but with narrower or less significant responsibilities, than in level 1. Suggested criteria are:

a. Medium-level responsibilities, for self and others, both with regard to importance and variety.
b. Policy interpretation.
c. Education at or above the bachelor level, but below the doctorate.

3. *Semi-Professional and Small Business.* The criteria suggested here are:

a. Low-level responsibility for others.
b. Application of policy, or determination for self only (as managing a small business).
c. Education: high school plus technical school or the equivalent.

4. *Skilled.* This and the following levels are classic subdivisions. Skilled occupations require apprenticeship or other special training experience.

5. *Semi-skilled.* These occupations require some training and experience but markedly less than the occupations in level 4. In addition, there is much less autonomy and initiative permitted in these occupations.

6. *Unskilled.* These occupations require no special training or education and not much more ability than is needed to follow simple directions and to engage in simple repetitive actions.

Further, Roe divided occupations into eight categories of interest which are to some extent contiguously arranged. The eight interest categories are as follows:

1. *Service.* These occupations are primarily concerned with serving and attending to the personal tastes, needs, and welfare of other persons. Included are occupations in guidance, social work, domestic and protective services.

2. *Business Contact.* These occupations are primarily concerned with the face-to-face sale of commodities, investments, real estate, and services. Also included are such occupations as demonstrator, auctioneer, and some kinds of agents. A distinction is made in sales occupations between those in which the job

is personal persuasion, which belong here, and those in which the selling is routine, and the person-to-person relation relatively unimportant, which belong in the next group.

3. *Organization.* These are the managerial and white collar jobs in business, industry, and government, the occupations concerned primarily with the organization and efficient functioning of commercial enterprises and of government activities.

4. *Technology.* This group includes occupations concerned with the production, maintenance, and transportation of commodities and utilities. Included are occupations in engineering, crafts (including repair work), and the machine trades, as well as transportation and communication.

5. *Outdoor.* This group includes agricultural, fishery, forestry, mining and kindred occupations: the occupations primarily concerned with the cultivation, preservation and gathering of crops, or marine or inland water resources, of forest products, and other natural resources, and with animal husbandry.

6. *Science.* These are the occupations primarily concerned with scientific theory and its application under specified circumstances, other than technology.

7. *General Cultural.* These occupations are primarily concerned with the preservation and transmission of the general cultural heritage. They include occupations in education, journalism, jurisprudence, the ministry, and linguistics. All elementary and high school teachers are included in this group.

8. *Arts and Entertainment.* These occupations include those primarily concerned with the use of special skills in the creative arts and in the field of entertainment. Both creators and performers are included.

At the time Roe published her book, she classified approximately 350 occupations in this way. In 1966, Dr. Roe and her associates at Harvard reworked the list of occupations in accordance with the new *Dictionary of Occupational Titles,* and the new list consists of 650 occupations. An example of the classification system follows (see figure 1).

RELATIONSHIP OF THE STUDENT RECORD

Given this two-dimensional classification system, the Willowbrook Committee began to study the ways in which objective data available about every student could be related to it. It was decided to put student permanent records in computer storage, so that parts of the record could be used in helping a student make realistic vocational choices. In beginning operation, the Committee decided to make use of cumulative class rank, the composite score on a battery of tests, and the Kuder Preference Record scores. After data are gathered over several years, other items on the student record, such as grades in specific courses and personality ratings, could be used. The battery of tests which will be administered to sophomores, Scholastic Testing Service's Educational Development Series, yields a verbal and nonverbal ability score and six achievement scores (mathematics, science, reading, English, social studies, solving everyday problems). The relationship of data to Roe's six levels would be as follows (see figure 2).

LEVEL	SERVICE	BUSINESS CONTACT	ORGAN- IZATION	TECH- NOLOGY	OUTDOOR	SCIENCE	GENERAL CULTURAL	ARTS & EN- TERTAINMENT
I	Psychiatrist, Psychologist					Anthropologist, oceanographer	Economist, lawyer	Architect
II	Social workers, counselors	Public relations worker	Hospital administrator, C.P.A.	Airplane pilot, engineer	Surveyor, landscape architect	Nurses, R.N., pharmacists	Clergymen, teachers, high school and elementary	Actor, actress, designer
III	Police chief, recreation worker	Sales, auto, insurance	Hotel manager, stenographer	Draftsman, flight engineer	Forest ranger, county agent	Dental hygienist, x-ray technician	Radio announcer, TV announcer	Interior decorator, photographer
IV	Policeman, practical nurses	Driver-salesman	Bookkeeper, salesclerk	Electrician, jeweler	Forestry technician, miner	Lab technician, optician		Letterer, paste-up man
V	Taxi driver, waiter		Typists, cashiers	Truck driver, plasterer	Chainman, rodman			
VI	Orderly, bellman		Mail machine operator, sort- ing machine operator	Bulldozer operator, cement mason	Roustabout, lumberjack			Pinboy

Figure 1 An example of Roe's classification system.

Cumulative rank in class		1	2	3	4	5	6	7	8	Composite test battery score (%)
I	Top one quarter									Top quartile (76-99%)
II	1st-2nd quarter									1st-2nd quartile (51-99%)
III	2nd-3rd quarter									2nd-3rd quartile (26-75%)
IV	2nd-3rd quarter									2nd-3rd quartile (26-75%)
V	3rd quarter									3rd quartile (26-49%)
VI	4th quarter									4th quartile (1-25%)
Kuder		Social service	Persuasive	Clerical, computational	Scientific, mechanical computational	Outdoor	Scientific	Literary	Artistic, musical, literary	

Figure 2 The relationship of the data to Roe's six levels.

The computer will be instructed to use the higher of the two criteria (rank or composite score) for its reactions, which will be explained later, in case of discrepancy. Should the test score be considerably higher than rank in class, the computer will record the discrepancy and will bring it to the attention of the student.

THE STUDENT EXPERIENCE

Before the student comes to the computer equipment, he will have been oriented to the classification system in a vocational unit in sophomore English classes. The six levels of training will be described to him in detail. The meaning of the eight interest categories will be explained and supplemented by audio-visual aids and guest speakers.

Sophomores, juniors, and seniors will be invited to use the computer system on a voluntary basis during their free time. In beginning operation, there will be two student terminals. These consist of a cathode ray tube and an automatic typewriter. The IBM 360-30 computer system will allow as many as 16 to 20 student terminals on one central processing unit.

When the student comes to this terminal equipment, he will first be asked to type in his student number. When he does so, the computer recalls for its use the student's permanent record. Messages to the student which should be kept by him will be typed to him on the typewriter. The "conversation" will be flashed on the cathode ray tube, and the student will respond by selecting multiple choice answers.

In order to acquaint the student with the use of the gadgetry, the computer will invite the student to a game of tic-tac-toe. It will then ask the student to do a limited self-analysis by asking him the following four questions:

1. Choice of occupation is related to your ability to learn. Try to remember how you did on the last tests you took. If you can't remember, I'll help you. How do you think you did compared to students of your grade level in the nation?
   1. Top Quarter
   2. Second Quarter

   3. Third Quarter
   4. Bottom Quarter

Possible Computer Reactions

1. Good show! You have a good memory!
2. Whoops! The last tests you took placed you in the _____ quarter. You may want to check this out with your counselor.

2. Grades in school are also related to your vocational choices. Think about your semester grades in all subjects since you entered Willowbrook and indicate where you think you stand in relation to the rest of your class on grade average.

1. Top Quarter

2. Second Quarter

3. Third Quarter
4. Bottom Quarter

3. Work can be fun if it's interesting to you. The occupations in my memory are divided into eight broad areas of interest. I'm going to give you a brief description of each area. Then I'll give you the whole list again and ask you to choose one interest area which you wish to explore today.
   1. Service
   2. Business contact
   3. Organization
   4. Technology
   5. Outdoor
   6. Science
   7. Cultural
   8. Arts and entertainment

4. Keeping in mind your abilities and interests, select the amount of education and job training you are planning immediately after high school.
   1. No further training after high school.
   2. Some training (2-6 months) after high school.
   3. Trade school (6-18 months) or apprenticeship.
   4. Technical school (6-18 months) or junior college technical program (2 years)
   5. Four years of college.
   6. Advanced degrees beyond college.

1. You're right. You may ask your counselor for your exact grade point average and rank if you'd like to.
2. (a) Maybe you forgot about some of your semester grades. Actually you are in the _____ quarter of your class. Talk this over with your counselor if you'd like to.

   or

   (b) I have a pleasant surprise for you! You're in the _____ quarter.

1. The results of the interest inventory which you have taken agree with your choice.
2. The interest inventory which you have taken indicates that your highest areas of interest are _____, _____, and _____. You may, however, look at the occupations in the interest area which fit the category you have chosen.

O.K. message: The plan you have chosen seems fine.

Minor discrepancy: Your record indicates that you could undertake a higher level of education than you have chosen. You may wish to discuss this with your counselor. You may, however, look at the jobs in the category you have chosen.

or

The level of education you have chosen may be quite difficult for you unless your grades begin to improve in high school. You may want to discuss this with your counselor. You may, however, look at the jobs in the category you have chosen.

Major discrepancy: Your choice puzzles me somewhat. I've compared it with your high school record, and the two don't seem to match. The best way to clear up this problem would be to see your counselor.

The script for the computer "conversation" is obviously much longer than quoted here. The Project Director tested the script with a group of students and altered it in accordance with their reactions to it.

Once the student has made a selection of interest category and training level, the computer chooses a "box" of occupations for him. The number of occupations in that box varies from none to as many as seventy-five. The typewriter types out this list of occupations for the student. At this point the student may choose to explore occupations on that list or to go back and make different decisions about interest and education, which will produce a new list for him. If he chooses to explore occupations on the list he has, he is asked to type in the number of the first occupation. As soon as he does so, a fifty-word definition of the occupation flashes on the screen. He may then ask for further information about that same occupation, begin to explore another on his list, or go back and make different decisions about education and interest. If he chooses to request additional information about the same occupation, the typewriter types a 300-word description. The format of these descriptions will be standard, including job duties, training requirements, recommended high school courses, working conditions, beginning salary range, and employment outlook. At the end of each description, reference will be made to sources of further information. The fifty-word definitions will be those which appear in the *Encyclopedia of Careers,* published in 1967 by the J. G. Ferguson Publishing Company of Chicago. This same company is preparing the 300-word job descriptions for Willowbrook without charge.

For students exploring occupations in:	Computer system will provide:
Levels I and II	1. Decision-making conversation about college (cost, distance from home, size, major fields, control, etc.).
	2. List of suggested colleges for investigation, based on the above decisions, student record, and testing information.
	3. Sources of scholarship aid.
Levels III and IV	1. Information about technical programs in local College of Du Page.
	2. Information about trade and technical schools within 100 mile radius.
	3. Information about local apprenticeships.
Levels V and VI	1. Information about how to choose first job gaming approach.
	2. List of companies in Du Page County which hire high school graduates (or leavers) in the field of interest specified by the student.

The student may then continue this process as long as he has time and interest. After the student has used the system once, he will not again play the game of tic-tac-toe or go through the self-evaluation. Rather, the computer will respond, "The last time you used CVIS (Computerized Vocational Information System) you were exploring jobs in the area of science (flashing list on the screen). Do you want to continue exploring this list, or do you wish to make different decisions about interest and training?" The student may also recall any single job description by typing in the code number of that occupation.

If plans continue on schedule, this part of the computer system will be in operation in November, 1968.

FURTHER DEVELOPMENTS

In another phase of development, which will hopefully be in operation for the school year 1969–70, other types of information will be stored in the data bank to be accessed by students in the same conversational mode. This information would be primarily intended for juniors and seniors. The following is a summary of plans for future developments.

COUNSELOR BENEFITS

By means of a terminal hook-up to the computer, counselors and other pupil personnel workers can have access to any information stored in the data bank. Counselors at Willowbrook will have cathode ray tube (TV screen) terminals in their offices. By typing in specified code numbers, the counselor can recall information about the occupations, colleges, scholarships, local technical and trade schools, local entry jobs, and student records. The counselors are currently expanding the traditional student permanent record to include such items as health disabilities, discipline record, record of work skills and experience, and information about the student gained from one- and five-year follow-up studies. The counselor will also be able to recall the path of decision-making followed by each of his counselees. Part of this student record will be printed out for transcripts and other purposes. Some block of it will never be printed out, and only designated professional personnel will have access to it.

Also for the counselors the computer will print out daily a list of counselees who have received minor and major discrepancy messages on the system during that day.

All of the information mentioned above can be readily and easily updated. Some items, like attendance and tardiness record, will be updated daily at the data-processing center. Others, like occupational briefs and college information, will be updated yearly.

EVALUATION AND RESEARCH

A block of computer storage space will be set aside for data which will provide evaluation on the project. Such data as the following will be stored.

1   The number of times a student makes different decisions about level of education and interest area during his high school career.

2   The number of minor and major discrepancy messages given.

3   The result of these messages, i.e., do they cause students to move toward more realistic goals?

4   The last 10 occupations explored in depth by each student. This can be compared with results of one- and five-year follow-up studies to see what degree the system is helping students to choose an occupation.

5   The number of times each occupation is explored by students.

6   The number of times each student uses the system.

The Committee has given much thought to the inclusion of all kinds of data which will be needed for evaluation and research. A doctoral candidate has been recruited to design a plan for evaluation. The evaluation will include:

1   Student reaction questionnaire.
2   Student interview.
3   Counselor reaction questionnaire.
4   Control group approach.

CONCLUSION

Computer technology will continue to revolutionize the field of counseling. Willowbrook's project committee views the computer as a valuable tool for the organization, updating, and retrieval of masses of information. In this sense, the computer becomes an automated library and filing system. The staff does not think that it can or should replace the counselor. Rather, the computer will allow him to become a more professional person, because he can have time to do personal, educational, vocational, and college counseling in depth. The computer's purpose, then is to provide instant information for human consideration.

FOLLOW-UP FOR SECTION TWO

Questions

1 The following pertain to "Trait-and-Factor Counseling: Yesterday and Today" by Weinrach.

 a Define and give an example of:

 (1) traits, (2) factors, (3) interest inventory, (4) performance test.

 b Name three people who were influential in the development of this model, and their respective contributions.

 c Describe how the three-step model works.

 d State one advantage and one disadvantage of this model.

2 Two contradictory methods for test interpretation are presented by Bixler and Bixler in "Test Interpretation in Vocational Counseling," and Stephenson in "Client Interpretation of Tests." What are the advantages and disadvantages of each approach? Describe the approach you would use and explain your reasons for selecting it.

3 The following pertain to "The Holland Model: What It Is and How It Works" by Weinrach and "Practical Applications of the Holland Occupational Classification" by Helms.

 a Define and give an example of:

 (1) hexagon, (2) consistency, (3) differentiation, (4) congruence, (5) calculus.

 b How does the saying, Birds of a feather flock together, relate to this theory?

 c To what extent are Holland's *personality types* similar to the *traits* the trait-and-factor theorists describe?

 d Describe the process by which one measures an environment. Discuss two different uses of such a technique.

4 The following pertain to Roe in "Early Determinants of Vocational Choice" and "The Computerization of Vocational Information" by Harris.

 a Define, identify and give an example of:

 (1) Maslow's basic needs, (2) hierarchical arrangement, (3) need intensity, (4) emotional concentration on child, (5) groups and levels.

 b What effect do early child-rearing practices have on vocational choice?

 c Describe how the six-by-eight classification system can be functionally applied to a school's guidance program.

 d Compare Roe's classification system with Holland's.

5 Complete the Career Development Theory and Practice Worksheet for any of the theories in this chapter. It may be found in Appendix C.

Learn by Doing

1 Practicing with a classmate. The purpose of this exercise is to provide the counselor-trainee with hands-on experience with a variety of psychometric instruments in a low-threat situation. These exercises should be completed in collaboration with a classmate.

 a Administer any or all of the following to one another:

 (1) The Self-Directed Search (Consulting Psychologists Press)*, The Kuder DD (Science Research Associates)*, or the Strong-Campbell Interest Inventory (The Psychological Corporation).*

 b Interpret the results of these surveys to one another.

*See Appendix H for additional information.

c Based on the results of the inventories, identify five appropriate pieces of occupational information.

d Evaluate these five pieces of information according to the Guidelines for the Systematic Selection, Evaluation, and use of Simulated Vocational Guidance Materials, which may be found in Appendix F.

e Use only those pieces of occupational information which were rated as satisfactory or better in a follow-up interview. Integrate the survey results and the occupational information into this counseling session.

2 Linking people to the world of work. The structural theories rely heavily upon an explicit worker–world-of-work relationship. The following activities are designed to help counselor-trainees conceptualize the functional qualities of that relationship.

a Arrange a visit to a local business or industry. See Appendix E, Activity no. 2.

b Prepare a *Community Resource Survey* based upon the guidelines found in Appendix E, Activity no. 3.

3 How can USES help? The United States Employment Service (USES), better known as State Employment, has been a major contributor to the delivery of vocational guidance services in the United States. Find out what it has to offer by arranging a field visit to a state employment office or a viewing of *Jobs* (Stuart Finley, Inc.)* or a similar film.

4 Does testing make a difference? The purpose of this assignment is to provide the counselor-trainee with some indication of the extent to which tests are used in the delivery of vocational guidance services. Conduct an interview with a counselor who is employed at a state employment office, vocational-technical school, or similar institution or agency. Consult Appendix A for the Taped Interview Format.

5 Do traits and factors really exist? The purpose of this assignment is to provide the counselor-trainee with some appreciation of the relationship between an individual's traits and the factors required for that individual's particular job. Consult the Taped Interview Format in Appendix A.

6 How do students react? The purpose of this exercise is to provide the counselor-trainee with the experience of presenting a group guidance lesson which includes the interpretation of an interest inventory. Select a group of junior high school students and administer the Kuder E General Interest Survey (Science Research Associates)*. Follow up with a presentation featuring KEYS (Science Research Associates)* or a similar package of materials.

7 Which theory fits best? Case studies provide a means to determine the extent to which any one theory sufficiently explains the vocational behavior of a given individual. Select a subject and prepare a case study. Consult the Guidelines for a Case Study in Appendix D.

8 To learn more. Prepare an abstract based upon one of the articles listed below under Additional Resources. Consult Appendix G for the suggested format.

Additional Resources

American Personnel and Guidance Association (Producer). *Don't blame the test: It may be the interpretation.* Washington, D.C.: American Personnel and Guidance Association Press, undated. (cassette, order #72933).

Calia, V. F. Vocational guidance: After the fall. *Personnel and Guidance Journal,* 1966, *45,* 320–327.

*See Appendix H for additional information.

Campbell, D. P., Crichton, L., Hansen, J. I., & Webber, P. A new edition of the SVIB: The Strong-Campbell Interest Inventory. *Measurement and Evaluation in Guidance,* 1974, *7,* 92–95.

Conley, J., & Wernick, W. *Interview strategies for career development.* Niles, Illinois: Argus Communications, 1976.

Goldman, L. Test and Counseling: The marriage that failed *Measurement and Evaluation in Guidance,* 1972, *4,* 213–220.

Harris, J. The computer: Guidance tool of the future. *Journal of Counseling Psychology,* 1974, *21,* 331–339.

Holland, J. L. A theory of vocational choice. *Journal of Counseling Psychology,* 1959, *6,* 35–45.

Holland, J. L. *Making vocational choices: A theory of careers.* Englewood Cliffs, N.J.: Prentice-Hall, 1973.

Holland, J. L. *The psychology of vocational choice.* Waltham, Mass.: Blaisdell, 1966.

Hollifield, J. If we divide the world into personality types . . . and each declares open war against the others . . . where will it ever end? *Human Behavior,* 1972, *1,* 46–50.

MacKay, W. R. The decision fallacy: Is it if or when? *Vocational Guidance Quarterly,* 1975, *23,* 227–231.

National Vocational Guidance Association. *NVGA bibliography of current career information.* Washington, D.C.: American Personnel and Guidance Association Press, 1977.

Parsons, F. *Choosing a vocation.* Boston: Houghton Mifflin, 1909.

Prediger, D. J. Data-information conversion in test interpretation. *Journal of Counseling Psychology,* 1971, *12,* 306–313.

Roe, A. *Psychology of occupations.* New York: Wiley and Sons, 1956.

Shoppeel, D. L., Hall, L. G., & Tarrier, R. B. An application of Roe's vocational choice model. *School Counselor,* 1971, *19,* 43–48.

Strong, E. K., Jr. *Vocational interests of men and women.* Stanford: Stanford University Press, 1943.

Whiteley, J. M. (Producer). *A dialogue on vocational development theory, parts I. and II. with John Holland and Donald Super.* Washington, D. C.: American Personnel and Guidance Association Press, 1970. (films)

Williamson, E. G. An historical perspective of the vocational guidance movement. *Personnel and Guidance Journal,* 1964, *42,* 854–859.

Williamson, E. G. Counseling and the Minnesota point of view. *Education and Psychological Measurement,* 1968, *7,* 147–157.

Williamson, E. G. *Counseling of Adolescents.* New York: McGraw-Hill, 1950.

Williamson, E. G. *How to counsel students.* New York: McGraw-Hill, 1939.

Williamson, E. G. Trait-factor theory and individual differences. In B. Stefflre and W. H. Grant (Eds.), *Theories of counseling* (2nd ed.). New York: McGraw-Hill, 1972.

Williamson, E. G. Vocational counseling: Trait-factor theory. In B. Stefflre (Ed.), *Theories of counseling.* New York: McGraw-Hill, 1965.

Section Three

Process Approaches

The process approaches can be distinguished from the structural approaches in that the process approaches do not provide any explicit link between the individual and the world of work. The process approaches have in common a belief that career development is a process that occurs over a period of time rather than an event that occurs at one definite point in an individual's life. The theories presented in this section are similar in that none of them posits an explicit link between the individual and the world of work, but they differ on many other points. This section contains approaches influenced by such diverse schools as the humanists and the behaviorists.

In 1951 Eli Ginzberg and his associates were among the first to speak of occupational choice as a *process*. This was startling to a profession that up to that time believed that occupational choice occurred as a single event in each person's lifetime. Ginzberg revised his original position in 1972; it is that revision which is presented here. It states that occupational choice is a developmental process which spans a lifetime. Ginzberg originally identified three developmental stages: Fantasy, tentative, and realistic. Referring to these developmental stages can help counselors identify the relative maturity of a client's career choices. The role of fantasy in career choice has been largely ignored. In 1970, Holland included a section dealing with fantasy in his Self-Directed Search. At the present there seems to be renewed interest in the intentional use of fantasy as a vehicle for helping clients clarify their thinking. In "Using Inner Experience: Fantasy and Daydreams in Career Counseling," Morgan and Skovholt suggest several ways in which fantasy can be incorporated into vocational counseling.

Like Ginzberg, Super also subscribes to a developmental framework. In 1953 he identified five developmental stages: Growth, exploration, establishment, maintenance, and decline. It is interesting to note that Super subdivided the exploratory stage into fantasy, tentative, and realistic, which are the three stages originally identified by Ginzberg and his associates. In Super's article "A Theory of Vocational Development," he criticizes Ginzberg's original statement and then presents his own ten propositions.

Super was also among the first to write on career development as a process. His work over the past quarter century qualifies him as an authority, and, in the eyes of many, Super is the leading figure on the subject today. Probably more is written about his approach than about any other. No one has had greater impact on vocational counseling over the past twenty-five years.

The trend toward K–12 career education is based largely on Super's developmental model. Films and other simulated materials often reflect his influence. His conceptualization of how careers develop has had a decisive influence on vocational counseling and curriculum. His theory is developmental, stressing the need for early and continuous experiences which help individuals clarify their self-concepts and views of the world of work. Hansen's "A Model for Career Development Through the Curriculum" integrates Super's use of the self-concept as a determining factor in career choice with the curriculum as a vehicle for career development. Hansen views the curriculum as a natural medium by which educators can have an impact on students. Although her approach is predicated upon Super's developmental model, many of her strategies are behavioral.

The hallmark of Super's research has been studying career patterns. He has been concerned with how careers develop. In "Career Development of Youth: A Nationwide Study," Prediger, Roth, and Noeth investigate, among other things, the impact counselors have on career decision making of high school students. One of the major limitations of many research studies is the limited sample on which the results are based. Not so in this case. According to Prediger et al., students indicated an overwhelming preference for assistance from counselors in making career plans. Far fewer students wanted their counselors to help them with personal problems. The implications of such a finding are far-reaching. If the services counselors provide are a function of client-expressed need, vocational counseling will receive higher priority than personal counseling. At present, this is not often the case.

Behavioral approaches to vocational counseling are included in this section because they too lack the person–world-of-work link which characterizes the structural theories. Yet they differ appreciably in philosophical outlook from the works of Ginzberg and Super. Behavioral counseling is easily distinguished from nondirective counseling by its emphasis on goal-directed behavior. Goal setting is an integral part of behavioral counseling. Typically, clients present several concerns which motivated them to see a counselor. The counselor asks the client to rank the concerns according to their relative importance, or to pick out one with which to begin. Once a goal has been selected, the counselor needs to assist the client in determining if the goal is (a) ethical, (b) attainable, and (c) measurable. If the answers to all three criteria are affirmative, the counselor and client may begin working on ways for the client to achieve the goal. Once a goal is attained, behavioral counselors, in conjunction with their clients, evaluate the relative success of counseling so far. If counseling has not been successful, clients are encouraged to select a new goal, whether or not it was included on the original list. If counseling has not been entirely satisfactory, the counselor and the client need to discuss the obstacles and ways to overcome them. This process is repeated as many times as the client expresses a concern. Typically, with the attainment of one central goal, the need to deal with other goals may be obviated.

As mentioned by Morrill et al. in the first section of this book in "Dimensions of Counselor Functioning," there are several possible targets and purposes of intervening. The following two articles, both behavioral in approach, look at the targets and purposes of intervention differently. In "Clarifying the counseling mystique," Herr, Horan, and Baker identify their targets as *primary* and *associational groups* (in this case, students in a school), and their purposes as *prevention* and *development*. Their method of intervention is based on a systems approach. (The terms *behavioral counseling* and *systems approach* are often interchangeable. Both refer to the setting of specific goals, the articulation of strategies to be employed toward the attainment of the goals, and the development of criteria to be employed in measuring the extent to which the goals have been met. A systems approach to vocational counseling employs behavioral objectives.) As one might expect, Herr, Horan, and Baker provide specific career-related behavioral objectives for clients at different ages.

In "Vocational counseling with behavioral techniques," Woody focuses on *remediation* as the purpose of intervention with the *individual* as its target. He explains how several classical behavioral counseling strategies can be implemented within a vocational counseling framework, among them social recognition and object rewards, verbal reinforcement, systematic desensitization, and assertive practice. One of the concerns addressed is the integration of behavioral techniques into existing theories of vocational development. Woody deals with the problem by demonstrating how various behavioral *techniques* can be applied to vocational counseling.

Others have approached the problem from a *theoretical* perspective. One such approach focuses on vocational decision making. Decision-making theorists are concerned with the effect different *variables* have on vocational decisions. There are several decision-making models. In "Vocational Decision-Making Models: A Review and Comparative Analysis," Jepsen and Dilley present the major decision-making approaches. Katz's is another approach. According to him, individuals need to identify and define their *values* before wise vocational decisions can be made. This contrasts sharply with other decision-making approaches that rely upon exploring alternatives rather than values.

What makes Katz's approach of particular interest here is SIGI. SIGI (pronounced *siggy)* is an acronym for System of Interactive Guidance and Information. It is a computer-based system for assisting young adults in vocational decision making. Specifically, its purposes are: To increase students' freedom of choice; to expand awareness of the variables involved in making a choice; and to improve rational and informed decision-making behavior. In "Career Decision Making: A Computer-Based System of Interactive Guidance and Information (SIGI)," Katz discusses his rationale for employing a decision-making model, and then explains how SIGI works. For a list of the locations throughout the United States where SIGI is currently in use, write: SIGI, Educational Testing Service, Princeton, New Jersey, 08540.

In summary, process theories have, over the past quarter century, attracted a lot of attention because of the developmental and humanist appeal of Super's work. By definition, process approaches emphasize the nature of the choice process; more often than not they contain no mechanism for linking the individual with the world of work. Katz's System of Interactive Guidance and Information comes close to bridging the gap between the process and structural approaches.

15. Toward a Theory of Occupational Choice: A Restatement*

Eli Ginzberg

In 1952, the editor of *Occupations* invited me to summarize [3] the theory of occupational choice that had been set forth by Ginzberg, Ginsburg, Axelrad, and Herma in our recently published book, *Occupational Choice: An Approach to a General Theory* [6]. Now, two decades later, the editor of its successor journal has suggested that I reformulate our theory in light of the intervening research undertaken by the Conservation of Human Resources Project at Columbia University. The editor was alerted to the need for such a restatement by certain comments in my Foreword to Dale L. Hiestand's *Changing Careers After 35* [9], which included the statement that, in contrast to my earlier view that saw the process of occupational choice as coming to a permanent closure when an individual begins to work in his early or middle 20's, I now believe that the choice process is coextensive with a person's working life; he may reopen the issue at any time. The editor appreciated that this was not a minor gloss, but, instead, pointed to a fundamental restatement of our earlier position.

REVIEW AND REVISION OF 1951 THEORY

To set the stage for the general restatement outlined below, I will summarize the key elements in our original theory. There were three. Occupational choice, we said, is a decision-making *process* that extends from pre-puberty until the late teens or early 20's when the individual makes a definitive occupational commitment. Many educational and other preparatory and exploratory decisions along the way have the quality of *irreversibility:* A student who is pursuing a pre-law curriculum cannot suddenly shift tack and seek admission to medical school, for example. Thirdly, the resolution of the choice process always ends in a *compromise,* since the individual seeks to find an optimal fit between his interests, capacities, and values and the world of work.

"Process" Reappraised

A first effort at restructuring must start with the statement made above that we no longer consider the process of occupational decision-making as limited to a decade; we now believe that the process is open-ended, that it can coexist with the individual's working life. Some men, particularly those with professional or managerial backgrounds, often enter new fields after their retirement.

We came to this revised conclusion about the choice process as a result of our continuing research. Our original study focused primarily on young men from upper income homes who had time, money, and options with which to work out their choice problems—with the result that many ended up in professional

*Source: Reprinted with permission of the author and publisher from *Vocational Guidance Quarterly*, 1972, *20*, 169–176. Copyright 1972 The American Personnel and Guidance Association.

careers. At that time we did not appreciate, as we did after our research into *Talent and Performance* [7], that even of those who enter a profession, sooner or later many move on into related and occasionally into different types of work.

A related factor that pushed us to reappraise the matter of timing was our research into the *Life Styles of Educated Women* [5] and other investigations that centered on the occupational choices and career development of women. These studies forced us to realize that the male model of preparation and choice followed by a clear-cut shift to full-time work and a career did not fit the female prototype. Many women interrupted their educational preparation for marriage, and their career development was frequently marked by shifts between work and home. Moreover, because the employment of their husbands took precedence over their own, many women modified their career objectives. In fact, we labeled two important types of educated women as "recasters" and "adapters"—see *Educated American Women: Self-Portraits* [8].

The Hiestand study also contributed to our deeper understanding of matters of timing. This study told us that many people who had decided on a career early in life and who had pursued it for a number of years—even decades—with marked success might, as a result of changes within themselves or within their work environment, seek a new career that held forth the promise of greater satisfactions.

If we were asked to identify the principal factors that lead to a lifelong dynamizing of the choice process, we would be inclined to stress the following three. The first and most important is the feedback mechanism that exists between a man's original career choice and his work experience. If the satisfactions that he sought originally are not forthcoming, or if as a result of his working he becomes aware of new career possibilities that promise greater satisfactions, it is likely that he will endeavor to make a new choice. The probability of his venturing the attempt and succeeding in carrying it out will be affected by two related factors: (a) the degrees of freedom that he has as a result of changing family circumstances, i.e., if his children are grown and his savings allow him to take a year off to explore a new field; and (b) the pressures or options arising out of his job situation that force him to look for new employment or which enable him to accept early retirement.

"Irreversibility" Reversed

With respect to the second critical element of irreversibility, our later research underscored the need for modification. While we still feel that the multiple educational and occupational decisions that a young person makes between his childhood and his 21st or 25th year have a cumulative effect on his occupational prospects, we now feel that it is wrong to see these decisions as having an irreversible impact on his career.

There are several reasons why this facet of our theory must be revised. The first is the elongation of the preparatory process. Since 80 percent of the age group graduates from high school and since half of all graduates continue with their education and training, the decisions made prior to age 20 do not appear to have great potency, at least for the two out of five who have kept their broad options open.

To a lesser degree, the same is true of those who do not have the qualifications for or the interest in continuing their formal education or training after high school. Many of these young adults spend two to four years in military service during which their horizons are broadened; they acquire some skill, and, if honorably discharged, they are entitled to valuable benefits that will enable them to pursue specialized training. Others among this noncollege population have an opportunity to enter one or another type of publicly supported training, as a result of which they are likely to reassess their occupational objectives.

Most important, we have come to recognize, largely as a result of the work of our colleague, Marcia Freedman, *The Process of Work Establishment* [2], that the career development of the noncollege group will be materially affected by whether or not they succeed in obtaining employment with a large company that has an internal labor market with training and promotional opportunities geared to seniority. If a young worker succeeds in joining such a work force, the key decisions about his career follow. The occupational decisions that he made earlier will be of relatively little significance.

Little is left of our original emphasis on irreversibility. The principal challenge that young people face during their teens is to develop a strategy that will keep their options open, at least to the extent of assuring their admission to college or getting a job with a preferred employer.

"Compromise" Reconsidered

This brings us to a reconsideration of the third element of our original theory that held that the individual, in crystallizing his occupational choice, must compromise between his preferences and the constraints of the world of work. While we believe that no one ever makes an occupational choice that satisfies all of his principal needs and desires, therefore giving validity to the concept of compromise, we now believe that a more relevant formulation would be that of *optimization*. Men and women seek to find the best occupational fit between their changing desires and their changing circumstances. Their search is a continuing one. As long as they entertain the prospect of shifting their work and career, they must consider a new balance in which they weigh the punitive gains against the probable costs. Our studies of talented men, educated women, and career shifts after age 35 have persuaded us to move from the static concept of compromise to the dynamic counterpart of optimization.

REFORMULATION OF OCCUPATIONAL CHOICE THEORY

The reformulation of our theory of occupational choice, then, follows in brief:

- Occupational choice is a process that remains open as long as one makes and expects to make decisions about his work and career. In many instances, it is coterminous with his working life.

● While the successive decisions that a young person makes during the preparatory period will have a shaping influence on his later career, so will the continuing changes that he undergoes in work and life.

● People make decisions about jobs and careers with an aim of optimizing their satisfactions by finding the best possible fit between their priority needs and desires and the opportunities and constraints that they confront in the world of work.

Our reformulated theory is that *occupational choice is a lifelong process of decision-making in which the individual seeks to find the optimal fit between his career preparation and goals and the realities of the world of work.*

The fact that a man remains in the same occupation does not imply that he has not altered his occupational choice. Consider the professor who, after being granted tenure, radically reduces his inputs into scholarly endeavors and looks to consulting or the golf course for his major satisfactions. Or the colonel who, passed over for promotion to brigadier general, spends his last four years in the service attempting to avoid trouble while he qualifies for retirement.

It is also true that many who make one or more radical changes in their organizational employment—the professor who leaves the campus to become a government administrator and who, after a few years, shifts again to a senior staff position in private enterprise—may be pursuing the same occupational goals. If, as we now believe, the process of occupational choice determination is lifelong, it is necessary to distinguish between the individual's latent and overt occupational behavior if the critical elements of continuity and change in his career development are to be isolated and evaluated.

Also important in this connection is the fact that the passage of time is a critically important factor. On the one hand, the passage of the years implies that the individual is undergoing important changes: He is accumulating skill and work experience; his interests and values are likely to shift; his personal and family circumstances will not remain the same. Moreover, prospective employers look differently at a young adult just out of school, at a man in his working prime, and at a middle-aged person who is entering the last third of his working life.

In the original version of our theory we paid little attention to these facts as we focused primarily on young men from middle and upper middle-income homes who were college-bound or college-educated. We had deliberately selected this group because it had a wide range of options based on family income, sex, intelligence, race, and educational opportunity. In the two intervening decades, our research was increasingly directed at disadvantaged populations—the under-educated, the ineffective soldier, Negroes, women, low income groups—with the consequence that we became sensitive to the manner in which inequalities in income, malfunctioning institutions, and prejudice and discrimination reduce the options and increase the constraints that people face in making their occupational choice.

CONSTRAINTS ON OCCUPATIONAL CHOICE

We paid particular attention to the inhibiting, constraining, and often crippling role of dysfunctional institutions on the occupational choice of large segments of the population in our recently published book on *Career Guidance* [4]. Children born into low income families have relatively little prospect of developing and accomplishing an occupational goal that requires graduating from college or professional school. The exceptional person can make it, but the vast majority will be unable to surmount the multiple hurdles along the way.

Important as parental income is for broadening options for young people, we found that parental education and values—aside from income—are often constraining. We are impressed with the fact that many parents in relatively high-earning, blue-collar families fail to encourage their offspring to acquire more than a high school diploma. This, in turn, cuts them off from entrance into many professional occupations and careers.

Educational Inadequacies

We are unsettled by our review of the widespread malfunctioning of the educational system. All too frequently young people from low income homes fail to develop interests, acquire skills, or formulate aspirations. Our summary conclusion is that the school, instead of liberating these youngsters from the adverse environment into which they have been born and brought up, operates so that at the end of their educational experience they are even more firmly entrapped.

We noted further that while considerable progress has been made in the lowering of discriminatory barriers in the world of work against women and minority groups, this progress is often not reflected in the educational system with respect to either curriculum or guidance. Consequently, a great many able young women, Negroes, and other minority group members are encouraged to pursue programs that will restrict their later career options. The school authorities are not keeping up with the changes in the marketplace, therefore contributing to faulty decision-making of many young people.

Linkages Lacking

While we believe that a significant improvement in the occupational decision-making process, particularly for the less affluent members of the community, requires major reforms in the educational system, we concluded from our inquiries that, for this end, exclusive attention on the reform of the school is wrong. We reached this conclusion through our new understanding about the important role played by the individual's experiences in the world of work in an open-ended occupational decision-making process. Particularly important in our view are the linkages among institutions, such as between the different levels of the educational system, between high school and post-secondary training, between high school and the armed forces, between military and civilian careers, between home and work, between hospitals and prisons and the labor market. As we sought to make clear in our new typology of career patterns [1], movements between and among these different sectors are the essence of adult work experience. Consequently if the transition from one sector to another is facilitated, there is less likelihood of slippage with waste of talent and personal frustration.

We were especially impressed with the marked elongation of the preparatory process. When Parsons wrote his pioneering book early in the century, he focused on the transition of young people who left school at the age of 12 or 14 to go to work. Increasingly, full-time commitment to the labor market occurs in the early or middle 20's after a young person has moved back and forth one or more times between school, the military, the civilian labor market, homemaking. Hence the importance of smoothing the pathways among these sectors.

The work of our colleague Ivar E. Berg, author of *Education and Jobs: The Great Training Robbery* [1], called attention to one of the deleterious consequences of faulty transitional mechanisms. While it is true that education is the open sesame to many prestigious occupations and careers, it is not necessarily true, as Berg's research makes clear, that the more education a man has, the better worker he will be. There is a marked difference between evaluating a man's educational background to determine that he has the basic knowledge required for his present or prospective assignment and a screening procedure that accepts those with the most education and rejects those with the least. Yet Berg found that many employers hurt themselves and inflict hardships on many poorly educated persons by confusing certification with performance.

Guidance Gaps

Another type of malfunctioning that we identified in the arena of occupational decision-making relates to the quality of informational and other supportive services. On the basis of our three-year investigation we concluded that most of the information currently provided by governmental and private sources to help people in their occupational decision-making is too general to be of much value, and that the information they need about training and employment opportunities in their locale is not available. Lacking are assistance in such mundane matters as filling out a job application, training in how to conduct oneself during an employment interview, little or no information about how to assess current wages versus deferred benefits, and many other unexciting but relevant considerations in career decision-making.

We were also disturbed to find that the majority of all guidance counselors are employed in junior and senior high schools. Consequently, young adults who are still in the throes of making a career commitment, adult women returning to work, mature men seeking to change their employment, released patients and prisoners, and many others who could profit from job and career advice are hard pressed to find it. There appears to us to be a misallocation of guidance services, particularly because most high school counselors are engaged in appraising student programs, assisting students in filling out their applications for college, and acting on behalf of their principals in dealing with disciplinary cases.

CONCLUSION

The reformulation of our theory of occupational choice delineated in the first part of this essay grows out of our two decades of empirical research in manpower economics, much of which has been focused on the occupational problems of disadvantaged populations. This later effort helped us to realize that the model we used in our original investigation, that of a group with maximum options, could not support our subtitle—"An Approach to a General Theory." Consequently, our efforts have been to deepen our knowledge and understanding of the ways in which such critical reality factors as income, sex, and race—especially in their institutionalized forms—operate to constrict and limit the occupational choices of large numbers of the population.

While our original formulation was based on a developmental approach, our reformulated theory stands on sociopsychological formulations. We have sought to make room not only for the individual as the principal actor in the decision-making process but also for the reality factors, past and present, that set the parameters within which he must resolve his choice.

Our greater sensitivity to reality factors in our present formulation of a theory of occupational choice does not obscure our conviction that the individual remains the prime mover in the decision-making process. While young people who grow up in adverse circumstances have fewer effective options through which to shape their lives and careers, all people have some options and the majority has a great many.

The critical issue is whether or not they take advantage of the options. An option, however, can never be exploited without some cost. The crucial questions, therefore, are whether the individual has sufficiently clear objectives and goals and whether he is able and willing to put forth the effort to realize them. While many people would like to be rich or famous, only a few are willing to make the sacrifices required to accomplish this goal.

While inequalities based on sex, race, income, and intelligence are pervasive in American society of the 1970's, and while such inequalities, particularly in their pathological manifestations, have a crippling impact on the career and life choices of many people, the fact remains that most Americans have career options. The existence of options is a precondition for a successful resolution of one's occupational choice. But more than options is required. The individual must be willing to make the investment required to realize these options. Options that are not exercised might never have existed. People who do not seek to optimize their satisfactions from their work are unlikely to do so. Many apparently place priority on other goals.

REFERENCES

1 Berg, I. E. *Education and jobs: The great training robbery.* New York: Praeger, 1970.
2 Freedman, M. *The process of work establishment.* New York: Columbia University Press, 1969.

3   Ginzberg, E. Toward a theory of occupational choice. *Occupations,* 1952, *30,* 491–494.
4   Ginzberg, E. *Career guidance.* New York: McGraw-Hill, 1971.
5   Ginzberg, E., et al. *Life styles of educated women.* New York: Columbia University Press, 1966.
6   Ginzberg, E., Ginsburg, S. W., Axelrad, S., & Herma, J. L. *Occupational choice: An approach to a general theory.* New York: Columbia University Press, 1951.
7   Ginzberg, E., Herma, J. L., *et al. Talent and performance.* New York: Columbia University Press, 1964.
8   Ginzberg, E., & Yohalem, A. M. *Educated American women: Self-Portraits.* New York: Columbia University Press, 1966.
9   Hiestand, D. L. *Changing careers after 35.* New York: Columbia University Press, 1971.

16. Using Inner Experience: Fantasy and Daydreams in Career Counseling*

James I. Morgan and Thomas M. Skovholt

Recent inventories and papers have promoted the use of fantasy and daydreams[1] in career counseling (Dolliver & Nelson, 1975; Figler, 1975; Holland, 1970; Klairreich, 1973; Sanz & Hoffman, 1973; Skovholt & Hoenninger, 1974). There is an extensive literature supporting the use of fantasy in psychotherapy, and research is beginning to be reported which supports its use in career counseling. In this paper we encourage the continued use of fantasy techniques by delineating issues in the use of fantasy and describing some techniques we have used.

When fantasy and daydreaming are mentioned, many career counselors flinch a bit, believing that the terms *fantasy* and *daydreaming* are indicative of personal problems or psychopathology. Such beliefs are not surprising since many career counselors were taught about fantasy and daydreaming in educational psychology courses. In these courses, personal maladjustment is a common topic and fantasy is often considered one characteristic of personal maladjustment. Labeling fantasy a suspect human activity is especially prominent in the introductory educational psychology texts of the 1950s and 1960s. Personality inventories of the 1950s also tended to describe fantasy as a negative activity. For example, the 1950 version of the Mooney Problem Check List—Form HS indicates that fantasy is a problem area.

Perhaps the most productive way to view fantasy, however, is to see fantasy activity as being on a continuum of sorts, with one end representing unhealthy activity and the other representing healthy activity. It is the healthy end which has recently begun to be emphasized in personality research. Recent research indicates that fantasy and daydreaming can be—and often are—positive, life-enriching, stress-reducing, creativity-increasing human activities that should be encouraged in many instances. Kripke and Sonnenschein (1973) discovered in human behavior an ongoing 90-minute daytime cycle of dream-like mentation that is similar to the well-established nighttime dreaming cycle. Singer and McCraven (1961) found that 95% of their subjects daydreamed daily, often concerning plans for future actions and interpersonal contacts. Schaefer (1969) and Segal (1975) believe that the fantasy life of children leads to their later development of creative ability. Klinger (1971) provides a wealth of data concerning the positive nature of fantasy. Perhaps the most exciting recent work that suggests the positive nature of fantasy and daydreaming is the work of Singer (1971, 1974, 1975, 1976). Recently Singer (1976) said,

> Fantasies and daydreams, far from being irrelevant and insubstantial, may be the foundation of serenity and purpose in our lives. My recent experiments . . . suggest

[1] The terms *fantasy* and *daydream* are used interchangeably in this paper.

*Source: Reprinted with permission of the authors and publisher from the *Journal of Counseling Psychology*, 1977, 5, 391–397. Copyright 1977 The American Psychological Association.

that fantasy plays a basic role in the healthy development of any man or women. (p. 32)

When discussing fantasy and career planning, many career counselors think immediately of the well-known theory of vocational development proposed by Ginzberg, Ginsburg, Axelrad, & Herma, (1951). In their theory, Ginzberg and his associates suggested that fantasy was an age-segregated activity reserved for young people. Ginzberg et al. believed reality would eradicate fantasy in the mature person. Fortunately, in his 1972 revision, Ginzberg does not limit the usefulness of fantasy and daydreaming to the lives of young people.

Thomas (1976) offers an example of a misunderstanding of the use of fantasy in career planning. In his study of the occupational plans of male adolescents, Thomas distinguishes between fantasized hopes and reality-bound plans. In order to assess the occupational fantasies of students he asked them the following:

> People sometimes think about what they would like to be although they don't really believe it could ever come true. If by some magic you could be anything you want what would you like to be? (p. 47)

Such questions tend to stress the magic, pie in the sky, unreality of fantasy rather than the important problem solving and planfulness of fantasy. Although the word "fantasy" will continue to connote unrealizable dreams, we hope career counselors will also realize that fantasy and daydreaming are important activities in problem solving and decision making (Giambra, 1974).

Fantasies and daydreams play a central role in career planning. In *Working* a stonemason who loves his craft is engaging in a fantasy about his future work. His thoughts are aptly captured by Terkel (1975):

> I daydream all the time, most times it's on stone. Oh, I'm gonna build me a stone cabin down on the Green River . . . I've got to figure out how to make a stone roof. That's the kind of thing. All my dreams, it seems like it's got to have a piece of rock mixed in them. (p 20)

In another work setting, a photographer discusses her plans. She says, "They're all dreams now, but if I didn't have dreams, then I couldn't make them come true" (Carlin, 1975).

Further evidence is found in research by Holland and Gottfredson (1975). Using a large sample, they found that occupational aspirations or daydreams are important in predicting future occupational choice. In fact, they found that an individual's top occupational daydream tends to be more predictive than that individual's Self-Directed Search Summary Code. They said,

> Taken together, the findings imply that a person's vocational aspirations [occupational daydreams] have considerable psychological meaning; a pattern of related aspirations implies decision-making ability, psychological integration and predictability. (p. 360)

It is our observation that fantasy and daydreams are a rich resource for individuals to use in their career planning. We believe career counselors can harness this activity and deliberately use the data of fantasy and daydreams to help their clients.

Some of the parameters for the use of guided fantasy in career counseling have come from the areas of psychotherapy and personal counseling. Wilkins (1974) provides a classification of imagery scenes and procedures as well as "a classification of diagnostic entities relevant to the application of imagery procedures" (p. 164). Schutz (1967) devotes 25 pages to describing and illustrating a guided fantasy technique. Kelly (1972) describes a guided fantasy technique in which the therapist intervenes during the fantasy to ask the client to attend to particular material which is being recounted by the client.

Research is just beginning in the use of fantasy in career counseling. However, a pioneering effort was made by Kline and Schneck in 1950. They used hypnotic scene visualization for investigating the nature and characteristics of occupational interests and choices. With the exception of the clients being placed in hypnosis, the technique used by Kline and Schneck is similar to the guided fantasy technique for career exploration described by Skovholt and Hoenninger (1975). (It should be emphasized, however, that guided fantasy is not the same thing as hypnosis.)

Holmes (1975), Nelson (1975), and Nicholson (1975) researched the use of guided fantasy in career counseling groups and found the fantasy technique to be an effective one. Nicholson (1975) said, "Thus it was demonstrated that the GF (guided fantasy) experience had an extremely powerful effect." Holmes (1975) found a series of guided fantasy exercises superior to test-feedback procedures in career exploration. Nelson (1975) believes that guided fantasy is especially effective when used in conjunction with other group techniques.

We are encouraged by this recent research using guided fantasy and hope that more research will emerge.

USING FANTASY

In this paper we have discussed fantasy and daydreams. Some fantasies are free, spontaneous, unstructured; other fantasy activity is structured, directed, guided. The relationship between structured fantasies and free fantasies has yet to be fully explored (Blume, Note 1). We believe that both spontaneous fantasies and guided fantasies can provide valuable information in career counseling.

Spontaneous Fantasy

We suggest that counselors ask clients about their present and past spontaneous occupational fantasies and daydreams. Questions like the following may be helpful: "What occupations do you fantasize or daydream about now?" "As a child, what were your occupational daydreams and how do you feel about these daydreams now?" "When you fantasize about accomplishments, what do you consider?" "What kind of work seems to be excluded from your fantasies or daydreams?" Career counselors can use the data from spontaneous daydreams just like they use other data (i.e., test scores, occupational information) to help clients.

Guided Fantasy

The guided fantasy experience, as we practice it, consists of three parts: (a) inducing relaxation, (b) the fantasy itself, (c) processing the fantasy experience.

Relaxation   We believe that participants must have a relaxed and receptive attitude. Often we start by telling the participants that we are going to ask them to try out a new, interesting method to gain self-understanding. We tell them that they need to relax as much as possible and to let their imaginations take over. The lights are dimmed and the participants are asked to assume a comfortable position sitting up or lying down. Then we use relaxation training à la Jacobsen (1964), varying the relaxation training by use of muscle tensing and relaxing, breathing exercises, and relaxation imagery to produce a sufficient level in the participants. Typically, we might ask the people to first tense, then relax, their toes, leg muscles, thigh muscles, and so on, until they have tensed and relaxed each major muscle group. We have them pay special attention to relaxing the muscles of their jaws, faces, foreheads, and scalps. We might further ask them to imagine lying on a fluffy, but firm and supportive, cloud that allows them to drift lazily through the sky. We ask them to take several deep breaths and let the air out slowly.

The Fantasy   As the participants remain passive and relaxed, we again ask them to let their imaginations take over. At this point we begin the guided fantasy. Our "bread and butter" guided fantasy is "A Day in the Future" fantasy. In this fantasy we ask participants to imagine events during a typical work day, 5, 10, or 15 years from now. Skovholt and Hoenninger (1974) describe one script that counselors may use for this future fantasy. The following is another:

> Let your imagination take you 10 years into your future. As I talk, just let any images come that will. Don't answer my questions aloud. Just let the images form. (pause) . . . You are just awakening from a good night's sleep. You lie in bed just a minute longer before getting up and doing the things you usually do before going to breakfast. (pause)
>
>   On your way to breakfast now, look around you to see where you are—what this place is like. . . . Perhaps you can begin to sense things now. See if there is anyone with you. Eat your breakfast now and notice how you experience it. (pause) It is nearly time to go to work . . . perhaps you stay at home, perhaps you leave. If you leave, notice how you get there. Do you walk? . . . drive? . . . take a train or bus? How do things look along the way? Do you see anyone you know? (pause)
>
>   You are approaching where you work if you are not already there. What do you notice? What do you feel as you enter and start about doing your work? Who else is there? What are they doing? Complete your morning's work right up to your lunch time. (pause)
>
>   It is lunch time now. Do you stay in or go out? What do you have to eat? Taste it. Smell it. Are you alone or with someone? Is this lunch like your usual one? (pause)
>
>   Return to work now and finish the work day. See if anything is different or if it

stays the same. Notice what the last thing is that you do before you get ready to quit work for the day. (pause)

Leave your work place and go to where you live. See what you notice along the way. As you arrive where you live, notice how you feel and how your living place looks. Do what you do before your evening meal. (pause) Eat your meal, paying attention to how it tastes, how it feels in your mouth, how many helpings you have, who, if anyone, is with you. (pause)

After your meal do what you do during the evening before going to bed. (pause)

Go to bed now. Just before dropping off to sleep, review your day. Was it a good day? What pleased you in particular? Go to sleep now. I'll help you awaken in a moment. (pause)

You're awakening now . . . but not in your bed . . . in (this place). Open your eyes when you're ready, and just sit quietly for a minute.

It is important for leaders to phrase instructions in such a way so as to allow the maximum amount of individual expression for each participant. One of the central strengths of this technique is the way a common guided fantasy produces such diverse and rich experiences for participants. In order to produce the variety of experiences we would say, for example, "Do you work alone? If not, what are your fellow workers like?" rather than "You are working with a small group of people whom you seem to enjoy." We agree with Singer (1971) that the greater the range of sensory modalities which can be used (sight, smell, touch, taste, hearing) the more varied and valuable the fantasy experiences to the participant.

"The Award Ceremony" Fantasy In this guided fantasy, participants are asked to imagine themselves the recipient of a special award at a gala banquet. The award is for a special competence the participant possesses. This fantasy attempts to help participants crystallize their own goals and think about their motivations. It attempts to tap what White (1959) calls competence motivation, the central motivation of human behavior.

"The Opposite Sex" Fantasy There are two ways we proceed here. In one method, the leader asks participants to imagine themselves growing up as the opposite sex. Here the content of the guided fantasy takes participants from the preschool years through adolescence and early adulthood and asks them about interests, competence, values, and decisions they make as they proceed.

A second method is to ask participants to imagine a job, usually held by the opposite sex (i.e., nurses, elementary teachers, secretaries, for males; insurance agents, engineers, welders, for females). Then the leader takes the participants through a typical work day.

We believe the opposite sex fantasy exercises help participants examine occupational choices they may naturally rule out because of their own sex role socialization. In these days when many occupations are hard to enter, individuals have an advantage if they have been socialized with characteristics most common to the opposite sex (i.e., nurturance in men, analytical ability in women; Bardwick, 1971). When an individual can cross stigmatized boundaries, there are career opportunities. For example, males who enter nursing and females who enter engineering often have many opportunities.

"Another Race" Fantasy As in the opposite sex fantasy, the purpose of this fantasy is to help participants to open new vistas they may naturally close. In this fantasy the leader asks participants to imagine themselves growing up from pre-school years to early adulthood as a member of another race.

"Mid-Career Change" Fantasy This fantasy is aimed at individuals who have been in the work force a number of years and now want to change. Also, this fantasy can be used with women who want to return to outside employment after being at home while their children are small. The content of this fantasy can be similar to the "A Day in the Future" fantasy.

"Retirement" Fantasy This fantasy is an effective technique to use with individuals who are beginning to think about and plan their retirement from active work. A variation is to use this fantasy with young people, asking them to imagine looking back over their working years and their interests, competencies, values, and decisions.

There are other areas in which leaders can develop guided fantasies. We suggest you use your own creativity to develop other guided fantasy exercises. The possibilities seem to be limited only by the imagination of the user!

Processing the Fantasy In processing the fantasy experience, the leader helps the participants examine and reflect upon the fantasy experience. When we process the experience, we do not aim for a structured, focused result. Processing is simply a time to discuss the impressions and feelings of the participants. Group processing is best. In this context, participants hear each other and realize the great variety of possible reactions to the guided fantasy instructions. The discussion provides a framework for the participants' own processing of the experience. We end the fantasy experience by telling the participants that knowing about the content of a guided fantasy is one more piece of information for them, as valuable in making career decisions as other information such as inventoried interests, grades, and parental influences.

THE BENEFITS

We believe there are many benefits in the use of guided fantasy, and others seem to agree (Holmes, 1975; Kelly, 1972, 1974; Nelson, 1975; Nicholson, 1975; Saltz & Johnson, 1974; Singer, 1974).

First, it is fun. It is a pleasurable and novel alternative to the more traditional career counseling methods.

Second, it is safe. Since each participant's fantasy is a private experience, the participants can choose how much of it to share with others. The indirect expansion of emotions, goals, and beliefs is controlled by the participant.

Third, it allows for great sharing of feelings. Scheidler (1972) wrote

> The directed daydream gives the experience of sharing a deep part of ourselves with others; yet, through the use of symbols the technique prevents self-conscious embarrassment or psychological nudity. The sharing (in a group) evokes a feeling of community which allows meaningful interaction to happen. (p. 301)

Fourth, it allows contact with oneself that is usually ignored or repressed. Singer (1971) notes that day dreaming and vivid imagery have usually been regarded as symptoms of neurotic dispositions in America, although in Europe the intrinsic value of one's images has long been widely accepted. The guided fantasy experience gives credence to the notion that to have fantasies, far from indicating craziness or idleness, implies that one is capable of tuning into and using one's inner experiences for one's benefit—including enhancing creative problem-solving abilities (DeVoge, Note 2).

Fifth, it provides valuable career counseling information. Of most importance, fantasy provides data for career counseling, data that are valuable and sometimes difficult to obtain in other ways.

Areas of Difficulty

Problems for the participant in using guided fantasy for career exploration are minimal. The two which seem to occur are (a) not being able to "get into it" and (b) trying to make it *mean* something. It has been our experience that those people who "can't get into it" the first time around often can do so after hearing of other people's experiences during the processing phase. As to what an experience "means," usually it becomes clear to participants through discussion that an experience "means" what the person experiencing it says it means. What is more important is to answer the question, What does this information allow me to do that I couldn't do before?

The areas of difficulty for leaders typically concern the mechanics of the technique: the variety of relaxation exercises, voice quality, pacing, and fear of eliciting too much emotion from clients. The fear of arousing intense emotion is reduced because we are using the technique for career exploration. Usually participants automatically filter out intense emotions. However, leaders should be prepared to deal with their participants' intense emotions.

Occasionally, counselors learning the fantasy technique will express their concern about clients not awakening at the end of the session. It is sometimes true that clients go to sleep or are reluctant to return from this very pleasant experience. However, this is rare and easily handled if it does occur. In these instances, the counselor can say, in a slightly louder voice, "Some of you are still completing your fantasy. Finish it now and return to the room." The clients will invariably open their eyes in a minute or so.

A concern involves the lack of external restraints on the fantasy experience. Thomas (1976) conceptualizes fantasy this way and he has a valid point. For some clients there is a gap between their high status fantasies and other data; counselors may need to help clients integrate this material.

Perhaps the greatest area of difficulty for potential users of the technique lies with their own uncertainty. This uncertainty usually concerns the leader's feelings of competence and the usefulness of guided fantasy. We are hopeful that this article will provide information to increase feelings of competence in career counselors.

Our experiences, buoyed by the self-reports of participants, lead us to suggest that others try this technique in order to gauge its effectiveness. We believe fantasy adds another dimension to career counseling, a field existing at present with a minimum of powerful intervention techniques. Fantasy, more than any other technique, permits participants to include their private, internal experience in the data of career counseling. It is an entertaining and enjoyable technique for leaders and participants. It promotes openness and sharing rather quickly in groups, while also allowing participants to control the depth of and sharing of their private experiences. It is a safe and easy technique to learn and to practice. In short, we feel fantasy techniques are very helpful in career counseling, and that their usefulness will continue to increase as more practitioners use them and report their experiences.

REFERENCE NOTES

1   Blume, G. *A comparative study of dreams and related fantasies.* Unpublished manuscript, 1976. (Available from Department of Clinical Psychology, University of Florida, Gainesville, Florida 32611).

2   DeVoge, S. *The uses of visual imagery in behavioral rehearsal: A group hypnosis treatment method.* Paper presented at the American Society of Clinical Hypnosis annual workshop and scientific meeting, Seattle, October 1975.

REFERENCES

Bardwick, J. *Psychology of women.* New York: Harper & Row, 1971.

Carlin, J. Look and see is this photographer's motto. *Gainesville Sun,* March 2, 1975, p. 7F.

Dolliver, R. H., & Nelson, R. E. Assumptions regarding vocational counseling. *Vocational Guidance Quarterly,* 1975, *24,* 12–19.

Figler, H. E. *A career workbook for liberal arts students.* Cranston, R.I.: Carroll Press, 1975.

Giambra, L. M. The working world of Walter Mitty—Daydreams: The backburner of the mind. *Psychology Today,* December 1974, pp. 66–68.

Ginzberg, E. Toward a theory of occupational choice: A restatement. *Vocational Guidance Quarterly,* 1972, *20,* 169–176.

Ginzberg, E., Ginsburg, S. W., Axelrad, S., & Herma. J. L. *Occupational choice: An approach to a general theory.* New York: Columbia University Press, 1951.

Holland, J. L. *The self-directed search: A guide to educational and vocational planning.* Palo Alto, Calif.: Consulting Psychologists Press, 1970.

Holland, J. L., & Gottfredson, N. G. Predictive value and psychological meaning of vocational aspirations. *Journal of Vocational Behavior,* 1975, *6,* 349–363.

Holmes, J. *Differences between clients and nonclients and a comparison of two vocational counseling procedures.* Unpublished doctoral dissertation, University of Colorado, 1975.

Jacobsen, E. *Anxiety and tension control.* Philadelphia, Penn.: Lippincott, 1964.

Kelly, G. F. Guided fantasy as a counseling technique with youth. *Journal of Counseling Psychology,* 1972, *19,* 355–361.

Kelly, G. F. Mental imagery in counseling. *Personnel and Guidance Journal,* 1974. *53,* 111–116.

Klarreich, S. Counseling young women: Some new techniques. *Impact,* 1973, *2*(4–5), pp. 61–64.

Kline, M., & Schneck, J. An hypnotic experimental approach to the genesis of occupational interests and choice: I. Theoretical orientation and hypnotic scene visualization. *The British Journal of Medical Hypnotism,* 1950, *2*(2), 2–11.

Klinger, E. *Structure and functions of fantasy.* New York: Wiley-Interscience, 1971.

Kripke, D., & Sonnenschein, D. A 90 minute dream cycle. *Proceedings of the Association for the Psychophysiological Study of Sleep,* 1973, *2,* 177.

Nelson, R. D. *A comparison of the effects of three career group counseling techniques on measures of self-information, cognitive self-information seeking behavior and group process factors.* Unpublished doctoral dissertation, University of Missouri, 1975.

Nicholson, J. A. *A comparison of the effects of three career development group techniques on measures of self information and process variables.* (Doctoral dissertation, University of Missouri, 1974). *Dissertation Abstracts International,* 1975, *35,* 4659B. (University Microfilms No. 75-5778, 9)

Saltz, E., & Johnson, J. Training for thematic-fantasy play in culturally disadvantaged children: Preliminary results. *Journal of Educational Psychology,* 1974, *66,* 623–630.

Sanz, D. L., & Hoffman, S. D. The future group experience. *Proceedings of the 5th World Congress of the International Association for Educational and Vocational Guidance,* 1973, *5,* 499–510.

Schaefer, C. E. Imaginary companions and creative adolescents. *Developmental Psychology,* 1969, *1,* 747–749.

Scheidler, T. Use of fantasy as a therapeutic agent in latency age groups. *Psychotherapy: Theory, Research and Practice,* 1972, *9,* 299–302.

Schutz, W. *Joy: Expanding human awareness.* New York: Grove Press, 1967.

Segal, J. The gentle art of daydreaming. *Family Health,* March 1975, pp. 22–25.

Singer, J. L. The viscissitudes of imagery in research and clinical use. *Contemporary Psychoanalysis,* 1971, *7,* 163–180.

Singer, J. L. *Imagery and daydream methods in psychotherapy and behavior modification.* New York: Academic Press, 1974.

Singer, J. L. Navigating the stream of consciousness: Research in daydreaming and related experience. *American Psychologist,* 1975, *30,* 727–738.

Singer, J. L. Fantasy: The foundation of serenity. *Psychology Today,* July 1976, pp. 32–34; 37.

Singer, J. L., & McCravern, V. Some characteristics of adult daydreaming. *Journal of Psychology,* 1961, *51,* 151–164.

Skovholt, T. M., & Hoenninger, R. W. Guided fantasy in career counseling. *Personnel and Guidance Journal,* 1974, *52,* 693–969.

Terkel, S. *Working.* New York: Avon, 1975.

Thomas, M. J. Realism and socioeconomic status (SES) of occupational plans of low SES black and white male adolescents. *Journal of Counseling Psychology,* 1976, *23,* 46–49.

White, R. W. Motivation reconsidered: The concept of competence. *Psychological Review,* 1959, *66,* 297–333.

Wilkins, W. Parameters of the therapeutic imagery: Directions from case studies. *Psychotherapy: Theory, Research and Practice.* 1974, *11,* 163–170.

17.   A Theory of Vocational Development[*]

Donald E. Super

Two and one-half years ago a colleague of mine at Columbia, Dr. Eli Ginzberg, an economist, shocked and even unintentionally annoyed many members of the National Vocational Guidance Association by stating, at the annual convention, that vocational counselors attempt to counsel concerning vocational choice without any theory as to how vocational choices are made. A year later Dr. Ginzberg published his monograph on *Occupational Choice*, in which he stated:

> Vocational counselors are busy practitioners anxious to improve their counseling techniques . . . the research-minded among them devote what time they can to devising better techniques. They are not theoreticians working on the problem of how individuals make their occupational choices, for, though they have no bias against theory, they have little time to invest in developing one (10, p. 7).

Ginzberg continues, apropos of the fields of psychology and economics:

> . . . there are good reasons why the problem [of how occupational choices are made] has not been a focus of investigation for psychology or economics. . . . The process has roots in the interplay of the individual and reality, and this field is only now beginning to be included in the boundaries of psychological inquiry. The obverse formulation applies to economics, which as a discipline concentrates on a detailed analysis of reality forces and satisfies itself with a few simplified assumptions about individual behavior (10, p. 7).

These conclusions were based partly on a review of the research literature which I did at his request, and partly on a number of discussions in which he, his research team, and I participated. Consequently, I have a feeling of responsibility, not for the conclusions which he drew, but for drawing my own conclusions and for sharing them with my colleagues in psychology and guidance.

Basis of Ginzberg's Criticisms   It may help to point out that Ginzberg's conclusions were based on a review of the research literature which was designed to provide answers to specific questions asked by his research team in order to help them plan their own research project. What synthesizing of results I did was undertaken to answer these questions. I did not attempt to answer the question "What theories underlie the principles of vocational guidance now generally accepted by practitioners?"

But I do agree with his analysis of the situation with regard to theory construction: we have done relatively little of it, and for the reasons he has suggested. However, this does not mean that we have operated without theory. It is the principal purpose of this paper to set forth a theory of vocational development, a theory inherent in and emergent from the research and philosophy of psycholo-

*Source: Reprinted with permission of the author and publisher from the *American Psychologist*, 1953, *8*, 185–190. Copyright 1953 The American Psychological Association.

gists and counselors during the past two decades. But first I should like, as a help in formulating a more adequate theory, briefly to present the theory of occupational choice put forth by Ginzberg and his associates, to show how each of its elements had already been set forth by psychologists doing research in this field, and to point out some of its limitations.

THE GINZBERG THEORY

As Ginzberg, Ginsburg, Axelrad, and Herma summarize their theory of occupational choice, it contains four elements:

1. *Occupational choice is a developmental process which typically takes place over a period of some ten years.* This theory of Ginzberg's, it should be noted, is one of the points made by the official statement of the *Principles and Practices of Vocational Guidance* (33), first formulated by the National Vocational Guidance Association 25 years ago; it is a point stressed by Kitson in his *Psychology of Vocational Adjustment* (14), published in 1925; and, in 1942, in my own *Dynamics of Vocational Adjustment* (28) several pages are devoted to a discussion of the fact that "choosing an occupation . . . is a process which . . . may go on over a long period."

2. *The process is largely irreversible:* experience cannot be undone, for it results in investments of time, of money, and of ego: it produces changes in the individual. This second theory of Ginzberg's is clearly implied in Charlotte Buhler's 20-year-old theory of life stages (5), in Lehman and Witty's equally old studies of play interests (15), in Pressey, Janney, and Kuhlen's 13-year-old discussion of adolescent and adult development (20), and in my own 10-year-old text on vocational adjustment (28).

3. *The process of occupational choice ends in a compromise between interests, capacities, values, and opportunities.* This third theory of Ginzberg's is well illustrated in the practices of individual diagnosis developed by the Minnesota Employment Stabilization Research Institute 20 years ago and described by Paterson and Darley (19); it was further demonstrated and described by the Adjustment Service experiment 17 years ago (2); and it is basic to presentations of the use of diagnostic techniques in texts such as Bingham's (3) and mine (29), both of which appeared before the completion of Ginzberg's study. In fact, Frank Parsons (18), in 1909, discussed vocational counseling as a process of helping the individual to study both himself and possible occupational opportunities, and to work out a compromise between his abilities, interests, and opportunities. He called this last process "true reasoning."

4. Ginzberg's final theoretical formulation is that *there are three periods of occupational choice:* the period of *fantasy* choice, governed largely by the wish to be an adult; the period of *tentative* choices beginning at about age 11 and determined largely by interests, then by capacities, and then by values; and the period of *realistic* choices, beginning at about age 17, in which exploratory, crystallization, and specification phases succeed each other. Those who are acquainted with Lehman and Witty's early research in the change of interest with

age (15), with Strong's more searching work (25) in the same area, with Sisson's research in the increasing realism of choice with increasing age (23), with Charlotte Buhler's research in life stages (5), and with the use made of these data by Pressey (20) or by me (28), will find these three choice periods familiar. The special contribution of Ginzberg and his associates is the postulation of the successive dominance of interests, capacities, and values as determinants of choice before reality begins to play a major role.

It is easy, and perhaps even rather petty, thus to take a theoretical contribution and demonstrate its ancestry, showing that there is nothing particularly original about it. This is, undoubtedly, the normal reaction to claims of originality. But originality is more generally the result of a rearrangement of the old than the actual creation of something new: the rearrangement is original because it brings out details or relationships which have been missed or points up new applications. Ginzberg's theory is indeed an important contribution: this seems clear to me, at least, as I recollect the struggle I had in writing parts of my *Dynamics of Vocational Adjustment* (a struggle which resulted from the lack of a theoretical structure and from inadequate research), and as I work on its revision in the light, among other things, of Ginzberg's theoretical formulation and the thinking which it has stimulated. I have used this critical approach to Ginzberg's work in order to demonstrate that we have not entirely lacked a theoretical basis for our work in vocational guidance, and to show that the elements of theory on which we have based our practice have been sound, at least in that they have foreshadowed the elements which one group of theorists used when they went about constructing a theory of occupational choice.

Limitations of Ginzberg's Theory
But this is not the whole story. Ginzberg's theory is likely to be harmful because of its limitations, limitations other than those of research design and numbers in his basic study.

First, it does not build adequately on previous work: for example, the extensive literature on the nature, development, and predictive value of inventoried interests is rather lightly dismissed.

Second, "choice" is defined as preference rather than as entry or some other implementation of choice, and hence means different things at different age levels. To the 14-year-old it means nothing more than preference, because at that age the need for realism is minimized by the fact that the preference does not need to be acted upon until the remote future. To a 21-year-old student of engineering, on the other hand, "choice" means a preference which has already been acted upon in entering engineering school, although the final action will come only with graduation and entry into a job. No wonder that reality plays a larger part in choice at age 21, when, unlike choice at age 14, it is by definition a reality-tested choice!

A third defect in Ginzberg's theory emerges from these different meanings of the term "choice" at different ages: it is the falseness of the distinction between "choice" and "adjustment" which he and his research team make. The very fact that choice is a continuous process going on over a period of time, a process rather far removed from reality in early youth but involving reality in increasing degrees with increasing age, should make it clear that there is no sharp distinction between choice and adjustment. Instead, they blend in adolescence, with now the need to make a choice and now the need to make an adjustment predominating in the occupational or life situation.

Finally, a fourth limitation in the work of the Ginzberg team lies in the fact that, although they set out to study the process of occupational choice, and although they properly concluded that it is one of compromise between interests, capacities, values, and opportunities, they did not study or describe the compromise process. Surely this is the crux of the problem of occupational choice and adjustment: the nature of the compromise between self and reality, the degree to which the conditions under which one yields to the other, and the way in which this compromise is effected. For the counseling psychologist's function is to help the individual to effect this compromise. He must not only know the factors which must be compromised and how these have been compromised in the experience of others, but also the dynamics of the compromising process, so that he may facilitate this process in his counselee with constructive results.

ELEMENTS OF AN ADEQUATE THEORY OF VOCATIONAL DEVELOPMENT

An adequate theory of vocational choice and adjustment would synthesize the results of previous research insofar as they lend themselves to synthesis; it would take into account the continuity of the development of preferences and of the differences in the stages, choices, entry, and adjustment; it would explain the process through which interest, capacities, values, and opportunities are compromised. The second part of this paper will be devoted to a sketch of the main elements of such a theory of vocational development as they appear in the literature, and the third and final part will consist of an attempt to synthesize these elements in an adequate theory. The term "development" is used rather than "choice," because it comprehends the concepts of preference, choice, entry, and adjustment. There seem to be a dozen elements to a theory of vocational development: they are taken up in sequence.

Individual Differences   One of the basic elements of a theory of vocational development has been the theory of individual differences, a cornerstone of modern educational and vocational psychology. Kitson based much of his early *Psychology of Vocational Adjustment* (14) on this theory and on the findings on which it was based. It was essential to the work of the Minnesota Employment Stabilization Research Institute (19). It is surely unnecessary to document the fact of individual differences in aptitudes, interests, and values, or the significance of these differences for vocational development.

Multipotentiality   A second basic element of theory has been the concept of the occupational multipotentiality of the individual. It was first documented for intelligence by Army psychologists in World War 1, and was stressed by Kitson in his early textbook. It was documented for interests by Strong's work on the classification of occupational interests (26). It is a well-established fact and a basic assumption of vocational counseling that each person has the potential for success and satisfaction in a number of occupations.

Occupational Ability Patterns   The existence of occupational ability patterns, that is, the fact that abilities and interests fall into patterns which distinguish one occupation from another, was established by the Minnesota Employment Stabilization Research Institute (19) and has been confirmed in other studies, particularly those of the United States Employment Service (8). People have been found to prefer, enter, remain in, like, and succeed most consistently in occupations for which they have appropriate patterns of traits. The theory of the patterning of aptitudes and interests within individuals and within occupational families and the significance of this patterning for choice, entry, and adjustment are widely accepted and applied by counselors and psychologists today.

Identification and the Role of Models   Much has been made of the importance of identification with parents and other adults in individual development by psychoanalytically oriented writers, and this concept is widely used by counseling psychologists regardless of orientation. It has been little documented, however, in psychological research in the vocational choice and adjustment process. The work of Friend and Haggard (9) and a study by Stewart (1) do, however, provide some objective basis for the theory that the childhood and adolescent identifications play a part in shaping vocational interests, and also provide role models which facilitate the development and implementation of a self-concept, provided that the required abilities and opportunities are present.

Continuity of Adjustment   The continuity of the adjustment process was stressed by Kitson in his 1925 textbook as a result of his analysis of the careers of men whose success was attested to by being listed in *Who's Who in America*. The fact that adolescents and adults face a succession of emerging problems as they go through life, and that some of these problems are peculiar to the various life stages, was brought out by the studies of life stages made by Charlotte Buhler (5) and by those of occupational mobility conducted by Davidson and Anderson (7), Strong (26), and Miller and Form (16). And theories of the development of interests have been formulated by Carter (6) and by Bordin (4), theories which I modified slightly in my book on testing and upon which I drew in describing the process of vocational choice and adjustment in a speech first made at Ft. Collins, Colorado, in 1949, revised several times, and later published in the journal *Occupations,* under the title of "Vocational Adjustment: Implementing a Self-Concept" (30). These formulations are drawn on again as the cement for the various elements which need to be brought together in a theory of vocational development and as an explanation of the process of compromise between self and reality.

Life Stages   The work of psychologists and sociologists in describing the stages through which growth and development proceed, and in showing how these stages bear on the process of vocational choice and adjustment, has already been referred to. It was drawn on heavily in the text by Pressey, Janney, and Kuhlen (20), in my own first text (28), in Ginzberg's research (10), and in a recent text on *Industrial Sociology* by Miller and Form (16) which is as important for its original contribution and synthesis as it is annoying for its bias against anything that does not conform to sociology as they conceive of it. Buhler's theory of development through the exploratory, establishment, maintenance, and decline stages is translated into occupational terminology by Miller and Form, who also documented the theory for American careers, while Ginzberg, Ginsburg, Axelrad, and Herma have developed in more detail the phases of the exploratory stage. This latter theory needs confirmation with a larger sample and more objective procedures, in view of Small's (24) recent failure to confirm it with a somewhat different adolescent sample, but the general theory of life stages is basic to vocational guidance and will be drawn on heavily in my attempt at synthesis.

Career Patterns   The formulation of a theory of career patterns resulted from the occupational manifestations of life stages first documented by Davidson and Anderson (7), added to for a select group by Terman's genetic studies of gifted persons (31), and then pointed up by Ginzberg and his associates (10) and by Miller and Form (16). Career pattern theory appears to be a key element in the theoretical basis of vocational guidance, for it gives the counselor basic assumptions concerning the social, educational, and occupational mobility of his counselees, and it enables him to foresee types of problems which a given client is likely to encounter in establishing a career.

Development Can Be Guided   Another basic element in a theory of vocational development is the theory that development through the life stages can be guided. Although there is ample evidence that ability is to some extent inherited, and that personality is to some extent inherited, and that personality too has its roots in inherited neural and endocrine make-up, there is also good evidence that manifested aptitudes and functioning personality are the result of the interaction of the organism and the environment. It is a basic theory of guidance as we know it today that the development of the individual can be aided and guided by the provision of adequate opportunities for the utilization of aptitudes and for the development of interests and personality traits.

Development the Result of Interaction   That the nature of the interaction between the individual and his environment is by no means simple has been brought out by a variety of investigations ranging from studies of the effects of foster homes and of education on intelligence (17) to evaluations of the effects of occupational information and of test interpretation on vocational plans and on self-understanding (13). The realization of this fact and the acceptance of this principle have led to a greater humility in our claims for counseling and to a greater degree of sophistication in our use of guidance techniques.

The Dynamics of Career Patterns   The interaction of the individual and his environment during the growth and early exploratory stages, little understood though the process actually is, has been much more adequately investigated than has this same process during the late exploratory, establishment, and mainte-nance stages. We still know relatively little about the dynamics of career patterns. Terman's work (31) tells us something about the role of intelligence, Strong's (26) about interests, and Hollingshead's (11) about social status, but no adequate studies have been made of the interaction of these and other factors in determin-ing whether the individual in question will have a career pattern which is typical or atypical of his parental socioeconomic group. It was partly with this objective that an investigation known as the Career Pattern Study was launched in Middle-town, New York, last year.

Job Satisfaction: Individual Differences, Status, and Role   Early theories of job satisfaction stressed the role of intelligence and interest in adjustment to the occupation or to the job, building on studies of the relationships between these traits and occupational stability such as those made by Scott (22, ch. 26) and by Strong (26). More recently other investigations such as the Hawthorne (21) and Yankee City studies (32), anticipated in this respect by Hoppock's work (12) and by a minor study of mine (27) in job satisfaction, have played up the importance of the status given to the worker by his job, status both in the sense of group membership or belongingness and of prestige.

While researchers interested in the role of one kind of factor or another have tended to emphasize the signal importance of that type of factor, there is nothing inherently contradictory or mutually exclusive in these findings. They can all be included in a comprehensive theory of job satisfaction or work adjustment. This is the theory that satisfaction in one's work and on one's job depends on the extent to which the work, the job, and the way of life that goes with them, enable one to play the kind of role that one wants to play. It is, again, the theory that vocational development is the development of a self concept, that the process of vocational adjustment is the process of implementing a self concept, and that the degree of satisfaction attained is proportionate to the degree to which the self concept has been implemented.

Work Is a Way of Life   This leads to a final theory, one that has been more widely accepted and stressed by sociologists than by psychologists, but familiar to most counselors and considered basic by some writers in the field. This is the theory that work is a way of life, and that adequate vocational and personal adjustment are most likely to result when both the nature of the work itself and the way of life that goes with it (that is, the kind of community, home, leisure-time activities, friends, etc) are congenial to the aptitudes, interests, and values of the person in question. In the estimation of many, this is a basic element in a theory of vocational development.

A THEORY OF VOCATIONAL DEVELOPMENT

Now that we have surveyed the diverse elements of a theory of vocational development, there remains the final task of organizing them into a summary state ment of a comprehensive theory. The theory can be stated in a series of ten propositions:

1. People differ in their abilities, interests, and personalities.

2. They are qualified, by virtue of these characteristics, each for a number of occupations.

3. Each of these occupations requires a characteristic pattern of abilities, interests, and personality traits, with tolerances wide enough, however, to allow both some variety of occupations for each individual and some variety of individuals in each occupation.

4. Vocational preferences and competencies, the situations in which people live and work, and hence their self concepts, change with time and experience (although self concepts are generally fairly stable from late adolescence until late maturity), making choice and adjustment a continuous process.

5. This process may be summed up in a series of life stages characterized as those of growth, exploration, establishment, maintenance, and decline, and these stages may in turn be subdivided into *(a)* the fantasy, tentative, and realistic phases of the exploratory stage, and *(b)* the trial and stable phases of the establishment stage.

6. The nature of the career pattern (that is, the occupational level attained and the sequence, frequency, and duration of trial and stable jobs) is determined by the individual's parental socioeconomic level, mental ability, and personality characteristics, and by the opportunities to which he is exposed.

7. Development through the life stages can be guided, partly by facilitating the process of maturation of abilities and interests and partly by aiding in reality testing and in the development of the self concept.

8. The process of vocational development is essentially that of developing and implementing a self concept: it is a compromise process in which the self concept is a product of the interaction of inherited aptitudes, neural and endocrine make-up, opportunity to play various roles, and evaluations of the extent to which the results of role playing meet with the approval of superiors and fellows.

9. The process of compromise between individual and social factors, between self concept and reality, is one of role playing, whether the role is played in fantasy, in the counseling interview, or in real life activities such as school classes, clubs, part-time work, and entry jobs.

10. Work satisfactions and life satisfactions depend upon the extent to which the individual finds adequate outlets for his abilities, interests, personality traits, and values; they depend upon his establishment in a type of work, a work situation, and a way of life in which he can play the kind of role which his growth and exploratory experiences have led him to consider congenial and appropriate.

REFERENCES

1 Barnett, G., Handelsman, I., Stewart, L. H., & Super, D. E. The Occupational Level scale as a measure of drive. *Psychol. Monogr.*, 1952, **65**, No. 10 (Whole No. 342).
2 Bentley, J. H. *The Adjustment Service.* New York: American Association for Adult Education, 1935.
3 Bingham, W. V. *Aptitudes and aptitude testing.* New York: Harper, 1937.
4 Bordin, E. S. A theory of vocational interests as dynamic phenomena. *Educ. psychol. Measmt,* 1943, **3**, 49–66.
5 Buhler, Charlotte. *Der menschliche Lebenslauf als psychologisches Problem.* Leipzig: Hirzel, 1933.
6 Carter, H. D. Vocational interests and job orientation. *Appl. Psychol. Monogr.,* 1944, No. 2.
7 Davidson, P. E., & Anderson, H. D. *Occupational mobility.* Stanford: Stanford Univer. Press, 1937.
8 Dvorak, Beatrice. The new U.S.E.S. General Aptitude Test Battery. *Occupations,* 1947, **25**, 42–49.
9 Friend, J. G., & Haggard, E. A. Work adjustment in relation to family background. *Appl. Psychol. Monogr.,* 1948, No. 16.
10 Ginzberg, E., Ginsburg, J. W., Axelrad, S., & Herma, J. L. *Occupational choice.* New York: Columbia Univer. Press, 1951.
11 Hollingshead, A. B. *Elmtown's youth.* New York: Wiley, 1949.
12 Hoppock, R. *Job satisfaction.* New York: Harper, 1935.
13 Johnson, D. G. The effect of vocational counseling on self-knowledge. Unpublished doctor's dissertation, Teachers College, Columbia University, 1951.
14 Kitson, H. D. *Psychology of vocational adjustment.* Philadelphia: Lippincott, 1925.
15 Lehman, H. C., & Witty, P. A. *Psychology of play activities.* New York: Barnes, 1927.
16 Miller, D., & Form, W. *Industrial sociology.* New York: Harper, 1951.
17 National Society for the Study of Education, G. M. Whipple (Ed.). *Intelligence: its nature and nurture.* Bloomington, Ill.: Public School Publishing Co., 1940.
18 Parsons, F. *Choosing a vocation.* Boston: Houghton-Mifflin, 1909.
19 Paterson, D. G., & Darley, J. G. *Men, women, and jobs.* Minneapolis: Univer. of Minnesota Press, 1936.
20 Pressey, S. L., Janney, J. E., & Kuhlen, R. G. *Life: a psychological survey.* New York: Harper, 1939.
21 Roethlisberger, F. J., & Dickson, W. J. *Management and the worker.* Cambridge: Harvard Univer. Press, 1939.
22 Scott, W. D., Clothier, R. C., & Mathewson, S. B. *Personnel management.* New York: McGraw-Hill, 1931.
23 Sisson, E. D. An analysis of the occupational aims of college students. *Occupations,* 1938, **17**, 211–215.
24 Small, L. A theory of vocational choice. *Vocat. Guid. Quart.,* 1952, **1**, 29.
25 Strong, E. K., Jr. *Change of interest with age.* Stanford: Stanford Univer. Press, 1931.
26 Strong, E. K. Jr. *The vocational interests of men and women.* Stanford: Stanford Univer. Press, 1943.
27 Super, D. E. Occupational level and job satisfaction. *J. appl. Psychol.,* 1939, **23**, 547–564.
28 Super, D. E. *Dynamics of vocational adjustment.* New York: Harper, 1942.
29 Super, D. E. *Appraising vocational fitness by means of psychological tests.* New York: Harper, 1949.

30 Super, D. E. Vocational adjustment: implementing a self-concept. *Occupations,* 1951, **30,** 88–92.

31 Terman, L. M., & Oden, M. H. *The gifted child grows up.* Stanford: Stanford Univer. Press, 1947.

32 Warner, W. L., & Low, J. D. *The social system of the modern factory.* New Haven: Yale Univer. Press, 1947.

33 *Principles and practices of vocational guidance.* Cambridge, Mass.: National Vocational Guidance Association, 1927.

18. A Model for Career Development Through Curriculum*

L. Sunny Hansen

In the last few years a variety of models and programs have emerged that attempt to integrate career development concepts into the school curriculum. Although many of these are developmental, few have been comprehensive; many deal with only one aspect of career development (e.g., occupational information) rather than with the broad dimensions that go far beyond the world of work (Hansen 1970).

Many of the programs created in the mid-sixties were essentially piecemeal, fragmented efforts—someone's good idea that worked. Recent efforts seem to be characterized by more solid conceptual bases, more sophisticated program designs, and more comprehensive systems approaches that give major attention to content, process, and evaluation (Campbell, Walz, Miller & Kriger 1972). Among the salient characteristics of these programs are: (a) integration of career development through subjects and curriculum, K–12 or K–adult; (b) exploratory work or volunteer experiences in community sites; (c) hands-on experiences that integrate academic and vocational subjects; (d) career resource centers; (e) inservice training for faculty; (f) counseling, placement, and followup.

This article describes one model of career education, that in K–12, that might be appropriate in a variety of settings and school systems. Parts of it have been and are being tried at Marshall-University High School in Minneapolis and other school systems. The model is based on considerable evidence that students do not get the help they need or want in exploring themselves and careers and that the help they get often is based on outmoded matching models of vocational guidance that do not adequately take into account knowledge about the changing nature of the individual and his values, the changing world of technology and work, the lifelong process of career development and career decisions, and the psychological meanings of work and leisure to different groups and individuals.

The model assumes that career development is self-development, that it is "a process of developing and implementing a self-concept, with satisfaction to self and benefit to society [Super & Overstreet 1960]." It provides for exploration of self in relation to educational and vocational pursuits and in consideration of the place that work and leisure have in a person's life. It assumes that a career covers a variety of roles people play in life, including those of student, spouse, parent, and worker. It sees career development as one aspect of human development that forms a natural core for unifying curriculum and brings into consciousness what many teachers already are doing unconsciously. It sees career education as the systematic, comprehensive intervention for meeting career development needs.

*Source: Reprinted with permission of the author and publisher from the The Personnel and Guidance Journal, 1972, 51, 243–250. Copyright 1972 The American Personnel and Guidance Association.

OBJECTIVES

With this framework in mind, what are the objectives of a developmental career education program? It is expected that students who experience this program would become more vocationally mature persons who

- are aware of their own preferred life styles and work values and can specify skills, abilities, attitudes, roles, and values congruent with those preferences;
- exercise some control over their own lives through conscious choices and planning and can choose from alternatives a specific goal that is achievable and will be satisfying;
- are familiar with the occupational options available in this society (major families or clusters of occupations grouped in some meaningful way), including the opportunity structure, entrance requirements, and potential psychological satisfactions;
- know the educational paths to and financial requirements for preferred occupations and careers;
- are familiar with the process of career decision making;
- know the major resources available in the school and community and are able to identify, use, and expand those resources (printed, human, and nonhuman) most appropriate for their particular goals;
- can organize and synthesize knowledge about themselves and the work world and can map strategies for achieving their goals and modifying them if desirable.

The strategies described here for accomplishing these objectives are, for the most part, not new. In fact, many of them have been selected from promising practices around the country. Although a few of the strategies are new, it is rather their organization, level placement, and sequencing that comprise the originality of this article. Their description here is intended merely to stimulate developmental efforts in local schools and not to provide a complete or finished pattern. Together the strategies form a suggested illustrative framework for maximizing career development through career education in a sequential curricular-community program.

THE STRATEGIES

Strategy One: Orientation and Awareness (Primary Years)

It is in the elementary years that attitudes about self and work are formed; during these years, therefore, the focus needs to be on beginning to develop self-awareness and a positive self-concept. Very early in life students get images of what they can and cannot do. It is crucial that the early years concentrate on helping children feel good about themselves and helping them communicate what they are learning to value and to do. There needs to be emphasis at this stage on building communications and interpersonal skills for everyday functioning and for potential satisfaction in work and other roles. Elementary children also need ideas and information about the work world in a broad sense. Following are strategies that might be used at this level.

Parent Role Models   Mothers and fathers might be invited into the classroom, wearing the uniforms and carrying the tools of their trade, to talk with students about their jobs. Such a technique could give students a feeling of self-worth, provide information and knowledge about workers, and instill respect for people and the work they do. If parents are unavailable, other significant adults in the child's life might be invited.

Learning Parents' Jobs   Each pupil might be invited to spend half a day with his parents on the job to obtain a clearer picture of his mother's and father's occupation and work setting. Since this might not be feasible for all, some children could be invited to visit the work setting of a friend's parent.

Use of Subjects   Children could be exposed to career development concepts and occupations through the variety of subjects offered at the elementary level. Several sets of materials and media are available, including the DUSO Kit (Dinkmeyer 1970); Our World of Work (Wolfbein & Goldstein 1970); Texas Career Development Curriculum, K–6 (Laws 1971); Career Development and the Elementary School Curriculum (University of Minnesota 1971); and Project BEACON (Stiller 1968), which offers excellent suggestions for providing local role models and improving the self-concepts of inner-city elementary school children.

Tele-Lecture Systems   These systems might be especially useful at the elementary level in providing telephone interviews with workers in a variety of fields and settings. Since primary children may not be able to have many direct experiences in business and industry (especially in rural areas), the tele-lecture arrangement, where 30 or more students can talk with a famous or a local person about his work satisfactions, life style, job requirements, and leisure opportunities, offers another medium for students to develop awareness and obtain information.

Strategy Two: Prevocational Self-Exploration Experiences (Intermediate or Middle School Years)

With the middle or junior high school student's orientation toward social and physical development, appropriate focuses here could be on (a) recognition of personal strengths and emerging values and goals; (b) awareness of individual potentials and the ultimate need to choose those that need to be more fully developed in order to achieve life goals; (c) awareness of the influence of friends, family, other role models, and significant others on emerging goals; (d) awareness of emerging personal styles; and (e) exploration of the worlds of education, occupation, and work, with emphasis on an activity-oriented program. Following are strategies that might be used at this level.

Strength Groups   Coeducational strength groups, well planned and structured, could meet weekly to focus on "What I can do and what I can do best." They could be led by counselors, teachers, or paraprofessionals with some training in career development and group process. A restructured homeroom model, using teacher-counselors in life planning labs, might be one approach.

Career Resources   Regular use of human and multimedia resources can be facilitated in a career resource center. Teachers can plan field trips that help students begin to get realistic information about the occupational world, with the emphasis on workers and processes rather than products. Teachers can also arrange for speakers—including parents of their students—to come into the classroom and talk about their work, its satisfactions, and its dissatisfactions. It is at this level that students begin their orientation to occupational clusters or families, and teachers can plan special interest career tours such as "Know your local merchants."

Broadening Role Models   In this systematic one-to-one or small group program, boys and girls get a chance to see men and women in nontraditional careers. The tendency toward too early a narrowing of career choices might be offset by identification with men and women in atypical careers (telephone repairwomen; female auto mechanics, dentists, computer programmers, and executives; male nurses, physical therapists, elementary teachers, and day care workers) and workers in emerging careers (environmental careers, health sciences, alternate schools). Filmstrip cassettes such as *Jobs and Gender* (Guidance Associates, Inc. 1971) might facilitate this strategy if live role models are not available. A directory of such life style models might be prepared.

Tentative Career Hypothesis   Each junior high student would have an opportunity to examine and assess a tentative career hypothesis through case study group approaches, autobiographical career lifelines, and group and individual counseling. He could begin to reality test present achievements and goals in relation to tentative educational and vocational plans. Emphasis would be on opening up rather than narrowing down possibilities at this level.

Strategy Three: Career Exploration Module (8th or 9th Grade)

In this module the cooperation of volunteers, aides, counselors, parents, and other community resources would be sought to assist the eighth or ninth grade teachers (English, social studies, core, or interdisciplinary team) in developing and implementing a career exploration learning package that would give junior high students exposure to the kinds of data and experiences described below.

Decision Making Process   Students would learn about the elements in the process of decision making—values, alternatives, probabilities, possibilities, consequences of choosing or not choosing certain options, and action plans. Such resources as *A Task-Oriented Course in Decision-Making* (Wilson 1967) and the

College Entrance Examination Board's junior high program *Deciding* (Varenhorst, Gelatt & Carey 1972) would be helpful tools at this level.

Simulation Experiences   Experience in motivational job problem solving through use of the *Job Experience Kits* (Krumboltz 1969) could provide one means of job-task tryout. Simulated adult decision making in the areas of family, education, occupation, and leisure, through use of the *Life Career Game* (Boocock 1967, 1968), has been demonstrated to be of value in promoting career development, especially with academically marginal youth.

Manpower and Economic Trends   Students need information about trends in the work world—manpower trends, poverty, occupational status of women, opportunity structure, emerging and obsolescent jobs, and effects of automation and cybernation. Such media as the U.S. Department of Labor's (1970) brochure *Manpower Trends in the 70's* and its accompanying slides would be appropriate.

Classifying the Work World   An important part of any career education program is information about the organization and classification of the world of work. Such information gives students a conceptual map of the occupational world, bringing its vast possibilities down to manageable and comprehensible size. It would be important to begin with some grouping of occupations by job families, interests, subjects, clusters, fields, or levels. Suggestions for groupings are offered by the Human Resources Research Organization's occupational clustering system (Taylor, Montague & Michaels 1972), the Science Research Associates' *Job Family Booklets* (1965), and the Ohio Vocational Interest Survey (D'Costa, Winefordner, Odgers & Koons 1968). The 15 U.S. Office of Education career clusters (Hardwick 1971) also could be considered for their functionality, appropriateness, and meaning for students.

Using Multimedia Resources   Enriching personal growth experiences can be gained through visits and orientation to career resource centers and other information centers. This can increase students' awareness of the many possibilities for door-opening contacts with business and industry. Familiarity with the many kits, films, filmstrips, cassettes, and other media available for a career exploration program can help accelerate the vocational planning process. Volunteers and paraprofessionals could be of immeasurable help in this aspect of a program. The Newton, Massachusetts, Career Information Center (Circle, Clemens, Kroll & Overholt 1968) and the Marshall-University High Resource Center (Hansen 1971) offer models to consider.

Career Development Contract   An alternate approach would be to have students create their own career development contract, in which they (a) specify tentative goals, (b) determine where they are now, (c) identify what they have to change in order to get where they want to go, and (d) develop an action plan with a teacher, friend, or counselor in order to bring about that change. This kind of approach could be repeated at many stages, including the senior high level. It has potential as a vehicle for helping students modify their own behavior and for bringing real and ideal self-concepts into greater congruence.

Strategy Four: Senior High Career Information Program (9th–12th Grades)

This aspect of the program would move away from traditional career day formats to a series of career information speakers, interviews, and field trips available to all students on a regularly scheduled basis. Such a program, which might include content relating to self, educational-vocational alternatives, the decision making process, and the job market outlook, could be built into the curricular program of a high school in the following ways:

1. The program would provide an orientation for all students to human and nonhuman resources available in the school (e.g., a career resource center) and community. The first year of the program all senior high grades would need to be included; thereafter only freshmen and other new students would need to participate. An elective course in the psychology of careers could be offered to those students interested in indepth exploration.

2. The program would consist of occupational information programs given throughout the school year, organized and implemented by paraprofessionals or volunteers under the aegis of school counselors. It would develop the mechanics for getting students out into business and industry and for bringing representatives from business and industry into the school. Where representatives are unable to come to the school, a tele-lecture system would enable students to have life style interviews with a variety of individuals, obtain direct information about manpower (and womanpower) supply and demand, and interview key people about their particular fields or about issues and trends.

3. Each month the program would focus on broad occupational families or job clusters. Choice of grouping or clustering of occupations should take into account local industries and fields in which a school's graduates tend to find employment. All levels of skills, abilities, and training would be included for all the broad educational paths available in the post-secondary years.

4. As part of his or her own career exploration and decision making, each student would be encouraged to attend at least two information sessions per quarter; a one- or two-hour block of time would be scheduled each week, for which students would sign up in advance. Sessions would be tape recorded and put in a cassette library of educational-vocational information so that those missing a particular program could listen at a later time. Volunteers and students could help monitor the program. The model developed by the Vancouver, Washington, Public Schools (Lothspeich 1967) can serve as a useful prototype.

5. Besides the scheduled weekly programs, a career resource center would be open to students engaged in self-directed searches or class projects. These students would come in to use kits, printed materials, computers, films, filmstrips, and cassettes. Volunteers or paraprofessionals, under the leadership of counselors, would be available to assist in the process and to arrange personal contacts, field trips, and interviews with workers in business and industry.

Strategy Five: Exploratory Occupational Information Interviews (10th–12th Grades)

With some training and modeling, a structured, exploratory interview between a trained volunteer and a senior high student could be scheduled. The purposes of this occupational information interview would be to (a) determine where the student is in his career planning; (b) obtain information about the student's vocational planning; (c) facilitate and accelerate the student's thinking about and acting on imminent decisions; (d) identify types of information the student needs that could be provided through volunteers and a career resource center; and (e) inform the student about the information and resources available in the school and community to assist in planning and exploration. Arranged by the counseling department as part of the counseling program, the interviews could be scheduled on a half-hour basis. Students would be informed that information is confidential and will be shared only with the student's counselor. Any student who chose not to have such an interview could do so. The volunteer would try to follow through with each student in identifying information and resources for exploration (Hansen 1971).

Strategy Six: Career Contracts with Counselor or Teacher-Counselor (11th–12th Grades)

Typically each high school junior and senior has at least one interview with his counselor about his post-high-school goals, plans, and decisions. In some schools a teacher-counselor or teacher-advisor assumes this function. Goals of this contract would be to help students (a) examine and synthesize their goals and values; (b) become aware of the forces and events that influence their decisions; (c) reality test their tentative decisions through a variety of tryout experiences—on the job, as volunteers, and through directed observation; (d) use the many resources available to them to obtain specific information about post-high educational and work options; and (e) modify their goals and plans as appropriate.

The "career competency contract" that has been tried out in the Wisconsin schools (Drier 1971) offers an excellent model for this phase of an individual's development. Students have their own individual advisory committee, consisting of a teacher, a counselor, a parent, and a representative from their occupational interest field, to help them identify and develop the career competencies needed to meet their goals.

Strategy Seven: Exploratory Work Experience (10th–12th Grades)

During the senior high years all students—especially seniors—should have the option of getting involved in a directed exploratory work experience to help them reality test their goals and work values. An Antioch-type high school program is envisioned, in which students have an opportunity for guided work or volunteer experience in a local business or industry as part of their curricular experience. Such a program would include the cooperative work program but be much broader in scope, including *all* students—not just the selected few typically reached. It could be scheduled in a variety of ways throughout the school year and summer (interim program, Christmas experience, semester option, etc.). A program of this nature already has been operational for some years in the Whittier, California, Unified School District (Eisen 1966) and could serve as a model for other high schools. Implementation of this strategy would require long-range planning, with commitments from teachers and administrators to allow part of the school day or school year to be used for this experience. It would also require extensive collaboration with business and industry and a commitment from them to hire, host, or supervise students in these exploratory capacities.

Strategy Eight: Career Development Subject Teams (Junior and Senior High)

To help integrate career development concepts into the curriculum, career development subject teams could be organized to help identify ways in which school subjects could be related more closely to careers and the world of work. Teams could consist of a teacher from the subject area, a counselor, a volunteer, a parent, a worker in a field related to the subject, and two or more students. The teams would brainstorm possible programs and ideas that would create in students a greater awareness of and sensitivity to (a) the career possibilities of a subject area—both the broad range of occupations related to the field and the potential self-actualizing (or debasing) features of the occupations; (b) the educational paths leading to those fields; (c) the leisure implications of the subject; and (d) the way the subject relates to the development of one's personal goals and identity. Special programs to develop the potentials of girls, minorities, and populations with other special needs could be created at various levels and stages. Program ideas could be screened for feasibility and carried out jointly by the teams, the department involved, and a career development advisory committee. Learning packages for career development through curriculum are being developed at the University of Minnesota (Tennyson, Klaurens & Hansen 1970) and are available for field testing through subjects.

A METHOD OF ORGANIZATION

While there is no best way to assure development and implementation of a systematic career development/career education program, an organizational strategy that might facilitate such implementation is the formation of a career development advisory committee or task force, K–12. Such a group could help monitor, implement, evaluate, and revise a developmental plan. The committee could include one teacher from each subject or cluster area, a student from each grade level, a counselor, an administrator, a parent, and representatives from business and industry. A steering committee, consisting of a vocational teacher, an academic teacher, a student, a parent, an administrator, a community representative, and a counselor, could serve as a core group to make recommendations to the larger group.

A CAUTION

No systematic career development/career education program can emerge full-blown at any given time. Some strategies might be more feasible and appropriate with some populations and settings than with others; students of the same age might be at different stages of readiness for planning and exploration; and some school systems initially might be better able to handle one part of a program than absorb a total plan. Although the goals and possibilities may be apparent, each school will have to select those portions of the program or create other developmental strategies that are most appropriate to the needs of its students and most adaptable to its facilities, personnel, and resources.

It is likely that the process of developing a comprehensive program of this scope would require the services of a full-time career guidance specialist. But the starting points and the possibilities for implementation will have to be decided by a number of people—representing key groups within the system—who are interested in and concerned about the career (self-)development of students and the help they are getting in this vital and pervasive aspect of their lives. Attention to strategies for the change *process* is imperative. It seems that the probability for success would be heightened if all groups within the school, particularly those most affected by such a program—the students themselves—are well represented in the decision making process from the very beginning.

REFERENCES

Boocock, S. The life career game. *Personnel and Guidance Journal,* 1967, *46,* 328–334.

Boocock, S. *Life career game.* New York: Western Publishing Co., 1968.

Campbell, R. E.; Walz, G. R.; Miller, J. V.; & Kriger, S. F. *Career guidance: A handbook of methods.* Columbus, Ohio: Center for Vocational and Technical Education, 1972.

Circle, D. F.; Clements, D. B.; Kroll, A.; & Overholt, D. *The career information service: A guide to its development and use.* Newton, Mass.: Bureau of Vocational Education, Department of Education, 1968.

D'Costa, A.; Winefordner, D. W.; Odgers, J. G.; & Koons, P. B., Jr. Ohio Vocational Interest Survey. New York: Harcourt, Brace & World, 1968.

Dinkmeyer, D. *Developing understanding of self and others (DUSO).* Circle Pines, Minn.: American Guidance Services, 1970.

Drier, H. N. Implementing career development programs in senior high schools. Paper presented at Workshop on Developing Guidelines for Planning Career Development Programs, K–12, Ohio State University, Columbus, Ohio, June 1971.

Eisen, N. B. Work experience education report. Whittier, Calif.: Whittier Union High School District, 1966.

Guidance Associates, Inc. *Jobs and gender.* New York: Harcourt Brace Jovanovich, 1971.

Hansen, L. S. *Career guidance practices in school and community.* Washington, D.C.: American Personnel and Guidance Association, 1970.

Hansen, L. S. Promoting student career development through utilization of volunteers in a career resource center. Volunteers in Career Guidance, Project Report, August 1971, Marshall-University High School, University of Minnesota.

Hardwick, A. L. Career education—A model for implementation. *Business Education Forum,* 1971, *25,* 3–5.

Krumboltz, J. *Job experience kits.* Chicago: Science Research Associates, 1969.

Laws, L. Career development curriculum, K–6. Austin, Texas: Texas Education Agency, 1971.

Lothspeich, W. F. Career guidance conferences. Career planning development committee. Vancouver, Wash., 1967. (mimeo)

Science Research Associates, Inc. *Job family booklets.* Chicago: SRA, 1965.

Stiller, A. *BEACON lights.* New York: Project BEACON, Rochester City School District, 1968.

Super, D. E., & Overstreet, P. L. *The vocational maturity of ninth grade boys.* New York: Teachers College Press, 1960.

Taylor, J. E.; Montague, E. K.; & Michaels, E. R. An occupational clustering system and curriculum implications for the comprehensive career education model. Technical Report 72–1. Columbus, Ohio: Human Resources Research Organization, The Center for Vocational and Technical Education, 1972.

Tennyson, W. W.; Klaurens, M. K.; & Hansen, L. S. *Career development curriculum: Learning opportunities packages.* Minneapolis: Departments of Counseling Psychology and Distributive Education, College of Education, University of Minnesota, 1970.

University of Minnesota, EPDA Institute. *Career development and the elementary school curriculum.* Minneapolis: Departments of Counseling Psychology and Distributive Education, College of Education, University of Minnesota, 1971.

U.S. Department of Labor. *Manpower trends in the 70's.* Washington, D.C.: U.S. Government Printing Office, 1970.

Varenhorst, B.; Gelatt, H. B.; & Carey, R. *Deciding: A program in decision-making for grades 7–8–9,* New York: College Entrance Examination Board, 1972.

Wilson, E. H. A task-oriented course in decision-making. Information System for Vocational Decisions, Project Report No. 7, April 1967. Harvard University, Graduate School of Education, Cambridge, Mass.

Wolfbein, S., & Goldstein, H. *Our world of work.* Chicago: Science Research Associates, 1970.

19. Career Development of Youth: A Nationwide Study*

Dale J. Prediger,
John D. Roth, and Richard J. Noeth

Career education and career guidance are currently high-priority items on the national agenda. Many believe student career development to be the unifying theme and primary goal of career education efforts. It was in the context of this national interest and the new developments in career education and career guidance that the Nationwide Study of Student Career Development (Prediger, Roth & Noeth 1973) was conducted. The primary purpose of the study was to assess and summarize core aspects of the career development of American youth enrolled in grades 8, 9, and 11. This is a particularly crucial period in the career development of students, one in which many experiences and decisions related to the post-high-school transition occur. Information on students' preparation for these decisions is certainly desirable as a basis for determining what is being done now and what needs to be done in the future.

The purpose of this article is to present some of the more significant findings of the study, findings that have implications for all counselors, but especially for those in school guidance programs. The article focuses primarily on what students *say* about their career development and about their current guidance needs. In addition, what students have *done* about career planning and what they *know* about career development are covered briefly.

Because the large amount of data obtained in the study precludes a complete discussion, we have attempted to identify some of the more salient findings and to draw some implications from them. Admittedly, this is a subjective process. Readers are therefore reminded that judgments concerning the implications of the findings are the authors' and that detailed study results are available for readers who wish to draw their own conclusions after inspecting the data.

SAMPLE AND ASSESSMENT PROCEDURES

The target population for the study was defined as all full-time 8th, 9th, and 11th grade students enrolled in public or Catholic schools in the United States in the spring of 1973. The sample, which consisted of approximately 32,000 students in 200 schools located in 33 states, was selected by Research Triangle Institute using sampling frame data developed for the National Assessment of Educational Progress. Stratification variables included region of country and size and socioeconomic status of community. When it was not possible to test all students, students in the specified grade within each selected school were randomly chosen. Weights were applied to sample data to insure that study results would be

*Source: Reprinted with permission of the authors and publisher from the *Personnel and Guidance Journal*, 1974, *53*, 97–104. Copyright 1974 American Personnel and Guidance Association.

nationally representative. A detailed description of sampling procedures has been provided by Bayless, Bergsten, Lewis, and Noeth (1974).

Under the supervision of local school personnel, students in the sample completed the Assessment of Career Development (ACD), a 267-item paper-and-pencil inventory/test. The ACD, which was developed from detailed content specifications drawn from career development theory and guidance practice (American College Testing Program 1974), covers the following core components of career development: (a) occupational awareness, including occupational knowledge and exploratory experiences; (b) self-awareness, including career plans and perceived needs for help with career planning; and (c) career planning and decision making, including career planning knowledge and involvement in career planning activities. The ACD also elicits student reactions to career guidance experiences, provides scores for 11 scales, and summarizes student responses to 42 specific questions.

RESULTS AND DISCUSSION

Student-Perceived Needs for Help

One of the most striking findings of this study is students' apparent receptivity to receiving help with career planning. As shown in Table 1, more than three-fourths of the nation's high school juniors would like such help; the proportion is almost as high for 8th graders. In both grades, more girls than boys are looking for career planning help. If recognition of the need for help with career planning is interpreted as an indicator of readiness, then American teenagers appear to be anxious to get on with career development.

Table 1 Student-Perceived Needs for Help

	Grade 8			Grade 11		
	"Yes" responses			"Yes" responses		
Area of student concern*	% M	% F	% Tot.	% M	% F	% Tot.
Improving study skills	74	72	73	68	61	65
Improving reading skills	65	60	63	61	56	58
Improving math skills	71	74	73	63	58	60
Choosing courses	62	66	64	57	58	58
Discussing personal concerns	38	40	39	29	32	30
Discussing health problems	31	26	29	17	13	15
Making career plans	71	75	73	76	80	78
Obtaining money to continue education after high school	57	57	57	56	55	56
Finding after-school or summer work	72	73	73	64	70	67

* Directions to students were as follows: "The list below covers several things with which students sometimes would like help. If you would like help with any of these things, mark A for YES. Otherwise mark B for NO."

Help with "making career plans" is by far the major area of need indicated by 11th graders; "finding after-school or summer work" is in second place. Far down on the list is "discussing personal concerns," the primary task for which many school counselors have been trained.

Reactions to School Guidance Services

The incidence of student-expressed need for help with career planning is in sharp contrast to the amount of help students say they receive. Item 1 in Table 2 shows that only 13 percent of the 11th graders feel that they receive "a lot" of help with career planning from their school. Another 37 percent feel that they receive "some" help. However, half of the 11th graders and slightly more 8th graders state that they receive little or no help with career planning. Yet, in a separate item not shown in the table, 85 percent of the 11th graders indicate that they recognize that career planning must begin before the final year of high school. It would appear, then, that a need exists that remains for the most part unfulfilled.

One explanation for the large number of students who feel they receive little or no career planning help might be the unavailability of school counselors. However, item 2 in Table 2 shows that only 3 percent of the 11th graders do not have a guidance counselor. An overwhelming 84 percent say that they can usually or almost always see a counselor when they want to. The implication, then, is that many counselors are simply not providing help with career planning, either on a one-to-one basis or through group guidance activities. Perhaps time constraints and conflicting responsibilities are the chief cause. We believe, however,

Table 2   General Reactions to School Guidance Services

Paraphrased questions and summary of student responses

1. Overall, how much help with career (educational and job) planning has your school (teachers, counselors, principal, librarian, etc.) given you?

	Grade 8			Grade 11		
	% M	% F	% Tot.	% M	% F	% Tot.
A. None	25	24	24	20	15	17
B. Little	31	30	31	33	32	32
C. Some	33	34	33	36	39	37
D. A lot	12	12	12	11	15	13

2. Do you feel you can see a guidance counselor when you want to or need to?

	Grade 8			Grade 11		
	% M	% F	% Tot.	% M	% F	% Tot.
A. Hardly ever	17	14	16	13	14	13
B. Usually	35	34	34	41	41	41
C. Almost always	31	31	31	43	44	43
D. We don't have a guidance counselor	17	20	19	4	2	3

that many counselors and administrators have failed to accept and communicate career planning as an appropriate responsibility of the school and that, as a result, students do not expect or request help with career planning.

Table 3 summarizes student reactions to some of the career guidance activities commonly described in textbooks and implemented in schools. Item 1 supports the notion that many counselors—for whatever reasons—are not providing career guidance help. Over half of the 11th graders (56 percent) indicate that they

Table 3   Reactions to Typical Career Guidance Activities

Paraphrased questions and summary of student responses

General directions: "Some of the ways schools help students with career planning are listed below. For each, show how you feel about the help provided at your school."

1. Discussion with a counselor about education and job plans for after high school.

	Grade 8			Grade 11		
	% M	% F	% Tot.	% M	% F	% Tot.
A. Help not provided/used	56	56	56	38	32	35
B. Of little help	19	17	18	21	21	21
C. Of some help	17	16	17	29	28	28
D. A lot of help	8	11	10	12	18	15

2. Class discussion by teachers of jobs related to their subjects.

	Grade 8			Grade 11		
	% M	% F	% Tot.	% M	% F	% Tot.
A. Help not provided	38	40	39	37	34	35
B. Of little help	28	27	27	27	23	25
C. Of some help	24	23	24	27	28	27
D. A lot of help	10	10	10	10	15	12

3. Films on jobs, talks by workers (in person or on tape), "career days," tours.

	Grade 8			Grade 11		
	% M	% F	% Tot.	% M	% F	% Tot.
A. Help not provided/used	46	51	48	44	43	44
B. Of little help	21	20	20	22	18	20
C. Of some help	23	20	21	24	25	24
D. A lot of help	11	11	11	11	14	12

4. File of job descriptions, pamphlets, or books on jobs.

	Grade 8			Grade 11		
	% M	% F	% Tot.	% M	% F	% Tot.
A. Help not provided/used	46	48	47	38	30	34
B. Of little help	25	21	23	24	20	22
C. Of some help	21	22	21	30	37	33
D. A lot of help	9	10	9	9	13	11

receive little or no help with career planning in discussions with counselors. As would be expected, the percentage is substantially higher for 8th graders. The number of 11th graders indicating that they receive some or a lot of help from counselors (43 percent) is somewhat lower than the number indicating that they receive some help or a lot of help from their school (50 percent; see Table 2). It appears that counselors provide most, but not all, of the career planning help received by 11th graders. In the 8th grade, the relative contribution of the school as a whole is substantially higher.

For many years teachers have been urged to make their subjects relevant to the "real world." More recently, and particularly in career education programs, attention has shifted to "the world of work." While the emphasis of these efforts is on instructional effectiveness and career awareness rather than on career planning, certainly help with the latter would be a reasonable concomitant to expect. Item 2 in Table 3 shows that about 35 percent of the 11th graders and 8th graders do indeed say that class discussions of jobs related to the subjects they are studying provide some help or a lot of help with career planning. However, a similar proportion of students indicate that help is "not provided" in class discussions of this type—possibly because a large number of teachers have yet to accept the career-relevance approach to instruction.

Items 3 and 4 in Table 3 summarize student reactions to other types of common career guidance practices. Tables 2 and 3 indicate that somewhat less than one-fifth of the 11th graders feel that they receive a lot of help with career planning through the various educational programs and guidance services offered by schools.

Career Plans

One of the questions in the study asked students to indicate their first occupational preference and then to select, from a list of 25 job families, the job family appropriate to this preference. While several discrepancies with U.S. Department of Labor employment projections are evident in the distributions of student preferences, the most striking feature of the data is the evidence of differences in responses of the two sexes. The nature of these differences is not surprising, but their extent is quite dramatic. For example, over half of the 11th grade girls choose occupations falling in only 3 of the 25 job families: clerical and secretarial work, education and social services, nursing and human care. By contrast, 7 percent of the boys prefer occupations in these areas. Nearly half of the boys' choices fall in the technologies and trades cluster of job families, in contrast to only 7 percent of the girls' choices. Results for 8th, 9th, and 11th graders are essentially the same. It is obvious that efforts to broaden the career options and choices of both males and females must overcome the pervasive influence of work role stereotypes related to sex.

Table 4 provides evidence of the amount of thought students give to their occupational preferences and career plans. Slight trends in favor of 11th graders appear for the first two questions but not for the third question, which taps the

Table 4   Self-Evaluation of Career Planning

Paraphrased questions and summary of student responses

1. Have you given much thought as to why your first two job choices are right for you?

	Grade 8			Grade 11		
	% M	% F	% Tot.	% M	% F	% Tot.
A. A little	16	13	15	13	8	10
B. Some	36	37	36	38	32	35
C. A lot	49	50	49	50	60	55

2. Is the amount of education you are planning in line with what is needed for the jobs?

	Grade 8			Grade 11		
	% M	% F	% Tot.	% M	% F	% Tot.
A. Yes	52	52	52	58	60	59
B. Not sure	39	42	41	34	34	34
C. Probably not	9	6	7	7	6	7

3. Students often change their minds about job choices. How sure are you that your "First Job Choice" will be the *same* in a year?

	Grade 8			Grade 11		
	% M	% F	% Tot.	% M	% F	% Tot.
A. Very sure	41	39	40	31	33	32
B. Fairly sure	46	48	47	45	47	46
C. Not sure at all	13	13	13	24	20	22

Note—Directions for items 1 and 2 were as follows: "A few minutes ago, you were asked to print the names of your first two job choices on the answer folder. The rest of the questions on this page all refer to these two jobs. THINK ONLY OF THESE TWO JOBS as you answer each of the following items."

certainty of the students' first occupational preference. Only 13 percent of the 8th graders answer "not sure at all" to the question, whereas 22 percent of the 11th graders choose that response—a substantial proportionate increase. Perhaps, with the approach of major career decisions, 11th graders take the task of career choice more seriously and begin to weigh more heavily the reality factors involved.

Whether more 11th graders should be "very sure" of their first occupational preference depends on one's views about the career development process. Certainly there is ample testimony in the professional literature and labor market projections that youth should "stay loose" occupationally and keep doors open as long as possible. However, if vocational choice is the zeroing-in process that some believe it to be (Super 1963), one might expect that students finishing the 11th grade would be "fairly sure" of their occupational preferences. This would imply that they have at least given them a lot of thought; 55 percent of the 11th graders say they have (Table 4, item 1).

What Students Do and Know about Career Development

The following are capsule highlights of conclusions based on a large amount of additional information gathered in the study.

1. As indicated by a 32-item self-report inventory, 20 percent of the nation's 11th graders exhibit what can only be called a very low level of involvement in career planning activities. Another 50 percent barely approach a minimally desirable level. Responses to specific items indicate that a substantial number of 11th graders have had very little involvement in frequently recommended career guidance practices (e.g., field trips, worker interviews, role-play job interviews).

2. As indicated by six scales covering job-related activities and experiences organized by occupational cluster, the exploratory occupational experiences of most students appear to be quite limited. Although many of these experiences occur outside of the school, none requires actual employment. Rather, they represent a component of career awareness that schools can do much to develop.

3. When the exploratory occupational experiences of males and females are compared, the results suggest distinct patterns related to sex roles endemic to American society. Again, schools can do much to broaden these experiences through the career awareness and career exploration programs now being developed.

4. Results obtained from a 40-item career planning knowledge scale show both a lack of knowledge and a substantial amount of misinformation. For example, 53 percent of the 11th graders believe that *more* than one-third of all job openings require a college degree; 41 percent of the 8th graders believe that *few* women work outside of the home after marriage; and 61 percent of the 11th graders believe that *most* persons remain in the same jobs throughout their adult lives.

IMPLICATIONS

What, then, can be said about the career development of the nation's youth? First and foremost, student-expressed need for help with career planning is in sharp contrast to the amount of help students feel they receive. This discrepancy is reflected in what students have (and more often, have not) done to prepare for the difficult career decisions they face. Their lack of knowledge about the world of work and about the career planning process also testifies to their need for help. We believe that, considered together, these vantage points for viewing student career development—what students say, do, and know—provide a consistent and dismal picture. If we were speaking of physical development rather than career development, we would describe American youth as hungry, undernourished, and physically retarded.

Does this mean that 11th graders will be unable to cope with the career development tasks posed by society at the difficult high school to post-high-school transition point? Certainly youth in the past have been able to muddle through. However, we believe study results presage unfortunate amounts of floundering and prolonged states of indecision that are costly both to the individual and to society. Perhaps society can continue to absorb these costs while it avoids the costs inherent in the remedy. This is the course of least resistance, and its acceptance may involve the least controversy, especially since the remedies currently receiving attention are largely untested. However, thoroughly researched and proven effectiveness is seldom a prerequisite for programs designed to meet demonstrated human need. If it were, most of what is provided in the name of education (both lower and higher) would be recalled for further research and development. While efforts to facilitate student career development should not proceed haphazardly, it would appear from the results of this study that current attempts to implement new approaches to career guidance and career education are amply justified.

We firmly believe that the traditional one-to-one counseling model for helping youngsters "choose their life's work" can no longer be justified. This model must be reoriented to encompass what is known about how careers develop and must be broadened to include the resources of the classroom and the community. As counselors and counselor educators come to recognize work as one of the central experiences of men and women, as the making of a life as well as a living (Super 1957), we are hopeful that they will accept the challenge posed by the career development needs of American youth.

REFERENCES

American College Testing Program. *Handbook for the assessment of career development.* Iowa City: Author, 1974.

Bayless, D. L.; Bergsten, J. W.; Lewis. L. H.; & Noeth, R. J. *Considerations and procedures in national norming: An illustration using the ACT assessment of career development and the ACT career planning program, grades 8–11* (ACT Research Report No. 65). Iowa City: American College Testing Program, 1974.

Prediger, D. J.; Roth, J. D.; & Noeth, R. J. *A nationwide study of student career development: Summary of results* (ACT Research Report No. 61). Iowa City: American College Testing Program, 1973.

Super, D. E. *The psychology of careers.* New York: Harper & Row, 1957.

Super, D. E. The definition and measurement of early career behavior: A first formulation. *Personnel and Guidance Journal,* 1963, *41*(9), 775–780.

20. Clarifying the Counseling Mystique*

Edwin L. Herr,
John J. Horan, and Stanley B. Baker

Throughout most of its short history, the guidance profession has consisted essentially of a collection of services (e.g., testing, information dispensing, individual and group counseling). These services have been directed toward global goals (e.g., helping students find satisfaction with themselves and with their educational experience). That achievement of such goals actually did result from exposure to guidance services was accepted by many on faith rather than on empirical evidence.

During the past decade school counselors, like other educational personnel, have felt intense pressure to identify in precise terms what effect they have on student behavior. This growing pressure for accountability, coupled with increased awareness of what student behaviors might be affected by guidance services, has given rise to greater specificity in the objectives sought by school counselors.

New labels such as "behavioral counseling," "performance based counseling," or "systematic counseling" have appeared in the literature. Such terms affirm both the possibility and the intent of pursuing specific goals in structured and direct ways.

EMPHASIS ON DECISION MAKING

Widespread efforts toward building a national model of career education all seem to stress the importance of developing decision making skills in students. Clearly, a priority in career education is to help students develop self-awareness, career awareness, and the planning skills to link the two. Vocational guidance is a major component of career education directed toward the attainment of such goals.

Vocational guidance can be further broken down into more specific components (counseling, testing, etc.), each directed toward the attainment of different goals with different age or grade groups. For example, we may decide that one goal should be that students upon completion of high school have the ability to distinguish between occupations, educational alternatives, and self-characteristics such as interests and aptitudes. However, different behaviors representing movement toward such a goal can be identified at the elementary, junior high, and senior high levels.

The objectives of a vocational guidance program might look like the examples shown in Table 1.

*Source: Reprinted with permission of the authors and publisher from the American Vocational Journal, 1973, 48, 66–72. Copyright 1973 The American Vocational Association, Inc.

Table 1   A Sample of Objectives at Different Educational Levels for a Vocational Guidance Program

	Elementary school	Junior high school	Senior high school
Condition	Stating how different workers contribute to student's well-being.	Demonstrating how certain knowledge and skills acquired in subjects are applied in work roles.	Differentiating major occupations in terms of their relationship to his interests and values.
Purpose	That students understand the way in which occupations and careers relate to the goals, needs and functions of society.	That students will understand the variety and complexity of occupations and career opportunities in the world of work.	That students will recognize the relationship between their pattern of personal characteristics and decision-making as it relates to their future.
Methods	Select from: discussion, class visitations, counselor or teacher presentations, vocabulary lessons, oral exercises, audiovisual presentations.	Select from: field trips to observe workers in action, fictional and non-fictional reading, illustrative films and filmstrips, exploratory work experience, career days.	Select from: reading current occupational literature, audio-visual materials, work experience, individual and group counseling related to interest and values, inventory results.
Outputs (Outcomes)	Students can successfully complete assignments associated with methods selected for use.	Students can successfully complete assignments associated with methods selected for use.	Students can state tentative plans which indicate an awareness of their values and interests.
Quality measures to use	Observed behavior, counseling contacts (individual or groups), objective tests and inventories, controlled and experimental group comparison.	Observed behavior, counseling contacts (individual or groups), objective tests and inventories, controlled and experimental group comparison, book reports and themes, frequency in use of occupational resources.	Observed behavior, counseling contacts (individual or groups), objective inventories, controlled and experimental group comparison.
Time limits or priority ratings to use	Optional (dependent upon methods and criterion measures which are selected).	Optional (dependent upon methods and criterion measures which are selected).	Optional (dependent upon methods and criterion measures which are selected).
Prerequisite abilities to learn the task	Ability to read and to verbalize or print desired responses.	Ability to read, write, and to see relationships between skills and roles.	Ability to read and write and to comprehend concepts such as interests and values.

"SYSTEMATIC COUNSELING"

Of all the vocational guidance subsystems, vocational counseling is perhaps the most widely practiced and yet the most misunderstood. "Systematic counseling" is a recent attempt to clarify the counseling mystique through the process of systems analysis. A system can be briefly described as an interacting set of components (subsystems) organized for the purpose of attaining specific objectives. Writers today tend to speak of the "systems approach" (1), thus describing how it works rather than what it is.

Several publications have described how the systems approach can be applied to counseling and vocational guidance (2, 3, 4, 5). Perhaps the most conspicuous characteristic of systematic counseling is its goal direction: What is it that the student will be able to do, or do better, as a result of counseling?

Once such goals are identified, as shown in Table 1, the systematic counselor helps the student attain them in the most efficient manner possible. In essence, he brings to bear on a problem or desired behavioral change any resource in the individual, the school, or the community which seems relevant. In this context, the counselor is concerned with individualizing his responses to students.

BEHAVIORAL GOALS

Systematic counselors are generally confronted with two major tasks: promoting adaptive behavior and eliminating maladaptive behavior. The former, of course, constitutes the stimulus or developmental role; the latter implies a remedial or treatment function (4, 6). For example, students may seek help in learning how to get a job or to study more effectively, or they may wish to overcome certain self-defeating fears and anxieties.

Counseling goals may be overt or covert. Overt goals are readily observable to anyone (e.g., development of effective work habits). Covert goals, on the other hand, are generally observable only to the student himself (e.g., the elimination of a troublesome thought or feeling). Hence, counselors must rely on verbal self-reports for verification.

The characteristics of a well-stated vocational counseling goal are identical to those of a well-written instructional performance goal. These characteristics or steps are (a) to identify the terminal behavior performance goal by name; (b) to describe the important conditions under which the behavior will be expected to occur; and (c) to specify the criterion of acceptable performance. The letters in parentheses in the following example indicate those portions of a counseling goal that correspond to the steps just listed.

"At the conclusion of the counseling process the client will be rid of his overwhelming fear of talking to prospective employers. Goal attainment will be evidenced by the client's engaging in at least three different job interviews (a) of at least 15 minutes duration (b) and reporting no anxiety or discomfort (c)."

Unlike other counseling goals involving the acceleration or deceleration of particular behaviors, helping a student arrive at a "good" decision poses a unique and often neglected problem for the systematic counselor. Getting married or taking a job can be easily defined in performance terminology. But "what spouse?" and "which job?" are questions for which no correct behavioral solution exists.

The appropriateness of a particular decision must be inferred from the behaviors which precede the decision rather than from the events which follow it. Many people make choices on impulse which eventually prove quite fortunate. But luck is capricious. Random decisions that are consistently good are highly improbable.

In order to increase the likelihood of making an appropriate choice, the counselor can help the student engage in a number of preparatory behaviors. To paraphrase IBM: No one can take the ultimate weight of decision making off a student's shoulders. But the more he learns about how things really are, the lighter that burden will be. Certain behaviors which imply knowing about "how things really are" in the world of work are easily definable in performance terminology. Some of these will be illustrated later in this paper.

Even if it were possible for a counselor to determine on an a priori basis the best possible choice among many possibilities, teaching the student decision-making skills is more predictive of future independent action than is outlining a solution for him. Given a framework for making wise choices, the student should be able to solve future dilemmas autonomously.

PROTOTYPE ILLUSTRATED

The prototype of systematic vocational counseling depicted in Table 2 is tentative. It suggests specific behaviors in which counselors ought to engage in order to contribute to the development of decision making skills in students.

The content of this performance based process is most applicable to students at the secondary level. However, with some modifications it can be generalized to students at other age or grade levels. Its format was derived from the work of Mager (7) and Byers and Huffman (8).

Essentially, then, vocational guidance is a subsystem of career education, and vocational counseling, in turn, is a subsystem of vocational guidance. Performance based goals in vocational guidance and counseling will contribute to the establishment of accountability in career education.

Table 2   Sequential Counselor Behaviors in Systematic Vocational Counseling

Counselor behavior	Necessary conditions	Criteria for successful performance
1 Counselor defines the purpose of counseling, and the roles of the counselor and student.	At the outset of the initial interview (unless the student discusses his concerns immediately, then before the end of the initial interview).	Definitions should correspond to a predetermined standard.
2 Counselor helps the client define the problem via specific counseling skills (see Ivey).	During the initial interview and in as many subsequent interviews as are required.	The problem is defined when the student so indicates (e.g., "Yes, that's it," or "You really do understand me!")
If the problem is one of vocational choice then the following counselor behaviors ought to ensue. Other kinds of student problems may require different types of counselor activity.		
3 Counselor determines if vocational choice is the primary concern (e.g., "It seems that although you have a lot of things on your mind, you're mainly interested in coming to some sort of vocational decision")	After the student has expressed all he cares to concerning his problem or his reason for seeking counseling.	The student responds in an affirmative manner.
4 Counselor explains the decision-making paradigm (e.g., "Arriving at a good vocational decision means that we have to look at all the alternatives, then weigh them in the light of information about you and the advantages and disadvantages of each course of action. I can't make the decision for you, but together we can arrive at and implement one.")	Immediately following Counselor Behavior No. 3.	The student indicates that he understands the process.
5 Counselor explains the preparatory behaviors needed to make a good decision (i.e., he provides an overview of the counselor behaviors depicted below).	Immediately following Counselor Behavior No. 4.	The student states that he understands the process.

Table 2 (Continued)

Counselor behavior	Necessary conditions	Criteria for successful performance
6 Counselor determines if the student has sufficient motivation, (e.g., "How do you feel about proceeding along these lines?")	Usually after Counselor Behavior No. 5. May be repeated after subsequent Counselor Behaviors.	The student indicates willingness to proceed. (If the student hesitates, or is unwilling to proceed, then recycle to Counselor Behavior No. 2 or terminate.)
7 Counselor asks the student to identify all possible alternatives which come to mind.	The alternatives may be identified in the interview and/or as a between-interviews assignment.	The student compiles a complete list of alternatives (oral or written).
8 Counselor identifies any additional alternatives which come to his mind and are ethically appropriate.	Counselor exhibits this behavior only if criterion for No. 7 is considered to be inadequate by either the counselor or the student.	A joint list of alternatives is compiled.
9 Counselor assembles all relevant information about the student (e.g., test scores, academic performance, vocational experience and interests) from records and/or from student inquiry	This information may be gathered during the interview or, if not immediately available, between interviews.	All existing relevant information about the student is available for discussion.
10 Counselor assembles additional information about the student (e.g., schedules further testing).	Counselor exhibits this behavior only if the criterion for No. 9 is considered to be inadequate by the counselor.	All relevant information is compiled.
11 Counselor presents to the student any information about the student relevant to the potential vocational decision (e.g., predictive statements derived from expectancy tables).	Immediately following Counselor Behaviors No. 9 and/or 10.	The student indicates that he understands this information.
12 Counselor requests that the student identify the advantages and disadvantages of the alternatives which have been identified.	During the interview (in the context of counselor-student discussion) and/or as a between-interviews assignment.	The student provides a set of such statements.
13 Counselor identifies any additional advantages and disadvantages which come to his mind.	Counselor exhibits this behavior only if the criterion for No. 12 is considered to be inadequate by either the counselor or the student.	A joint list of such statements is compiled.

Table 2 (Continued)

Counselor behavior	Necessary conditions	Criteria for successful performance
14 Counselor asks the student to evaluate the alternatives (e.g., "In terms of what we know about you and the various alternatives, which alternatives seem most promising?")	Immediately following Counselor Behaviors No. 12 and/or 13.	The student rank orders the alternatives from most to least preferred.
15 Counselor helps the student obtain additional information about the most promising alternative(s) (e.g., He verbally reinforces the student for reading about the prospective profession(s) and talking to members of the prospective profession(s). He may also schedule modeling or simulation experiences for the student.)	The additional information is usually accumulated outside of the counseling interview.	The student gathers this information or participates in the scheduled experience.
16 Counselor helps the student implement the most promising alternative.	Immediately following Counselor Behavior No. 15	A tentative course of action is selected and tried out.
17 Counselor determines if the selected alternative is satisfactory.	Immediately following Counselor Behavior No. 16	The student reports that he is happy with the decision. (If not, recycle to Counselor Behavior No. 16, "next most promising alternative.")
18 Counselor terminates the counseling relationship.	Immediately following Counselor Behavior No. 17	The student has learned the decision-making paradigm and is able to engage in independent action.

178

REFERENCES

1 Silvern, Leonard C. " 'Systems Approach'—What Is It?" *Educational Technology,* 1968. Vol. 8, No. 8, pp. 5-6.
2 Yelon, Stephen T. "Toward the Application of Systems Analysis to Counselor Education." *Educational Technology,* 1969. Vol. 9, No. 3, pp. 55-60.
3 Stewart, Norman R., et al. *Systematic Counseling* (Flowchart, Fifth Revision). College of Education, Michigan State University, 1970.
4 Herr, Edwin L., and Cramer, Stanley H. *Vocational Guidance and Career Development in Schools: Toward a Systems Approach.* New York: Houghton Mifflin, 1972.
5 Thoresen, Carl E. "Training Behavioral Counselors." *Implementing Behavioral Programs in Educational and Clinical Settings.* (Edited by F. W. Clark, D. R. Evans, and F. A. Hamerlynck.) Champaign, Ill.: Research Press, 1972, pp. 42-62.
6 Horan, John J. "Counselor Behavior in Behavioral Counseling." *Pennsylvania Personnel and Guidance Association Journal,* 1973. Vol. 1, No. 1. (In Press).
7 Mager, Robert F. *Preparing Instructional Objectives.* Palo Alto, Calif.: Fearon, 1962.
8 Byers, Edward E., and Huffman, Harry *Writing Performance Goals: Strategy and Prototypes.* New York: McGraw-Hill, 1971.
9 Ivey, Allen E. *Microcounseling: Innovations in Interviewing Training.* Springfield, Ill.: Thomas, 1971.

21. Vocational Counseling with Behavioral Techniques*

Robert H. Woody

Behavior therapy, which is based on learning theory principles, has recorded significant success in the treatment of a wide variety of problem behaviors. For the most part, applications of behavioral techniques have been in clinical settings, but there are examples that support its applicability to educationally related problems, such as those school counselors and school psychologists might encounter [15].

In regard to counseling, there seem to be four points that justify, and almost demand that counselors consider the use of behavioral techniques. First, evidence has been presented that counselors practice nonselective reinforcement; that is, the counselor may reinforce certain classes of verbal responses given by the client and thereby encourage or reinforce indiscriminately. Indeed, this has been found to be true of the client centered counseling of Carl R. Rogers [9]. If this reinforcement is an inevitable intrinsic concomitant of counseling, then obviously the logical preference would be to make efforts to reduce the unselective nature of the reinforcement and instead to schedule or make the counselor's reinforcement selective. This would assure, at least to some degree, that the counseling processes adhered to the goals of the counselor-client relationship and not merely to the counselor's personal (unselective) preferences. Second, there is reason to believe that counseling follows a desensitization model; in other words, counseling begins on a relatively superficial level and as it progresses the client becomes more able to deal with the anxiety-provoking or threatening elements, i.e., he becomes desensitized to them [10]. If it is true that desensitization is a component of counseling *per se,* then it is essentially identical to one of the main techniques of behavior therapy: systematic desensitization [12]. Third, the efficacy of behavioral procedures, as measured by the duration of therapy (e.g., the number of sessions) and the therapeutic success (e.g., the percentage of patients "cured"), appears to be greater than that of insight-oriented procedures [13]. This efficacy factor is an important consideration if the counselor is to fulfill his responsibility to the client. Fourth, there have been experimental studies that document that behavioral techniques, such as verbal reinforcement, can be used in counseling; some of these will be subsequently described. These four points and their ramifications for school counseling have been described in greater detail elsewhere [17].

BEHAVIORAL TECHNIQUES

The following are descriptions of the primary behavioral techniques and some brief examples of how they have been or could be used in vocational guidance and counseling.

*Source: Reprinted with permission of the author and publisher from the *The Vocational Guidance Quarterly,* 1968, *17,* 97–103. Copyright 1968 American Personnel and Guidance Association.

Social Recognition and *Object Rewards* are given to the client when he performs an acceptable or approved behavior; they are withheld, thereby constituting "punishment," when an unacceptable behavior occurs. An example of use might be in a junior high school career planning class: if the student carried out certain assigned tasks, such as reading a number of career pamphlets or writing the required essay on a job or talking to an adult employed in the position he was studying, then he would receive a reward to give positive reinforcement for productivity in the class (the reward might be extra time in the school library for free-reading or permission to go on a special field trip). If he did not perform well or if he misbehaved, the reward would be withheld. The careers teacher might use social recognition by ignoring the student when he did not apply himself and by smiling, praising, and showing approval when he worked diligently in the class.

Social Modeling is the technique which presents a client with a recorded or filmed model of a desired behavior; if desired behaviors are gradually presented, according to a hierarchy of difference from the client's present behavior, the client will progressively modify his behavior towards that of the model [1]. In a sense this principle is involved when a careers teacher presents a film describing a job and depicting a worker in his daily activities; the viewer, the student in the class, is being figuratively asked to project himself into the role of the worker in the film and feasibly to pattern his own behavior after that of the model. This technique, via audio and video tape recordings, has also been used to influence counselees to model their counseling behavior. For example, a filmed model vocational counseling session could lead to more initial counseling productivity than a session in which there was no model-preparation.

Verbal Reinforcement has been subjected to extensive research, and particularly as it is applicable to counseling and psychotherapy [11]. In verbal reinforcement, the counselor selects certain classes of words, such as self-references, and then during the counseling sessions responds positively, such as with a praise-giving comment, e.g., "good" or "I approve of that idea", or an approving physical gesture, e.g., such as a smile. The counselor ignores, that is he makes absolutely no response to, other types of responses from the client. The principle is that the client-responses that receive reinforcement from the counselor will occur more frequently and the unreinforced responses will occur less and may even be extinguished from the client's counseling responses. This technique has received relevant application in the research of Krumboltz and his associates [3, 4, 5, 8]. These studies have supported that verbal reinforcement from the counselor, when used singly or in conjunction with filmed counseling models, produces significant alteration in the in-counseling and out-of-counseling behaviors of the client. For example, when Krumboltz and Thoresen [5] verbally reinforced information-seeking behavior of high school students in individual and group counseling, the students engaged in more information-seeking outside of the counseling sessions than those students who were not reinforced. Similar success has occurred when deliberation and decision-making responses were reinforced. Relevant to vocational counseling, verbal reinforcement appears to be capable of influencing such areas as bringing the client to actively seek occupational and/or educational information to read and consider materials relevant to career planning and eventually to be able to take the initiative in making a vocational choice.

Systematic Desensitization techniques have proved to be highly successful in the treatment of phobic fears and anxiety [13, 14]. Systematic desensitization is based on the reciprocal inhibition principle: ". . . If a response inhibitory of anxiety can be made to occur in the presence of anxiety-evoking stimuli it will weaken the bond between these stimuli and the anxiety." [13, p. 10]

The procedure is to create a hierarchy of fear-producing or anxiety-provoking situations, that is, a list of acts that begins with a situation that has little power of provocation and progresses to a situation with a great deal of power (perhaps one that would even provoke an overwhelming degree of anxiety). Then gradually, through imaginary or actual experiencing of the threatening situations (pausing at each stage and repeating it until it no longer has provocation power), the person becomes desensitized to these situations. The use of this technique in vocational counseling seems somewhat limited, unless it is for the purpose of facilitating work adjustment: this approach has been successfully applied to numerous on-the-job situations that provoked anxiety or fear in the employee and thus impaired his productivity.

Assertive Practice techniques are similar to systematic desensitization in that they involve the use of a hierarchy (of interpersonal situations related to assertion) and are based on the reciprocal inhibition principle. In brief, assertive techniques employ role-playing, assigned actual experiencing, and other forms of real and imagined behavior that gradually train the person to be more assertive; thus its alternate name: behavioral rehearsal. There is a host of potential uses for behavioral rehearsal in vocational counseling; to name but a few: the client could be trained to show positive assertion during a job interview or in meetings of a labor union or in his interpersonal relations with his work-colleagues; the client could develop new personal characteristics that would qualify him for job advancements, e.g., promotion into a leadership role; or the client could gain assertive skills that would foster improved self-respect or self-concept reformation. Clinical experience has also revealed this approach to be effective for dealing with certain pathological situations, e.g., phobias, that might develop in the job setting; for example, an employee who dreaded to go to work because he was afraid his fellow workers would criticize his work, was treated by a combination of insight-therapy, systematic desensitization, and behavioral rehearsal [10].

Clinical Suggestion, although seldom applied alone (it is usually combined with insight-counseling), has proved successful in promoting behavioral change. Subtle, clinically-derived suggestions are made in the context of counseling or psychotherapy; the suggestions are designed to build gradually the client's ability to cope with problem situations, or to provide what Hartland [2] calls "ego strengthening." As an adjunctive technique, clinical suggestion could feasibly be employed with essentially any problem typically encountered in vocational counseling.

Those who are familiar with behavior therapy techniques are no doubt aware that no mention has been made of aversive conditioning (the use of an unpleasant stimulus, e.g., mild electric shock, when an unacceptable behavior occurs, thereby fostering subsequent avoidance of that behavior) and massed practice (repetition of the unacceptable behavior so many times that it becomes unsatisfying to the person). Because of the punitive nature of the former and the questionable validity of the latter, both of these seem unsuited for use in counseling and have been purposefully ignored.

It should be emphasized that while each of the behavioral techniques can be used alone, they may also be combined. Moreover, there is reason to believe that behavior therapy can be integrated with insight-oriented counseling and psychotherapy, despite theoretical differences. That is, regular counseling or psychotherapy continues until there is a special need for a behavior technique; after the behavioral technique is used and the special need has been fulfilled, counseling and psychotherapy continue [7, 16].

Another unique characteristic of behavior therapy is that frequently there are concomitant changes in behaviors other than the one being treated. One example of special relevance occurred in a psychiatric project on sexual deviations where electric shocks were being used in an aversive conditioning format to eliminate sexual problems, e.g., sexual fetishes and transvestism; it was not unusual to find the patient re-examining his vocational attitudes (losing such a chronic and influential behavior could, of course, have far-reaching implications in the patient's personal-vocational adjustment).

VOCATIONAL DEVELOPMENT THEORY

Perhaps the most difficult problem to resolve in considering the use of behavioral techniques in vocational counseling is the seeming incongruity between these techniques and a theory of vocational development. To generalize, vocational development theories typically emphasize the client's progressing through a series of self-determined vocational choices. It might seem that the client is deprived of the decision-making when behavioral techniques are used, that is, that the behavioral counselor decides what to reinforce and that the client is left at the mercy of the professional skills and personal whims of the counselor.

The behaviorist, however, would deny that such a conflict is paramount, and indeed that a conflict exists at all. Behaviorists believe that the client does perform the decision making, but that this occurs when he decides to come to the counselor and when he decides what the problem or the goal of counseling should be. Then it is up to the behavioral counselor to apply his professional skills to fulfill the client's request optimally. Thus the counselor might conduct a diagnostic interview, administer tests, e.g., aptitude and vocational interest measures, and then establish a counseling format in which he can reinforce the client toward accepting the trait-and-factor analysis and initiating this into career planning or a career choice.

Probably the major concern of the non-behaviorist is that behavioral counseling means total manipulation of the client and depriving him of his individuality: a forerunner to Big-Brotherism. This position might even be extended hypothetically to the point that governmental conducted research would be fed into a computer, the names of potential candidates with suitable characteristics would be spewn out, and behavioral counselors would be assigned clients to interview and to reinforce them into accepting and even liking a vocational choice made for them by the Establishment: the manpower needs of the society would be met at the expense of individuality.

Such an alarmist position, although making interesting fictional reading, is not at all in accord with behavioral counseling. In fact, behavioral counselors and therapists would probably raise the cry of dissent and condemnation even louder than non-behaviorists if this impersonal approach were erroneously aligned with them. Behaviorists steadfastly maintain that they are humanists, and that their therapeutic activities are in the best interest of their clients. Some even maintain that their approach may be the most ethical. That is, the insight-oriented approaches to counseling do not always stress resolution of the problem that brought the client to the counselor, but rather emphasize striving for personal understanding. One can only speculate as to how many clients seek counseling for vocational reasons, but encounter a counselor who says to himself: "This client may say he wants vocational counseling, but what he really wants is personal-social counseling." The behavioral counselor, on the other hand, would not make a value judgment about the goals for counseling, but would accept what the client states *per se* and then establish the goals accordingly. There is reason to believe that if a client does have a personal-social problem defensively hidden under his request for vocational counseling and the vocational goals are effectively dealt with, he might be even more apt to request and enter into further counseling for the personal-social problem subsequently.

THE COUNSELING RELATIONSHIP

There is no denying that the behavioral counseling relationship differs to some degree from that of insight counseling. But, there are probably more commonalities than there are differences. Both approaches share a commitment to helping the client, and that is, of course, the factor of prime importance. Communication, the therapeutic essential, is via the verbal medium in both, but the behaviorist might tend to use other stimuli, such as films, more than the insightist. In vocational counseling, however, it is probable that both approaches would employ a variety of materials, but the way of using them would differ: the behaviorist would systematically program their use from the beginning to insure optimal learning.

The two primary differences are in the areas of determining the goals for counseling and the respective responsibility of counselor and client for the counseling processes. As mentioned above, the "insightists" believe the goals should evolve during the course of counseling, while the behaviorists believe in determining the goals from what the client requests initially, unless there is some subsequent intervening event that would alter this client-request. This difference in goal determination seems to be due to two things: insightists believe the problems mask an underlying neurotic conflict and this conflict must be dealt with by helping the client achieve self-understanding, and the behaviorists believe that all problems stem from maladaptive learning and that unlearning the problem can best be achieved by deconditioning and/or reconditioning. In view of the dissonance in definitions of etiology, it is logical that the goals and, moreover, the criteria for success of treatment will be different. In regard to the latter, the theoretical differences and particularly the factor of goal-determination limit the value of any comparison of the efficacies of insight and behavioral counseling. As might be assumed, the second major difference, the responsibility for the counseling processes, stems from conflicting theories: the insightists maintain that the client is primarily responsible for movement and direction, whereas the behaviorists believe that the client's request for help and the counselor's professional training behoove the counselor to assume command of or responsibility for the counseling processes and to apply his expertise at his own discretion. Which approach is the more effective depends, of course, on the criteria used by the assessor. What bears emphasis, however, is that both insight and behavioral counselors, despite their theoretical differences, establish a *counseling relationship;* there is feeling communicated between the counselor and client, regardless of what the counseling goals are or who has assumed responsibility for the counseling relationship.

ETHICAL CONSIDERATIONS

As previously discussed, many professionals view behaviorism as a step toward cybernetics or automated, impersonal manipulation of others. And as was also noted, behaviorists disagree with this accusation and instead maintain that their approach is highly ethical because they do not inflict their own uncontrolled influences, but rather use the stated wishes of the client as the determinants for the counseling format. Admittedly, the responsibility for the counseling is removed from the client's hand once he has made his specific request to the counselor. London [6] has presented this controversy in greater detail.

It seems wise to caution against allowing the factors unique to behaviorism to go unchecked. For example, the counselor must develop self-imposed safeguards against accepting a request from a client that he is uninterested in or unqualified to deal with or which goes against his own professional code of ethics [3]. While behaviorism itself does not violate common ethical boundaries, it must be acknowledged that the greater responsibility placed on the counselor and the *action*-oriented conditioning techniques could easily exceed the controls of the unprepared counselor.

IMPLICATIONS FOR COUNSELOR EDUCATION

With behavioral counseling earning a new and diversified usage in counseling, counselor educators must accordingly modify their training programs to accommodate the relevant needs of the trainees. In most cases, this will not involve an extensive modification of the existing curriculum. Counselors should be exposed to theories of learning and perhaps to a behavioral modification seminar. The only other primary change will be to assure that the trainee receives supervised practicum and internship experiences with behavioral techniques as adequate and as well as with the other standard counseling procedures [18]. It should be emphasized that the objective is not to train behavioral counselors, but rather to prepare generic counselors who are able to number behavioral techniques within their spectrum of counseling skills.

DISCUSSION

This paper has reviewed the various behavioral techniques that seem appropriate for counseling, and their application to vocational guidance has been discussed and exemplified. There is little doubt that these action-oriented techniques have a valid claim to inclusion in counseling, and indeed their high degree of efficacy virtually demands that counselors give immediate consideration to their usage.

These behavioral techniques seem especially well suited to vocational counseling. In fact, analysis of existing vocational guidance practices reveals a great deal of reinforcement. For example, it is safe to say that most counselors probably emphasize with a student those areas in which he scored high on a vocational interest test, perhaps by having him more thoroughly investigate those areas of interest rather than the ones in which he scored low; and it is probable that students are led to consider a very small percentage of colleges and universities, those with which the counselor has the most familiarity. Behavioral counseling differs from these practices only in that the counselor would strive for the most efficacious format by scheduling his reinforcements.

Although these techniques are relatively new in vocational counseling, such studies as those on verbal reinforcement for information-seeking and decision-making with students coming for career counseling lend strong support for their immediate use. University training programs will have to accommodate these new procedures, but their use in the hands of the well trained counselor, one who has training with both insight and behavioral techniques, should facilitate increased effectiveness in vocational counseling.

REFERENCES

1 Bandura, A., and Walters, R. H., *Social Learning and Personality Development*, New York: Holt, Rinehart and Winston, 1963.
2 Hartland, J., "The General Principles of Suggestion," *American Journal of Clinical Hypnosis*, 1967, *9*, 211–219.
3 Krumboltz, J. D., "Behavioral Counseling: Rationale and Research," *Personnel and Guidance Journal*, 1965, *44*, 383–387.
4 Krumboltz, J. D., and Schroeder, W. W., "Promoting Career Planning Through Reinforcement," *Personnel and Guidance Journal*, 1965, *44*, 19–26.
5 Krumboltz, J. D., and Thoresen, C. E., "The Effect of Behavioral Counseling in Group and Individual Settings on Information-seeking Behavior," *Journal of Counseling Psychology*, 1964, *11*, 324–333.

6 London, P., *The Modes and Morals of Psychotherapy*, New York: Holt, Rinehart & Winston, 1964.

7 Marks, I. M., and Gelder, M. G., "Common Ground Between Behavior Therapy and Psychodynamic Methods," *British Journal of Medical Psychology*, 1966, *39*, 11–23.

8 Ryan, T. A., and Krumboltz, J. D., "Effect of Planned Reinforcement Counseling on Client Decision-making Behavior," *Journal of Counseling Psychology*, 1964, *11*, 315–323.

9 Truax, C. B., "Reinforcement and Nonreinforcement in Rogerian Psychotherapy," *Journal of Abnormal Psychology*, 1966, *71*, 1–9.

10 Truax, C. B., "Some Implications of Behavior Therapy for Psychotherapy," *Journal of Counseling Psychology*, 1966, *13*, 160–170.

11 Williams, J. H., "Conditioning of Verbalization: A Review," *Psychological Bulletin*, 1964, *62*, 383–393.

12 Wolpe, J., *Psychotherapy by Reciprocal Inhibition*, Stanford: Stanford University Press, 1958.

13 Wolpe, J., "The Comparative Clinical Status of Conditioning Therapies and Psychoanalysis." In J. Wolpe, A. Salter, and L. J. Reyna (Eds.), *The Conditioning Therapies*, New York: Holt, Rinehart and Winston, 1964, 5–2.

14 Wolpe, J., and Lazarus, A., *Behavior Therapy Techniques*, Oxford, England: Pergamon Press, 1966.

15 Woody, R. H., "Behavior Therapy and School Psychology," *Journal of School Psychology*, 1966, *4*, 1–14.

16 Woody, R. W., "Integrating Behavior Therapy and Psychotherapy," *British Journal of Medical Psychology*, in press.

17 Woody, R. H., "Reinforcement in School Counseling," *School Counselor*, 1968, *15*, 253–258.

18 Woody, R. H., "Preparation in Behavioral Counseling," *Counselor Education and Supervision*, in press.

22. Vocational Decision-making Models. A Review and Comparative Analysis*

David A. Jepsen and
Josiah S. Dilley

Vocational development has been described as the processes of preparation for and entry into a series of education and work roles over a lifetime. During the 1960s, a number of vocational theorists speculated that these processes could be understood better by employing concepts suggested by psychological decision theory. Indeed the promise that fundamental decision concepts have for enriching our understanding of vocational development received early acclaim (Blau, Gustad, Jesser, Parnes, and Wilcock, 1956; Brayfield, 1963, 1964; Super, 1961; Tyler, 1961). Recent reviews of vocational development theories have concluded that this promise remains largely unfulfilled (Crites, 1969; Kroll, Dinklage, Lee, Morley, and Wilson, 1970; Osipow, 1968).

One major problem in integrating this literature is that various theorists have not employed either the framework or the language of their predecessors. Several questions can be raised: Among the various theories, are there similarities in the basic concepts that are observed by the differences in language? Do the theories fit the same population of decision situations? Do certain theories better describe certain types of decisions? How do the theories vary in terms of assumptions about characteristics of decision-makers and their resources?

The authors believe that psychological decision theory provides a useful framework for clarifying the relationships among various vocational decision-making theories and between these theories and the population of decision situations with which people are faced. This paper outlines psychological decision theory; summarizes eight prominent vocational decision-making (VDM) models; compares and contrasts VDM models on basic assumptions and fundamental concepts; and suggests applications of theory to theoretical decision types. Implications for research, theory, and practice are discussed.

PSYCHOLOGICAL DECISION THEORY

Psychological decision theory seeks to "describe in an orderly way what variables influence choices [Edwards and Tversky, 1967, p. 7]." A set of concepts common to a wide-ranging literature were described in an early review by Edwards (1954), and more recently by Edwards (1961), Taylor (1963), Becker and McClintock (1967), and Lee (1971). Feather (1959) compared the central constructs used in "utility-expectancy theories" (that is, theories by Atkinson, 1957; Edwards, 1954; Lewin, 1951; Rotter, 1954; Tolman, 1959) and found that the given meanings were similar but the labels differed. (For example, what Edwards named as "sub-

*Source: Reprinted with permission of the authors and publisher from the *Review of Educational Research*, 1974, *44*, 331–344. Copyright 1974 The American Educational Research Association.

jective probability" serves the same function as the concept Atkinson called "expectancy.") Cellura (1969) extended the comparison and showed that, although constructs have similar meanings, their theoretical interrelationships differed in important ways (for example, relationship between expectancy and utility). Despite these differences, it is clear that decision theory stems from markedly different traditions and assumptions than do "behavior theories" (for example those of C. Hull and K. Spence), psychoanalytic theories, or developmental theories.

The form of theory construction reviewed in this paper is the model—a conceptual analogue chosen (or erected) for its heuristic value in organizing the ideas and/or observed phenomena it represents (Marx, 1963). Decision theory provides "an orderly way" to describe conceptualizations of vocational behavior in sequence and juxtaposition. Theoretical models serve as conceptual frameworks or "schematic maps" that often result from efforts to identify and to clarify the major concepts in an area of study. It is assumed that the decision-maker processes information relevant to his goals. Bross (1953) helped to clarify the conceptual framework by describing the functional categories into which the information is sorted. Edwards, Lindman, and Phillips (1965) attempted to list all functions necessary for designing future decision-making systems. What follows is primarily a synthesis of the two.

A decision-making conceptual framework assumes the presence of a *decision-maker,* a *decision situation* (social expectation), and relevant *information* both from within and outside the person. The information is arranged into decision-making concepts according to the functions it serves. Two or more *alternative actions* are considered, and several *outcomes* or consequences are anticipated from each action. Each outcome has two characteristics: *probability,* or likelihood of occurrence in the future, and *value* or relative importance to the decision-maker. The information is arranged according to a strategy so that the decision-maker can readily recognize an advantageous course of action and make a *commitment* to this action. Strategies, also called rules or criteria, guide the assembling of the above concepts into an array so that straightforward judgments can reveal the commitment. Strategies are not concepts but structures; that is, they are aspects of the personality acquired prior to initiating the decision process and, as such, function as properties of the organism (for example, the disposition called "risk taking").

VOCATIONAL DECISION-MAKING (VDM) MODELS

The eight VDM models reviewed here were selected because each employs concepts that appear to be similar to concepts in psychological decision theory and because each attempts to provide a picture of the entire VDM process. Each model will be labelled by the authors' names, for example, the Tiedeman-O'Hara model.

Since this review is limited to models related to decision theory, several important vocational development theories are not discussed. For example, Super's treatment of career development (for example, Super, Starishevsky, Matlin and Jordaan, 1963) does not lend itself to analysis as a decision theory. The same can be said for Holland's work (1966). By making this distinction, we have focused on one of four major types of vocational choice theory according to Crites' (1969) descriptions. Osipow (1968), Crites (1969), and Zaccaria (1970) have reviewed the other types thoroughly.

Decision theory has been applied to human situations as both a prescriptive model to be emulated and a description of actual decision-making behavior (Becker and McClintock, 1967; Taylor, 1963). In order to facilitate comparisons, the eight VDM models are divided into two groups. *Descriptive VDM models* purport to represent the ways people generally make vocational decisions, that is, the "natural" phenomena. This classification includes models by Tiedeman and O'Hara (1963), Hilton (1962), Vroom (1964), Hsu (1970), and Fletcher (1966). *Prescriptive models* represent attempts to help people make better decisions— rules people should use—to reduce decision errors. Models in this group were written by Katz (1963, 1966), Gelatt (1962), and Kaldor and Zytowski (1969).

The distinction between prescriptive and descriptive approaches is slippery and depends on the conditions of a decision situation. For example, as the "stakes" are increased, the decision-maker tries harder to approximate the prescriptive model in order to maximize returns (Edwards et al., 1965).

Descriptive VDM Models

Tiedeman-O'Hara Model   Tiedeman (1961), and Tiedeman and O'Hara (1963) developed a VDM model which they named a "paradigm of differentiation and integration in attempting rational solutions to the problems of one's vocational situation [1963, p. 37]." The problem-solving process is initiated by the experiencing of a vocational problem and by the recognition that a decision must be made. In later writings, Tiedeman refers to vocational problems as "discontinuities" (Tiedeman, 1964, 1965; Tiedeman and Field, 1961).

Tiedeman and O'Hara divide the process into two periods, called Anticipation and Implementation-Adjustment, that distinguish between behavior prior to and following instrumental action on the decision. (Only the Anticipation period will be discussed here.) The Anticipation period is subdivided into four stages, representing discrete changes in the condition of the decision. The decision-maker may reverse himself in the order of stages, but advancement predominates over time. Since decisions interconnect, a person may be at an advanced stage on one particular decision, yet at an earlier stage with regard to another decision.

The first stage, called Exploration, accounts for trial-and-error efforts to differentiate among alternate goals. Activity is principally imaginary as the decision-maker attempts to give order and meaning to several possible goals and to the context (Tiedeman calls it "field") of each goal. During exploration, fields are relatively transitory, highly imaginary ideas about what the self might be like in later situations—situations specifically associated with a possible goal. In short, the decision-maker attempts to take the measure of himself in relation to each alternative goal as he senses it.

The next three stages, Crystallization, Choice, and Clarification, are relatively inseparable. Crystallization describes attempts to clarify the order and pattern of goals and their fields. Assessment of personal values and their bases is a primary activity. Goals are compared on the basis of competing demands, costs and returns, advantages and disadvantages, and take on the qualities of definiteness, clarity, complexity, and rationality. Thought about the problem becomes more stable (less random), durable, reliable. The Choice stage involves commitment to one goal and its field, which, in turn, orients the person to act. The particular commitment is probably a function of qualities of the alternatives such as complexity, clarity, and "degrees of freedom." The certainty of a choice orientation (its "motive power") is probably the product of the complexity and antagonism of alternatives. The Clarification stage, brought on by doubt experienced during the waiting period between choice and action, involves attempts to perfect the image of self in the later situation.

Hilton's Model   A career decision-making model based on complex information-processing mechanisms was outlined by Hilton (1962). Although clearly influenced by Herbert Simon's work in human problem solving (Newell, Shaw and Simon, 1958; Simon, 1955, 1958), Hilton borrowed the concept of "plans" from Miller, Galanter and Pribram (1960) and the concept of "cognitive dissonance" from Festinger (1957). The key elements in the model are premises, plans, and cognitive dissonance. Premises are beliefs and expectations about self and the world, for example, self-perceptions, attributes of occupational roles, needs, perceptions and social structure, and things important to the decision-maker. Plans are not explicitly defined, but apparently they denote an image of sequential actions associated with entering an occupational role. Cognitive dissonance accounts for a method of testing out plans against current premises.

Hilton's decision-making process is initiated by an input from the environment that alters the decision-maker's present plans. The decision-maker "tests" to see if the input has raised dissonance sufficiently above the satisfactory threshold—that is, whether an imbalance or inconsistency among plans and premises has been created. If dissonance has been raised above threshold, the decision-maker examines his premises, and if there is no imbalance, he continues acting on the present plan for action. If the premises can be revised, they are, and then submitted (with the plans) for a dissonance test, and the cycle is complete. If, on the other hand, premises cannot be revised, the person searches his stored knowledge or his surroundings for another behavioral plan. Future work roles, not previously tested as plans, are scanned to find one that may now "pass the test." The new plan is tested and, if dissonance is below threshold, it becomes the controlling plan for future action.

Hilton's mechanism for testing cognitive dissonance determines whether the outcomes of tentative plans and/or premises remain acceptable or not, that is, whether dissonance is below or above the threshold level. The operation of the mechanism assumes that people classify outcomes dichotomously as satisfactory or unsatisfactory. The basis for such an assumption rests on Simon's (1955) critique of classical economic models. He suggests substituting "satisficing" for maximizing in problem-solving models where imperfect knowledge is available. Simon argues that the decision-maker does not have enough information to order the value of all possible outcomes at one time, therefore the decision-maker simply determines whether each is satisfactory or not as he considers them one at a time.

Vroom's Model   Vroom (1964) outlined a cognitive decision-making model that included algebraic equations to define principal concepts: the concept of Valence, the concept of Expectancy, and the concept of Force. Vroom drew upon psychological theories where similar concepts had been employed, for example, Lewin (1951), Rotter (1955), Peak (1955), Davidson, Suppes, and Siegel (1957), Atkinson (1957), and Tolman (1959).

Valence refers to the decision-maker's preferences among outcomes (future states of nature) or, more specifically, to the affective orientations toward particular outcomes. It is the anticipated satisfaction from an outcome, as contrasted with the actual satisfaction. An outcome acquires Valence from the decision-maker's conception of its instrumentality for attaining more distant and prized goals. Instrumentality is a belief about the association between immediate and eventual outcomes. The mathematical definition of Valence says that Outcome A's Valence is a function of the summed products of affect associated with prized, distant goals and the cognized instrumentality of A for attaining each goal.

Expectancy refers to the degree to which a decision-maker believes outcomes are probable. It is defined as "the momentary belief concerning the likelihood that a particular act will be followed by a particular outcome [Vroom, 1964, p. 17]." Expectancies range from subjective certainty that an outcome will follow an act to subjective certainty that it will not. Expectancy is differentiated from Valence in that the former is an action-outcome association and the latter is an outcome-outcome association.

Behavior, or the decision commitment, is controlled by the direction and magnitude of forces to perform particular and competing acts. Force is the hypothetical cognitive factor that controls behavior—it is the product of Valence and Expectancy, and consequently controls which alternative is acted upon. It is a function of the sum of the products of Valences and Expectancies over all outcomes.

Hsu's Model   Hsu (1970) presented a VDM model based on familiar concepts—largely those used by Vroom—but included major variations in the relationships among concepts. The concept of Force (as defined by Vroom) is employed by Hsu to describe all alternative occupations considered and is assumed to have maximum value for the decision-maker's unique vocational goal. The vocational goal is defined as the algebraic sum of Valence-Expectancy products of all outcomes for an occupation where the Expectancy of each outcome is unity. The essential difference between Vroom and Hsu is that the Hsu model suggests a final step in the VDM process where the Force for vocational choices is subtracted from the Force for the vocational goal. Hsu assumes that the decision-maker is attempting to minimize the disparity between a choice and a goal.

Hsu assumes that the decision-maker can be represented as a "system" where information in the form of occupational values, occupational information, and evaluative information about the self serves as the environmental "input" and occupational choice is the "output."

Fletcher's Model   Although his purpose was not to explain decision, Fletcher (1966) "roughs out" a VDM paradigm based on conceptual learning ideas. He assumes that decision processes are not wholly rational and that commitment is as much a function of timing as it is of the data available to the decision-maker. Motivation for VDM is, initially, to satisfy basic human needs but later may derive from curiosity or conceptual conflict.

Fletcher hypothesized that the formulations for career decisions are concepts about the future. These concepts are based on experiences associated with one or more basic human needs (for example, Maslow's hierarchy). A career concept system is the composite of several concepts, such as self-concept, interests, attitudes, and values—all derived from experiences that the decision-maker associates with a given career alternative. Each career concept has an affect charge defined as the particular feeling or emotional tone associated with, or actually a part of, the concept. Affect charges for a complex career concept system may be the summed resultant of several affect charges related to several experiences both positive and negative. The career chosen is that one for which the career concept's affect charge is the highest at the time of decision.

Career concepts have two additional dimensions, with the opposite poles being degree of specificity contrasted with degree of generalization and degree of concreteness vs. degree of abstractness. Specific concepts are directly related to particular experiences but become generalized as they interact with other concepts. The movement from concrete to abstract concepts follows an inferential process toward higher levels of classification identity.

Other Descriptive Models   Loughary (1965), Dolliver (1967), and Simons (1966) have each described aspects of the VDM process but have not proposed complete models.

Prescriptive VDM Models

Katz Model   Katz (1963) sketched a "general model for career decision-making" and later added detail in his "model of guidance for decision-making (1966)." The model emphasizes a structure to be used in the practical art of helping people. Indeed Katz (1969c) suggested that career development theory contributes the content and outcome for guidance theory. In this sense, it prescribes preferred VDM behavior. The major difference from other models is that the entry point into the VDM process is the identification and definition of values (rather than the listing of alternatives).

Values are regarded as the satisfying goals or desired states that are sought but not in terms of motivating drive or specific instrumental action (Katz, 1963, 1969a). The decision-maker develops his own list of dominant values and scales them according to their relative "magnitude of value." For each value a "threshold level" that meets his personal requirements is identified. For each option (or alternative) the decision-maker estimates the "strength of return" it offers in respect to each value's threshold level. This refers to probabilities inherent in the option itself (for example, the proportion of people earning the desired "threshold level" income in an occupational option). The sum of products of "strength of return" and "magnitude of values" provides a "value return" for each option.

Objective probabilities regarding success or entry for each option are multiplied by the value return to obtain an "expected value." The strategy is to select that option for which the expected value is greatest.

Gelatt Model   Assuming that one important purpose of counseling is to help students make "good" decisions, Gelatt (1962) suggested that a decision be evaluated by the process it follows rather than the outcome alone. He described a "proposed decision-making framework" derived from Bross' (1953) design for statistical decisions and Cronbach and Gleser's (1957) description of decision sequences. The model assumes a decision-maker who requires information as "fuel" and who produces a recommended course of action which may be terminal (that is, final) or investigatory (that is, calling for more information) depending upon how it relates to his purposes. Information is organized into three systems: (1) *predictive system*, information about alternatives actions, possible outcomes, and probabilities linking actions to outcomes; (2) *value system*, relative preferences among outcomes; and (3) *decision criterion*, or rules for evaluation.

A "good" decision includes adequate and relevant information in each system (Clarke, Gelatt, and Levine, 1965; Gelatt, 1962). Clarke et al. argued that, since the content of prediction and value systems is more readily observable and far less complex than the decision criterion, improving information services would increase the likelihood of good decisions. Gelatt and Clarke (1967) emphasize the importance of subjective probabilities, the place of objective probability data in modifying subjective estimates, and the indeterminable, but significant effect of subjective probability estimates on preferences. In effect, the Gelatt model prescribes characteristics of adequate informational inputs and suggests an organization to be imposed on it. No specific rules are offered for proceeding from information to commitment.

Kaldor-Zytowski Model   A model of occupational choice derived from the tenets of economic decision making was developed by Kaldor and Zytowski (1969) to specify classes of determinants and to describe their interrelationships in producing a final choice.

The occupational choice process is assumed to approximate maximizing behavior and, as such, can be described in terms of inputs and outputs. The inputs include personal resources, e.g., intellectual and physical characteristics. When applied to a given occupational alternative (in imagination), certain outputs, or consequences, follow as a function of the inputs and the alternative. Likewise, the inputs are priced in terms of what the decision-maker foregoes in using them in a particular occupational alternative. The chosen alternative is the one offering the greatest net value—the highest value when input costs are balanced against output gains

Kaldor and Zytowski present detailed forms for assessing the values of outcomes and inputs. "Occupational utility functions," the extent to which a person obtains the outcomes he wants in the proportion he wants them, are computed for successive pairs of values. An aggregate occupational utility function can be derived from each alternative. This method assumes that a decision-maker can rank order relevant values for each available alternative and that he can assign a value to the sacrifices made to attain each alternative. Once these assumptions are accepted, the authors provide elaborate graphic techniques (for example, indifference curves) to plot the information and determine the maximal occupational alternative.

Other Prescriptive Models Prescriptive models dealing specifically with college choice decisions have been offered by Hills (1964) and Hammond (1965). Thoresen and Mehrens (1967) describe variables relevant to vocational decisions and suggest research questions about the influence of information on decisions.

Comparisons of VDM Models: Assumptions

Decision theorists make assumptions about the decision-maker or his surroundings. In this section VDM models are examined in terms of five of these assumptions.

1. *Assumptions about the amount of information available to decision-makers.* Specifically, how much does the decision-maker know about possible alternatives, how much is known about a given alternative, what is known about the projected outcomes and the probabilities connecting alternatives to outcomes?

The most apparent contrast is between the Hilton and Kaldor-Zytowski models. On the basis of his research on the careers of teachers (Hilton, 1960; Hilton, Levin, and Leiderman, 1957) and business administration graduate students (Hilton, Baenninger, and Korn, 1962), Hilton assumed decision-makers have limited knowledge about alternatives. Kaldor and Zytowski, on the other hand, assume that the decision-maker has relatively unlimited knowledge about alternatives, outcomes, resources, and values. They recognize the difficulties in accepting this assumption but report that hypotheses derived from their model are consistent with the occupational plans of farm boys (Kaldor, Eldridge, Burchinal, and Arthur, 1962).

The other models apparently assume that more moderate but unspecified amounts of information are available to the decision-maker. For example, the Gelatt model encourages a thorough information search, but in the absence of "stop" rules, we can only guess at how much information is considered sufficient. As long as only one model (Kaldor-Zytowski) suggests that values be assigned to each new "bit" of information received this assumption is argued at a very general level.

At least two models have been implemented through computer-assisted information systems. The Tiedeman-O'Hara model was applied through the Information System for Vocational Decisions (ISVD) (Tiedeman et al., 1967, 1968), and the Katz model has been translated to the System of Interactive Guidance Information (SIGI) (Katz, 1969a). Both systems supply considerable information to the decision-maker.

2. *Assumption of conditions of risk or uncertainty in VDM processes.* The models can be roughly divided into two groups on this issue. The risk group sees vocational decisions as among those where probabilities about future events are assigned. The *uncertainty* group sees vocational decisions as among those to which no generally accepted probabilities of future events can be attached. Put another way, the difference refers to the amount of so-called "objective" data directly applied to the VDM process.

The risk models utilize "objective" probability statements based on other persons' experiences (for example, expectancy tables or regression equations), where available, in the VDM process. This procedure was suggested in the Katz and Kaldor-Zytowski models and implied in the Gelatt model. Perhaps the extreme risk advocates are Gelatt and Clarke (1967) who assume that "objective data" is the base-line against which subjective probabilities are compared for "distortions."

The uncertainty models suggest that the probability statements about future events are filtered through the decision-maker's subjective judgments before fitting into the array of information used to make a final commitment. Tiedeman's (1967) distinction between data (facts) and information (interpreted facts) seems to capture the essence of the different assumptions. Hilton, Vroom, and Hsu appear to incorporate information rather than facts into their VDM models.

The arguments probably boil down to choosing between beliefs about the differences between the contemporary experiences of the decision-maker and the experiences of several past decision-makers. Those who prefer the risk assumption find this difference insignificant for decision purposes, whereas those preferring the uncertainty assumption attach considerable importance to these differences.

3. *Assumptions about the decision strategy being implemented by the decision-maker.* Decision strategies in VDM models can be considered of two general sorts: the *classical models* that attempt to select the alternatives with maximum subjective expected utilities, and the *satisficing models* that attempt to minimize the difference between an alternative and some preconceived standard (for example, level of aspiration). The former group includes Vroom, Gelatt, and Kaldor-Zytowski. All see the decision-maker as comparing several alternative actions and selecting the one that is "best"—usually the one with the greatest multiplicative products of values and subject probabilities summed over all outcomes. Kaldor-Zytowski add the concept of net value which is the aggregate value less the aggregate costs for a given occupation. From the satisficing group, Hilton and

Hsu assume that the decision-maker has a standard in mind that must be met. This standard is usually not fixed and fluctuates as a result of the decision-maker's experiences. The alternative selected is the one that first meets the standard (Hilton) or the one that comes closest to meeting the standard (Hsu).

Katz uses strategies from both classical and satisficing models. The latter approach is used when the decision-maker is asked to estimate the "threshold level" of a value dimension. The former applies to comparisons of expected value sums across options.

Fletcher does not develop a complete strategy but rather suggests that people decide upon the alternative with the greatest "affect change" at the time a commitment is required.

4. *Assumptions about the level of precision in combining information to make a commitment.* The pivotal concern here usually has to do with assumed performance by the decision-maker in ordering his value preferences. Hilton assumed a simply binary grouping of "yes" or "no" on all outcomes. Others discussed means for ordering value preferences that increase in complexity from Katz and Hsu's constant-sum method to Kaldor-Zytowski's indifference curves.

Perhaps the models break down into those that include mathematical computations as necessary to descriptions of the process of combining information and those that do not. Vroom, Kaldor-Zytowski, Hsu, and Katz use algebraic formulas to define concepts. Gelatt strongly suggests it would be included in a more specific statement of his model.

5. *Assumptions regarding the relationship between two conceptualizations about anticipated future states (outcomes).* The relationship between the subjective probability that the state will obtain and the value attached to it constitutes another issue upon which there are basic differences among VDM models. Two aspects of the relationships are involved: (a) how much distinction a model assumes between the two concepts; and (b) the direction of influence, if any, between them. Kaldor-Zytowski, Vroom, Hsu, Fletcher, Gelatt, and Katz assume that the two concepts are distinctive, whereas Tiedeman-O'Hara and Hilton blend the two together into one nearly inseparable concept. Gelatt and Clarke (1967) gather evidence to show interrelated effects between the concepts, but most of the models avoided the knotty problems of isolating values and subjective probabilities.

Comparison of VDM Models: Concepts

Table 1 shows a comparison of VDM models on the decision concepts presented earlier. VDM concepts appear to be quite similar although their labels are different. For example, alternative actions are labelled as "goals," "plans," "actions," "options," "career concepts," and "occupational alternatives." Generally speaking, the definitions describe cognitions of anticipated behaviors relevant to vocational goals. A notable exception occurs where the function of alternatives is applied to roles rather than actions, for example, occupational roles. If we assume that the roles designation applies to role entry behavior, the differences fade into insignificance. If, on the other hand, the roles designate relatively stable

Table 1 A Comparison of Major Decision Concepts across Selected VDM Models

Decision concepts	Vocational decision-making models			
	Tiedeman-O'Hara (1963)	Hilton (1962)	Vroom (1964)	Hsu (1970)
A. Awareness of decision situation	*Awareness* that present situation is or will become unsatisfactory.	*Input* that alters present vocational status.		
B. Alternative actions	*Goals* which can possibly be attained from opportunities.	*Plans*	*Actions*—behavior within repertoire of the person.	*Alternatives*—behavior associated with vocational choice.
C. Outcomes	*Psychological field*—imagined situations including attitudes.	*Premises* about attributes of vocational roles.	*Outcomes*—more distant and less controlled events (than actions).	*Outcomes*—anticipated rewards from an occupation.
C1. Subjective probability	*Commitment or orientation*		*Expectancy*—an action-outcome association.	*Expectancy*—probability of chosen behavior leading to particular outcome.
C2. Value	*Personal values*	*Satisfactoriness*	*Valence*—anticipated satisfaction.	*Valence*—attractiveness or desirability.
D. Commitment	*Choice*	*Plan accepted*	*Force*	*Force*

Table 1 (Continued)

		Vocational decision-making models		
Decision concepts	Fletcher (1966)	Katz (1963, 1966, 1969A, 1973)	Gelatt (1962)	Kaldor-Zytowski (1969)
A. Awareness of decision situation	*Need satisfaction*	*Disequilibrium*—motivated by needs and anticipation of societal pressures.	(Statement of) *Purpose* or *objective*	
B. Alternative actions	*Career concepts*—composite of concept system associated with a career.	*Options*	*Possible alternative actions*	*Occupational alternatives*
C. Outcomes			*Possible outcomes*	*Outputs*
C1. Subjective probability		*Strength of return*—probabilities that an option will satisfy value dimension. (Objective) probability of entry.	*Subjective probabilities*—estimates of how likely that certain actions will lead to certain outcomes.	*Subjective probabilities*
C2. Value	*Affect charge*	*Values*—goals or satisfactions sought.	*Desirability* of outcomes	*Occupational utility*—extent of obtaining outputs in the proportion desired.
D. Commitment			*Investigatory decision* or *terminal decision.*	*Occupational choice*

future *situations* rather than behavior, then they serve different functions: roles as more distant ends, and actions as more immediate means. Indeed roles would be more properly considered as outcomes.

Not all VDM models fit comfortably into the decision theory array of concepts. Models proposed by Hilton, Fletcher, and Katz are particularly difficult. None has a concept that clearly fulfills the "outcomes" function. Hilton's "plans," though not explicitly defined, apparently refer to rather complex actions lasting over a long period of time. Katz starts with personal values and works towards actions—a reversal of the order used to explain behavior in other models. Consequently Katz' "options" may fulfill the functions of both alternative actions and outcomes. Fletcher's "career concepts" may be comfortably viewed as spanning the decision theory function for both alternative actions and outcomes.

Key differences among models appear to be related to notions about time. Some models combine outcomes (thoughts about somewhat distant events) with actions (thoughts about more immediate events), and others separate the two at some point on the conceptualized time-line. This difference (which may constitute a sixth set of separate assumptions) may account for the variation in conceptualizations of "alternative actions." "Situations" or roles may be more temporally distant descriptions of actions.

There are concepts important to some VDM models that cannot be neatly placed into Table 1. For example, Hilton's "dissonance test" and "premises," Kaldor-Zytowski's "costs," and Katz' "expected values" are not included. In addition, varied emphasis is placed on concepts from model to model. Emphases on values by Katz and plans by Hilton have already been reviewed. Tiedeman-O'Hara emphasize the psychological field, Fletcher the career concept, Kaldor-Zytowski the occupational utilities, and Gelatt the information about probabilities.

VDM Models and Decision Types

By utilizing an analytic model introduced by Braybrooke and Lindblom (1963), a clearer picture emerges of the purposes VDM models serve. Earlier it was proposed that VDM models differed on assumptions about (1) the amount of understanding—information and computational skill—assumed to be available to the decision-maker, and (2) the distance in time from the present situation to the imagined futures under consideration (for example, the choice of an occupational role has long-range effects, but selection of a part-time job has short-range consequences). By imagining these two assumptions on continua and describing the extremes, four recognizable decision types appear:

    1 Decisions that effect long-range changes and are guided by considerable information and understanding.

    2 Decisions that effect long-range changes but are based on limited information.

    3 Decisions that effect short-range changes and are based on minimal information.

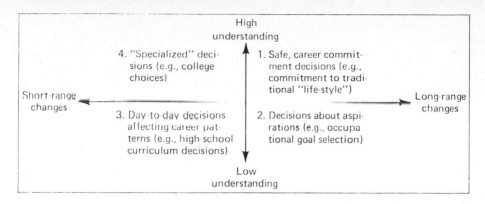

Figure 1   Theoretical vocational decision types.

4   Decision that effect short-range changes and are based on considerable information and high understanding.

In Figure 1 these types appear as quadrants 1, 2, 3, and 4 respectively.

The four decision types generally refer to vocational behaviors described in the VDM models. Type 1 vocational decisions occur where decision-makers have rich informational and computational resources and are ready to make long-range commitments. These decisions are rarely observed. Perhaps the closest approximations are those decisions faced by upper-class, bright males, such as the Harvard undergraduates studied by McArthur (1954), who were found to be highly predictable occupational decision makers. At least one VDM model, Kaldor-Zytowski, describes Type 1 decisions. In order to apply such a model, a considerable amount of computation is required which necessitates "intelligent" resources such as brilliant thinkers, computers, or both. With the full operation of computer information systems, such as ISVB and SIGI referred to previously, the Tiedeman-O'Hara and Katz models can be applied to Type 1 decisions.

Type 2 decisions apply to long-range commitments rather than commitments to immediate action, but require lesser amounts of information and computational skill. There are several "unknowns," but situations often hold out the prospect of some highly-prized rewards. Such decision processes may precede setting career goals that function as "levels of aspiration" in shorter-term decisions. Braybrooke and Lindblom included under Type 2 decisions those that led to "grand opportunities" on the one hand, or crises on the other.

Fletcher's model appears to operate under the condition of Type 2 decisions—selection of an occupational goal where less-than-complete information is necessary. Perhaps the "career concepts" that Fletcher describes are functioning as "aspirations."

Type 3 decisions assume short-range changes and relatively low understanding—the day-to-day decisions that make up a career. Osipow (1968) refers to these decisions as links in a complex decision network. Type 3 decisions lead to incremental moves that often make headway but sometimes retrogress. They

are characteristically exploratory and serial, that is, they effect gradual changes
on short-range goals as decisions are made in sequence.

Among the VDM models reviewed, those by Tiedeman-O'Hara, Hilton, and
the investigatory portion of the Gelatt model come closest to describing Type 3
vocational decisions. They assumed relatively low levels of knowledge and computational skill. Most of the decision situations for which these models were
intended cover shorter periods of time than the usual "occupational choice."
Tiedeman-O'Hara have assumed that their model would be applied to several
vocational decision situations simultaneously. Hilton's model was intended to
deal with decisions in sequences.

Type 4 vocational decisions are those for which many VDM models have
been adopted. Such decisions involve elaborate and detailed information utilized
by exacting processes to accomplish a more immediate change. Consequently,
Type 4 decisions are referred to as "technical" decisions such as college choices
where sufficient data are sometimes available. Hills (1964), Hammond (1965),
and Gelatt (1967) describe models especially for college selection. Vroom, Gelatt,
and Katz appear to offer the most applicable VDM models. Each requires considerable and detailed information, and each is intended to apply to short-range
decisions. Machine and mathematical technologies have been developed to assist
the decision-maker with Type 4 decisions. Ehling (1966) developed an elaborate
computer model describing high school students' decision processes when considering whether or not to enroll in a college. Marshall (1967) has described applications of "Bayesian decision" to vocational problems. Novick and Jackson (1970)
discussed a mathematically sophisticated "Bayesian guidance technology" that
would increase the accuracy of prediction about two or more career opportunities. The authors note that the time is ripe to use this technology. Perhaps the
precise thought behind the Novick-Jackson "technology" can be wedded to hardware in computer-assisted vocational decision programs (for example, those described in Super, 1970, and United States Dept. of Health, Education, and Welfare, 1969) to yield meaningful assistance in making vocational decisions of this
type.

Conclusions

We have shown that the VDM models are similar in many ways to decision
theory and to each other but certainly not to the point where parts of one can be
interchanged for parts of another.

We have shown that VDM models vary substantially on their assumptions
about the decision-maker and the conditions under which the decision is made.

We have shown that VDM models are applicable to different types of decisions.

The models are not clearly enough defined nor is there sufficient research
evidence to consider discussions about which might be the better explainer or
predictor. As a matter of fact, the models appear to be more complementary than
competitive. For example, Fletcher's model explains the derivation of "career
concepts" that, in turn, may function as "goals" in the Tiedeman-O'Hara model.

Thus, they may connect. Likewise the Katz model may suggest strategies suitable for "technical decisions," whereas Hilton's model would apply to decisions where less information is available.

Although we have not been able to make evaluative conclusions about the various VDM models, we think we have been able to sift through the semantic jungle and isolate some of the fundamental issues with which future theorists and researchers must come to grips if VDM models are ever to achieve their promise in describing vocational development over a lifetime.

REFERENCES

Atkinson, J. W. Motivational determinants of risk-taking behavior. *Psychological Review,* 1957, **64,** 359–372.

Becker, G. M., and McClintock, C. Value: Behavioral decision theory. *Annual Review of Psychology,* 1967, **18,** 239–286.

Blau, P. M., Gustad, J. S., Jesser, R., Parnes, H. S., and Wilcock, R. C. Occupational choice: A conceptual framework. *Industrial Labor Relations Review,* 1956, **9,** 531–543.

Braybrooke, D., and Lindblom, C. E. *A strategy of decision: Policy evaluation as a social process.* New York: The Free Press, 1963.

Brayfield, A. H. Counseling psychology. *Annual Review of Psychology,* 1963, **14,** 319–350.

Brayfield, A. H. Research on vocational guidance: Status and prospect. Part I: A critical examination of research issues. In H. Borow (Ed.), *Man in a world at work.* Boston: Houghton Mifflin Co., 1964.

Bross, I. *Design for decision: An introduction to statistical decision-making.* New York: The Free Press, 1953.

Cellura, A. R. The application of psychological theory in educational settings: An overview. *American Educational Research Journal,* 1969, **6,** 349–382.

Clarke, R., Gelatt, H. B., and Levine, L. A decision-making paradigm for local guidance research. *Personnel and Guidance Journal,* 1965, **44,** 40–51.

Crites, J. O. *Vocational psychology.* New York: McGraw-Hill, 1969.

Cronbach, L. J., and Gleser, G. C. *Psychological tests and personnel decisions.* Urbana, Ill.: University of Illinois Press, 1957.

Davidson, D., Suppes, P., and Siegel, S. *Decision-making: An experimental approach.* Stanford, Calif.: Stanford University Press, 1957.

Dolliver, R. H. An adaptation of the Tyler Vocational Card Sort. *Personnel and Guidance Journal,* 1967, **45,** 916–920.

Edwards, W. H. The theory of decision-making. *Psychological Bulletin,* 1954, **51,** 380–417.

Edwards, W. H. Behavioral decision theory. *Annual Review of Psychology,* 1961, **12,** 473–498.

Edwards, W. H., Lindman, P., and Phillips, L. Emerging technologies for making decisions. In *New directions in psychology, II.* New York: Holt, Rinehart & Winston, 1965.

Edwards, W. H., and Tversky, A. *Decision-making.* Baltimore: Penguin Books, Inc., 1967.

Ehling, W. P. *Development of a computer model of the factors which influence school students to continue or discontinue their education.* Syracuse University, 1966.

Feather, N. T. Subjective probability and decision under uncertainty. *Psychological Review,* 1959, **66,** 150–164.

Festinger, L. *A theory of cognitive dissonance.* Stanford, Calif.: Stanford University Press, 1957.

Fletcher, F. M. Concepts, curiosity and careers. *Journal of Counseling Psychology,* 1966, **13,** 131–138.

Gelatt, H. B. Decision-making: A conceptual frame of reference for counseling. *Journal of Counseling Psychology,* 1962, **9,** 240–245.

Gelatt, H. B. Information and decision theories applied to college choice and planning. In *Preparing school counselors in educational guidance.* New York: College Entrance Examination Board, 1967.

Gelatt, H. B., and Clarke, R. B. Role of subjective probabilities in the decision process. *Journal of Counseling Psychology,* 1967, **14,** 332–341.

Hammond, J. S. Bringing order into the selection of a college. *Personnel and Guidance Journal,* 1965, **43,** 654–660.

Hills, J. R. Decision theory and college choice. *Personnel and Guidance Journal,* 1964, **43,** 17–22.

Hilton, T. L. Alleged acceptance of the occupational role of teaching. *Journal of Applied Psychology,* 1960, **44,** 210–215.

Hilton, T. L. Career decision-making. *Journal of Counseling Psychology,* 1962, **19,** 291–298.

Hilton, T. L., Baenninger, R., and Korn, J. H. *Cognitive studies in career decision-making.* Cooperative Research Project No. 1046. Pittsburgh: Carnegie Institute of Technology, 1962.

Hilton, T. L., Levin, H., and Leiderman, G. L. Studies of teacher behavior. *Journal of Experimental Education,* 1957, **26,** 81–91.

Holland, J. L. *The psychology of vocational choice.* Waltham, Mass.: Blaisdell, 1966.

Hsu, C. C. A conceptual model of vocational decision-making. *Experimental Publication System,* 1970, **8,** Ms. #270–276.

Kaldor, D. R., Eldridge, E., Burchinal, L. G., and Arthur, I. W. *Occupational plans of Iowa farm boys.* Research Bulletin 508. Ames, Iowa: Iowa State University, 1962.

Kaldor, D. R., and Zytowski, D. G. A maximizing model of occupational decision-making. *Personnel and Guidance Journal,* 1969, **47,** 781–788.

Katz, M. R. *Decisions and values: A rationale for secondary school guidance.* New York: College Entrance Examination Board, 1963.

Katz, M. R. A model of guidance for career decision-making. *Vocational Guidance Quarterly,* 1966, **15,** 2–10.

Katz, M. R. Can computers make guidance decisions for students? *College Board Review,* Summer, 1969, **12,** 13–17. (a)

Katz, M. R. Interests and values: A comment. *Journal of Counseling Psychology,* 1969, **16,** 460–461. (b)

Katz, M. R. Theoretical formulations of guidance. *Review of Educational Research,* 1969, **39,** 127–140. (c)

Katz, M. R. The name and nature of vocational guidance. In H. Borow (Ed.), *Career guidance for a new age.* Boston: Houghton Mifflin, 1973.

Kroll, A., Dinklage, L. B., Lee, J., Morley, E. D., and Wilson, E. H. *Career development: Growth and crisis.* New York: Wiley, 1970.

Lee, W. *Decision theory and human behavior.* New York: Wiley, 1971.

Lewin, K. *Field theory in social science.* New York: Harper & Row, 1951.

Loughary, J. W. Some proposed new developments in vocational aspects of counselor education. In C. McDaniels (Ed.), *Conference on vocational aspects of counselor education,* 1965.

Marshall, J. C. Bayesian decision. *Journal of Counseling Psychology,* 1967, **14,** 342–345.

Marx, M. H. The general nature of theory construction. In M. H. Marx (Ed.), *Theories in contemporary psychology.* New York: Macmillan, 1963.

McArthur, C. Long term validity of the Strong Interest Test in two subcultures. *Journal of Applied Psychology,* 1954, **38,** 346–353.

Miller, G. A., Galanter, E., and Pribram, K. *Plans and the structure of behavior.* New York: Holt, Rinehart and Winston, 1960.

Newell, A., Shaw, J. C., and Simon, H. A. Elements of a theory of human problem-solving. *Psychological Review,* 1958, **65,** 151–166.

Novick, M. R., and Jackson, P. H. Bayesian guidance technology. *Review of Educational Research,* 1970, **40,** 459–494.

Osipow, S. H. *Theories of career development.* New York: Appleton-Century-Crofts, 1968.

Peak, H. Attitude and motivation. In M. R. Jones (Ed.), *Nebraska Symposium on Motivation.* Lincoln, Neb.: University of Nebraska Press, 1955.

Rotter, J. B. *Social learning and clinical psychology.* Englewood Cliffs, N.J.: Prentice-Hall, 1954.

Rotter, J. B. The role of psychological situation in determining the direction of human behavior. In M. R. Jones (Ed.), *Nebraska Sympsosium on Motivation.* Lincoln, Neb.: University of Nebraska Press, 1955.

Simon, H. A. A behavioral model of rational choice. *Quarterly Journal of Economics,* 1955, **49,** 99–118.

Simon, H. A. *Administrative behavior.* New York: Macmillan, 1958.

Simons, J. B. An existential view of vocational development. *Personnel and Guidance Journal,* 1966, **44,** 604–610.

Super, D. E. Book reviews. *Journal of Counseling Psychology,* 1961, **8,** 190.

Super, D. E. (Ed.) *Computer-assisted counseling.* New York: Teachers College Press, Columbia University, 1970.

Super, D. E., Starishevsky, R., Matlin, N., and Jordaan, J. P. *Career development: Self-concept theory.* New York: College Entrance Examination Board, 1963.

Taylor, D. W. *Decision-making and problem-solving.* New Haven: Dept. of Psychology and Dept. of Industrial Administration, Yale University, 1963.

Thoresen, C. E., and Mehrens, W. A. Decision theory and vocational counseling: Important concepts and questions. *Personnel and Guidance Journal,* 1967, **46,** 165–172.

Tiedeman, D. V. Decision and vocational development: A paradigm and its implications. *Personnel and Guidance Journal,* 1961, **40,** 15–21.

Tiedeman, D. V. Purposing through education: The further delineation of goal and program for guidance. In E. Landy and P. A. Perry (Eds.), *Guidance in American education: Backgrounds and perspectives.* Cambridge: Harvard Graduate School of Education, 1964.

Tiedeman, D. V. Career development through liberal arts and work. *Vocational Guidance Quarterly,* 1965, **14,** 1–7.

Tiedeman, D. V. Predicament, problem, and psychology: The case for paradox in life and counseling psychology. *Journal of Counseling Psychology,* 1967, **14,** 1–8.

Tiedeman, D. V., and Field, F. L. Guidance: The science of purposeful action applied through education. *Harvard Educational Review,* 1961, **32,** 483–501.

Tiedeman, D. V., and O'Hara, R. P. *Career development: Choice and adjustment.* New York: College Entrance Examination Board, 1963.

Tiedeman, D. V. et al. *Information system for vocational decisions: Annual report, 1966–67.* Cambridge, Mass.: Harvard Graduate School of Education, 1967.

Tiedeman, D. V. et al. *Information system for vocational decisions: Annual report 1967-68.* Cambridge, Mass.: Harvard Graduate School of Education, 1968.

Tolman, E. C. Principles of purposive behavior. In S. Koch (Ed.), *Psychology: A study of a science.* Vol. 2. New York: McGraw-Hill, 1959.

Tyler, L. E. Research exploration in the realm of choice. *Journal of Counseling Psychology,* 1961, **8**, 195–201.

United States Dept. of Health, Education, and Welfare. *Computer-based vocational guidance systems.* Washington, D.C.: U.S. Govt. Printing Office, 1969.

Vroom, V. H. *Work and motivation,* New York: Wiley, 1964.

Zaccaria, J. S. *Theories of occupational choice and vocational development.* Boston: Houghton Mifflin, 1970.

23. Career Decision-Making: A Computer-Based System of Interactive Guidance and Information (SIGI)*

Martin R. Katz

Socrates' comment in the dialogue with Protagoras seems apropos today: ". .Since our salvation in life. .(lies). .in the correct choice of pleasure and pain—more or less, greater or smaller, nearer or more distant—is it not in the first place a question of measurement. .?" He goes on to say, ". .when people make a wrong choice of pleasures and pains . . . the cause of their mistake is a lack of knowledge . . ."

What knowledge do they lack for wise choice? Socrates, of course, gave first rank to knowledge of self, assuming that people were free to control their own behavior.

Does knowledge make us free? In modern times, the social and behavioral sciences have seemed to discover ever narrower limits on individual freedom. For example, here are just a few of the high spots from which these sciences have observed behavior and have tried to understand, explain, and, in some cases, influence it:

1 The ethologist notes similarities that link human beings to other species and differences that demarcate them. Behavior is explained largely in terms that may be called instinctual. The primary determinant of change in behavior is natural selection of behaviors that have survival value, although some promise is also held for adapting environments to biological equipment.

2 The geneticist seeks to explain similarities and differences between people as a function of their genes. He focuses on behavior that stems from inherited characteristics. Changes in behavior can be effected through breeding, perhaps eventually through genetic engineering.

3 The anthropologist and sociologist look to culture to account for similarities and differences between groups or subgroups of people. Behavior depends largely on roles in the culture and is shaped by acculturation.

4 Many psychologists focus more specifically on the reinforcements experienced by each person in his environment. Behavior is modified by controlling the contingencies of reinforcement.

5 Nevertheless, there still survives a doctrine in psychology that emphasizes the autonomy of each person, his free will, his capability of making purposive, intentional decisions about his own behavior. Subscribers to this school of thought believe that a person can change his own behavior by understanding himself better, by taking thought about himself and the options open to him, by getting and interpreting appropriate information, and then by making plans and taking action to achieve the goals he has chosen.

As even this hasty and oversimplified outline must make clear, these various approaches to human behavior are not mutually exclusive. Perhaps, though, in the tradition of the aphorism, "Ontogeny recapitulates phylogeny," we may discern a maturational trend in the extent to which the various forces implied by these approaches govern behavior at successive stages of a person's development. At the earliest stage, the infant's behavior seems dominated by instinctual drives, with the behavior of one individual relatively less differentiated from that of another. Then, hereditary differences become more evident, and behavior appears more clearly differentiated. Increasing socialization of the child gives the culture more opportunity to affect his behavior. Meanwhile, a number of persons (such as parents, teachers, peers) have been exercising the power to reinforce selected behaviors. But at some point, usually in adolescence, most people in our culture emerge into a stage in which autonomy becomes the name of the game.

As a person progresses through these stages, his behavior seems capable of variation up to the limits established by preceding stages. Thus, within whatever constraints are allowed by being a member of the human species, having inherited a given set of genes, being brought up in a certain culture, and being subjected to selected arrays of reinforcements, most young men and women seem to want to become as independent as possible. They seem to want to use as much space as is left them for making their own decisions, for determining their own behavior—even those who decide to become behaviorists. We have not yet progressed, if that is the word, entirely "beyond freedom and dignity."

It is to this striving for individual freedom in decision-making that our computer-based System of Interactive Guidance and Information (SIGI) addresses itself, specifically in the area of career decision-making. But freedom without competence may be frustrating. We have set out to enhance the freedom of the decision-maker by helping him to increase his competence in the process of making informed and rational decisions.

Time does not permit me to repeat here the rationale for this approach; it has been explicated in various papers I have written over the last 20 years (Katz, 1954, 1963, 1966, 1969, 1973). Instead, let us get on with a description of the system, including a slide sequence that illustrates the track of a real student through SIGI. We will show selected key frames that the student saw on the terminal in the course of his interaction with SIGI two summers ago. Then you can judge for yourself how far we have progressed from the heyday of trait-and-factor theory or—as it has been dubbed—"Test 'em and tell 'em."

The current version of SIGI is designed for use at community and junior colleges. Development was supported by grants from the Carnegie Corporation, and a small-scale field trial last spring was funded by the National Science Foundation. In this guidance system, the student interacts with a computer in such a way as to examine and explore his own values, obtain and use relevant information, interpret predictive data, and formulate plans. This interaction helps the student to arrive at tentative career decisions and to modify them as he gains new insights and additional information. The decisions involve both educational and occupational options. Remember, however, that emphasis is not merely on the content of decisions, but on the process of decision-making. As the student progresses through SIGI, he learns to move freely within the structure of the system. In gaining control of the system, he develops competencies and masters strategies for rational behavior in the face of uncertainty—which may be the closest we can get to wisdom.

The keyboard of the cathode-ray tube terminal is covered, except for 10 numbered response keys at the right, a "Print" key which the student presses to get hard copy of a display, and the space bar, which is marked NEXT and is used to bring on the next slide when no other response is appropriate. The hardware configuration for SIGI was chosen by William Godwin; he and Ronald Bejma did the programming, assisted by Christine Sansone; Frederick Kling served as an advisor.

The test on the terminal is not legible in photographs. So the following slides are simulations. For the most part, they are summary slides and give no sense of the dynamic interaction between student and terminal.

Early in the introduction, the student sees a list of the four major sections of SIGI (see slide 1). Each section deals with distinctive topics, later brought together in a section called Strategy. The first section of SIGI asks the student about his values. After the Values section has helped the student to define what he wants in an occupation, the Information section helps him identify occupations that may fit his values and allows him to get a great deal of relevant information. The Prediction section deals with his probabilities of success in programs at his own college that tend to prepare him for entry into various occupations. The Planning section helps him figure out how to get from here to there; it deals with educational requirements, courses of study, financial aid, and so on.

SIGI emphasizes the primacy of individual values. There are, of course, different points of view about values, the subjective ordering of "pleasures and

Slide 1

SIGI includes 4 systems that you can use in making career decisions:

I. VALUES

What satisfactions are most important to you in an occupation? Some examples of Values are: Income, Independence, Security, Helping Others, etc.

II. INFORMATION

Where can these satisfactions be found? Which occupations fit your values best?

III. PREDICTION

What are your chances of success in preparing for each occupation? How well are you likely to do in various major programs at your school?

IV. PLANNING

What are your next steps? What courses should you take? What problems are you likely to face and how can you handle them?

Press NEXT

pains" of which Socrates spoke, SIGI devotes a great deal of attention, right from the start, to the student's exploration and examination of values. Why is this necessary? Why can't we assume that each student already knows his own values? Socrates speaks of "latent knowledge." It is this kind of latent knowledge that SIGI tries to help the student uncover, bring into full awareness, and make explicit. SIGI provides him with useful categories and definitions. Each of a series of 10 occupational values is defined in operational terms. As illustrated (see slide 2), the student weights each value in accordance with its importance to him. Here, the row of asterisks indicates that this student has given a weight of 6, indicating "strong" importance, to security.

After this independent weighting of one value at a time, the weights for all 10 values are gathered, in graphic form (slide 3), and the student has a chance to make comparisons, have second thoughts, and make adjustments in the weights. If he elects to change the weight for any value, he sees a short form of the definition first.

You may wonder where those 10 values dimensions come from. We did a number of studies of our own, and, of course, took into account the research of others. For example, we asked students, in structured interviews, a series of questions designed to elicit the dimensions along which they construed occupations. We asked them to tell us what they knew about an occupation of interest to them, and to indicate what other information they would like to have; what appeals to them most about it, and what least; what events or additional information might make them change their preference for that occupation; what characteristics an "ideal" or "dream" occupation and also a "nightmare" occupation—the worst they could imagine—would have. In a simulated occupational choice procedure, we gave students an opportunity to ask us questions about a set of unknown occupations; from the information we gave them, they would choose one as most attractive. Classifications of their questions and their evaluations of the occupa-

---

Slide 2   **WEIGHT (IMPORTANCE)**

None (∅)	(1)	Slight (2)	(3)	Medium (4)	(5)	Strong (6)	(7)	Highest (8)

, ———— , ———— , ———— , ———— , ———— , ———— , ———— , ———— ,

  *   *   *   *   *   *

SECURITY: In the most SECURE occupations, you will be free from fear of losing your job and income. You will have tenure—that is, you cannot be fired very easily. Employment will tend to remain high in spite of recessions, and there will be no seasonal ups and donws. Your income will generally remain stable and predictable; it will not vanish with hard times. Your occupation is not likely to be wiped out by automation or other technological changes.

Press one of the numbers (∅-8) to show how important it is to you to work in an occupation that offers steady employment and income.

Slide 3

WEIGHT (IMPORTANCE)

VALUES	None	Slight	Medium	Strong	Highest

```
                         None        Slight      Medium      Strong      Highest
                       ,----,----,----,----,----,----,----,----,----,

(1) HIGH INCOME        *    *    *    *    *    *    *    *
(2) PRESTIGE           *    *    *    *    *
(3) INDEPENDENCE       *    *    *    *    *    *    *    *
(4) HELPING OTHERS *   *    *    *    *
(5) SECURITY           *    *    *    *    *    *    *
(6) VARIETY            *    *    *    *    *
(7) LEADERSHIP         *    *    *    *    *    *
(8) INTEREST FIELD *   *    *    *    *    *    *
(9) LEISURE            *    *    *    *    *    *
(Ø) EARLY ENTRY        *    *    *    *    *
```

The rows of stars, above, show how much weight you gave each of the ten Values. The longer a row of stars, the more important you said that Value is.

Are you satisfied that the Values with longer rows of stars are more important to YOU than Values with shorter rows? Do ONE of the following:

To make any row longer OR shorter, press its number (1, 2, 3, 4, 5, 6, 7, 8, 9, Ø).
Or, to keep all the rows just as they are now, press NEXT.

tions in light of the information they received gave us an additional check on the comprehensiveness and relevance of our values dimensions. In a variation on Kelly's Role Construct Repertory test (Kelly, 1955), we gave them triads of occupations and asked them to indicate which two of the three seem to offer satisfactions and rewards that are more nearly alike than the satisfactions and rewards offered by the third. From their responses, we were able to determine the dimensions along which they construed similarities and differences in occupational satisfactions.

In addition, as part of a questionnaire follow-up of a large national sample of secondary school students one year after completion of high school (Norris & Katz, 1970), we asked them to weight the importance of some dozen values dimensions; we computed the intercorrelations among the weights, and did an unrestricted maximum likelihood factor analysis of the intercorrelation matrix. (We also put aptitude and interest scores into the matrix and found that the three domains—aptitudes, interests, and values—were independent.)

Despite all this research, I am sure there will not be universal agreement with some of our omissions. For example, we decided that we could not formulate a good enough operational definition of Creativity for this program. And a value called Sense of Accomplishment, or Pride in Work, although it might differentiate between specific jobs or positions within an occupation and clearly differentiated between many unskilled and higher-level positions, did not seem useful in differentiating between occupations of concern to community college students. Incidentally, in our field-testing of SIGI, we found that students perceive the dimensions as independent (intercorrelations of the weights tend to be quite low), each of the values is regarded as important by many students (as indicated by the mean weights), the weight given each value varies greatly across students (as indicated by the standard deviations of the weights), and students did not feel that values of importance to them had been omitted (as determined by interviews after their use of SIGI).

The inclusion of Interest Field as one of the values dimensions may be a bit confusing. This value is defined in terms of the importance to the individual of working in a field in which the activities are of primary intrinsic interest rather than in some other field. The student indicates his preferred interest field from six options, each defined and illustrated: scientific, technological, administrative, personal contact, verbal, and aesthetic. The designation of these six areas obviously takes cognizance of the massive body of research on interest measurement and dimensions of occupational interests.

To help the student scrutinize his values more closely and probe into them more deeply (slide 4), we then go on to challenge him on the weights he has assigned to the 10 values. This Values game was written and flow-charted by Warren Chapman.

In a clearly playful and gamelike context, the student is confronted with a series of values dilemmas (slide 5), in which he first makes choices between hypothetical occupations that represent a pure manifestation of each value.

Some of the other occupational titles found at Strive Employment Agency include Bucksman, Autonomist, Benefician, Tenurist, Charismat, and so on. These are paired at random for the student's initial choice.

Having made his choice, he finds—as in the real world—new decisions to be made. He encounters a series of problems or opportunities, each featuring a different value (slide 6). For example, this student finds that his occupation is deficient in opportunities for leadership. The "hurdle," as we call it, is selected at random; whether it comes up as a deficiency (like the one shown) or a temptation (not shown) is also randomized. The student's decision to keep his job or switch indicates the relative importance to him of the two competing values in a given context.

Slide 4

You may not be sure which values are truly more important to you and which are less.

One way to find out is to choose between two values when you can get only one of them.

You are now going to play a game in which you do that: You will make choices between competing values.

After the game you will come back and adjust your original value weightings again in light of what you learned in the game.

Press NEXT.

Slide 5

Welcome to the Strive Employment Agency.
The jobs currently available are listed below.

TORPIST

(1) Torpist is a choice job for a person who values leisure strongly. The hours are short, the schedule has been arranged to provide for a four day work week, the annual paid vacations are long, and every national and state holiday is observed, giving you many extra long weekends. As a result, you have lots of free time to follow your own interests.

VARISATOR

(2) Varisator is a great job if you want variety. You work with your hands, adjusting the varimeter, or with your brains, solving the priority flow. You travel, work with people, work alone, deal with varied tools and problems. If routine is your enemy, this is the job for you. But you need a cool head, for you never know what will come up next.

Press (1) or (2) to show which job you prefer.

Slide 6

You have the following job:

TORPIST

Torpist is a choice job for a person who values leisure strongly. The hours are short, the schedule has been arranged to provide for a four-day work week, the annual paid vacations are long, and every national and state holiday is observed, giving you many extra long weekends. As a result, you have lots of free time to follow your own interests.

As you work, you get the following information about your job:

The boss's stupid son-in-law has been appointed supervisor of your group. He is a poor leader. You are sure you could do better than he, for you have been successful in directing new employees who were breaking in. But you have few opportunities for leadership on this job.

What do you do? Press (1) or (2) to show your choice.

(1)   Keep your present job.
(2)   Go to the Srtive Employment Agency and take a job featuring a
different Value.

At the end of each "round" of the game, the student sees a display in the form of a balance scale (slide 7). In this student's case, Leisure prevailed successively over each of the five values listed on the left.

But then, as shown in the balance scales at the right (slide 8), Helping Others outweighed Leisure.

The student then sees a display which ma comprehensive study of the influence on mothers and their infants of early separation during the each value, or—

Slide 7

This ends your career as torpist, featuring the Value leisure.

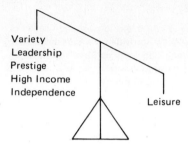

Look at the balance scales above.
Your choices in the game suggest
that leisure was more important
to you than any of the Values on
the left side of the scales.

Press NEXT.

Slide 8

This ends your career as torpist, featuring the Value leisure.

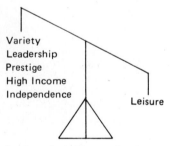 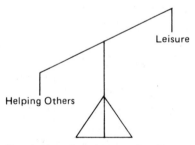

Look at the balance scales above.
Your choices in the game suggest
that leisure was more important
to you than any of the Values
on the left side of the scales.

Press NEXT.

Now look at the balance scales above.
Your choices in the game suggest that
leisure was LESS important to you
than the Values on the left side of
the scales.

Press NEXT.

as in this case—that they have been inconsistent (slide 9). The inconsistencies are merely pointed out. This is just a game, intended to stimulate further thinking, and the student is not held accountable for his behavior. His own evaluation of the inconsistencies is likely to show up when he reweights his values.

After each value has been represented at least once, either by a job or a hurdle, the student can exit from the game, or he can play as many rounds of the game as he wants; there are three versions of every temptation and of every deficiency, making 60 hurdles in all before the student would encounter any repetition.

When he has had enough of the game, he readjusts the weights he previously gave the 10 values (slide 10). Besides taking into account whatever insights he has gained from the values game, he must also consider a new constraint: to distribute a fixed sum (40 points) among the 10 values. This constraint reflects the sad

Slide 9

Some of your choices in this game disagree with the way you felt about your Values earlier. Think back to the rows of stars you made to show the importance of your Values.

You gave more stars to the Values listed below than you gave to liesure.

     High Income   Independence

But when you played the game, you showed that leisure was more important.

You gave more stars to leisure than to the Value listed below.

     Helping Others

But when you played the game, the listed Value became more important.

Did you notice the disagreement?

You will get a chance to weight your Values again later on.

Press NEXT.

Slide 10

WEIGHT (IMPORTANCE)

VALUES		None	Slight	Medium	Strong	Highest
(1)	HIGH INCOME	7	* * *	* *	* *	*
(2)	PRESTIGE	3	* * *			
(3)	INDEPENDENCE	6	* * *	* *	*	
(4)	HELPING OTHERS	3	* * *			
(5)	SECURITY	6	* * *	* *	*	
(6)	VARIETY	4	* * *	*		
(7)	LEADERSHIP	5	* * *	* *		
(8)	INTEREST FIELD	6	* * *	* *	*	
(9)	LEISURE	5	* * *	* *		
(Ø)	EARLY ENTRY	3	* * *			

Sum = 48

Choose any Value that you want to change. In order to add OR subtract points, first press the number BEFORE that Value (1, 2, 3, 4, 5, 6, 7, 8, 9, Ø).

But if the sum already equals 4Ø, and you want to keep all the weights just as they are now, press NEXT.

Slide 11   WEIGHT (IMPORTANCE)

VALUES		None	Slight	Medium	Strong	Highest
(1)	HIGH INCOME	6	*	*	*	*	*
(2)	PRESTIGE	3	*	*	*		
(3)	INDEPENDENCE	5	*	*	*	*	*
(4)	HELPING OTHERS	2	*	*			
(5)	SECURITY	6	*	*	*	*	*	*
(6)	VARIETY	4	*	*	*	*	
(7)	LEADERSHIP	5	*	*	*	*	*
(8)	INTEREST FIELD	6	*	*	*	*	*	*
(9)	LEISURE	5	*	*	*	*	*
(Ø)	EARLY ENTRY	3	*	*	*		
	Sum = 45						

SECURITY: Freedom from fear of losing job or income. You cannot be fired easily.
Employment high even in recessions, no seasonal ups and downs. Income
stable. Occupation not likely to be wiped out by new technoolgy.

To ADD a point to the Value you have chosen, press the number 1.
To SUBTRACT a point from that Value, press the number Ø.

Press 1 to add or Ø to subtract as many points as you want.
When you are satisfied with the weight you have given that Value, press NEXT.

truth that one can rarely expect to get all there is of everything in the real world.
He must make some hard choices and give up a little of something that is slightly
less desirable in order to retain what he considers more important.

In this frame, the student has already reduced his weights for some of the
values and is about to change the weight for Security (slide 11). Note that he gets
the short form of the more detailed definition that he saw earlier. The result of
the adjustments, when the values sum equals 40 and the student is satisfied with
all the weights, is a profile of his "examined" values.

It is not sufficient in career decision-making to know one's values. Occupational information does not generally appear in a form that is isomorphic with
the domain of values. This slide finds the student in the Locate mode of the
Information section of SIGI (slide 12). In Locate, the computer will retrieve
occupations that meet his specifications on any set of five values taken simultaneously. He can start with the five values that he had previously given the highest
weights, as listed on the left, or he can substitute any set of five that he wishes to
use. Our student elected to stay with his top five values for the first round in
Locate, and he is now about to specify the minimum amount or the kind of
satisfaction he will accept on each one. For example, this slide asks for his specification on income.

When he has filled in his specifications on all five values, at the left, a list of
occupations in the system that meet or exceed his specifications appears at the
right (slide 13). If his specifications had been so demanding or anomalous that no

occupations in the system fit, he would be invited to loosen up on one or more of the specifications. Note that by pressing the PRINT key he can get a hard copy of this display as of many others.

Most students learned to use Locate in a systematic and logical way, fishing for different sets of occupations with seines of alternately tighter and looser mesh. This student extended his list over several rounds, always staying—as it happened—in the technological field of interest (slide 14). Satisfied with this list of occupations worthy of further consideration in the light of his values, he decided to get extensive and specific information about them, querying the system about three occupations at a time.

In the section called Compare, the student can ask as many as he wants of this array of pointed questions about three occupations at a time, substituting

Slide 12

Values for locating occupations:	Specifications for INCOME:
	The list of occupations should include only those with average salary of:
Income	(5) More than $14,000
Security	(4) More than $12,000
Independence	(3) More than $9,000
Interest Field	(2) More than $7,000
Variety	(1) $7,000 or less will do
	Press the number (5-1) for the specification you choose.

Slide 13

Values for locating occupations:	These occupations meet your specifications:
	Broadcast Technician
	Chemical Engineer
	Civil Egnineer
Income	Industrial Engineer
More than $12,000	Electrical Engineer
	Meteorologist
Security	Mechanical Engineer
An average amount	
Independence	
A more than average amount	
Interest Field	
Technological	
Variety	
A more than average amount	

For a copy of this information, press PRINT; otherwise press NEXT.

Slide 14

(11) Broadcast Technician
(12) Chemical Engineer
(13) Civil Engineer
(14) Industrial Engineer
(15) Electrical Engineer
(16) Meteorologist
(17) Mechanical Engineer
(18) Airline Pilot
(19) Flight Engineer
(2∅) Appliance Repair Technician
(21) Automobile Mechanic

(22) Aircraft Mechanic
(23) Business Machine Repair Tech.
(24) Electronics Technician
(25) Instrument Repair Technician
(26) Machinist
(27) Optician
(28) Radio/TV Technician
(29) Science Laboratory Technician
(3∅) Telephone Crafts Worker
(31) Draftsman

You can choose any three of the occupations you got from LOCATE. (Later you can substitute any of the 12∅ occupations now in SIGI.)
Press the numbers of the 3 occupations you want to ask questions about first.

Slide 15

Now you can get information about the three occupations.
Press the number for the question you would like to have answered.
(After you get the answer, you can keep coming back to this list to ask more questions.)

DEFINITION AND DESCRIPTION
(11) Definition of occupation?
(12) Description of work activities?
(13) Level of skill in interacting
    with data, people, things?
(14) Where to get more information?

EDUCATION, TRAINING, OTHER REQUIREMENTS
(15) Formal education beyond high school?
(16) Specific occupational training?
(17) Related college courses?
(18) Personal Qualifications?
(19) Other requirements?

INCOME
(2∅) Beginning salary?
(21) Average income of all people in this occupation?
(22) Top salary possibilities?
(23) How salaries vary?

PERSONAL SATISFACTIONS
(24) Opportunities to help others?
(25) Opportunities for leadership?
(26) What fields of interest?
(27) Prestige level?

CONDITIONS OF WORK
(28) Physical surroundings?
(29) Leisure (hours)?
(3∅) Independence on the job?
(31) Variety?
(32) Fringe benefits?

OPPORTUNITIES AND OUTLOOK
(33) Employment outlook?
(34) Where are the jobs?
(35) Job security?
(36) Advancement?
(37) How many women?

occupations as he sees fit (slide 15). The questions cover such areas as work activities, entry requirements, income, personal satisfactions, conditions of work, opportunities, and outlook.

Where did all this information come from, and how accurate is it? It came from more sources than I have time to list, and it is as accurate as we can make it with the help of specialists in many fields—including national sources such as the Bureau of Labor Statistics and various other bureaus of the federal government, professional organizations, labor unions, occupational briefs and monographs; a similar variety of regional and local sources, including many state agencies; plus a miscellany of sociological and psychological studies of occupations, college handbooks, assorted publications, and a wealth of cooperative and informed people in the various occupations.

Data from different sources sometimes failed to agree. We searched into such discrepancies very carefully. For example, when data were derived from different surveys, we evaluated sampling procedures and response rates, and made some judgment about the trustworthiness of each source. Although SIGI emphasizes national rather than local occupational information, we checked national data against representative regional and local data, and often incorporated regional differences when they were significant.

Documentation for all the information is on file in our office library, and is continually brought up to date, with changes edited into the computer periodically. While all of our SIGI staff has participated somewhat in this work, the main digging has been ably done by Katharine Bode, Karen Boyle, Gretchen Bullock, and Elizabeth Cogswell.

All but four of the questions can be answered by hard data found in solid studies from multiple sources. To single out one, by way of acknowledgement of the kind of cooperation we received: A prepublication copy of Paul Siegel's University of Chicago doctoral dissertation *Prestige in the American Occupational Structure* gave us most of our prestige ratings. The four that required more active inference on our part are questions 24, 25, 30, and 31. For each of these soft areas, four levels of degree were operationally defined. Then, in addition to our readings, we directed questions, based on these definitions, to representative members of each occupation to elicit their experiences and observations. For example, concerning Variety: How many different problems and activities do you (and others in your occupation) typically work on each week, month, or

Slide 16

Employment outlook?

Mechanical Engineer
Favorable, even though there is temporary unemployment due to cutbacks in aerospace and defense. Fewer mechanical engineers are being trained, and industry is expanding in new areas, such as atomic energy and environmental control, creating a demand that may be greater than the supply within a few years.

Civil Engineer
Favorable through the 1970's. Expansion in the field will come from increased construction, transportation, and urban environment needs. Since the work is not related to aerospace and defense activities, there is little fear of unemployment resulting from government spending cutbacks.

Electronics Technician
Good because of expansion of industry, increasing complexity of technology, trend toward automation of industrial processes, and growth of new areas of work, such as atomic energy.

For a copy of this information, press PRINT; otherwise press NEXT.

Slide 17

VALUE	WT.	OCCUPATION		
		MecEng	CivEng	ElcTec
(1) Income	6	5	5	5
(2) Prestige	3			
(3) Independence	5			
(4) Help Others	2			
(5) Security	6			
(6) Variety	4			
(7) Leadership	4			
(8) Interest Field	5			
(9) Leisure	3			
(Ø) Early Entry	2			

A rating of 5 = average salary over $14,ØØØ per year; 1 = $7,ØØØ or less.

Which of the following do you want to do?

If you want to see the ratings for Prestige, press NEXT.
If you want more detailed information about Income, press the number 1.

year? How many different people do you deal with? To how many places does your work take you? We did not have time or resources to poll a large sample from each occupation on these questions. (We hope to extend our activities in that direction later.) So the responses for each occupation were pooled with our readings as a basis for inference and consensus among our own staff.

One of the questions our student asked was 33, employment outlook. This was the display he got for the three occupations he was then inquiring about (slide 16). This information came from our old data base, now being revised. At the beginning of this section, a display gives the sources of information, the limits of accuracy, and the date of last revision.

The student then had a chance to put his values and occupational information together, in summary form, to see the relative desirability of each occupation (again in sets of three at a time) (slide 17). This arithmetic algorithm suggests how well each occupation fits his values, as he has weighted them. The weights, retrieved from the values system, show how important each value is to him. The rating in each cell indicates the opportunity offered by that occupation for the kind of satisfaction represented by that value. The scale on which the ratings are based is defined below as each rating appears. The student has the option of going on immediately to the next rating or of seeing the particular data which substantiate the rating he has just seen.

When all the ratings have been filled in, the computer multiplies what the student wants (the weight for each value) by what he can get from each occupation (its rating on that value) (slide 18). These products are summed to show the desirability of each occupation, and the sums are compared with previously expressed preference for the three occupations. A cluster analysis, done by Lila

Norris, showed that the occupations in SIGI are distinct from one another in terms of the values dimensions used.

Of course desirability should be moderated by probability or success in entering each occupation. The closest we can come to this is the student's probability of success in appropriate programs or courses at his college. These probabilities are essentially experience tables: They tell a student the proportion of students at his institution with test scores and previous marks like his who received a grade of A or B, C, or below C in each curriculum or key course. These tables are derived from local data. For example, Mercer County Community College, where the first field test was conducted, has required all entering students to take the Comparative Guidance and Placement battery. We used scores on these tests and previous scholastic record as predictor variables. Mercer furnished us with the criterion data, and we computed prediction equations. We were able to get predictive validities greater than .40 for each criterion, and these did not shrink on cross-validation. The prediction studies were made by Lila Norris.

The Prediction section starts with a series of didactic frames, explaining how probabilities are derived and used. This one (slide 19) gives the student's predictions for the program called Humanities and Social Sciences and emphasizes the limits of such information. Throughout the Prediction section, it is made clear that a given probability statement can have different implications for different students.

Having seen three such sample predictions, the student is then free to call in

Slide 18

	VALUE	WT.	MecEng	CivEng	ElcTec
(1)	Income	6	5 3Ø	5 3Ø	3 18
(2)	Prestige	3	3 Ø9	4 12	3 Ø9
(3)	Independence	5	3 15	4 2Ø	2 1Ø
(4)	Help Others	2	1 Ø2	3 Ø6	1 Ø2
(5)	Security	6	3 18	3 18	3 18
(6)	Variety	4	3 12	4 16	2 Ø8
(7)	Leadership	4	2 Ø8	4 16	1 Ø4
(8)	Interest Field	5	4 2Ø	3 15	4 2Ø
(9)	Leisure	3	3 Ø9	3 Ø9	3 Ø9
(Ø)	Early Entry	2	2 Ø4	2 Ø4	3 Ø6
		Sum =	127	146	1Ø4

Your weight for Income (6) X the rating of MecEng on Income (5) = 3Ø, etc.

The sum of the products appears at the bottom of each column.
The occupation with the highest sum is probably the one that would fit your values best. The highest possible sum is 168; the lowest is 4Ø.
In general, a difference of 1Ø points or more between sums is significant.

You will want a copy of this chart. Press PRINT.

Slide 19

MAJOR FIELD	Chances in 1ØØ for GPA of:			Notice that this SIGI prediction
PROGRAM	4.Ø-3.Ø A-B	2.9-2.Ø C	Below 2 Below C	does NOT tell you for certain what will happen to you.
Hum.&Soc.Sci.	Ø5	35	6Ø	It does tell you the probabili-

Notice that this SIGI prediction does NOT tell you for certain what will happen to you.

It does tell you the probabilities (chances in 1ØØ) for various outcomes. These probabilities are based on the experience of previous students.

Remember: Will you be one of Ø5% with abilities like yours who get an A or B in Humanities and Social Sciences? Or one of the 35% who get a C? Or one of the 6Ø% who get less than C? No one can tell.

These probabilities are the best predictions that can be made. It is up to you to decide whether a given probability is a good risk or a bad one.

To see predictions for two other programs, press NEXT.

Slide 20

Press the number of the program for which you want a prediction. If you want pre-
dictions for all the programs in a group, press the number (ending in Ø) for that group.
(Example: Press 11 to get Accounting. Or press 1Ø to get all six programs listed under
Business.)

(1Ø) Business
11   Accounting
12   Business Administr.
13   Marketing
14   General Business
15   Secretarial Science
16   Data Processing

(2Ø) Health & Human Serv.
21   Laboratory Technology
22   Nursing
*23 Dental/Assisting
*24 Library Tech. Asst.
*25 Commnuity Serv. Asst.
*26 Education Assistant

(3Ø) Developmental
31   General Studies

*No prediction available.

(4Ø) Liberal Arts and
          Science
41 Humanities & Social Sci.
42 Engineering Sci.,
      Mathematics,
      Physics,
      Chemistry
43 Biology

(5Ø) Technology
51 Architectural Tech.
      Civil Eng. Technology,
      Electro-Mech. Eng Tech,
      Electric Power Tech,
      Mechanical Eng. Tech
52 Drafting & Design Tech.
53 Electric Eng. Tech.,
      Electronics Tech.

(6Ø) Fine/Applied Arts
61 Architecture
62 Fine Arts,
      Advertising Design
63 Communications Media

(7Ø) Agriculture
*71 Ornamental Horticulture

* (8Ø) New Programs
*81 Aviation Instr.
*82 Aviation Electronics
*83 Flight Technology
*84 Industrial Supervsn.
*85 Law Enforcement
*86 Government Aide

predictions for any program of interest to him. This frame (slide 20) shows all the
programs available at that time at Mercer. In some instances (42, 51, 53, 62),
prediction equations for several programs were virtually identical; so these programs were combined. The asterisked programs had not been in existence long
enough to provide criterion data, so no predictions could be computed for them.

In the future, a centralized prediction system may make it possible to predict new programs on the basis of pooled data from similar institutions.

This student, as you can see (slide 21), called in predictions for a number of programs in his area of technological interest. He will be able to shuttle back to the Prediction section from the Planning section if he decides to get predictions for other programs.

The Planning section helps the student see how to get from here to there for any occupation in the system that he may be considering. It was written and flow-charted by Warren Chapman. The steps are presented in reverse chronological order. For example, if the student is interested in a professional occupation, he begins by deciding whether he is willing and able to undertake the necessary amount of education (slide 22). The final step is the specific program of courses he will take at his own community college to begin the journey. Between these first and last steps, he may consider alternative programs and pathways to prepare for a given occupation. He may, at any time, decide to drop the occupation he is considering and start planning for another one. In this case, the student decided he was willing to undertake a four-year degree program for mechanical engineering.

Slide 21

MAJOR FIELD PROGRAM	Chances in 1∅∅ for GPA of:		
	4.∅-3.∅ A-B	2.9-2.∅ C	Below 2 Below C
Hum.&Soc.Sc.	∅5	35	6∅
Data Proc.	15	5∅	35
Acctg.	3∅	5∅	2∅
Engr. Sci.	15	4∅	45
Drafting	1∅	4∅	5∅
Biology	1∅	5∅	4∅
Arch. Tech., etc.	2∅	4∅	4∅
Electronics	35	4∅	25

When you have finished, you can get a copy of this chart.
For a copy, press PRINT.
Otherwise, press NEXT.

Slide 22

Mechanical Engineer

You have to graduate from a four-year college to enter this occupation.

Are you willing to spend at least four years preparing for the occupation?

(1)   Yes, willing to spend the time.

(2)   No, not willing. I want to switch to another occupation.

The student then sees a list of generally required courses for mechanical engineering and makes an estimate of his ability to get through them with at least a C average (slide 23).

He has the option of seeing a prediction for the appropriate program at his college (slide 24), and he can also see a "key course" prediction. If more than one curriculum is suitable for the occupation, he sees predictions for each.

Having seen the predictions, he is asked whether he wants to revise his estimate of ability (slide 25). Indication of any doubts about his ability leads to a

Slide 23

Mechanical Engineer

For most occupations, you can take the first two years at a junior college. Then you can transfer to a four-year college.

Now think about your ability. You should have AT LEAST a C average in junior college to transfer. (That won't be enough in some cases.) Also, many colleges will not give credit for a course if your grade in it is below C. The better your grades, the easier it is to transfer.

Do you think you have the ability to get AT LEAST a C average in the 2-year college courses in the list below?

2-YEAR COLLEGE: 4 semesters university-level math and physics, chemistry, engineering graphics, computer languages, plus courses for Associate degree and transfer to 4-year college accredited by Engineers' Council for Professional Development. 4-YEAR: Solid mechanics, fluid mechanics, thermodynamics, heat transfer, systems & controls, materials, electricity & magnetism, design, computer languages.

(1)   Yes, I think I have the ability.

(2)   No, I probably don't have the ability.

Slide 24

PROBABILITY OF SUCCESS IN PROGRAM OF STUDY FOR MECHANICAL ENGINEER

Chances in 1ØØ that you will get a GPA of

PROGRAM OF STUDY	4.Ø-3.Ø A-B	2.9-2.Ø C	Below 2.Ø Below C
Engr. Sci.	15	4Ø	45

EXAMPLE: The first time means that you have 15 chances out of 1ØØ to getting A or B, 4Ø chances of getting C, and 45 chances of getting a grade below C. Adding 15 and 4Ø gives you 55 chances of getting C or better.

To get a printed copy of this information, press PRINT. Otherwise, press NEXT.

Slide 25

Mechanical Engineer

You estimated that you could get a C average in junior college.

Now that you have seen a prediction, do you think your estimate was right?

(1)   No. I would change my estimate.

(2)   Yes. I would stick with my original estimate.

Slide 26

CAREER PLAN FOR MECHANICAL ENGINEER:

1.   Enroll in engineering science program in junior college.

2.   Check catalogs of 4-year schools offering bachelor's degree in mechanical engineering. Include in junior college program courses they require for transfer.

3.   Complete Associate degree; transfer to 4-year school; complete bachelor's degree in mechanical engineering. (In some schools this requires a fifth year of study.)

4.   Check licensing or registration laws in the state where you wish to work. You may be required to pass an examination to become registered.

5.   Graduate training required for most teaching positions.

For a copy press PRINT; otherwise press NEXT.

special interaction showing risks and rewards of taking a trial semester of the program in question versus switching to a different program.

The student decided to stick with Mechanical Engineering, and saw this step-by-step career plan, which would apply to students at any college (slide 26). He will next see a list of high school prerequisites for entering this program, and will be urged to check out any deficiencies with his counselor.

Then he sees this specific suggested two-year program of courses, that takes into account requirements and electives at his own school (slide 27). This frame will be followed by a list of four-year or advanced-level colleges in the region that offer majors in the field he is considering. He can also see information about financial aid. The detailed information in the Planning section, like that in the Prediction section, is of course based on local data, reflecting the distinctive characteristics and curricula of each institution.

Once the student has completed a round in the Planning section, he gets this list of choices (slide 28). He is no longer a novice, but an initiate, on SIGI. His path is not prescribed. He can go to whatever section he wants, bypassing intro-ductory and explanatory material, use as much as he wants of that section, and then go on, by way of this list to any other section. If he signs off now, and later

Slide 27

A suggested ENGINEERING SCIENCE program includes:

FIRST SEMESTER

EG 101 Language & Lit. I
MA 111 Math Analysis I
CH 101 General Chemistry
EN 103 Engineering Graphics
PH 103 Univ. Physics I
MA 113 Computer Program. I
EN 501 Engineering Orient.
      Health & Phys. Ed.

THIRD SEMESTER

MA 211 Math Analysis III
PH 213 Univ. Physics III
CE 205 Statics
      Soc. Sci. Elect.
      Technical Elect.

SECOND SEMESTER

EG 102 Language & Lit. II
MA 112 Math Analysis II
CH 102 Gen. Chem. & Qualitative Analysis
EN 106 Descriptive Geometry
PH 104 Univ. Physics II
MA 114 Computer Program. II
      Health & Phys. Ed.

FOURTH SEMESTER

MA 212 Math Analysis IV
PH 214 Univ. Physics IV
CE 206 Dynamics
      Soc. Sci. Eelctive
      Technical Elective

For a copy press PRINT; otherwise press NEXT.

Slide 28

What do you want to do next?

(1) Sign off.

(2) Go to VALUES and examine your Values again.

(3) Go to the LOCATE mode of the Information System and look for
     occupations that meet your Values.

(4) Go to the COMPARE mode of the Information System and ask
     questions about cocupations.

(5) Go to the DESIRABILITY mode of the Information System and
     see how occupations can offer different amounts of what you want.

(6) Go to PREDICTION and get probabilities of success in various
     programs of study.

(7) Go to PLANNING and plan how to prepare for various occupations.

(8) Go to STRATEGY and put Values, Information, and Predictions
     together in decision charts that help you choose an occupation.

reenters, he starts with this array of choices. (Sign-off after any subsection during
his first time through the system would enable him to start only at the next
subsection, in order.)

The one section you have not yet sampled is called Strategy. In our next
revision, this is going to be attached directly to the section on desirability. Again,
the student can choose any three occupations. Here we see him using the same set
of three that appeared previously (slide 29). Strategy brings together Values,
Information, and Prediction. The student first has an opportunity to revise his
values weights. Then the desirability sum for each of the occupations is multi-

plied by the probability decimal. The resultant index combines subjective utility and objective probability. Its main function is heuristic, not deterministic. The student is not pushed to choose the occupation with the highest index.

There are four possible displays, depending on the outcome. In this instance, the highest index has the highest desirability but not the highest probability (slide 30). So the student is reminded to consider his feelings about risks.

This student continued to express a preference for Mechanical Engineer. Students were asked to bear in mind that there is no special magic in the arithmetic. What is important is not the numbers, but the thinking and information that underlie them. Some students go back to the Values section after a round of Strategy, make changes in their weights, and then return to Strategy to see what effect the changes may have on the indexes for various occupations.

Now, then, what is SIGI? It is a career decision-making "treatment" defined by the record of each student's interaction with the system. The treatment is *structured* by the courseware, software, and hardware (along with whatever human counseling may be joined to it), but it is not a fixed treatment. Rather, it is

Slide 29

OCCUPATIONS	DESIRABILITY	X PROBABILITY	= INDEX
Mechanical Engineer	127	.55	7Ø
Civil Engineer	146	.55	8Ø
Electronics Technician	1Ø4	.75	78

The Index combines chances for satisfaction and for success.

Does that mean you should always choose the occupation with the highest index?
Not necessarily.

Press NEXT.

Slide 30

OCCUPATIONS	DESIRABILITY	X PROBABILITY	= INDEX
Mechanical Engineer	127	.55	7Ø
Civil Engineer	146	.55	8Ø
Electronics Technician	1Ø4	.75	78

For many people with Values and abilities like yours, the occupation with the highest index would be the best choice, on the average. The chance for greater gain would outweigh the higher risk.

But how do YOU feel about risks? You may be so concerned with getting through your courses that you will choose a program with higher Probability of success, even though it does not have the highest index.

Press the number to show which occupation you would choose right now.

(1) Mechanical Engineer
(2) Civil Engineer
(3) Electronics Technician

variable, responsive to individual needs and uses. It is interesting to observe that no two students used the system in the same way. As novices, some made copious, others only cursory, use of various sections. Then, as initiates, their use of the system was even more distinctive. They availed themselves of the freedom they had to move from one section to another in a sequence and at an interval of their own choosing. From the record of their behavior at the terminal, one can infer their conceptions of their own status and needs in career decision-making, as they made free and variable use of the resources available to them in the different sections of SIGI (Chapman, Norris, and Katz, 1973).

How will their choices come out? We don't know. Can we say they have chosen wisely when we don't know the long-range results of their decisions? I suggest that to define wise decisions in terms of such outcomes is not only difficult; it is presumptuous. Tennyson wrote, "No man can be more wise than destiny."

The problem in identifying wise decisions by outcomes is not just the time lag between the choice point and the judgment day—the day when all the evidence on consequences of the choice is in. Nor is the problem just a matter of insufficient predictive validity. Predictive data are really historical data, and our predictions are manifestations of what we have learned from history. So if our predictors had perfect validity, we could extend the aphorism "Those who do not learn from history are condemned to repeat it," by adding, "And those who do learn from history are also condemned to repeat it." But, in fact, we don't repeat history, even when events materialize as we have predicted. For there is always a surplus of events—there are more events than predictions. Any decision that is not trivial has ramifications without end.

In fact, what one learns from the multitude of real-life outcomes may or may not be relevant to wisdom. Like Mark Twain's cat, who learned from sitting on a hot stove never to sit on any stove again, we may learn from these outcomes more "wisdom" than is in them.

It is these tendencies to "generalize" that lead the behaviorists to concern themselves with *contingencies* of reinforcement. Or as O. H. Mowrer once put it, "You've got to be smarter than the rat." Well said, since such an approach to defining wisdom in terms of outcomes requires that wisdom reside in the experimenter (or counselor), not in the subject (or student). But this is where the presumption comes in: Do counselors, or computers, know which decisions are wise?

In shunning a definition of wise decisions solely in terms of content or predicted outcome, I have assumed that experience does not teach us what will be best for the individual (or society) except freedom to work things out. Thus, I have defined the best choice as the choice that is most nearly free. But freedom does not mean *laissez-faire*. Rather, I speak of the freedom that comes from competence in the process of decision-making. If I may quote from my 1963 monograph on *Decisions and Values:*

Decision-making at each stage may be regarded as a strategy for acquiring and processing information. If a decision is truly to be made, if it is not a foregone conclusion, it must involve some novel elements. The person confronted with the problem of decision-making either does not know what information he needs, does not have what information he wants, or cannot use what information he has. Thus, the pressure for making a decision creates a discrepancy between the individual's present state of knowledge (or wisdom) and the state that is being demanded of him (Katz, 1963, p. 25).

To know what information he needs, a student must know his own values. If we grant that students will vary in the weights they attach to any occupational value, we must allow for variation in the importance that any item of information will have for each student. Thus, a student should be free to seek the information that is most significant and salient to him at any stage in his career decision-making. He should know what the "right" questions are for him.

To get the information he wants implies not just that he seeks information from an appropriate domain. He must also know how to select questions so that appropriate connections can be made between his values and such occupational information as may be accessible. For example, if a student values job security, he must be able to see the relevance to this value of information about tenure, seniority provisions, occupational outlook projected over a period of years, vulnerability to economic conditions or to technological developments, and so on.

Finally, *to use the information that he receives* means that the information makes a noticeable difference in moving toward a decision. The impact of each item of information on the student's decision must be made visible.

This, then, is what SIGI tries to do.

Without directing the *content* of an individual's choice, we do think we can help him in the *process* of choosing. This emphasis on process does not pretend to insure the "right" choice—except insofar as the right choice is defined as an informed and rational choice. Our bias—our conviction—is that in education enlightened processes are intrinsically important. Therefore, we bend our efforts to increase the student's understanding of the factors involved in choice (imperfect though our own understanding may be) so that he can take responsibility for his own decision-making, examine himself and explore his options in a systematic and comprehensive way, take purposeful action in testing hypotheses about himself in various situations, and exercise flexibility in devising alternate plans.

In short, we don't want to play the decision-making game for him. We want to help him master the strategies for rational behavior in the face of uncertainty so that he can play the game effectively himself.

Horace, in one of his satires, asked "Who then is free?" and answered "The wise man who can govern himself."

Let me make "free" with Horace, and interchange the descriptors, to ask, "Who then is wise?" and answer "The man who can govern himself freely."

REFERENCES

Chapman, W., Norris, L., & Katz, M. *SIGI: Report of a pilot study under field conditions.* Princeton, N.J.: Educational Testing Service, 1973.

Katz, M. A Critical Analysis of the Literature Concerned with the Process of Occupational Choice in High School Boys, *Harvard Studies in Career Development,* No. 6, 1954.

Katz, M. *Decisions and Values. A Rationale for Secondary School Guidance,* New York: College Entrance Examination Board, 1963.

Katz, M. A model of guidance for career decision-making. *Vocational Guidance Quarterly,* **15,** 2-10, 1966.

Katz, M. Theoretical foundations of guidance. *Review of Educational Research,* **39,** 127-140, April 1969.

Katz, M. Can computers make guidance decisions for students? *College Board Review,* **72,** 13-17, Summer, 1969.

Katz, M. The name and nature of vocational guidance. In H. Borow (Ed.), *Career guidance for a new age.* Boston: Houghton-Mifflin, 1973. Pp. 83-133.

Kelly, G. *The Psychology of Personal Constructs,* New York: W. W. Norton, 1955.

Norris, L. & Katz, M. *The Measurement of Academic Interests: Part II. The Predictive Validities of Academic Interest Measures.* College Entrance Examination Board Research and Development Report 70-71, No. 5 and Educational Testing Service Research Bulletin 70-67, 1970.

Siegel, P. Prestige in the American Occupational Structure. Unpublished doctoral dissertation, Department of Sociology, University of Chicago, 1971.

FOLLOW-UP FOR SECTION THREE

Questions

1 The following pertain to Ginzberg's "Toward a Theory of Occupational Choice: A Restatement."

   a Define, identify, and give an example of:

   (1) Fantasy, tentative, and realistic; (2) compromise; (3) lifelong dynamizing, (4) optimal fit; (5) constraints on occupational choice.

   b What are the social, economic and political implications of Ginzberg's concept of irreversibility?

2 The following pertain to Super's "A Theory of Vocational Development."

   a Define, identify, and give an example of:

   (1) process; (2) compromise between interests, capabilities, values, and opportunities; (3) life stages; (4) individual differences; (5) multipotentiality; (6) role models; (7) career patterns; (8) life satisfactions; (9) self-concept; (10) developmental tasks.

   b How does Super's position differ from the trait-and-factor approach?

   c Basing your remarks on Super's theory, respond in 250 words or less to the following statement: "Vocational counseling should be separated from educational and personal counseling."

3 Compare and contrast the theories of Super and Ginzberg.

4 What, according to Hansen in "A Model for Career Development Through the Curriculum," are the advantages and disadvantages of integrating career-development concepts into the curriculum of elementary, secondary, and postsecondary educational programs?

5 According to Prediger, Roth, and Noeth in "Career Development of Youth: A Nationwide Study," what type of help do students most frequently want from their counselors? What are the implications for policies governing the administration of a school guidance program? Why do counselors tend to prefer providing personal rather than educational or vocational counseling?

6 According to Herr, Horan, and Baker in "Clarifying the Counseling Mystique," how does a systems approach differ from other approaches? What are the advantages and disadvantages of this approach for the delivery of vocational guidance services?

7 Distinguish between counseling, vocational counseling, and behavioral counseling. Where does vocational counseling with behavioral techniques fit into this scheme?

8 According to Woody in "Vocational Counseling with Behavioral Techniques," how does behavioral vocational counseling differ from other approaches? List and describe three behavioral techniques appropriate to vocational counseling.

9 According to Jepsen and Dilley in "Vocational Decision-Making models: A Review and Comparative Analysis," what do various career decision-making models have in common with the position described in Over's "The Interaction of Vocational Counseling with the Economic System"?

10 Compare and contrast the role of the computer in the systems described by Katz in "Career Decision-Making: A Computer-Based System of Interactive Guidance and Information (SIGI)" and Harris in "The Computerization of Vocational Information."

11 Which theory fits best? Case studies help determine the adequacy of a theory to explain the vocational behavior of a particular individual. Select a subject and prepare a case study. Consult the Guidelines for a Case Study in Appendix D.
12 Complete the Career Development Theory and Practice Worksheet for any of the theories in this chapter. The worksheet appears in Appendix C.

Learn by Doing

1 Does fantasizing work? With a group of students, demonstrate several of the activities Morgan and Skovholt suggest in "Using Inner Experience: Fantasy and Daydreams in Career Counseling." Report your results.

2 What are students' priorities for help? The purpose of this exercise is to provide counselor-trainees with an appreciation of the kinds and sources of help students say they want. Conduct an interview with a group of high school students. Consult the Taped Interview Format in Appendix A.

3 Exposure can help. According to Super's sixth proposition, the number and type of opportunities students are exposed to influences career development. Arrange a Business and Industry Visit according to the guidelines found in Appendix E.

4 An extension of Super's theory. Super stresses the importance of viewing career development as a *process* as well as focusing on a client's values. Conduct a group guidance activity based upon the materials listed below or similar materials:

   Career Choice: A Lifelong Process (Guidance Associates)*
   Career Values: What Really Matters to You (Guidance Associates)*
   Work Values Inventory (Houghton Mifflin)*

5 The role of curriculum development. The purpose of this exercise is to provide counselor-trainees with the opportunity to translate career-development concepts into meaningful instructional objectives and activities. This assignment requires counselor-trainees to design a week-long unit which can be implemented within the confines of existing curricula.

   a Select and specify one of Super's ten propositions as the underlying rationale for the modification of the curriculum.
   b Select and specify the subject matter which will be the focus of the unit (e.g., English, science, history, physical education).
   c Select and specify the grade and ability level of the intended group.
   d Review articles 17 and 18 and Appendix E.
   e Develop lesson plans for five periods of 45 minutes each in duration, or their equivalent, specifying: (1) behavioral objectives and (2) activities designed to meet the behavioral objectives for each day's lesson.

6 How aware are counselors? Find out what counselors think about the role self-concept plays in career development by arranging to interview several counselors in state employment offices, vocational-technical schools, or similar agencies or institutions. Consult the Taped Interview Format which may be found in Appendix A.

7 Are computers in? Conduct a telephone survey and, based on your results, prepare a directory of local institutions that have computer-based guidance systems. Arrange to visit as many as possible. After each visit prepare a brief report which contains the following information:

   a name of system
   b name of developer
   c name of theorist on whose work the system is based
   d a brief description of how the system works
   e student reaction to the system

*See Appendix H for additional information.

  f advantages and disadvantages
  g counselor's role
  h role of paraprofessionals
8 Let's role play. Role playing is an established technique for efficiently and inexpensively exposing an individual to a wide range of experiences. Conduct a group guidance activity based upon the use of the Job Experience Kits (Science Research Associates*) or a similar set of simulated materials. Prepare a report describing what transpired, how students reacted, and the potential benefits of using such materials.
9 Let's review. Apply the Guidelines for the Systematic Selection, Evaluation and Use of Simulated Vocational Guidance Materials to the Job Experience Kits (Science Research Associates*). See Appendix F.
10 Complete the Career Development Theory and Practice Worksheet for each of the theories in this chapter. See Appendix C.
11 To learn more. Prepare an abstract based on one of the articles listed below under *Additional Resources.* Consult Appendix G for the suggested format.

Additional Resources

Bartsch, K., Yost, E., & Girrell, K. *Effective personal and career decision making.* New York: Westinghouse Learning Corporation, 1976.

Brown, O. H. "The client-centered approach to educational and vocational guidance." The Personal Counselor, 1947, *2,* 1–5.

Elliott, J. *Personal growth through guided imagery.* Berkeley, California: Explorations Institute, 1977. (outline and cassette)

Ginzberg, E. Toward a theory of occupational choice. *Occupations,* 1952, *30,* 491–494.

Ginzberg, E., Ginsburg, S. W., Axelrad, S., & Herma, J. L. *Occupational choice: An approach to a general theory.* New York: Columbia University Press, 1951.

Herr, E. L. *Decision-making and vocational development.* Boston: Houghton Mifflin, 1970.

Herr, E. L., & Cramer, S. H. *Vocational guidance and career development in schools: Toward a systems approach.* New York: Houghton Mifflin, 1972.

Ivey, A. E., & Morrill, W. H. Career process: A new concept for vocational behavior. *Personnel and Guidance Journal,* 1968, *46,* 644–649.

Jones, O. M., Hansen, J. C., & Putnam, B. A. Relationship of self-concept and vocational maturity to vocational preferences of adolescents. *Journal of Vocational Behavior,* 1976, *8,* 31–40.

Krumboltz, J. D., & Baker, R. D. Behavioral counseling for vocational decisions. In H. Borow (Ed.), *Career guidance for a new age.* Boston: Houghton Mifflin, 1973.

Krumboltz, J. D., Mitchell, A. M., & Gelatt, H. B. Applications of a social learning theory of career selection. *Focus on Guidance,* 1975, *8,* 1–16.

Krumboltz, J. D., & Sheppard, L. E. Vocational problem-solving experiences. In J. D. Krumboltz & C. E. Thoresen (Eds.), *Behavioral counseling: Cases and techniques.* New York: Holt, Rinehart & Winston, 1969.

Ryan, T. A. A systems approach to career education. *Vocational Guidance Quarterly,* 1974, *22,* 172–179.

Super, D. E. *Measuring vocational maturity for counseling and evaluation.* Washington, D.C.: American Personnel and Guidance Association, 1974.

Super, D. E. *The psychology of careers.* New York: Harper & Row, 1957.

Super, D. E. Vocational development theory: Persons, positions, processes. In J. M. Whiteley & A. Resnikoff (Eds.), *Perspectives on vocational guidance.* Washington, D.C.: American Personnel and Guidance Association, 1972.

Super, D. E., & Crites, J. O. *Appraising vocational fitness.* New York: Harper & Row, 1962.

Super, D. E., Starishevsky, R., Matlin, N., & Jordaan, J. P. *Career development: Self-concept theory.* New York: College Entrance Examination Board, 1963.

Thoresen, C. E., & Mehrens, W. A. Decision theory and vocational counseling: Important concepts and questions. *Personnel and Guidance Journal,* 1967, *46,* 165–172.

Tiedeman, D. V. Decision and vocational development: A paradigm and its implication. *Personnel and Guidance Journal,* 1961, *40,* 15–20.

Varenhorst, B., Gelatt, H. B., & Carey, R. *Deciding: A program in decision-making for grades 7–8–9.* New York: College Entrance Examination Board, 1972.

Westbrook, B. W. Content analysis of six career development tests. *Measurement and Evaluation in Guidance,* 1974, *7,* 172–180.

*See Appendix H for additional information.

Section Four

Special Treatment Groups

The theories presented in Sections Two and Three tend to be painted in broad strokes. The purpose of vocational theories is to account for as much vocational behavior as possible. Thus, the theories all suffer from being general in nature, and to varying degrees ignore the existence of certain critical periods that many people routinely encounter and specific problems some groups experience. Most approaches are better at *explaining* or *describing* vocational behavior than *prescribing* what to do when problems arise. Sections Four and Five are concerned with the specific vocational counseling needs of different populations. Women, men, the disadvantaged, and the disabled are discussed in Section Four. The normal developmental needs of all individuals at specific points across a life span are discussed in Section Five.

The groups represented in Section Four have many things in common. Most women and men are searching for roles with which they are comfortable. Few wish to accept *automatically* the traditional roles society ascribes to them. Women, the disadvantaged, and the disabled frequently face discrimination. Too often they are the last hired and first fired. All four groups would seem to be searching for roles different from those they presently play. The changes that members of these groups wish to bring about cause concern in our society. For all those who

wish to see change, there are also those opposed to change. Counseling historically has assisted clients in achieving their goals by helping them make changes in
their environments and/or life-styles. Today's counselors need to increase their
awareness of the wide diversity of needs various client groups present. The articles in this section are selected illustrations of the types of concerns counselors
will encounter.

L. Sunny Hansen states in the beginning of "Counseling and career (self)
development for women" that "Counselors today need to be concerned about the
career development of women as well as the career development of men." With
this in mind, she describes many of the societal trends that influence life patterns
of women today, including technology, legislation, and increased opportunities
for study and work. Despite increased opportunity, there remain many obstacles.
Sex-role conditioning, socialization, and role conflicts about fulfilling the multiple roles of marriage are among the obstacles she explores.

Counselors play a critical role in helping clients determine the nature of their
relationship with the world of work. Thus counselors need to explore their own
attitudes and values in relation to the vocational aspirations of female and male
clients. Unfortunately, research has tended to indicate that high school counselors "responded more positively to female clients with traditional (feminine) goals
than to female clients with deviant (masculine) goals." And male counselors have
tended to be less informed about alternative career options for female clients
than were female counselors.

Hansen concludes her article with two major sets of recommendations. First,
she provides a series of seven counseling interventions designed to make a positive difference in the lives of female clients. Second, she suggests a model for
curriculum infusion which features several examples from practitioners. Hansen's
recommendations are in many cases equally appropriate for expanding the
awareness of clients of both sexes.

Although many of the counseling interventions for sex-fair career counseling
are similar for men and women, the causes of the problems each sex experiences
are not always identical. In "Career counseling with men: The shifting focus,"
James I. Morgan, Thomas M. Skovholt, and James M. Orr, Jr. trace the evolution
of the traditional male role. They also provide a series of counseling interventions
designed to liberate the male client by offering him an opportunity to make an
informed choice on the basis of his desires and needs as opposed to conforming
to societal expectations.

All of the groups discussed in this section share one thing in common: Being
"discriminated against." But probably no group has consistently suffered as
much as the economically disadvantaged. The barriers that the poor encounter
are great. The obstacles to overcoming being poor may be greater than those of
being disabled or female. Eli Ginzberg succinctly identifies who the disadvantaged are and what needs to be done in their behalf. In "Guiding the disadvantaged," he dispels many of the myths associated with those who are commonly
referred to as "the disadvantaged."

Fortunately the line between what is considered *normal* and what is considered *abnormal* is fading. It may have as much to do with the setting in which a client is seen as it does with the client's characteristics. We know that some clients need more professional intervention than others. We further know that the schools are not the only institutions that provide vocational guidance. Community-based agencies are filling many of the gaps that schools are unable to fill. In "Agency settings for career guidance," Donn E. Brolin discusses the contributions of manpower, rehabilitation, and social service agencies. He proposes a competency-based model for improving the quality of services agencies provide.

24. Counseling and Career (Self) Development of Women*

L. Sunny Hansen

Counselors today need to be concerned about the career development of women as well as the career development of men. For, as we are well aware, women do not exist in a vacuum or make decisions in a vacuum; what women do and can do affects and is affected by the perceptions and actions of men. By the same token, the limitations put on female development also create obstacles and prescriptions for the way men act, behave, and grow. Yet, it seems appropriate that special focus on the career planning and counseling process for women is justified at this point in time, though perhaps it will not be necessary in another 12 or 15 years. And perhaps, as human liberationists have pointed out, both men and women eventually will have more options open to them as a result of the current attention to the concerns and development of girls and women.

It is an underlying assumption of this article that both men and women can have greater control over their lives and development if both males and females, counselors and teachers all accept some responsibility for doing something about women's untapped resources, talents, and potentials. It would seem logical that counselors, who are supposed to be facilitators of human growth and development, should be key persons in bringing about changes in this area, in public school, college, and vocational school settings, not only through counseling but also through curriculum interventions and consultation with teachers. This article attempts to make a case for such interventions by (1) reviewing some of the literature on female self-concepts, career patterns, and aspirations; (2) summarizing the facts about women in the work force and obstacles to women's career development; (3) suggesting practical approaches to facilitate female development through counseling and curriculum; and (4) offering a few multimedia resources to assist in the above task.

SOCIETAL TRENDS AND CHANGING LIFE PATTERNS

A number of societal trends and changing work and family patterns have contributed to the changing roles of women and particularly to their increased participation in work and community. While it is difficult to assess the rate and strength of movements, it seems reasonable to say that these trends (Hansen, 1974b) are having an impact on women's career development and the roles of men as well. A few of them are cited below:

1 Technology, labor-saving devices, and the "decline of motherhood" as a fulltime occupation.

2 The population explosion and birth control with its powerful effects on norms and decisions regarding number of children.

3 Legislation and federal regulations providing a legal context for improving the status of women in education and work.

4 The Women's Movement which has highlighted issues and concerns about equal rights in a variety of sectors and the concomitant movement for men's liberation.

5 New life styles and female sense of identity—the movement toward a more androgynous society in which roles in work and family are shared, diverse family patterns are acknowledged, and women are risking different kinds of patterns and self-definitions based on their own needs.

6 Increasing numbers of part-time jobs and day-care centers making part-time work and more humanized day-care facilities more available.

7 Continuing education with its opportunities for women to enter and re-enter education and/or work and to update or retrain for new fields.

8 Breakdown of occupational and career stereotypes so that continuous career patterns are becoming more common and both male and female occupational stereotypes are being reduced.

Female Career Patterns

There is no full-blown theory of female career development. While most of the career development literature has dealt with male populations, Super (1957) postulated a "Logical Scheme" of women's career patterns. He identified seven kinds of female patterns, including what he labels the stable homemaking, the conventional, the stable working pattern, a double-track pattern, and multiple trial pattern. The first attempt of any major theorist to direct his attention toward female participation in the world of work, Super's descriptive schema was prefaced with the somewhat prescriptive statement, "Woman's role as childbearer makes her the keystone of the home and, therefore, gives homemaking a central place in her career."

Others also have offered descriptions of women's patterns by socioeconomic divisions. In 1968, for example, Psathas suggested the importance of cultural and situational factors and chance elements in the environment which limit women's freedom of vocational choice. Anastasi (1969) identified the blue-collar pattern, the active volunteer, the interim job, the late-blooming career, and the double-life pattern. Zytowski (1969), like Super, began his "contribution toward a theory" with the assumption that the modal role of woman is homemaker. He then identified three factors which affect female vocational development: (1) age of entry into an occupation, (2) span of participation, and (3) degree of participation. Combinations of these elements yield three different vocational patterns which he labeled the mild vocational, the moderate vocational, and the "unusual" (the latter being the career-oriented woman).

These theories are important not because they provide the last word on women's career development but because they open the doors to research and provide some beginning attempts to understand women in other than traditional stereotypic roles. They also offer support for the thesis that women's life patterns are not uniform and that a variety of life styles and multiple roles are possible, desirable, and feasible for women as well as for men.

Sex Role Socialization

There is another growing body of literature on women's growth and development that offers startling evidence of the limits on that growth. Although space does not allow detailed summary here, the studies of early sex role socialization present convincing evidence of the programming of girls and boys for prescribed roles (Hochschild, 1973; Hartley, 1960; Maccoby, 1966; Weitzman et al., 1972). The textbook messages are clear: boys are active, outdoor, strong, and breadwinners; girls are passive, dependent, weak, and homemakers; boys need to be able to be smart, to take care of themselves, boss, do a variety of jobs; girls are to stay behind, watch, wait, work puzzles, help boys, and stay home (New Jersey Commission on Women, 1972). In one book of phonics, the 21 consonants are boys, the 5 vowels are girls. The girls all have something wrong with them; when put with the consonants, the girls lose their names and their identities. One book about girls shows a dejected little girl sitting on the steps asking, almost plaintively, "What can I do?" The parallel book about boys shows a standing, active, happy boy saying, What I *can* do. Girls grow up narcissistic, asking "How will I look? What will I wear?" Boys learn early that they can be, as one pre-school book for four-to-six-year-olds suggests,

> A pirate, a sailor, a gypsy, a knight,
>
> An actor, a cowboy, a king.
>
> I'll be strong, it shouldn't take long,
>
> I'll be five by spring.

That this programming is reinforced in early childhood became evident recently at my daughter's sixth birthday party. Having bought a variety of inexpensive role-free gifts for the children to fish out of an imaginary pond, I let the children fish randomly for such toys as police set, doctor set, binoculars, jump ropes, dental set, nurse set, etc. While the game was in progress, I was surprised to find one of the girls in tears. When asked what was the matter, she replied that she had gotten a dental set and that was for boys; she wanted jewelry instead. It was interesting, however, that one of the other girls, whose father was a dentist, also had randomly fished out a dental set; she was pleased because her father wanted her to become a dentist (she was one of three daughters).

Obviously, we are not trying to force children to make choices regarding what they want to be at the tender age of six; we *do* want them to fantasize and develop their sexual identity (as different from traditional sex roles). However, such examples are significant because as studies such as those by Goodman and Schlossberg (1972) have shown children link occupations with sexes and begin the premature occupational foreclosure process early in life.

Female Self-Concepts and Aspirations

What does this early conditioning do to female self-concepts and aspirations? Matthews and Tiedeman (1964) found that girls who had expressed strong vocational goals in junior high had shifted to marriage goals in senior high although the more recent study by Rand and Miller (1972) suggested that a new cultural imperative for women was being expressed in the options perceived by girls in junior high, senior high, and college—that of the dual role of career and marriage. Other studies have cited women's lack of vocational goals and realistic planning (Lewis, 1965; Zytowski, 1969) though more recent studies, such as the follow-up study on Project Talent population, reveal girls as showing more concern for career planning and wanting more control over their own lives (Flanagan & Jung, 1971).

Horner's widely quoted study of female career motivation (1968), though recently replicated with different results (Hoffman, 1974), does give cause for reflection. Academically talented college females, asked to complete a story about "Anne, who was graduating at the top of her medical class," revealed all kinds of "fear of success" themes, fantasies that it couldn't be true—having Anne drop to eighth in the class and marrying the boy at the top; seeing her as an acne-faced bookworm experiencing feelings of rejection, loneliness, and doubts about her femininity; having her see a counselor who suggests that she try nursing, and the like. The young women simply could not cope with the image of Anne as a competent, feminine person who might be able to have a successful career and marriage. In another oft-quoted study of Broverman et al. (1970), mental health practitioners were asked to describe a mature, well-adjusted man, woman, and person. The descriptions for the well-adjusted person and well-adjusted man coincided. However, the well-adjusted woman was described as more submissive, less independent, less adventurous, more easily influenced, less aggressive, less competitive, more emotional, excitable, and vain, and less interested in science and mathematics. While the results of self-concept studies are conflicting, some of the investigations of female self-concepts have found that girls tend to devalue themselves and other girls and that both boys and girls value males more than females. These studies seem to indicate a number of factors which mitigate against women feeling very good about themselves as achieving, motivated, participating human beings.

WOMEN IN THE WORK FORCE

What happens when we move from the theoretical descriptions of women's lives and the sociological and psychological studies of their self-perceptions and aspirations to the realities of their participation in the work world? Even here the data can be somewhat shocking, especially to the high school boy or girl who may find it difficult to internalize the information. While there are numerous myths about working women, there is an abundance of data available on the nature and extent of women's participation in education and work—data gathered by occupational analysts in the U. S. Department of Labor.

Women and Employment

It is well-known, for example, that there are some 32 million working women, comprising one third of the labor force; that 42% of all women are working, over half of them married; that most women work for economic reasons; that the number of employed mothers, even those with small children, has increased; and that there is an increasing proportion of female heads of households.

We are told that the average woman marries at 20 (although some women appear to be marrying later and having fewer children), has her last child at age 26, her last child in school by 32. The average age of women in the labor force is now 42. With a life expectancy of 74 or 75, the average woman can expect to have 30-35 years after children (if she has them) are in school to develop new meaning and interests in the second half of her life. A chart prepared by the California Advisory Commission on the Status of Women presents very vividly a typical married woman's life (Figure 1). Of course there is considerable variation in work force figures, dependent on whether the woman is from a minority or poverty family, her marital status, the number of children she has, the amount of education she has, and her work motivation. But the long-range Labor Department projections are that 9 of 10 girls will marry; 8 of 10 will have children; 9 of 10 will be employed outside the home for some period of time; 6 of 10 will work full-time outside their homes for up to 30 years; 1 of 10 will be widowed before age 50; 1 of 10 will be heads of families; probably 3 of 10 will be divorced; and 1 of 5 will obtain a college degree (Impact, 1972).

Figure 1 A woman's life.

The blank half could be filled in with "vegetation," employment, political activity, community work, church or club work, etc., but should it not be filled with productivity and the utilization of talents, abilities, and interests? Do people stagnate if they don't continue to grow? What happens to a woman who hasn't worked in 20 years if she is suddenly widowed or divorced at age 43? Shouldn't the full-time homemaker's child-raising years be devoted part-time to continued education and preparation for the last half of her life? *(Prepared by California Advisory Commission on the Status of Women, 1972.)*

Occupational Distribution

One of the hard realities is that women who are working are concentrated in a few occupations; many of them low-paying, low-level and dead-end. Although the *Dictionary of Occupational Titles* has classified approximately 23,000 different occupations in the United States, one-third of all working women are concentrated in only seven of them; retail sales clerk, secretary, household worker, elementary school teacher, bookkeeper, waitress and nurse. An additional one-third are found in 20 occupations: e.g., typist, cashier, cook, telephone operator, babysitter, assembler, hairdresser, stenographer, high school teacher, practical nurse, receptionist, maid, and file clerk (Bem & Bem, 1971). Only four million women—15% of all women workers—are professional or technical workers: women comprise only 7% of the physicians, 3% of the lawyers, 1% of the engineers. The proportion of women in professional jobs has declined over the past 30 years, from 45% in 1940 to 37% in 1969. Three of four clerical workers are women. The average full-time female worker makes ⅗ of the earnings of the full-time male worker in all occupational levels and fields. A more detailed presentation of these statistics appears in Kreps' (1971) *Sex in the Marketplace: American Women at Work* and Kievit et al. (1972) *Women in the World of Work* as well as in numerous pamphlets published by the Labor Department. Such are the realities of women and work.

OBSTACLES TO THE CAREER DEVELOPMENT OF WOMEN

It must be apparent that the obstacles to the development of women are real and pervasive. While they have been alluded to, the most common ones are summarized below:

1. *Sex-Role Conditioning and Socialization.* If it is true, as appears increasingly to be so, that on many of the major variables in human development (self-concept, moral development, career aspirations, peer evaluation) female development levels off in early adolescence, counselors need to be justly concerned. The image females get of themselves through our curriculum and child-rearing practices seems to have taken hold, the self-fulfilling prophesy comes true, and 78% of women end up in the same role despite their individual differences.

2. *Role Conflicts about Fulfilling Multiple Roles in Marriage and Work.* While there is a natural expectation that men will be able to fill multiple roles of employee, husband, and father, we do not have that same expectation for women. Thus the woman who is considering both career and family may experience role conflict. Besides the fear of success and concern about femininity which Horner (1968) found, the woman may be caught between trying to vie with men in jobs, career, and business and at the same time trying to find an identity as wife, mother, and woman. She may face the problem of meeting the multiple demands on her once she has accepted multiple roles and may find she has to be a superwoman to meet those demands—to organize her time, to manage the household, to attend to her children, to have an abundance of energy—unless she has a partner who recognizes that such roles and household tasks can be shared. If she

has small children, she may be criticized for not spending enough time with them—although the literature on the employed mother suggests that her children are no less well-adjusted than other children, that they are more independent, that they have more career aspirations and, when asked to name the person they would most like to be like, most frequently mention their mother (Bem & Bem, 1971).

Counselors increasingly must recognize that women's development is both a male and female concern, for when women increase their participation in work and community the lives of men and families will be affected. The problems of the re-entry woman with children, for example, may include the way in which her husband and children cope with her transition from a traditional to a contemporary woman. Problems associated with the changing roles and status of women require not only (1) the resocialization of men's attitudes towards women's roles, as Farrell suggests, but (2) the resocialization of women's attitudes towards men's roles and (3) of women's attitudes towards women's roles. As we move toward an androgynous society, we may see a greater variety of life patterns—the equal partnership marriage, in which both partners have professional careers and share that part of their career that is in the home; the two-person career, in which one job or appointment is shared by two partners who want to work 20 hours or so and have more time for other parts of their lives; the extended family, in which members develop alternative life patterns for work and family and leisure; or the single parent, who prefers not to marry but adopts a child. One of the ways we can reduce the role conflicts is to be more accepting of a variety of life patterns and life styles.

3. *Focus on Marriage or Its Prospect.* We know that the modal role is still marriage, in spite of increasing choices of the single life. But we as educators and parents need to make our young men and women aware of the fact that life does not end at 40 and that Prince Charming is not going to take care of his Princess forever. The modern fairy tale of "Atalanta" in *Free to Be You and Me* provides an excellent antidote to this myth. Young people need to be made aware of those last 25 to 35 years of a woman's life and to do some conscious planning for their preferred life style. Consistently studies have shown that girls lack planfulness, that they tend not to seek occupational information, that they lack realistic educational-occupational plans. If it is true that both boys and girls "do not know what information they need, do not have what they want, and cannot use what they have," we as counselors have a responsibility to help them get this information, to use it, and to internalize it in terms of their own goals, plans, abilities, preferred life styles, and self-images.

4. *Lack of Work Orientation.* While junior high girls and upward are beginning to see themselves in multiple roles, especially dual roles of career and marriage, women simply are not as work oriented as men, nor are they expected to be. Working outside the home in the past has not been as central to women as to men, and those who have career motives at the head of their motivational hierarchy are labeled "unusual" as Zytowski (1969) suggests. Concern for women's career development is not a movement to get every woman into the labor force

but, rather, a concern for her uniqueness and individuality as a person and for her right to have some freedom of choice in both her personal and work life. It is concern about the overwhelmingly subordinate nature of women's roles—as nurses rather than doctors, teachers rather than principals, assembly workers rather than supervisors, secretaries rather than bosses, bank tellers rather than lending officers, administrative assistants rather than deans. It is concern about the ancillary nature of women's careers, with only small numbers in banking, engineering, medicine, and management. It is concern about the passivity and dependence that keep her from finding room at the top even if she has ability. It is concern about fear of competency that keeps her from maximizing her potentials and from making what Tyler (1972) has called first-class rather than second-class contributions to society. It is concern about the complexity of demands, pressures, and conflicts facing women at different life stages and the limited reward system which denies them the range of options and rewards available to men. What counselors need to do here has to do with changing self-concepts and expectations, opening up opportunities, and upgrading aspirations so that more talented women will be able to say not "What can I *do*?" but "What I *can* do."

5. *Sexism and Sex Discrimination.* While it is true that some of the barriers between women's work and men's work are being broken down, the discrimination in hiring, wages, and promotion is still very real, affirmative action programs notwithstanding. The problems of conscious and nonconscious sexism (Bem & Bem, 1971) are as prevalent in education as in other parts of society. The Minnesota Board of Education passed a position paper offering nine suggestions for what school systems could do in "Eliminating Sex Bias in Education." There was little action in implementation until the Human Rights Division hired a person to coordinate implementation efforts around the state. Areas of concern include athletic budgets, promotion to administrative positions, curriculum texts and materials, counseling, career education, and the like. As educators, we need to look at ways in which we perpetuate discrimination and sexism through our actions, inactions, and even denials that a problem exists.

PRACTICAL APPROACHES TO FACILITATE FEMALE CAREER DEVELOPMENT

One of the things we know from organizational change literature is that it is futile to offer solutions before people recognize there is a problem. Unfortunately, to many parents and educators in higher education as well as K-12 settings, concern about women's career development is still considered a "ha-ha." It is an assumption of this paper that counselors view it as more than a "ha-ha."

Counselor Attitudes

Counselors have been indicted in the professional literature as being sexist. While we need much more data on this (and I do not assume that counselors are any more or less sexist than people in general), several studies have supported these charges. Thomas and Stewart (1971) found that secondary school counselors responded more positively to female clients with traditional (feminine) goals than to female clients with deviant (masculine) goals. Pietrofesa and Schlossberg (1973) found differences in counselor attitudes toward women entering "masculine" occupations. Fridersdorf (1973) examined attitudes of male and female secondary counselors toward college-bound and noncollege-bound girls and found males with more traditional expectations about female occupational choices. Bingham and House (1973a) found counselors to be misinformed on women's occupational status (on such issues as women in the work force, discrimination against women, income discrepancies, and the probability of women getting leadership jobs). Male counselors were found to be less well informed than female counselors (on such issues as the occupational alternatives needed by women, their general ability, women's ability to fill both worker and mother roles, and length of time in labor force). In a follow-up study on counselor attitudes toward women and work, the investigators (1973b) found that substantial numbers of male counselors had negative attitudes and agreed with such statements as "training women for high-level jobs is wasteful," "married men should receive more pay than single women doing the same work," and "boys should be better educated than girls." They also felt that motherhood is the primary function of woman. Hawley's study (1972), in contrast, suggested that female counselors hold a wider view of the roles of women. Such studies point up the need for counselors to become aware of their own attitudes and practices and ways in which these limit options for female clients.

Counseling Interventions

While the role of the counselor in school and college is changing in certain ways, it is likely that one-to-one counseling and group counseling procedures will still persist. Counselors can play a critical part (but not the only part) in counseling both boys and girls and men and women for changing roles in society. Matthews et al. (1972) have addressed themselves to the importance of counseling girls and women over the life span, from infancy through mature adulthood and old age. Tyler (1972) stressed the need for all individuals at various life stages to have counseling available regarding their multi-potentialities. Below are suggested a few counseling strategies that might help make a positive difference in the lives of females.

1. We need to become aware of our own conscious and nonconscious attitudes, expectations, and practices in the counseling interview.

There are a number of subtle and not-so-subtle things we do both verbally and nonverbally in our counseling that communicate to boys and girls what is acceptable or appropriate and what is not. In our interviews, how do we react when a girls says she wants to become a pilot, an engineer, or an auto mechanic? How do we help girls plan and choose their school courses and programs with open options? By the same token, how do we react when a boy says he wants to be a nurse? How much do our own sex-role stereotypes and expectations affect our counseling behavior? Among the things we might do to counteract our biases is to help females think of themselves as persons, to affirm their sense of personal worth, to face and work through their identity and role conflicts, to learn to say *"I can."* We need to be aware of the development stage the woman is at in her life span and "where she is coming from" as a person and as a woman.

2. We need to become increasingly aware of sex bias in guidance materials, tests and inventories, and our own bias in interpreting and using those materials.

Schlossberg and Goodman (1972) have called attention to the channeling that can occur through use of biased interest inventories. The National Institute of Education (NIE) sponsored a national conference on this topic, resulting in a manual of "Guidelines for Assessment of Sex Bias and Sex Fairness in Career Interest Inventories" (NIE, 1974). It seems to me counselors have to be equally sensitive to other kinds of instruments, especially in career planning and exploration. A recent study by Birk, Cooper, and Tanney (1973) of illustrations in an array of career literature—including the *Occupational Outlook Handbook*, the *Encyclopedia of Careers and Vocational Guidance*, Volumes I and II, 1972, and the Science Research Associates Occupational Briefs, 1973—revealed the same kinds of racial and sexual stereotypes that have been found in the children's textbooks and picture books: women and minorities appeared only infrequently in comparison with white males and often were in passive, helping, subordinate roles. If there is one major area in which counselors have been criticized, it is in our selection, use, and interpretation of tests, earlier with minorities and more recently with women; we would be well advised to examine our own test interpretation practices and to help eliminate from use those that are clearly biased in the way they present opportunities for men and women in the world of work.

3. We need to know and help clients obtain accurate information about trends both in the world of work and in the larger society.

We have to do a better job not only of getting accurate information ourselves but of helping boys and girls get the information they need and to use it. They need information about themselves, the labor force (present and projected), work environments, alternatives, and decision processes. Because of this expectation of marriage and the Prince Charming myth, many girls do not seek education-occupational information. Presumably if one is seeking a job merely as a stopgap until marriage, one does not need much information. When examining the human life cycle of woman today and the second half of her life, ask what kind of information does she need? When, how, and under what circumstances do we get across the reality of what is happening to the woman in American society—that she may be working 25-35 years out of her life even if she marries and takes time out for childbearing? And how do boys obtain and react to that same kind of information? How do we help him and her to internalize the information? One way might be to provide group guidance and group counseling experiences in which boys and girls can talk together about these trends and what they mean in relation to both male and female goals and roles and family patterns and the possible androgynous society of the future.

4. We need to help young men and women become increasingly aware of the

options available to them in a pluralistic society—in education, occupation, life styles, and career patterns.

We may have to help both boys and girls think through and plan for the multiple roles they may have as workers and parents. They need to be aware of the variety of life styles and family and work patterns from which they can choose and of potential conflicts involved in choosing one pattern over another (e.g., single life, multiple children, two-person career, dual career without children, etc.). Particularly, we need to help female clients consider a wide range of educational and occupational options in addition to the traditional stereotypic ones. This becomes extremely important at a time when the traditional options, such as teaching, for example, are becoming less available. Society is beginning to realize that college is not the only road to success and that other excellent opportunities exist in such institutions as vocational-technical schools. With the small percentages of women in the skilled trades, we should encourage adolescent girls to explore new and emerging training programs and occupations and expose them to contact with women in atypical fields. While we need competent secretaries, teachers, and nurses (of both sexes), we do not want women programmed into limited types, numbers, or levels of occupations; we want to help female clients choose from that larger pool of alternatives those appropriate to their abilities, goals, interests, and motivations.

5. We need to help young men and women learn the processes involved in decision-making.

If counselors really are concerned about human development, they have to help each individual, regardless of race, sex, or age, to know that s/he can choose in accord with his or her values, abilities, motivations, and preferences from a variety of life options. Clients need to be helped to explore the alternatives, the probability and possibility of achieving the alternatives, and the consequences of choices they make for both themselves and the significant others in their lives. They need to be able to examine themselves as risk-takers, to critically evaluate the information about self and options, and to synthesize or integrate it as they think about themselves in relation to society. They need to be encouraged to challenge traditional assumptions and expectancies about roles and to realize that changing women's opportunities for different life patterns also have implications for work, family, and leisure patterns of men.

The problems of decision-making for women have been cited often in the professional literature—the lack of planning orientation; the fear of loss of femininity if she chooses a career; the shift from vocational goals to marriage goals from junior to senior high; the assumption of marriage as the modal role and not perceiving the dual roles of marriage and work (or other patterns) as viable options. All of these contribute to the view that females do not have choices or decisions to make, that they do not have alternatives to choose from since they are programmed from early childhood for the one option of marriage and motherhood. If females are to develop their potentials to reduce the gap between what they do and what they can do, counselors must help them know and be able to choose and decide from diverse life patterns, from traditional nuclear family to single parent to single person to dichotomous or multiple roles; they need to be helped to know that they can have goals of their own and an identity of their own.

6. We need to provide female clients with a variety of role models with whom they can identify and from whom they can learn that multiple roles are possible, desirable, and real.

The importance of putting females in touch with women who are in nontraditional roles cannot be overemphasized. Many of the early and late adolescents we counsel today are familiar only with the female image to which they have been exposed at home, in their school books, and in the media. Counselors can help broaden their views and expose them to wider options by helping identify women in the school and community who have chosen all kinds of career and family patterns.

7. We need to involve parents more systematically and developmentally in the career development process of boys and girls.

Since parents still have the greatest impact on their children's self-concepts, goals, attitudes, and aspirations, it is exceedingly important they be oriented to the facts about the life span of women, changes in the labor force, the need for career planning for girls, and the trends in work and family. Orientation and information groups for parents regarding the development of women's potentials might be one vehicle; perhaps what we need is a career development counterpart to parent effectiveness training called CDTP, Career Development Training for Parents.

These are just a few strategies we might use as counselors to become facilitators not only of female career development but of the development of all human beings for a variety of life roles.

CURRICULUM INTERVENTIONS

The foregoing suggest modifications of traditional counselor roles in interviewing, in test interpretation, in career information, and in parent counseling. The other major thrust toward which counselors are moving today is a more central and direct involvement with curriculum, particularly through working with teachers in new ways. There seems to be a lot of support at every level of the educational process for counselors to move in the direction of outreach programs, to become a part of the mainstream of the teaching-learning process, and to take active leadership in changing the school system to more effectively promote the positive growth and development of students.

Career development or guidance-based career education offers an excellent vehicle for counselors to have some significant inputs. Since women, like minorities, by and large have been outside the educational and opportunity structure, special attention of counselors needs to be directed at this point in time to helping to eliminate the barriers and open up more opportunities. In a recent non-yet-finalized APGA Position Paper on "Counselor Role in Career Education," Hoyt (1974) recommends leadership in eliminating sexism and racism in career opportunity as one of six major counselor roles.

Elsewhere I have presented a career development conceptual framework for facilitating female growth (Hansen, 1974a). I would like to summarize it here. Such a framework is totally appropriate if one accepts the broad definition of career development as self-development over the life span. In our work on the Career Development Curriculum (CDC) at the University of Minnesota, Wes Tennyson, Mary Klaurens, and I have built on the concept of career development as a lifelong process of self-clarification, as a consequence of positions one holds in a lifetime, as the various choices and decisions one makes to implement a life style, and the ways work and leisure fit in with the kind of person one perceives herself or himself to be. This definition assumes that consideration of work is intimately related to family roles and patterns and to matters of career-marriage conflict and commitment. Drawing from career development theorists and developmental psychology, the definition includes such career management tasks as developing positive self-concepts, gaining control over one's life, and maximizing vocational possibilities; such goals as awareness of self, awareness of preferred life styles, formulation of tentative career goals, clarification of the decision process, obtaining employability skills, interpersonal skills, a sense of planfulness, and commitment with tentativeness within a changing world (Tennyson, Hansen, Klaurens, in press).

A Conceptual Framework

The CDC is a comprehensive unified curriculum model, presently K-12, to be used by counselors and teachers in implementing career education programs. An interdisciplinary staff refined a set of career management tasks for the primary, intermediate, junior high, and senior high years, developed performance objectives appropriate for the various life stages, and suggested enabling objectives to reach them. A number of supplementary objectives relating to emerging life patterns of women were incorporated into the curriculum model, many of them relating to men as well. The objectives provide a framework for sequential, developmental experiences for boys and girls, a guide from which resourceful teachers and counselors can create their own lesson plans and learning activities. Although there are many innovative women's programs, units, and courses emerging throughout the country at various levels of school systems, few have attempted to build their efforts around a theoretical framework of career development. Since the CDC is only a conceptual model (intended for students in general), the intervention strategies have yet to be developed. A few resource guides for teachers and counselors are available under such titles as "Life Styles and Work," "Self-Concept Exploration," "Women and the World of Work," "Significant Others," "Value Identification," and "The Social Contribution of Work" (Minnesota Department of Education, 1972).

Intervention Strategies

Several educators have suggested a variety of curriculum interventions which could be tied to developmental goals. In a recent article (1972) I urged that counselors work with teachers in creating, planning, and teaching units aimed at the career development of females in the elementary, junior high, and senior high. Among suggestions for the elementary years were positive reinforcement and hands-on experiences with tools, auto mechanics, home maintenance, and political leadership; putting girls and boys in contact with atypical role models to help females gain the political savvy they need to assure equal opportunity; equal assignment of chores and leadership tasks; and utilization of both male and female community resource persons and media to show the work that humans do.

At the junior high we can use such strategies as helping teachers provide broad exploratory action-oriented experiences to introduce both sexes to the vocational and avocational implications of subjects; continued exposure to atypical role models both directly and through resource directories and multimedia; strength groups in which both boys and girls focus on potentials and develop action plans to become the kinds of persons they would like to be. Elimination of sex-linked courses in home economics and industrial arts is essential to keeping educational paths open to all kinds of occupations. Values clarification experiences, cross-age teaching, and tryout experiences tutoring young children can increase awareness of work opportunities and satisfactions.

At the senior high we need to help girls and boys continue their values clarification and examine their needs, drives, goals, interests, and abilities as they face real decisions about life style preferences and life patterns. They need information about the reality of discrimination, trends in the work force, stereotypes, and sexism. Apprentice or shadowing experiences with a variety of role models in preferred occupations and tryout tasks will help them reality test their preferences and tentative decisions. They need more specific information about educational paths and exposure to vocational specialties or college majors related to subjects in which they have a continuing interest and success. Direct courses in Psychology of Self, Psychology of Interpersonal Relations, and Psychology of Careers as well as Women's Studies can facilitate such development. Life Planning Labs in which students have an intensive opportunity to examine values, potentials, goals, and priorities can also be helpful, as could a variety of well planned consciousness-raising and role reversal exercises. Strategies summarized by the author include infusion through curriculum, exploratory work experience (paid and unpaid), career resource centers and multimedia approaches, hands-on experiences, role models, counseling, cross-age teaching, and staff development.

Mitchell (1972) recommended that the miseducation of girls might be redressed through a variety of curriculum strategies not unlike those already mentioned. She also recommends special training for counselors to eliminate sexism in career counseling. Simpson (1972) offered 11 specific steps in "Career Education—Feminine Version," including efforts by elementary educators to enlarge girls' vocational self-concepts; a variety of single and married role models; new curriculum materials portraying women in a variety of constructive life styles and occupational roles; teacher orientation to vocational preparation of women; women's history courses in social studies; training programs including opportunity to prepare for dual roles; and alternatives and supplements to in-school instruction related to vocational preparation.

Practitioner Examples

A number of creative teachers and counselors have moved beyond the conceptual level and have developed units, courses, and strategies for promoting female development. A few examples are presented here.

Ann Schmid, a fourth grade teacher, uses "the teachable moment" to help her children become sensitive to sexism and sex-role stereotyping in their readers and other curriculum materials. They wrote letters of protest to Hallmark regarding ways in which boys and girls were portrayed on greeting cards; they examined their illustrated *ABC of Occupations* book and rewrote it when they found stereotypic presentations of occupations (A as in Astronaut, B as in Beautician) with new illustrations. Both boys and girls work at the tool bench, bake cakes, rewrite stereotyped materials, and interview workers in non-traditional occupations.

Suzanne Laurich, a first grade teacher, in a series of career development lessons has boys and girls look at such topics as "Who Am I?" "Workers Who Come to Our Home," "Our Parents' Jobs," "Day Workers and Night Workers," and "What I Can Do" in nonstereotypic ways.

Ronnie Tallen and Claire Allyn helped boys and girls get more in touch with their own feelings, values, and self-concepts through a three-week unit on Male and Female Images. Students learned to analyze sex-role images on TV, in newspapers, and on radio; read fact and fiction, biographies and autobiographies; did independent study on women's issues (including the school's athletic policies); studied women in nontraditional occupations; interviewed workers in sex-typed occupations; and even analyzed their teachers' and parents' sexist language. Anne Saxenmeyer taught a Women's Liberation Unit directly in her ninth grade civics class. A counselor and a teacher, Georgia Loughren and Helen Olson, teamed to develop a three-week group counseling course on Women in the '70s. Students built a support system and looked at their own attitudes and expectations through a variety of awareness exercises, did some values voting regarding their attitudes about women's roles, and were exposed to a variety of role models through class visitors and field interviews—e.g., the traditional homemaker, the dual career, the two-career family, the single adoptive parent, the single career woman.

Two senior high social studies teachers teamed to create a unit on Women in History under the Minnesota Council on Quality Education. Students investigate several facets of the role and status of women and look at the issues critically. A senior high counselor created a questionnaire for faculty to look at their own attitudes toward women's roles; another created a model for a faculty workshop on sexism in education; a group of counselors and teachers developed an interdisciplinary program called Women's Seminar in which senior women (and later senior men by their own request) spent 10 three-hour weekly sessions looking at women's changing roles and human sexuality. Another senior high counselor developed a Women in Literature course intended to facilitate female development by studying the lives of women who had functioned at higher levels of development based on the Kohlberg Scales of Moral Development and Loevinger Scales of Ego Strength. Erickson (1973) through a curriculum intervention found that it was possible to promote female growth through a positive program designed for that purpose.

Besides the K-12 efforts there has been a burgeoning of activity to promote female development at the post-high level, particularly on college and university campuses. Besides the traditional counseling, these interventions have taken such forms as women's resource centers; courses on assertive training, career planning, and women's search for identity; personal assessment and career planning groups; courses for the mature or adult student, women's support groups (counseling groups, job-seeking groups, feminist groups, human sexuality groups), and special seminars and conferences, women's study programs, creation of alternate study options, and the like; research topics related to women's development; units on sexism in human relations courses; creation of multimedia presentations and video cassettes for training of counselors; and creating and evaluating intervention models.

THE TASK FOR COUNSELORS

It is probably safe to say that we have just begun to chip away at the top of the iceberg of the enormous problems and implications of counseling and career development of girls and women. The topic, like the larger career development area itself, is still unfinished business; there is much we need to know about female career patterns, self-concepts, aspirations, and decisions. And yet we know enough to chart some humanistic paths which will lead to greater options and genuine freedom of choice for both men and women. The following poems express the essence of my concern—the first a negative example, the second a positive one.

Following is a song students are asked to learn in a career education program in a junior high school, sung to the tune "Jingle Bells":

> Styling hair, styling hair
> To make you gals look neat,
> So that hubbies when at home
> Will see their wives look neat.
> Fixing twirls, fixing swirls,
> Maybe a French bob,
> Don't let feminine society
> Look like crummy slobs.

Besides being bad poetry, this is not career education but career miseducation. This is not what we are about as teachers and counselors involved in career development programs. In contrast, the following poem appeared a few years ago in an elementary level career development project which offered a variety of methods to help children gain more positive self-concepts, to upgrade their aspirations, to feel good about themselves. The poem appeared on the cover of the project booklet.

DISCOVERY: A CHILD'S FIRST AWARENESS OF HERSELF

She looks into the mirror with eager eyes,
And all the world is bells, and she is wise.
The wonder of herself she sees therein.
And longs to play the world's violin.

Her name is written and no turning tide
Will wash it from the sand or oceans wide.
She feeds on knowledge and her mind is stirred,
Fed on the beauty of a thought, a word.

Where she must walk, a slant of light has shown,
Knowledge is the lamp her heart has known.
And when she thinks of all her eyes might find,
She says, "Quickly, pull the cord and lift the blind."

Adapted from Kaleen Sherman

This poem, adapted from Kaleen Sherman, is a beautiful expression of the openness to life, to knowledge, to growth that a child feels. And yet we do something to females in our society as they grow up, something that keeps the blinds drawn on many of their possibilities and potentialities.

When I say "adapted," I should hasten to explain that the poem originally was written using "he." But isn't it equally beautiful and equally meaningful with "she"? It is exciting to think what we as counselors could do, even with some slight changes, a few facts, some innovative approaches, and a commitment to open the blinds of the school and eliminate our own biases to promote the positive growth and career development of our female clients along with our male clients.

REFERENCES

Anastasi, A. "Sex Differences in Vocational Choices." *National Catholic Conference Journal, 13* (4), 1969 (63–76).

Bem, S. J. & Bem, D. J. "Training the Woman to Know Her Place: The Social Antecedents of Women in the World of Work." Palo Alto, California: Stanford University, 1971 (mimeo).

Bingham, W. C. & House, E. "Counselors View Women and Work: Accuracy of Information." *The Vocational Guidance Quarterly,*1973a (262–268).

Bingham, W. C. & House, E. "Counselors' Attitudes toward Women and Work." *Vocational Guidance Quarterly, 22,* 1973b (16–23).

Birk, J., Cooper, J. & Tanney, F. "Racial and Sex Role Stereotyping." In "Career Information Illustration." College Park: University of Maryland, 1973 (mimeo).

Broverman, I. K. et al. "Sex-Role Stereotypes and Clinical Judgments of Mental Health." *Journal of Consulting and Clinical Psychology, 34,* 1970 (1–7).

Erickson, L. V. "Personal Growth for Women: A Cognitive-Developmental Curriculum." University of Minnesota, March, 1973 (mimeo).

Flanagan, John D. & Jung, Steven M. *Progress in Education: A Sample Survey* (1960–1970). Palo Alto: American Institutes for Research, December, 1971.

Friedersdorf, N. "A Comparative Study of Counselor Attitudes toward the Further Educational and Vocational Plans of High School Girls." Paper delivered at American Personnel and Guidance Convention, San Diego, February, 1973.

Goodman, J. & Schlossberg, N. K. "A Woman's Place: Children's Sex Stereotyping of Occupations." *Vocational Guidance Quarterly, 20,* 1972 (226–270).

Hansen, L. Sunny. "We Are Furious (Female) But We Can Shape Our Own Development." *Personnel & Guidance Journal, 51,* October, 1972 (87–93).

Hansen, L. S. "A Career Development Curriculum Framework to Promote Female Growth." In M. A. Guttman & P. Donn (Eds.) *Women and ACES—Perspective and Issues.* Washington, D.C.: Association for Counselor Education and Supervision, 1974a.

Hansen, L. S. "The Career Development Process for Women: Current Views and Programs." In T. Hoshenshil (Ed.) *Career Development of Women.* Conference Proceedings, Virginia Polytechnic Institute, Blacksburg, Va., March 7–8, 1974b.

Hartley, R. E. "Children's Concepts of Male and Female Roles." *Merrill-Palmer Quarterly, 6,* 1960 (83–91).

Hawley, P. Perceptions of Male Models of Femininity Related to Career Choice. *Journal of Counseling Psychology, 19,* 1972 (308–313).

Hochschild, A. R. "A Review of Sex Role Research." In J. Huber (Ed.) *Changing Women in a Changing Society. American Journal of Sociology, 4,* 1973 (1011–1029).

Hoffman, L. "Replication of the Matina Horner Study." In D. McGuigan (Ed.), *New Research on Women.* Ann Arbor, Michigan: University of Michigan, 1974.

Horner, M. S. "Women's Will to Fail." *Psychology Today,* 1968 (36–38).

Hoyt, Kenneth B. "The Counselor's Role in Career Education." APGA Position Paper presented at National APGA Convention, New Orleans, Louisiana, March 11, 1974 (mimeo).

Impact. When I Grow Up I Want to Be Married. California Commission on the Status of Women, 1972 (simulation game).

Kievit, Mary Bach. *Review and Synthesis of Research on Women in the World of Work.* Columbus, Ohio: The Center for Vocational and Technical Education, The Ohio State University, 1972.

Kreps, Juanita. *Sex in the Marketplace: American Women at Work.* Baltimore: Johns Hopkins Press, 1971.

Lewis, E. C. "Counselors and Girls." *Journal of Counseling Psychology, 12,* 1965 (159–166).

Maccoby, E. E. "Sex Differences in Intellectual Functioning." In E. E. Maccoby (Ed.), *The Development of Sex Differences.* Stanford, California: Stanford University Press, 1966.

Matthews, E. E. & Tiedeman, D. "Attitudes toward Careers and Marriage and the Development of Life Style in Young Women." *Journal of Counseling Psychology, 11,* 1964 (375–384).

Matthews, E. E. et al. *Counseling Girls and Women over the Life Span.* Washington, D.C.: National Vocational Guidance Association, 1972 (375–384).

Minnesota Department of Education. *Career Education Resource Guides.* Seven Learning Packages, 1972.

Mitchell, E. "What About Career Education for Girls?" *Educational Leadership,* December, 1972 (233–236).

National Institute of Education. *Guidelines for Assessment of Sex Bias and Sex Fairness in Career Interest Inventories.* Washington, D.C. Department of Health, Education, and Welfare, 1974.

New Jersey Commission on Status of Women. *Dick and Jane as Victims.* Princeton, New Jersey, 1972.

Pietrofesa, J. J. & Schlossberg, N. K. "Perspectives on Counseling Bias: Implications for Counselor Education." *The Counseling Psychologist, 4,* No. 1, 1973 (44–54). (Special issue on Counseling Women)

Psathas, G. "Toward a Theory of Occupational Choice for Women." *Sociology and Social Research, 52,* 1968 (253–268).

Rand, Lorraine & Miller, Anna. A Developmental Sectioning of Women's Careers and Marriage Attitudes and Life Plans. *Journal of Vocational Behavior, 2,* 1972 (317–331).

Schlossberg, N. K. & Goodman, J. "Imperative for Change: Counselor Use of the Strong Vocational Interest Blanks." *Impact, 2,* 1972 (26–29).

Simpson, E. J. "Career Education—Feminine Version." Paper presented at Regional Seminar/Workshop on *Women in the World of Work,* Technical Education Research Centers, Chicago, Illinois, October, 1972.

Super, Donald E. *The Psychology of Careers.* New York: Harper Brothers, 1957.

Tennyson, W. Wesley; Hansen, L. S.; Klaurens, M. K. & Antholz, M. B. *Teaching and Counseling for Career Development.* St. Paul: Minnesota Department of Education, in press.

Thomas, H. & Stewart, N. R. Counselor Response to Female Clients with Deviate and Conforming Career Goals. *Journal of Counseling Psychology, 18,* 1971 (352–357).

Tyler, L. E. "Counseling Girls and Women in the Year 2000." In E. Matthews (Ed.) *Counseling Girls and Women over the Life Span.* Washington, D.C.: National Vocational Guidance Association, 1972 (89–96).

Weitzman, L. J. et al. "Sex-Role Socialization in Picture Books for Pre-School Children." *American Journal of Sociology, 77,* 1972 (1125–1150).

Zytowski, D. G. "Toward a Theory of Career Development for Women." *Personnel and Guidance Journal, 47,* 1969 (660–664).

25. Career Counseling with Men. The Shifting Focus

James I. Morgan, Thomas M. Skovholt, and James M. Orr, Jr.

Because of the ever increasing complexity of the Western world and the relatively new emphasis on equal rights for all kinds of groups, the traditional career roles and expectations of men have begun to change. The success of the women's movement has brought into sharper focus role expectations for both men and women in our society. Accepted career roles are less clear-cut than at any time in the past. We are now becoming aware that men as well as women have special career problems needing special attention.

THE EVOLUTION OF THE MALE ROLE

Historically, work has been at the center of men's identities, and often their whole worth has been inextricably intertwined with it. Jourard (1971) commented on the fact that many men in our society, following retirement, frequently disintegrate and die not long after they assume a new life of leisure. Few, if any, vocational roles seem in any way biologically ordained, although it is probably true that many vocational roles have become traditionally male or female primarily because of physiological differences such as reproductive capacity, strength, and stamina. As industrialization has increased, especially in the past century, physical prowess has come to mean less and less as a basis for differentiating between the work of women and men. The power of the earned wage—and therefore of the wage earner—has come to be the chief distinguishing characteristic of the male role. Through their vocations and their earnings, men have until recently maintained the position of head of the household.

The Depression of the 1930s dispelled the notion of the male as the sole economic support of the American family. Women worked because there was no work for men (Steinman and Fox, 1974). World War II showed beyond doubt that women were fully capable to perform much of the hard physical labor that previously had been the sole domain of men. Yet after the war, most women returned to their role of "housewives" because of the *still* strong belief that when a woman works outside the house, the husband is an inadequate provider (Steinman and Fox, 1974). From World War II onward, however, women as a group were aware of their new vocational and educational possibilities. They could aspire to careers which had not been open to them before, and to some degree they have been successful, although equal pay for equal work, equal access to promotions, and other factors are still to be resolved. Vocationally, women now have a place to go—toward formerly male-dominated occupations. For every three men planning to enter the traditionally male fields of business—engineering, law, and medicine—there is now one woman planning the same career. The ratio was eight to one just ten years ago (Flanders, 1977). Women may also choose from among traditionally female occupations.

NO PLACE TO GO

In contrast, men have no place to go. The historic division of labor whereby women have given birth and raised children during their adult lives and men have served as warriors, food gatherers, and wage earners has gradually changed, and is still changing. Raising young children is less and less the full-time adult occupation of women. Househusbands are probably little more than a contemporary occupational novelty. Likewise, the traditionally female occupations like secretarial work, elementary school teaching, and nursing offer men low pay, low status, and doubts about their masculinity.

Sexism affects men when they try to cross sex-typed occupational boundaries just as it does women. A recent Associated Press story in the *Charlotte Observer* (1977) tells of a man who has complained to a state Division of Human Rights about a prestigious secretarial school which "made only long-delayed, inadequate and insincere efforts to place [him] in a secretarial position" because, a school official said, employers wanted secretaries who wore "cute skirts—or words to that effect." The man who elects to be a homemaker, and who earns no income, is considered strange, even if the spouse's income is more than adequate for their needs.

Cohen and Bunker (1975) found that job recruiters at two university placement offices discriminated against both females and males in recruitment interviews when the applicants were applying for job positions against the traditional sex orientation. Individuals applying for sex-role–incongruent jobs had to be perceived as more qualified, in a task-oriented sense, in order to be hired for the job. Thus, for men there are few *new* occupational options. Women are entering the traditional jobs held by men, and men are continuing in them as well—but with much greater competition than ever before.

Some contemporary authors have noted a movement from a male-dominated career pattern to a male-and-female–shared breadwinner role in this country (Ginzberg, 1973; Steinman and Fox, 1974; Hoffman, 1977). By 1972 over 50 percent of women with school-aged children and husbands present were employed. Over 36 percent of women with pre-school–aged children and husbands present were employed. Husbands of working women help more with household tasks, including child rearing, than husbands of nonworking women (Hoffman, 1977). The direct career implications of these changes for men are unclear. Perhaps men will begin to welcome this increased opportunity to engage in more parenting and begin to place less emphasis on occupational achievement as *the* criterion of self-worth. And there is little question that for many men occupation success *is* the sole criterion of self worth. In her book *Passages*, Sheehy studied Americans as they passed from one life stage, or crisis, to another. She found that while women tend to recount the first half of their lives in terms of attachment to and detachment from people, men "reconstruct their tracks according to the career line they follow" (Sheehy, 1977, p. 167).

It is probably fair to observe that most men compete with other men to climb the occupational ladder. As in any hierarchy, there are few at the top and many at the bottom. This is unfortunate, since women as well as men often seem to engage in what Gould (1973) calls "measuring masculinity by the size of the paychecks." In a classic study, Lopeta (in Brenton, 1966, p. 172–173) found that wives value their husbands most as breadwinners, with the role of father second, and husband third. In the 1977 "Welcome Week" edition of the University of Minnesota student newspaper, the *Minnesota Daily* (Stempel, 177), one male reporter writes to male readers describing favorite techniques for picking up women in local bars. A favorite successful technique is the casual use of an American Express credit card to lure women students looking for financially successful males.

Work titles are also worn as badges of success. Commonly, the title of doctor or lawyer holds more prestige and is seen as having more worth than that of mechanic or plumber. The pressure to achieve this kind of worth can be tremendous, and is evidenced by the fact that the large majority of students, both male and female, currently entering colleges and universities say that they intend to major in medicine or law, even though the chances for their acceptance in these areas of study grow less and less almost daily. It is hoped that as new options for men develop, there will be more avenues for them to earn self-esteem. Unfortunately, many men are still caught up in the traditional self-worth equation: *Occupational success equals high self-esteem.*

The fact that changes have already occurred in this society with regard to the male as the sole breadwinner offers some promise for new flexibility in men's career possibilities. It is certain that both male and female children in households where the parents are both employed have more varied role models to observe than if only one parent is employed. One of the interesting prospects of having two wage earners in the family is that it opens up the possibility of more career changes for men. Dealing with this new flexibility can be an experience of great joy *and* great consternation. Great joy results from new opportunities. For the first time a man may have a chance to stop working a second job, or a chance to take a paternity leave to be at home for a short period with a new baby. He may have a chance to go to school again for training in a new field. The presence of two wage earners in one family lessens the pressures experienced by the primary wage earner; usually the male.

Great consternation results from new demands and changing responsibilities. Men feel uncomfortable dating women who are their intellectual equals (Komarovsky, 1973). How do these men now resolve the issue of professional competition with their wives? Whose career receives priority? If the wife receives a new professional opportunity in a distant location, does the family move? Dual-career couples must also resolve issues concerning child care and household responsibilities. Who will raise the children? Who will prepare meals? Who will maintain the automobile, paint the house, or wash the kitchen floor? Old divisions of labor must be renegotiated; hence, great consternation.

WHAT CAREER SPECIALISTS CAN DO

Examine Counseling Approaches   Career specialists may need to reexamine existing theories of career development and occupational choice. Career counseling theories, being by necessity general explanations of career behavior, have nothing specific to say about the special problems men encounter. There is also a growing recognition that for the individual client career choice is not a completely rational, systematic process or event (Holland, 1973; Dolliver & Nelson, 1975; Baumgardner, 1977; Morgan & Skovholt, 1977). This, of course, does not mean that the career specialist's approach needs to be nonrational; only that the specialist must recognize that personal attitudes, including role expectations, may heavily influence a man's career choices. The career specialist should be equally concerned with helping the male client explore these attitudes as with helping him learn to use occupational information, test scores, programs of training, and the like. Two structured and nonsexist ways to accomplish this are through the use of a vocational card-sort technique (Dewey, 1974a) and guided fantasy activities (Morgan & Skovholt, 1977). These techniques have the advantage of being task-relevant, structured and yet open-ended, novel, and fun for client and counselor alike. Professional journals routinely carry many articles describing other techniques with similar goals.

Career specialists should also actively dispute certain commonly held assumptions about when and how career choices *ought* to be made. Holland (1973) claims that only about 30 percent of the population requires extensive career counseling services, and that these services should be tailored or adopted to a person's special vocational needs and to the special populations institutions serve. Powell and Driscoll (1973) note that a trained, but only recently unemployed, man needs a list of jobs rather than counseling. A qualified man who has been unemployed for a longer period of time might require extensive counseling.

Deal With Their Own Sex-role Stereotyping   Sex-role stereotypes are "consensual beliefs about the differing characteristics of men and women" (Broverman, 1972, p. 64). They are an integral part of all cultures, and unless examined are treated as facts. Authors writing about contemporary sex roles point out the obvious: *Career specialists' role expectations for women and men in our society are heavily influenced by their own parents, teachers, and peers* (Broverman, et al., 1972; Dewey, 1974; Steinman & Fox, 1974; Cohen & Bunker, 1975; Campbell & Klein, 1975). The current push toward evaluating male career roles has come about largely as a response to the dramatic expansion of women's role possibilities in the past few years. Women's roles cannot change without some sort of change in men's roles as well. Career specialists must become sensitive to these shifts. Unfortunately, as a function of their own acculturation, counselors are susceptible to inadvertently providing sex-role–stereotyped alternatives to their clients. Broverman et al. conclude that "the sex orientation of this society is not only shared, but also promoted by its clinical personnel" (1972, p. 71).

Reading sex-role literature is one way for career specialists to become knowledgeable about sex-role stereotypes. There is a growing literature, although the amount of literature dealing especially with men is small. However, the types of questions being raised about women's roles can serve to raise counselors' awareness of sex-role stereotyping in general. Discussing sex-role literature and personal experiences with other career specialists and counselors can be a valuable means for dealing with stereotypes. Such discussions, sometimes called consciousness raising, can result in the sharing of important feelings and beliefs, making them more available for open examination.

Teach Clients About Sex-role Stereotyping   Career specialists can teach their clients about sex-role stereotyping in classroom settings, small groups, or individual counseling sessions. Bibliographies of readings can be compiled and used.

Men's consciousness-raising groups can be conducted. These groups should be established as essentially leaderless groups based on mutual trust and sharing. The focus should be on cooperative sharing, as opposed to the active competition which pervades most other social situations in which men gather together, such as sports, business contacts, school. A time limit on the group (six to eight sessions) helps maintain the sense of urgency of getting down to work. Any topic can become the focus of the group, although these areas might be suggested to the group for their consideration:

1   Growing up male
2   Work as worth
3   Men in traditionally female jobs
4   The househusband
5   The advantages and disadvantages of dual breadwinners
6   Women's expectations for men and men's expectations for women
7   Men's expectations for men

Men's consciousness raising is discussed more fully by Farrell in *The Liberated Man* (1975). Groups can be very valuable for increasing awareness, and with increased awareness come new alternatives.

Provide Alternate Role Models   Men at all stages of career development need alternate role models so they can begin to consider new possibilities for themselves (Broverman, et al., 1972; Tibbetts, 1975). One study indicates that, from kindergarten through college, attitudes of both females and males grow steadily more liberal in viewing various occupations as suitable for either sex (Shepard & Hess, 1975). This finding supports the belief that attitudes about nontraditional career roles can be modified as late as an individual's college years. Role modeling (bringing a male nurse and a househusband to class), role playing (having women make all the social approaches for a week), and trial work experiences (as secretaries, baby sitters, fashion designers) in nontraditional career areas can be arranged. Career specialists are bound here only by their *imagination* and willingness to take a *risk*—two of the same factors their clients need help with. However, consideration should be given to who is selected for these presentations and how these work experiences are arranged so as to allow their evaluation with as little sex bias as possible.

Consult With Others   Desey (1974b) sees the schools as playing a large part in the *teaching* and *maintenance* of sex-role stereotyping. Not only the personal values and attitudes of the teachers themselves, but also the curriculum design, text books, and other teaching materials contribute to perpetuating role rigidity. Vocational tests are only beginning to be revised and made "sex-free." Much of the vocational literature currently available is in serious need of reevaluation with regard to sex bias.

The career specialist is obligated to point out these biases whenever they are found, and may also offer training programs for various other professionals designed to help them identify how their practices or the materials they use might be made more bias-free. In-service workshops for school teachers and administrators built around the theme of motivating oneself to learn and teach in a nonsexist way (Hilliard, 1975) are often appropriate.

Career specialists can also offer to help screen test materials, text books, and vocational information. They may write articles for local newspapers, and offer to appear on local radio and television shows to discuss the importance of these issues. They may offer to help institutions, agencies, and local government analyze hiring practices in nontraditional sex-role positions. They can encourage employers to offer full-time jobs that can be occupied by either spouse on a half-time basis so that both men and women get the opportunity to earn wages and engage in homemaking and child-rearing tasks. Finally, career specialists must, through their own behavior, be models for others to emulate.

SUMMARY

Men's traditional career roles are beginning to change. Career specialists need to be aware of these changes and help men cope with them. They must provide men with experiences that help them explore alternatives previously closed to them, regardless of the choices they eventually make. This will require that career specialists become sensitive to sex-role stereotyping as it relates to men's career possibilities. It is important to keep in mind the notion that ". . . no job is a guarantee of human, let alone sexual, identity" (Steinman & Fox, 1974, p. 277).

REFERENCES

Associated Press. The man with the steno pad wants to keep his moustache. *The Charlotte Observer,* August 14, 1977, 6E.

Baumgardner, S. Vocational planning: The great swindle. *Personnel and Guidance Journal,* 1977, *56*(1), 17–22.

Brenton, M. *The American Male.* Greenwich, Connecticut: Fawcett Publications, Inc., 1966.

Broverman, I., Vogel, S., Broverman, D., Clarkson, F., & Rozenkrants, P. Sex-role stereotypes: A current appraisal. *Journal of Social Issues,* 1972, *28*(2), 59–78.

Campbell, D., & Klein, K. Job satisfaction and vocational interests. *The Vocational Guidance Quarterly,* 1975, *24*(2), 125–131.

Cohen, S., & Bunker, K. Subtle effects of sex role stereotypes on recruiters' hiring decisions. *Journal of Applied Psychology,* 1975, *60*(5), 566–572.

Dewey, C. Exploring interests: A non-sexist method. *Personnel and Guidance Journal,* 1974(a), *52*(5), 311–315.

Dewey, C. Sex typed division of labor is no accident: The roll [sic] of education in the perpetuation of sexual inequality. *Tennessee Education,* 1974(b), *4*(3), 17–26.

Dolliver, R. & Nelson, R. Assumptions regarding vocational counseling. *The Vocational Guidance Quarterly,* 1975, *24*(1), 12–19.

Farrell, W. *The Liberated Man.* New York: Random House, 1975.

Flanders, R. Work: The prospects for tomorrow. *Occupational Outlook Quarterly,* 1977, *21*(1), 2–7.

Ginzberg, E. Meaningful careers for educated people. *Journal of College Placement,* 1973, *34*(1), 34–39.

Gould, R. Measuring masculinity by the size of the paycheck. In J. Pleck and J. Sawyer (Eds.), *Men and Masculinity.* Englewood Cliffs: Prentice-Hall, 1974.

Hilliard, A. Motivating oneself to learn and teach in a non-sexist way. *Journal of Teacher Education,* 1975, *26*(4), 310–312.

Hoffman, L. Changes in family roles, socialization and sex differences. *American Psychologist,* 1977, *32*(8), 644–657.

Holland, J. Some practical remedies for providing vocational guidance for everyone. Invited address at the 23rd Annual Conference of the Minnesota Statewide Testing Programs, Minneapolis, September 20, 1973.

Jourard, S. *The Transparent Self.* New York: Van Nostrand, Reinhold Company, 1971.

Komarovsky, M. Cultural contradictions and sex roles: The masculine case. *American Journal of Sociology,* 1973, *78,* 873–884.

Morgan, J., & Skovholt, T. Using inner experience: Fantasies and daydreams in career counseling. *Journal of Counseling Psychology,* 1977, *24*(5), 391–397.

Powell, D., & Driscoll, P. Middle-class professionals face unemployment. *Society,* 1973, *10*(2), 18–26.

Sheehy, G. *Passages: Predictable crises of adult life.* New York: Bantam, 1977.

Shephard, W., & Hess, D. Attitudes in four age groups toward sex role division in adult occupations and activities. *Journal of Vocational Behavior,* 1975, *6,* 27–39.

Steinman, A., & Fox, D. *The male dilemma.* New York: Jason Aronson, 1974.

Stempel, Jeff. The love of a nighttime may await some bar hustler. *Minnesota Daily,* September 19–29, 1977, pp. 17, 30.

Tibbetts, S. Sex-role stereotyping in the lower grades: Part of the solution. *Journal of Vocational Behavior,* 1975, *6,* 255–261.

26. Guiding the Disadvantaged*

Eli Ginzberg

I. INTRODUCTION

No better justification for this effort can be found than the fact that such a presentation would have not been necessary in past generations. As late as World War I the typical employment screening process consisted of the guard or foreman at the factory gate requesting a prospective employee to roll up his sleeves so that the foreman could make a rough estimate of the worker's ability to meet the physical requirements of the job. These were often the only requirements.

To stay with the past a moment longer, it was accepted practice in New York City many years ago for employers to have their agents meet the immigrant ships arriving from Europe. Many of the new arrivals would be hired before they even left the docks, having received orders to report to work the next morning. The young native-born man who departed from his father's farm to seek his future in the city likewise had little difficulty in obtaining employment, except in periods when business was depressed. It might take him a day or two, but seldom more than that, before he was able to get work at wages which would enable him to support himself adequately.

How different things are now when we read in the first *Manpower Report of the President* that only one out of every ten young persons growing up on farms can look forward to making his living in agriculture; and we read in the second *Manpower Report of the President* that in 1963 unemployment among teenagers averaged around fifteen per cent, approximately thirty per cent in the case of Negro boys and girls. No longer is it true that the farm boy who sets out to seek his fortune in the city can be assured of finding a job. Even those youngsters growing up in the city may face difficulty in locating work.

While it may be true as the official statistics show, that there has been no significant increase over the decades in the percentage of the labor force that is unemployed, the shape of the unemployment problem and its social significance have been greatly altered. In earlier generations a high proportion of the farm population, particularly in the South but also in other sectors of the country, was, if not unemployed, seriously underemployed. The same was true for a substantial number of the women who lived with their families or who held domestic jobs.

Many of the underemployed rural persons of yesteryear are today the urban unemployed. Many of the domestics of years past are today the poorly educated women in urban communities looking for jobs, or those who have stopped looking because they could not find them.

Compounding these problems, which are related to the vast changes that have occurred in the American economy and the labor market, are the following

Source: Reprinted by permission of Harvard University Press from *Guidance in American Education II: Current Issues and Suggested Action,* Edward Landy & Arthur M. Kroll, editors. Cambridge, Mass.: Graduate School of Education, Harvard University, Copyright © 1965 by the President and Fellows of Harvard College.

developments: the proportion of unskilled jobs requiring physical labor has declined precipitously; correspondingly, the proportion of jobs for which a college degree is prerequisite has increased substantially. Women have become a preferred source of labor over men for a large number of jobs in operative and service occupations. Blue collar work has increasingly given way to white collar work. The office and the store are furnishing a much higher proportion of jobs, the factory a lesser proportion. These then are some of the facts of current occupational structure that must be kept in mind as we focus on the guidance of disadvantaged youth.

II. WHO ARE THE DISADVANTAGED?

Americans have a penchant for gadgets and for slogans. It is therefore not only desirable but essential to look with care at the concept of the disadvantaged so that one knows exactly what the term means. One can think of "the disadvantaged" in terms of children who come from families unable to provide them with adequate developmental opportunities. This may reflect a lack of moral, financial, emotional, intellectual or other basic prerequisites for child rearing. In this category, we would have to include the offspring of certain wealthy as well as poor families, of certain white as well as Negro families, of certain families whose roots go back to before the Revolutionary War as well as families who have only recently immigrated; of certain families whose English contains Elizabethan forms as well as families to whom English is an unknown tongue; of certain Protestant families as well as those who belong to religious minorities.

Alternatively, we can define the "disadvantaged" in terms of the children themselves. In that case we would have to include those who, by reason of heredity or environment, possess serious handicaps—whether physical, emotional, mental, social, racial, ethnic, religious, or others—which would interfere with their successful adjustment to the world of work.

While the two methods of classification—the disadvantaged family and the disadvantaged child—overlap, they are not necessarily identical. One illustration will make the point. There are many children born into middle class families who for one reason or another grow up with serious handicaps, making it difficult for them to find employment, while at the same time many children whose parents are poor and uneducated succeed in making highly satisfactory adjustments to the world of work.

For the purpose of this analysis we will focus on the children from families of lower socio-economic status but we will avoid the false postulate that all, or even most, of them are so severely handicapped by the time they enter school that they are unlikely to make a satisfactory adjustment to their studies or later to their work. Rather, the main thrust of the following analysis will be to suggest the various types of guidance which might enable the offspring from these families more nearly to realize their full potential.

III. PRE-SCHOOL YEARS

Many children growing up in rural and urban slums, as well as in less disadvantaged areas, have been born to parents who do not possess the minimum competence to rear them effectively. On the assumption that except in rare cases of gross incompetence it is better for a child to be brought up by his natural parents, the major challenge to public policy is to help these handicapped parents do a better job of child-rearing. At an optimum such guidance should start before the child is born and in many instances should be directed toward providing information as to how the conception of additional children can be prevented. The responsibility for assisting such handicapped parents should be shared by institutions ranging from government welfare and health agencies to ladies church auxiliaries and other types of voluntary social organizations.

In urban communities the mothers in low-income families frequently work out of the home all day, and many of those who do not are frequently unable to stimulate their children effectively. As a result, the child's potential for learning is often inadequately developed. The establishment of day care and nursery schools staffed by competent professionals who could help in the early socializing of the child, and at the same time provide guidance for the mother, would contribute much to compensating for the inherent limitations of the home. It should be stressed in passing that no system of compensation will prove adequate for children who grow up without sufficient food or who are unable to sleep properly because of overcrowded housing conditions.

IV. EARLY YEARS AT SCHOOL

There is a naive belief that guidance consists primarily in offering information and advice to individuals who are uncertain as to how they should act. In point of fact, a more meaningful definition of guidance is the sum total of influences to which an individual is exposed that operate to direct his behavior in one rather than another direction. Hence the young child in school is constantly guided by both his teachers and his peers, as well as, of course, by the influences within his home and in his neighborhood.

Among the important characteristics of the economic environment to which entirely too little attention has been paid until lately is the fact that those localities with the lowest per capita imcome are also likely to be localities with the lowest level of public services, including those of an educational nature. This is particularly true of the rural areas in the Southeastern United States. To compound these handicaps such regions also tend to have a very high birth rate. As a result, there is even less money available than elsewhere per child for instruction and supplemental school services. Moreover, low salaries mean less competent teachers. Many of these rural communities, because of changes taking place in the economy, are confronted with an erosion of their economic base. This means that they seldom have the capital funds necessary to refurbish their educational plant and equipment.

A frequently overlooked difficulty facing Negro youngsters in the South is the fact that the snail's pace at which school desegregation is proceeding implies that they continue to be taught almost exclusively by Negro teachers in a segregated environment. All the evidence points to the fact that these teachers, with relatively few exceptions, have themselves been inadequately trained. What is more, they have usually had little intimate experience with the folkways and behavior patterns of the majority—except as they bear on the relationships between the races under segregation. They are therefore ill-suited in many, if not most instances, to help these youngsters prepare themselves for living in a desegregated society.

The situation is only slightly better in the large urban centers of the North. Here the teaching staffs are better prepared in their respective fields, and Negro youngsters are from the start likely to be exposed to white as well as to Negro teachers. For the most part, however, the white teachers are likely to be young and inexperienced, without special sympathy for or understanding of the special problems facing these children. Because of segregation in housing most of the Negro youngsters are likely to attend schools which have few if any white students who could help demonstrate early in their schooling a set of values and behavior standards different from those prevailing in the disadvantaged subculture.

The schematic presentation just set out for Negro children applies, except for the very important consideration of color, equally as well to white children from low-income homes. While school authorities have become increasingly aware of the need to make sure that the consequences of neighborhood racial and income segregation are not mirrored within the school, progress to date has been very slow. With the more wealthy members of the white community ensconced in the suburbs, most metropolitan centers are hard pressed to raise the revenue required to run first rate schools; they have been loath to establish special incentives to encourage a superior teaching staff to work with youngsters who, because of multiple problems, usually respond more slowly to instructional efforts.

In addition to upgrading the teaching staffs and improving the school facilities attended by disadvantaged youngsters, action should be taken to extend the school day to cover supervised play and assistance with homework; Saturday activities and special summer programs must be developed. Anything less than such a major and sustained effort means that the oppressive weight of poverty and despair will not be lifted and that many youngsters will fail to acquire a positive attitude toward the school process, falling behind very quickly in the mastery of basic skills, above all, the ability to read.

As indicated earlier there is likely to be a substantial range in the potential and motivation to learn among any group of students, including those from disadvantaged backgrounds. It becomes very important therefore for school authorities not to see the group as a homogeneous unit but rather so to structure the first three years that the more able can be differentiated from the less able, making it possible to treat each according to his needs. Nothing is more destructive than the subtle labeling of all disadvantaged youngsters as poor pupils. Teachers who hold such opinions are likely to become unconscious to a self-fulfilling prophecy.

One additional point about the early school year: Any guidance, other than the influence and impact of the educational process itself, must be directed towards the parents of these children. Many parents, however straitened their circumstances, welcome advice and assistance from sympathetic teachers and others in the school system. While one must be quick to acknowledge that not all parents can be reached, this is no excuse for not trying to reach the largest possible number and working with them to help their youngsters adjust to and profit from their school experience.

There is an urgent need for all levels of government, as well as for the voluntary social welfare agencies, to see the problem as a whole to determine what gains can be made from a more integrated use of public and private funds. Undoubtedly more funds will be needed. But additional money without certain organizational changes and a broad-scale social commitment will fail in the future just as it has failed in the past. A minimum objective of guidance in the first six years of school is to convey to parents and child alike the essentiality of learning for a successful adult adjustment, and to establish as many of the preconditions as are necessary to enable the child to make as much progress in the mastery of basic skills as his endowment permits.

V. THE CHOICES INCREASE

The decision-making of young people with respect to their future work takes an important new turn around their eleventh year, a year that coincides more or less with their entrance into junior high school. At this age, the young person no longer thinks about the future in terms solely of fantasies but has reached a stage of development where his interests begin to provide a foundation for his future occupational plans. And in the years immediately following, his decision-making process is broadened as he also begins to take into account his capacities and later his values. Then in his middle and later teens he enters upon a period of exploration which gives him a firm basis for assessing what he likes or dislikes about the way in which work is organized.

While the choice of an occupation becomes even more prominent with the onset of puberty, the young person cannot operate directly with respect to it. The decisions which he must make relate almost entirely to schools and curricula, not to work itself. There are three major influences involved in the occupational choice of a student: the student himself, his parents, and school officials. As far as the student is concerned it should be clear at once that he is in a poor position to weigh alternatives either as to schools or to curricula. If forced to make a decision he is likely to fall back on his peers and go along with the crowd, or else make a choice on the basis of such irrelevant factors as whether the school has a superior sports record or whether the shop facilities are above average.

In the case of most youngsters from lower socio-economic backgrounds they cannot look for help from their parents or other adults in their immediate environment. The odds are strong that the adults whom they might consult have not gone far in school themselves, and are in a poor position to offer constructively meaningful advice.

This means that a particularly heavy burden of responsibility falls on teachers, guidance counselors and school administrators. They cannot fail to play a major role in the eventual outcome. As far as teachers are concerned, a major danger is that they will see their classes as an underpotential group of more or less disadvantaged children. Faced with large classes that are also likely by the sixth term to involve disciplinary problems, they have their hands full in keeping the group under control and in instilling in them some minimum of new knowledge and skills. Teachers are seldom motivated, nor do they possess the time, energy or techniques, to pick out the more talented minority who, if assisted and encouraged, might break out of the lockstep.

Hence a major challenge is to increase the resources available to those schools in which children from disadvantaged homes predominate. In that way, the teaching personnel will not be swamped by their routine assignments, preferring to take the easy road out and treat all as if they were without ability or promise. Not only should the classroom ratio of teacher to pupil be kept at a relatively low figure but, in addition, the whole gamut of services included in the Higher Horizons program of the New York City schools should be provided. These involve, among other things, lengthening the school day, the school week and the school year; furnishing supervised group activities both within the school and outside; hiring additional staff personnel for teaching and guidance and offering counsel to parents as well as to students.

There is a tendency in any school system, large or intermediate, to deal with pupils *en masse:* that is, to promote all students to the next grade, whether ready for it or not, and to fit them into curricula, whether suited for them or not. School administrators, like all other types of administrators, try to make their own lives more bearable by simplifying their tasks. One way they do this is by moving students *en block* from one school to another, from one course of studies to another, without taking into consideration the individualized needs of the students.

There is a great danger that many able young people from disadvantaged homes will be lost in the shuffle. At this point it might be best to use the diversity of a large city school system to enable children to attend some distant school better suited to their needs. In this connection, funds for carfare and lunches may have to be provided, especially to those from very poor homes.

Even more unfair is the tendency to assume that since those children come from homes where the parents are at the lower end of the occupational and income scale, there is little point in encouraging them to pursue an academic career; that since their ambitions, if they have them, are bound to be frustrated, it is the better part of wisdom to shunt the children early into programs that are more functional and which they are more likely to complete successfully.

Such an administrative attitude, often shared by the teaching personnel, the pupils and even their parents, is not at all sound. Its effect is to victimize a significant minority. Instead of being encouraged to pursue an academic course, instead of being informed of the many types of financial and other assistance available to them, instead of being told that college can be part of their future reality, these children from disadvantaged homes are all indiscriminately discouraged from lifting their aspiration levels. The ultimate result is to shunt all pupils, and therefore the minority who might succeed in an academic curriculum, to a different type of school and a different course of study. Seldom if ever is it realized that the best preparation for the world of work for the non-college student is the completion of an academic program.

All the influences in the disadvantaged young person's environment operate to diminish his interest and concern with an academic course of studies. Inevitably therefore a great many will have to be furnished other opportunities. The primary task of the school is not to go with the trend but rather to provide an optimum of educational opportunity for each child.

VI. LIMITATIONS OF OPPORTUNITIES

There are two groups of children from disadvantaged homes that are particularly handicapped by the present structure of the schools. The first are farm youth who are growing up in areas in which there is little prospect that more than a few will ever be able to find profitable employment. It is difficult enough for the urban youngster to find his way; it is much more difficult for the farm youth who eventually faces the task of relocating. To make matters worse, most farm counties have a low tax yield and the monies spent on education are frequently badly misallocated. Tradition insures that a considerable proportion of all vocational funds will be devoted to preparing youths for agricultural vocations that do not exist, except in very small quantities. The new Congressional legislation on vocational education is a promise of a better day but it will take a long time before it can be expedited.

As is so often the case, there are no direct and simple answers to this problem. Among the many reforms that would help are: more liberal support for farm schools; a revised curriculum and more imaginative guidance of pupils; and carefully structured programs to broaden farm childrens' knowledge of urban industrial life. The possibility of establishing regional boundary schools at the tenth or twelfth grade for a selected minority should also be considered. Such a radical shift is never easy and is always costly. However, it will probably prove less expensive in the long run to make the investment in those who must locate earlier rather than later in their lives.

On the urban front, the principal challenge is how to cope with the sizeable minority who by the time they reach fifteen or sixteen have had their fill of schooling. For the most part they are simply marking time, waiting to be released from the drudgery of sitting through and not participating in five hours of classes each day. For whatever the complex reasons, they have failed to learn to read effectively and to master the other essential skills which alone make further learning from books feasible. There is no question that they are ill prepared for work or life, that they need more "learning." But it is learning that must take place in the outside environment rather than in the classroom. What they really need is an opportunity to go to work, associate with adults, be stimulated by a new environment, earn some money—in short, an opportunity to grow up.

The great tragedy of our times is that, firstly, the educational system has failed in its basic mission to teach this group the fundamental skills without which further learning becomes very difficult; and secondly, because of the changes that have occurred in the economic environment, the educational system deprives this group of the only attractive opportunities which could aid their development, the opportunity to obtain meaningful employment. With proper financial and other public support, the schools, it is hoped, will eventually learn how to teach those they have previously failed to reach. But in the interim, the schools acting in concert with business, labor, communal organizations and government must seek to create the attractive opportunities which this group so badly needs. The President's Poverty Program holds out a promise of some programs aimed at this group; the Manpower Development and Training Act provides leverage; the follow-up of the Administration on its report, *One-Third of a Nation,* may provide still additional relief. Aside from these efforts of the Federal government there are numerous local and state efforts directed to broadening work-study opportunities. But a wide gap continues to exist between needs and opportunities. It must be closed—for otherwise many young people will be cheated of their birthright.

VII. THE WORLD BEYOND THE SCHOOL

For too long schoolmen have equated the school with education. In point of fact the educational process has always been more variegated than that. Never has this been more true than at present. From the viewpoint of guidance, two institutions are particularly important: the Armed Forces and industry. Entirely too little attention has been paid by high school counselors to those two institutions and to their potential for enabling many youths to add to their knowledge and skills, approaching adulthood better prepared for work and life.

One of the severe challenges that high school personnel face is to develop and maintain the interest of many students in their work. So many students see no point to it. But they might, if a bridge could be built between their present circumstances and what lies ahead in the military and in industry. Most adolescents will respond to challenges which are realistic. There is nothing unrealistic for the vast majority setting themselves a goal of doing enough work so as to be able to secure a better assignment in the military or to be able to enter an industrial training program which will bring them a better job and higher wages. Regrettably, many counselors have failed to relate those major institutional opportunities to their school charges. Probably the best way to do so is through group guidance in which students are given the opportunity to confront and talk with slightly older persons from their own environment who have been exposed to these new opportunities and have profited from them.

VIII. DIRECTIONS FOR ACTION

In brief recapitulation these are the challenges to the guidance of the disadvantaged presented by a rapidly changing economic and social environment, together with the preferred ways of meeting these challenges:

A. Communities must recognize that supportive action must start early, before the child enters school. This in turn requires working with parents on the one hand, and establishing preschool institutions such as nursery groups on the other.

B. Schools that are struggling to educate large numbers of rural and urban youth from disadvantaged homes require much more public support to improve their classroom performance and to add a galaxy of supplemental services.

C. Special care must be taken by the school authorities not to deal with disadvantaged youth as a homogeneous group whose potential for higher education and professional occupations is generally discounted. To the extent possible, capable youths should be encouraged to pursue an academic course.

D. Communities must take special measures to provide developmental opportunities for older adolescents who can no longer profit from classroom instruction. Job opportunities must be opened up for these youngsters, to which continuing education and training can be grafted.

E. The potential for skill development inherent in military service and industrial training should be pointed out to these youths. Group guidance, using successful former members of these groups as models should be undertaken.

F. The Federal government, as well as state and local governments, have a responsibility to provide a "second chance" for many disadvantaged youth by creating work-study opportunities. Otherwise, this group will be permanently handicapped throughout their adult lives as citizens and workers.

27. Agency Settings for Career Guidance*

Donn E. Brolin

Considerable need exists for community agencies to render quality career guidance services to a large portion of our population. Although many such programs do exist and are evolving around the country, the need for many more is evident. This article contains a review of some of the current career guidance agencies and services, recommendations for some needed changes, and suggestions for a more competency-based orientation by agency personnel.

CAREER GUIDANCE AGENCIES

Career guidance agencies are lodged primarily in manpower, rehabilitation, and public and private social service agencies, although business and industry are also moving more into this important area.

Manpower Agencies

In recent years special career guidance programs have evolved in state employment agencies—programs in basic education, classroom and/or trade training, training in job seeking skills, career exploration, paid on-the-job training, and specialized job placement assistance. These services have grown out of the needs of welfare clients and other disadvantaged persons, including youth, correctional inmates, and armed forces personnel. The Manpower Development and Training Act (MDTA), the Work Incentive Program (WIN), the Concentrated Employment Program (CEP), Job Opportunities in the Business Sector (JOBS), and the Job Corps are programs that were created to meet special needs.

    The agency also offers labor information, job banks, programs for handicapped and older workers, youth services, minority group programs, veterans' services, and other career guidance services. The Comprehensive Employment and Training Act (CETA) of 1973 has substituted a decentralized and decategorized program so that local needs can be better met by agency services.

Rehabilitation Agencies

Traditionally, rehabilitation agencies provide services to individuals who have a variety of physical, emotional, intellectual, sensory, and behavioral handicaps that prevent them from being assimilated into the labor market. The state vocational rehabilitation agency, due to large case loads and travel responsibilities, cannot always offer intensive career guidance. Its counselors therefore often depend on rehabilitation facilities (workshops) and rehabilitation centers to assist them in more extensive career guidance activities. Such facilities offer a work environment in which clients can learn about industrial work requirements, work habits, work skills, and work behaviors and can explore different jobs while receiving career guidance. Two such agencies are described below.

*Source: Reprinted with permission of the author and publisher from *The Personnel and Guidance Journal,* 1975, *53,* 686–690. Copyright 1975 The American Personnel and Guidance Association.

Vocational Counseling and Rehabilitation Services, in St. Louis, Missouri, offers two types of services to urban clients: (a) career guidance for any adult having problems clarifying educational goals, work abilities, or other job possibilities and (b) rehabilitation services, including comprehensive work evaluation, social security disability determinations, personal adjustment training, training for job seeking skills, and job placement. In the first case, vocational counselors test and counsel self-referred or agency-referred individuals about occupational possibilities. Individuals receiving the second service obtain remunerative work training in a realistic production setting operating under accepted business standards. The agency also offers a small-scale homebound work program for individuals capable of performing work but physically unable to leave the home situation; classes for clients who, despite adequate intellectual skills, need basic academic instruction to qualify for possible jobs; and family counseling, although the agency recognizes that even more emphasis is needed in this area.

Portal Programs, Inc., in Grafton, Wisconsin, has evolved from a small work activity center for severely retarded persons to a comprehensive county service for those with all types of handicaps, from mild to severe. All trainees, no matter how low their productivity, are guaranteed 50 cents an hour and receive more if their work warrants it. With this remunerative opportunity and a businesslike but accepting environment, often the agency's main problem is convincing those who have competitive employment potential to leave after they have acquired the necessary skills. The agency also offers basic living skills and academic instruction for those needing them. Mental health, special education, vocational education, and other programs cooperate closely with the agency's delivery of services and often send their own personnel to work intensively with Portal's staff. A summer program for handicapped public school youth has been a tremendous success, giving these youngsters an opportunity to learn about the world of work, develop vocational skills, and make money, rather than remaining home for the summer with nothing to do. This agency exemplifies what can be done in a small community if agencies, the community, and parents join together to better meet the career development needs of its citizens.

Social Service Agencies

Several social service agencies have become more active in providing career guidance to individuals. For example, counseling services are springing up for ex-offenders, alcoholics, drug addicts, and ex-mental patients to prevent the reoccurrence of their problems. Probation and parole agencies, courts, departments of corrections, mental health centers, halfway houses, and private agencies have established special programs for their clientele. Positive peer culture and other group techniques have gained considerable favor in recent years. The involvement of the entire family in career guidance problems is also receiving more attention.

An example of a dynamic program is that of the Roanoke (Virginia) Social Service Bureau for public assistance recipients, called the Job Orientation and Motivation Project (JOMP). The program, designed to help these individuals gain confidence and find jobs, uses group counseling to focus on the main obstacles to their employment. As a result of this program, the service worker is no longer being seen as a "fire fighter" but as a facilitator who uses "new-found goal-oriented vocational guidance tools and group dynamics expertise" (Frank & Martin 1974, p. 8). This clear-cut role has helped the professional worker by improving his or her job satisfaction through the elucidation of an identity, and it has helped the employer by providing better and more satisfied workers.

An innovative project is being conducted at the University of Arizona under the University Year for Action Program of the federal agency ACTION. ACTION brings together VISTA, the Peace Corps, SCORE, ACE, Foster Grandparents, and several other federal volunteer programs. College students sign up as VISTA volunteers for one year as part of their graduate program. Students work in a variety of areas—adult and juvenile corrections, alcoholism counseling, drug counseling, rehabilitation counseling, health and social services for Indians, and youth counseling with unwed mothers. Students assume many career guidance activities that agency staff members never seem to have enough time to do, particularly job development, job placement, and follow-up counseling. Thus they provide valuable career guidance services while gaining extensive field experience during their college training.

IMPROVING AGENCY SERVICES

Fortunately, hands-on experiences are being recognized and practiced as a more viable method of career guidance for many individuals than the traditional method of verbal interchange and paper-and-pencil testing. Although slow to evolve in many agencies, there is occurring more use of instructional packages, modules, job tryouts, and audio-visual techniques. Career guidance systems such as the JEVS Work Samples (developed at Philadelphia's Jewish Employment and Vocational Service), the Vocational Evaluation System, the Job Survival Skills Package, the Career Awareness Laboratory (CAL), and a new life skills program are emerging products. Despite the improvements that have resulted from the efforts of many agencies, much remains to be done. Here are some recommendations.

1. Agency personnel should help educational institutions rejuvenate and inject the educational system with a career development orientation, providing numerous educational offerings to meet the diverse learning styles and needs of students (rather than forcing them to fit into the system). It is important to initiate career guidance and development in the early years so it becomes infused throughout the educational system. It would be valuable for schools to secure more involvement with community agencies. This becomes especially important with the movement to mainstream special education students into regular classes.

2. Agency personnel should educate noneducational agencies about career education: what it is, how they can contribute to it, and how they can coordinate their efforts with each other and the educational system. Relevant and collaborative relationships between the school and the community agencies would enable this goal to be achieved.

3. Agency personnel should systematically identify those competencies individuals need in order to function successfully in the kind of environments in which they will be living and working. The contributions of schools and other agencies need to be specified to assure a continuum of career development services at the various stages of each individual's lifetime.

4. Agency personnel should effectively use different kinds of personnel so that those individuals with no college training can assist professional workers in the delivery of career guidance services. Volunteers, people in business and industry, and parents should be called on in these efforts.

5. Agency personnel should justify a program's efficacy by requiring the program's staff to define program objectives operationally, to specify how each of these objectives will be met and evaluated, and to measure the extent to which each of these objectives has been achieved. Agency workers need to spend most of their time on actual career guidance activities, not in shuffling papers and reporting esoteric figures to justify their existence.

6. Agency personnel should designate an existing agency in each large community and district (such as the Employment Service) to serve as a fixed point of referral for career guidance services. Carlucci (1974) has pointed out that we lack one good human service network to bring together the hundreds of narrowly based health, education, welfare, and manpower programs operating in virtual isolation from one another. He reported that 9 out of 10 people need several kinds of service rather than just one kind.

COMPETENCY-BASED SERVICES

Agencies need to become more concerned with the total individual than with crisis counseling. Agency personnel as well as educators should provide career guidance and development services that teach skills in daily living, personal-social skills, and occupational skills. Elsewhere (Brolin 1974) I have identified 22 competencies in these three areas as being absolutely essential for educable mentally retarded persons if they are to secure a satisfactory and satisfying level of vocational and community adjustment. The competencies and their respective areas are presented below.

Skills in daily living include: managing family finances; caring for home furnishings and equipment; caring for personal needs; raising children and living with family; buying, planning, and preparing food; selecting, buying, and making clothing; engaging in civic activities; utilizing recreation and leisure time; and getting around the community. Attainment of these nine competencies will enable individuals to manage a home, a family, finances, and themselves.

Personal-social skills include: attaining self-awareness and appraisal; acquiring self-confidence and a positive self-concept; achieving socially responsible behavior; developing and maintaining appropriate interpersonal relationships; achieving independence; making good decisions and solving problems; and communicating appropriately with others. Attainment of these seven competencies will enable individuals to learn those personal and interpersonal skills so vital to vocational and community functioning.

Occupational skills include: knowing about and exploring occupations; selecting and planning appropriate occupational choices; developing appropriate work behaviors; developing physical and manual skills; acquiring a specific job skill; and seeking, securing, and maintaining appropriate employment. Attainment of these six competencies will enable individuals to obtain employment commensurate with their abilities, interests, and needs.

CONCLUSION

Career guidance agencies can make a significant contribution by identifying special needs and assisting clients in moving toward occupations that will meet those needs. A primary need of many is to build self-confidence so that they believe they can be successful. Too many job failures result from job dissatisfaction due to a worker's having received poor guidance or having grabbed anything that was available.

Hundreds of exemplary programs and thousands of dedicated individuals are contributing to the improvement of career guidance in agency settings, but there is a need to make these educational, social, and vocational programs more coordinated, more responsive, and more relevant to a great number of people, no matter how limited or how brilliant they might be.

REFERENCES

Brolin, D. Programming retarded in career education. Working Paper No. 1, Project PRICE. Columbia, Mo.: University of Missouri, 1974.

Carlucci, F. New directions in service. *Social and Rehabilitation Record,* 1974, *1*(5), 6–8.

Frank, D. S., & Martin, D. Roanoke program helps clients find confidence and jobs. *Social and Rehabilitation Record,* 1974, *1*(9), 6–8.

FOLLOW-UP FOR SECTION FOUR

Questions

1 The following questions pertain to Hansen in "Counseling and Career (Self) Development of Women."

   a What effect have the eight societal trends had on your own career behavior?

   b How do female and male career *patterns* differ?

   c List three obstacles to the career development of women and strategies to overcome them.

   d Compare and contrast Hansen's recommendation for curriculum changes as presented in this article with those she presents in "A Model for Career Development through Curriculum."

2 The following questions pertain to Hansen in "Counseling and Career (Self) Development of Women" and Morgan, Skovholt, and Orr in "Career Counseling with Men: The Shifting Focus."

   a Both men and women experience unique problems in relation to the world of work as a function of their sex. How do the *causes* of these problems differ? What do they have in common?

   b Compare and contrast the interventions recommended to provide sex-fair counseling for women with those for men.

3 The following pertain to Ginzberg in "Guiding the Disadvantaged."

   a Who are the disadvantaged?

   b Compare the following statement by Ginzberg with Warnath's view as expressed in "Vocational Theories: Direction to Nowhere," of the potential for personal satisfaction that the world of work has to offer:

   There is nothing unrealistic for the vast majority setting themselves a goal and doing enough work so as to be able to secure better assignment in the military or be able to enter an industrial training program which will bring them a better job and higher wages.

   c Morrill, Oetting, and Hurst divide the dimensions of counselor functioning into *target of intervention, method of intervention,* and *purpose of intervention.* Using these terms, classify the recommendations presented by Ginzberg in "Guiding the disadvantaged."

   d React to the following definition of guidance:

   Guidance is the sum total of influences to which an individual is exposed that operate to direct his behavior in one, rather than another, direction.

4 How, according to Brolin in "Agency Settings for Career Guidance," do the services of manpower, rehabilitation, and social services agencies differ? What do they have in common?

5 Cite several examples of discrimination you have observed or personally experienced. Specify what you believe counselors might have done to either reduce the discrimination or assist individuals in dealing constructively with it.

Learn by Doing:

1 What's important? Conduct one of the following exercises with members of any of the groups discussed in this chapter. Both exercises may be found in *Values Clarification* (Hart Publishing Co., Inc.).*

Twenty things you love to do
Pie of life

2 What's available? Conduct a series of interviews with professionals in your community. Consult the Taped Interview Format in Appendix A, Set C. Determine the extent to which the following are available:
   a   Sex-fair counseling for women
   b   Sex-fair counseling for men
   c   Bias-free counseling for the disadvantaged
   d   Bias-free counseling for the disabled

3 The past as a predictor of the future. Select a group of high-school or post-secondary-school students and use the Career Logs Assignment which may be found in Appendix E, Activity no. 5. The purpose of this assignment is to provide the students and counselor-trainees with some insight about how past experiences relate to future goals. Upon completion of this activity, counselor-trainees should have some indication of how much more vocational counseling individual students need at the present time.

4 How it feels. Conduct a series of interviews with representatives from the groups listed below. Focus on the ways these individuals have experienced or observed discrimination. Consult the Taped Interview Format in Appendix A, Set B.
   a   Women
   b   Men
   c   The disadvantaged
   d   The disabled

5 Sex-fair counseling. Present a group guidance activity based on the use of the materials listed below or similar ones.
   Back to School, Back to Work (American Personnel and Guidance Association)*
   The Mature Woman (American Personnel and Guidance Association)*
   Man and Woman: Myths and Stereotypes (The Center for Humanities)*
   Jobs and Gender (Guidance Associates)*
   Women at Work: Choice or Challenge (Guidance Associates)*
   Anything you Want to Be (American Telephone and Telegraph)*

6 Information, please. Select one of the populations below and prepare a bibliography of both print and nonprint materials which would facilitate bias-free career awareness or career development:
   a   Women
   b   Men
   c   The disadvantaged
   d   The disabled

7 Let's review. Based upon the bibliography prepared above, select one item for review. Apply the Guidelines for the Systematic Selection, Evaluation, and Use of Simulated Vocational Guidance Materials, which may be found in Appendix F.

8 To learn more. Prepare an abstract based upon one of the articles listed below under *Additional Resources.* Consult Appendix G for the suggested format.

*See Appendix H for additional information.

Additional Resources

American Personnel and Guidance Association. (Producer). *Career education and the disadvantaged: Trick or treat.*Washington, D.C.: American Personnel and Guidance Association Press, undated, (cassette # 72910).

American Personnel and Guidance Association. (Producer). *Sexual bias in testing and job placement.* Washington, D.C.: American Personnel and Guidance Association Press, undated, (cassette # 72933)

Amos, W. E., & Grambs, J. (Eds.) *Counseling the disadvantaged youth.* Englewood Cliffs, N. J.: Prentice-Hall, 1968.

Ansell, E. M., & Hansen, J. C. Patterns in vocational development of urban youth. *Journal of Counseling Psychology,* 1971, *18,* 505–508.

Astin, H. S., & Myint, T. Career development of young women during the post-high school years. *Journal of Counseling Psychology,* 1971, *18,* 369–393.

DiMichael, S. G. (Ed.) *New vocational pathways for the mentally retarded.* Washington, D.C.: American Personnel and Guidance Association Press, 1966.

Dole, A. A. Aspirations of Blacks and Whites for their children. *Vocational Guidance Quarterly,* 1973, *22,* 24–31.

Eason, J. Life style counseling for a reluctant leisure class. *Personnel and Guidance Journal,* 1972, *51,* 127–132.

Farmer, H. S. Helping women to resolve the home-career conflict. *Personnel and Guidance Journal,* 1971, *49,* 795–801.

Hansen, L. S. *Career guidance practices in school and community.* Washington, D.C.: American Personnel and Guidance Association, 1970.

Hansen, L. S. We are furious (females) but we can shape our own development. *Personnel and Guidance Journal,* 1972, *51,* 87–92.

Ho, M. K. Cross-cultural career counseling. *Vocational Guidance Quarterly,* 1973, *21,* 186–190.

House, E., & Katzell, M. *Facilitating career development for girls and women.* Washington, D.C.: American Personnel and Guidance Association, 1975.

Jacques, M. (Ed.) Counseling the severely disabled. *Rehabilitation Counseling Bulletin,* 1975, *8*(4), 1–96.

Kuvlesky, W. P., & Patella, V. M. Degree of ethnicity and aspirations for upward social mobility among Mexican American youth. *Journal of Vocational Behavior,* 1971, *1,* 231–244.

Lewis, J. (Guest Ed.) Women and counselors. *Personnel and Guidance Journal,* 1972, *51,* Special Issue, 84–156.

Matthews, E. (Ed.) *Counseling girls and women over the life span.* Washington, D.C.: National Vocational Guidance Association, 1972.

Miller, J., & Leonard, G. *Career guidance practices for disadvantaged youth.* Washington, D.C.: National Vocational Guidance Association, 1974.

Muthard, J. E., & Salomone, P. R. (Eds.) The roles and functions of the rehabilitation counselor. *Rehabilitation Counseling Bulletin,* 1969, *13,* 1–96.

National Vocational Guidance Association. *Facilitating career development for girls and women.* Washington, D.C.: National Vocational Guidance Association, 1975.

Picou, J., & Campbell, R. (Eds.) *Career behavior of special groups.* Columbus, Ohio: Charles E. Merrill, 1975.

Sadker, M. (Producer) *Developing children's attitudes towards sex roles.* New York: Miller—Brody Productions, Inc., 1973. (2 filmstrips, 2 cassettes and instructor's resource book)

Sinick, D. Rehabilitation counselors on the move. *Personnel and Guidance Journal,* 1973, *52,* 167–170.

Stivala, A. M. Career guidance in the urban setting. *American Vocational Journal,* 1974, *49,* 32–34.

Tyler, L. E. The encounter with poverty—Its effect on vocational psychology. *Rehabilitation Counseling Bulletin,* 1967, *11,* 61–70.

VanDusen, R. A., & Sheldon, E. B. The changing status of American women—A life cycle perspective. *American Psychologist,* 1976, *31,* 106–116.

Vetter, L. Career counseling for women. *Counseling Psychologist,* 1973, *4,* 54–64.

Wittmer, J. Effective counseling of children of several American subcultures. *School Counselor,* 1971, *19,* 49–52.

Section Five

Counseling Across a Life Span

This section is concerned with the longitudinal needs of individuals as they relate to the world of work. The articles focus on the specific vocational counseling needs of the following groups: Children, non-college-bound young adults, college students, and older workers. Even those theories which are based on developmental psychology, like Super's and Ginzberg's, tend to emphasize the adolescent period, almost to the exclusion of other periods. Research has tended to focus on the vocational counseling needs of youth and young adults. Only recently have we experienced an interest in the vocational counseling needs of individuals across their entire life spans.

The younger the child the easier it is to bring about a change in behavior. Parents, classroom teachers, and counselors have thought this for a long time. Thus, it was only reasonable that counseling found its way into the elementary school. Counseling at the elementary level emphasizes the developmental needs of children. Prevention is the hallmark of counseling young children. Career guidance in turn at the elementary level is generally limited to awareness activities. Vocational guidance activities at the elementary school level are not designed to force children to commit themselves to a career choice. Children are encouraged to explore, not decide. In "Vocational Aspects of Elementary School

Guidance Programs: Objectives and Activities," Edward D. Smith discusses seven basic objectives. The sample activities he suggests are designed to prevent the lack of knowledge about self and the world of work which so many individuals experience at those points when decisions need to be made.

In this society, one of the prominent points at which a decision needs to be made occurs when students are about to graduate from high school. For the college-bound student, the urgency of a decision about a career is to some extent postponed for several years. But the majority of 17- and 18-year-olds do not attend college. In "Counselors and the Noncollege-bound Student," Leslie Cochran calls for counselors to embrace the career-education movement. Specifically, Cochran stresses the need for counselors to "integrate career-development theory, work experience outside of education, vocational knowledge, career-guidance skills, occupational information courses, and placement and follow-up techniques."

Until recently, the vocational-guidance needs of college students have been underestimated. College professors, traditionally caught up in the world of academia, have resisted lending students support in making career decisions. Counseling-center staffs are often not much different from their counterparts at the secondary level; they prefer helping students with personal problems as opposed to vocationally related ones. In "A Systematic Career Development Program in a Liberal Arts College," Richard Thoni and Patricia Olsson suggest an alternative. Their seven-stage model is based, in part, on the work of Ginzberg, Super, and Hansen.

The elderly have been the most ignored group of those commented on in this book. If the current shifts in population continue as they are expected to, there will be a greater need for counseling services for the elderly than for the very young. This is accounted for by the decrease in our birth rate and the increase in life expectancy. Daniel Sinick presents two issues: (1) The emergence of second careers; and (2) the unique problems associated with retirement. Sinick, like Ginzberg and Super, approaches his topic from the perspective of developmental tasks. Sinick points out that "closure comes only with death, the final developmental task." Each of these tasks is dealt with in terms of *special considerations* and *counseling emphases*. The former presents the issues counselors need know and the latter the appropriate counseling interventions.

According to Norman C. Gysbers and Earl J. Moore in "Beyond Career Development: Life Career Development," some of the more current definitions of career development are not broad enough to accommodate the expectations placed on counselors today. They propose an alternative—both in terminology and concept. For them,

> Life career development is defined as self-development over the life span through the integration of the roles, settings, and events of a person's life. . . . Life career development provides a comprehensive and integrated view of human growth and development over the life span. It has the potential of helping individuals link their past and present circumstances to possible future ones.

Gysbers and Moore suggest that we need to transcend those approaches that limit counseling to critical developmental points in each person's life. They contend that in addition to providing the services currently available, we need to reconceptualize the longitudinal counseling needs of individuals. They suggest that counselors need to become involved in helping clients with "self-knowledge and interpersonal skills; life career planning and self-placement competencies; and knowledge and understanding of their current and future life career roles, settings and events—especially those associated with family, education, work and leisure."

As we have recognized for some time, it is not possible to provide vocational counseling apart from educational and personal counseling. Vocational counseling involves the whole person—and its outcomes, career decisions, affect virtually every aspect of a person, including, as Gysbers and Moore suggest, career roles, work settings, family, and leisure. The future shape of counseling will be up to its practitioners. Hopefully, a more eclectic and expansive view of counseling will have a major impact on improving the quality of life for each of us.

28. Vocational Aspects of Elementary School Guidance Programs: Objectives and Activities*

Edward D. Smith

Career selection is a complex human process involving maturation on the part of the individual in terms of knowledge about self and environment, the integration and internalization of acquired knowledge, and finally some form of occupationally relevant behavior. Young children typically verbalize or act our "I wish I were" careers which are based upon current interests and/or familiarity with a person or job. Such behavior may be labeled fantasy, apparently bearing little relationship to reality. It is, however, a forthright and honest expression of interest, even though it is vulnerable to instantaneous change. This period of random fantasy is the basis of future career exploration; hence, it cannot be ignored by adults who are concerned with the career development of youngsters. Therefore, it is incumbent upon school counselors to capitalize on the inherent eagerness and curiosity of youth by developing sequential experiences designed to mold vocationally mature young adults.

Essentially, the mandates to vocational guidance programs in the elementary grades are to provide experiences by which youngsters can:

1 Expand their knowledge concerning the magnitude of the occupational world;

2 Appreciate the various broadly defined dimensions of work;

3 Systematically diminish their distortion about various occupations;

4 At the generalization level, understand those factors present in our society which cause change and, in turn, directly affect work and workers;

5 Identify, understand, and interpret the significance of interests, capacities, and values as dominant factors in the career process;

6 Establish meaningful relationships between education and future occupational endeavors; and

7 Acquire more effective decision-making skills.

Activities designed to enhance the student's skill in each of these areas must be an integral part of each elementary education experience. Nelson (1963) has indicated that youngsters start as early as age eight to reject certain occupations because of a lack of interest or distorted information concerning these occupations. This phenomenon takes on added significance since these rejections tend to solidify as the child grows older. Consequently, what we have are vocationally crippled youngsters who may be plagued by their handicap for the remainder of their lives. It is becoming increasingly urgent, in light of current and projected societal conditions, for young people to receive a broad, firm base of knowledge

*Source: Reprinted with permission of the author and publisher from the *Vocational Guidance Quarterly*, 1970, *18*, 273–279. Copyright 1970 The American Personnel and Guidance Association.

upon which to make realistic, individually meaningful educational and vocational decisions.

THE ELEMENTARY SCHOOL

In terms of the developmental stages of children, the words *elementary school* carry the implication of many different individual readiness levels. In structuring activities pertinent to career development, one would not attempt to implement the same activity for a first grader as for a fifth grader. In most elementary schools, perhaps it would be more appropriate to structure activities according to anticipated typical behavior for specific age groups with provisions for attending to individual differences rather than to plan specific activities for various grade levels.

Elementary school guidance programs should focus attention on the following areas in a manner compatible to the readiness levels of children involved. This would mean, therefore, that all children would not be plugged into a lock-step progression of so-called vocationally significant activities. The major areas previously listed for student exposure are presented in a sequential order which, if properly designed and implemented, should result in more vocationally mature middle and/or junior high school students. The spiral fashion approach suggested should provide a series of successful experiences for each individual. The notion of successful experiences, emphasizing student strengths, is crucial to fostering in young people positive attitudes toward work. It is easy for one to visualize the confusion and frustration experienced by elementary school aged youngsters when they do not have any assistance in sorting out this massive jig-saw puzzle called the world of work.

Before attempting to discuss some parameters of counselor involvement in the vocational aspects of an elementary guidance program, it must be clearly understood that this section will not be a how-to-do-it-by-the-numbers routine but essentially an opinion concerning what to do. It is quite obvious that one cannot do something well before he is clear on what should be done.

THE MAGNITUDE OF THE OCCUPATIONAL WORLD

Starting with the familiar (known) and going to unfamiliar (unknown) is a good strategy for building confidence and establishing a success pattern for youngsters. After determining the range of occupations with which the students are familiar and can describe in some manner, the next step is to expose youngsters to adult workers with whom they have had contact but do not recognize as workers. This group could include individuals such as housewives, physicians, professional athletes, entertainers, military men, and salesmen. Following a discussion of role and functions peculiar to those occupations with which the students are familiar, the expansion of the children's knowledge of the occupational world can be accomplished by demonstrating or graphically representing the array of related and/or support personnel for those workers originally discussed. For example, the physician is only one member of a much larger medical team (e.g., nurses, physical therapists, medical technicians, pharmacists, nurses aides, medical records librarians, etc.). It is just as easy to develop this occupational cluster concept for each of the familiar job titles. The entertainer, as another example, is supported by writers, costumers, sound and lighting technicians, set designers, producers, directors, and so on. Perhaps the newly acquired occupational knowledge could be successfully reinforced by a group art project such as a mural that would pictorially represent a group of workers at their job stations.

The intent of this activity is not to increase the child's knowledge of job titles *per se* but to clearly establish the diversity of work and workers, as well as to provide the student with some simple methods for identifying various occupations.

THE DIMENSIONS OF WORK

In this era of busy schedules, impressive titles, sophisticated products, and massive corporate structures, most youngsters have, at best, only a foggy notion of what people do when at work. In addition, many young people think that work is done only by those persons who are involved in some type of manual endeavor. The task of expanding the child's knowledge of different workers and the type of work in which they are involved is not an impossible one.

In an attempt to determine whether primary grade children could gain occupational awareness important to vocational attitude and value formulation, Wellington and Olechowski (1965) found eight-year-old youngsters able to:

1 Develop a respect for other people, the work they do, and the contributions made by providing production and services for everyone;

2 Understand that occupations have advantages and disadvantages for the worker;

3 Understand some of the interdependent relationships of workers.

The group of students that Wellington and Olechowski studied was first exposed to a unit of study entitled Shelter. The building industry and the variety of workers related to this industry were explored. Initial indications showed that youngsters, after studying the unit, still did not understand the workers' role and function. Follow-up discussions then focused on methods for increasing the children's understanding. It was decided to have the class interview a variety of workers. With the assistance of the teacher and counselor, the children developed questions they wished to ask people during the interview. The interviews and the resultant class discussions were taped. After the children listened to the tapes and completed their discussions concerning the building industry and its workers, there was a noticeable increase in the students' understanding and awareness of working people and their jobs. It was concluded that the initial lack of student awareness was a result of faulty techniques, not the lack of student ability to grasp the concept. Even though the available evidence is not complete, one should not underestimate the capacity of young people to comprehend some of the complexities of the modern work world.

STUDENT DISTORTION

When developing activities which are designed to expose young people to various facets of the world of work, counselors must be aware of the distortion of data that takes place in individuals during the learning (i.e., perceiving—internalizing—conceptualizing) process. The stimuli (various student exposures) which activate the learning process are subject to distortion as a result of being filtered through psychological sets present in each individual as a result of his unique experience. Hence, counselors need to consider the effect of each activity on the individual. Research evidence has suggested that a student's attitudes constitute the framework of his self-concept, which in turn is instrumental in career choice. Therefore, the dissemination of educational and occupational information cannot be considered as a sterile, mechanical process. In order to reduce student distortion of information and make it a viable part of the learning process, counselors must have a working knowledge of factors which influence the child, such as environmental conditions, parental attitudes, socio-economic conditions, and the types of adult worker models available to the youngster. Quite obviously this means that counselors must have frequent contacts with the home and certain segments of the community. Inasmuch as parents appear to exert a powerful influence on students during early stages of the career development process, an excellent investment of time may be to help parents become positive adult worker models for their children.

THE CHANGING NATURE OF OUR SOCIETY

It may well be that the only valid information that can be transmitted to students concerning their future is that it will be different from the life they are currently experiencing. As important as it is for individuals to be prepared to face an uncertain future, it is just as important to know something about factors causing the changing nature of our society.

Most adults find it easy to examine the past, but many become quite uncomfortable in speculating about the future. Adults must consciously guard against transmitting to children their anxiety about the uncertainty of the future. Young children with their present-time orientation have little or no disturbing concern for their immediate or distant future. Therefore, the task in this area is twofold: (a) to make students aware of the dynamic and evolving nature of our society as well as the responsible factors, and (b) to dramatize the concept of individual maturation. The point to be made is that both the individual and his environment will change.

The meaningful communication of societal conditions and changes may best be accomplished by a blending of classroom and field-trip experiences. For example, a unit on the automobile as a means of transportation would dramatize for students the speed with which changes have taken place in the past few years. Each youngster has a good understanding of the appearance of the family car(s). He also recognizes the difference among automobiles seen daily. A study of the development, appearance, speed, cost, numbers, and utilization of the automobile in our society would be a meaningful method of dramatizing the concept of change. This type of activity would necessitate an exploration of technological, economic, and sociological factors, thus bringing to the awareness of the individual some cause-and-effect relationships. Field trips to automobile museums, automobile dealerships, or an automobile assembly plant would reinforce the classroom activities as well as continue to expand the students' knowledge of the world of work and workers.

Segments of the in-school activities just discussed could and should be a joint effort of the entire professional staff of the elementary school. The music teacher, for instance, could supply examples of how the auto industry has influenced music in this country (e.g., the songs "In My Merry Oldsmobile" and "Little Deuce Coupe"). Another teacher could demonstrate the style and utility of the costumes worn during the various eras in the development of the automobile. The mushrooming effect of this approach should be obvious. The only limiting factor is the creativity of the staff.

Concurrent with this activity, the counselor should be structuring activities by which students could recognize changes in their interests, abilities, and values. It would be a relatively simple task to structure a group activity for typical 10-year-olds that involves all the conditions and physical surroundings normally provided for kindergarten youngsters. It would not be too long before the group members would verbalize their concerns, maybe complaints, for being treated like babies or about the nature of the activity. One could then initiate discussions concerning other changes that will occur in the individual.

After learning about environmental and individual change, the student should be better able to formulate a healthy attitude toward change as a social phenomenon.

INTERESTS, CAPACITIES, AND VALUES

Most theoreticians agree that interests play a vital role in career development. Verbal and nonverbal behavior manifested by young children concerning work and adult worker role models, regardless of its reality level, must be recognized and nurtured because from this fantasy evolves more realistic educational and vocational planning as the youngster becomes more aware of certain strengths and weaknesses he possesses. Interests and capacities as career determinants are later tempered by the individual's developing value system.

Both recorded information and data provided by teachers, if properly collected, analyzed, and interpreted, should constitute a developmental profile of the individual student's interests and capacities. Wise utilization of these data via group and individual sessions with parents and teachers will certainly enhance their understanding of the child. Contacts with the students concerning interest and capacity as factors in their career development must deal with the following attributes of those traits:

1   Meaning and significance;
2   Acquisition and development; and
3   Identification and effect.

Obviously, many approaches could be adopted to achieve the goal of self-understanding. A set of materials specifically designed for intermediate-age elementary school children was developed by the Abington, Pennsylvania, School District (1968). The model they developed, basically heuristic in nature, drew upon the resources of the school, home, and community. For example, six sessions were developed for grade five to explore the concept of interests. The sessions were constructed in such a manner that they could become a part of the language arts curriculum and contribute to student development in the area of spoken and written communications as well as being compatible with the objectives of the vocational guidance program. The dual objectives were met by developing:

1   A card game for the purpose of demonstrating how interests develop;
2   Short stories with characters with whom the students can identify;
3   An interest inventory to obtain a profile of the students' interests;
4   An "open-ended" play showing the influence of interests on personal relationships with the provision for the students to write the second act showing the outcome of the situation;
5   A taped series of role-played interviews with various people in which the students were to determine the occupation from the interests described by the person interviewed.

MEANINGFUL RELATIONSHIPS

It is generally agreed that when an individual can formulate some relationship between two worthwhile activities, each activity becomes more meaningful. The problem is then one of how to help youngsters draw meaningful relationships between educational experiences and work. Prerequisite to achieving any success in this area must be workable knowledge of the

1   Roots of the evolving value system of the youngster and the possible effect of the role of education and work in his life;
2   Significance of the educational program in terms of the individual;
3   Array of external factors influencing both the individual and the educational program.

The portion of the Abington project dealing with the exploration of student interests via the language arts curriculum is a pioneer effort at developing in youngsters the desirable relationships between learning and work which we are seeking.

Lockwood, Smith, and Trezise (1968) reported a technique appropriate to this concern. Their approach to occupational guidance was developed for the junior high school, but it could easily be adopted for use in the intermediate grades of the elementary school. The purpose was to expand students' knowledge of available occupational alternatives so the individual would be better prepared to make meaningful vocational decisions at appropriate choice points. This model consisted of systematically transmitting to students occupational information classified according to four worlds: the Natural, the Technological, the Aesthetic, and the Human World, which in turn correspond to the elements of a basic educational program. The array of activities that constituted this program was conducted by both teachers and counselors, and the results of the pilot activity were gratifying in terms of the objectives established for the project.

DECISION-MAKING SKILL

Decision-making is a learnable skill, and as such it may be taught to fairly young individuals. Regardless of the age level and the complexities of the decision, the essential tools for effective decision-making are accurate, understandable information and a plan for using the information. The information must contain data on external factors impinging upon the decision, insights concerning self, and clues to the probable utility for the individual of each option available. Teaching decision-making skills is a matter of providing the learner a model for the systematic analysis of situational and self-information which, when blended, will trigger some course of action.

One of the major obstacles to achieving the goal of effective student decision-making is the individual's anxiety over making poor and personally harmful decisions or decisions which will be judged inappropriate by peers and/or other significant individuals. Educational games, a fairly recent innovation, tend to reduce the level of anxiety by removing the "real" penalties for errors in judgment. Simulations which involve many of the situations experienced by the individual provide the opportunity for the youngster to test out certain behavior and observe the consequences of his action. As the result of his exposure to the reality-oriented, yet make-believe situation, the student is being taught the procedural steps of decision-making by the structure (rules) of the game.

CONCLUSION

In conclusion, don't be misled by the artificial separation in this presentation of the essential elements of the vocational aspects of elementary school guidance programs. The seven areas discussed are not separate entities capable of being managed in a neat, clean fashion at given points in time during the experience of the elementary school child. Each activity must be designed and conducted as an integrated, meaningful part of the child's total educational program while being vertically articulated to his developmental needs.

The goal of developing more vocationally mature preadolescents, better able to profit from their secondary school experiences and to ultimately cope in a successful manner with their uncertain future, is not an impossible job, but it is a difficult task well worth the time and energy of every elementary school counselor.

REFERENCES

Abington School District. Career development activities, grades 5, 6, 7. Report of a project supported by NDEA Title V-A funds, Abington, Pennsylvania, 1968.

Lockwood, O., Smith, D. B., & Trezise, R. Four Worlds: An approach to occupational guidance. *Personnel and Guidance Journal,* 1968, *46,* 641–643.

Nelson, R. Knowledge and interests concerning sixteen occupations among elementary and secondary students. *Educational and Psychological Measurement,* 1963, *23,* 741–754.

Norris, W. *Occupational information in the elementary school.* Chicago: Science Research Associates, 1963.

Smith, E. Innovative ideas in vocational guidance. *American Vocational Journal,* 1968, *43,* 19–22.

Wellington, J., & Olechowski, V. Attitudes toward the world of work in elementary schools. *Vocational Guidance Quarterly,* 1965, *14,* 160–162.

29. Counselors and the Noncollege-Bound Student*

Leslie H. Cochran

Since the turn of the century, most secondary schools have had a far-removed wing, basement area, or separate temporary building commonly referred to as the "shop" or the "kitchen." Typically, it has been the place where the "misfits," "dum-dums," "troublemakers," and the like are sent. It is usually poorly financed, has substandard equipment, and is loaded with safety hazards. Parents, teachers, administrators, and counselors see it as a degrading area where kids are sent only as a last resort, and then only when they are someone else's kids. Somehow the "shop teacher" has survived this era of misinformation, lack of support, degrading attitudes, and resulting poor image problems and has emerged—as has the vocational curriculum—as an integral aspect of the total educational program.

Guidance and counseling developed during this same period and grew in size to a cadre of over 70,000 members. On the surface the guidance profession presents a shining example as reflected in the raising of professional standards; the reduction in counselor-pupil ratios; the development of better research-based tools, techniques, and procedures; and the initiation of counselor education programs. When viewed by most vocational educators, however, the status of counseling in practice looks shaky and shabby. While most vocational educators willingly admit their own deficiencies in curriculum planning, course development, and program implementation, counselors are the one group that is almost unanimously singled out and that receives broad-based criticism for lack of understanding, lack of commitment, and unwillingness to work for and with the typical vocational education student. This general attitude is reflected in such comments as: "Counselors for the most part do not have an extensive background in or understanding of business and industry"; "Counselors are interested only in producing more 'academicians' like themselves"; "Counselors ignore the special needs and abilities of students who are not in college prep programs"; "Counselors devote about eighty percent of their time to a small group of students and to functions that are not related to the vast majority of the student population"; "Counselors are content to work with the easy-to-handle student rather than with the problem cases."

WHERE IS THE ACCOUNTABILITY?

There is no doubt that it is unfair to single out counselors as the scapegoats for vocational education or to imply that all counselors are guilty of such practices as those noted in the comments above, but it is significant to note that the general perception of vocational educators closely parallels these comments. If the counseling profession is not willing to accept this indictment or to admit to its role as

*Source: Reprinted with permission of the author and publisher from the *Personnel and Guidance Journal,* 1974, *52,* 582–585. Copyright 1974 The American Personnel and Guidance Association.

an accomplice in fostering such an image, guidance personnel must assume leadership responsibilities to correct the misconception. The urgency of the situation is apparent for students, and parents are aware that change is coming at an increasingly rapid rate. Change is occurring in the nature of occupations, in the skill levels required for job entry, and in work values. Educators know that adaptability is the key and that individuals can expect to change occupations somewhere between three to five times during their working life.

While most youngsters fully understand that education is a key ingredient in the preparation for employment, educators have passed on to them the societal myth that a college degree is the best and surest route to occupational success—even though less than 20 percent of all occupations existing in this decade will require a college degree. But youngsters have also been told, in contradiction to what the societal myth leads them to believe, that they should endorse the work ethic and enter vocational education. Because of this conflicting information, and because young people have never been supplied with hard facts that would provide a rational basis for making decisions about their future, it is little wonder that the National Advisory Council on Vocational Education (1972), in their *Sixth Report—Counseling and Guidance: A Call for Change*, cited the alarming facts that:

- Over 750,000 youths drop out of high school each year.
- Over 850,000 drop out of college each year.
- Fewer than 1 in every 4 high school students is enrolled in vocational education.
- Record numbers of high school graduates are enrolling in college during the very time when unemployment among college graduates is at a 10-year high.
- The ratio of youth to adult unemployment has risen each year since 1960.
- Student unrest is a strong and pervasive force among both high school and college students.
- Over 75 percent of all community college students are enrolled in the liberal arts transfer program, but less than 25 percent ever attain a baccalaureate degree.
- 38 percent of all Vietnam veterans are enrolled in vocational programs, while 60 percent are enrolled in 4-year college programs, in spite of the limited prospects of jobs for college graduates.

Those who work as practitioners in the field are—and should be—held accountable for both the successes and failures of students in specific programs. There is no doubt that a portion of the responsibility must also be placed on counselors themselves. There are others too who must share in the responsibility for providing sound counseling systems. Foremost among these are: (a) school administrators who assign an abundance of clerical and administrative tasks to counselors, (b) counselor education institutions that offer only one course in occupational guidance and require little or no work experience in their counselor preparation program, (c) school systems that fail to recognize the value of and need for a well-balanced guidance program, (d) state departments of education and professional associations that do not make work experience a part of the requirements for counselor certification, and (e) business and industry that do not work with counselors in an attempt to upgrade counselor knowledge regarding the world of work.

THE OBLIGATION OF GUIDANCE PERSONNEL

It is clear that the problem permeates education and that a total effort is needed to improve the quality and quantity of counseling and guidance services provided for all individuals. The career education thrust speaks strongly to this point, but it provides only general insight. There is no magical solution that will bring about the required changes in attitude, commitment, and understanding of occupationally oriented guidance. Personnel in the guidance profession, however, have specific responsibilities that must be assumed if significant reform is to be initiated. Basically these changes can be grouped into four major types: structural changes, preparation changes, programmatic changes, and directional changes.

Structural Changes. From an administrative point of view, major changes must be made all the way from the local level to the state department of education. Such changes should include: (a) the initiation of actions at the local school board level and in the corresponding administrative units within their jurisdiction confirming these groups' commitment to the importance of providing equal and sound counseling and guidance services to all individuals; (b) efforts to lower the counselor-pupil ratios to a point where all those needing counseling and guidance services can receive them either through individual or group processes; (c) the development by state departments of education of standards requiring at least one year of work experience outside of education for all school counselors; (d) the reorganization of the counseling staff to provide a coordinated team approach so special interests and competencies can be maximized, while still maintaining general guidance functions; (e) the infusion into the counseling system of individuals with rich backgrounds of experience in business, industry, and labor; and (f) the utilization of paraprofessional personnel to perform basic guidance functions under the supervision of professional counselors.

Preparation Changes. The counselor education institutions play a key role in the development of a new career awareness for individuals throughout the guidance and counseling profession. Changes must be made to insure that: (a) work experience outside of education is an integral aspect of all certified counselor programs, (b) career development and the career education thrust permeate the preparatory program, (c) vocational knowledge and career guidance skills of currently employed counselors are upgraded, (d) occupational information courses are integrated into all counselor education programs, and (e) prospective guidance personnel are strongly encouraged to take courses outside of education that will expand their career perceptions.

Programmatic Changes. Within the profession there is a need to provide an expanded continuum both horizontally and vertically. Teachers, outside resource persons, and individuals in the community provide horizontal ties, but a guidance continuum is inadequate if it does not do more. It must also. (a) permeate the entire teacher preparation program as part of the responsibility of *all* educational personnel; (b) provide adequate communication and articulation among personnel at various educational levels; (c) offer job placement and follow-up services as a major part of the counseling and guidance program; (d) serve as a major component within the career education movement; and (e) include backup systems that provide accurate, timely data concerning education, training, and career opportunities.

Directional Changes. The career education movement, along with social pressures, federal legislation, and distress among the educational community, further suggests the need for modifications in emphasis in guidance and counseling. Several needed changes can be cited, such as increased efforts to improve counseling and guidance services for minority populations, handicapped persons, and other disadvantaged persons. In many cases such transformations are already beginning to occur. The main thrust of the change in direction, however, can best be summarized by the goal to *provide equal and comprehensive counseling and guidance services for all individuals.* This requires response to the attitudes expressed by vocational educators, noncollege-bound students, and other groups of students who are given, at least on the surface, second-rate services in comparison to those provided for the college prep segment.

REALITY OR FANTASY?

While the societal myth that a college degree is the best and surest route to occupational success continues to permeate education, such theory and concomitant practice run contrary to all career and educational projections. Educators in general are guilty of fostering this myth, and counselors in particular have made little effort to accurately appraise prospects for youth in the future. This is why counselors in rehabilitation centers, employment centers, vocational guidance agencies, secondary schools, and higher education institutions have not implemented strategies to insure their competence in guiding and assisting individuals in the preparation for lifelong careers.

The inability of the guidance profession to successfully integrate career development theory, work experience outside of education, vocational knowledge, career guidance skills, occupational information courses, and placement and follow-up techniques has contributed significantly to much of the current criticism of education. Students and the educational system itself are therefore plagued by the failure of bond issues, an oversupply of professional personnel, employer-controlled models, the under-employment of large segments of society, and the scarcity of qualified personnel in many careers.

The career education thrust, which evolved as a direct response to these and other social pressures, has limited prospects for success unless the guidance profession is willing to accept the challenge for reform. These issues stress the need for all counselors to be committed to this goal and demonstrate their willingness to work with and for all students, and such a goal requires action-oriented effort to visually demonstrate a broad-based understanding of the world of work so that equal and comprehensive counseling and guidance services can be provided for all individuals.

REFERENCE

National Advisory Council on Vocational Education. *Sixth report—Counseling and guidance: A call for change.* Washington, D.C.: Author, 1972.

30. A Systematic Career Development Program in a Liberal Arts College*

Richard J. Thoni and Patricia M. Olsson

Commitment to one life style over another is a "super decision," according to *Future Shock.* At a time when many students are questioning the practical value of higher education, a central goal of a liberal arts education must be the preparation of the individual for a satisfying life style beyond the college experience. At Augsburg, a liberal arts college in Minneapolis with 1,700 students, the counseling staff had come to view life style preparation and career development as one and the same and, as a result, decided to take a hard look at career needs of Augsburg students.

In separate surveys of high school seniors, present Augsburg students, and Augsburg alumni, all three groups ranked career and human development goals highest; however, the latter two groups ranked the accomplishment of these goals low in degree of satisfaction. It was clear that a more comprehensive approach to career growth was needed.

THE ASSUMPTIONS

Although it was clear that career development concerns were uppermost in the minds of Augsburg students, what was not so clear was what exactly should be done. As Myers (1971) and others have noted, very little career development literature has been directed toward the college years. It was apparent that the Augsburg staff would have to piece together its own goals and principles for a career development program.

Career and liberal arts have not always dwelt comfortably together. Career smacks of "vocationalism" to some faculty and staff, and it was therefore necessary that the program planners consider the unique nature of career development in a liberal arts college. The following assumptions were made: (a) *career* is broadly defined to include those aspects of development that contribute to the individual's life style; (b) career development is a significant part of human development and is closely related to the formation and implementation of one's self-concept (Super et al. 1963); (c) there is no conflict between career development goals and the goals of a liberal arts education—a liberal arts view that has long been held is that education should promote the growth and development of the student (Heath 1968); (d) career growth is a sequential developmental process, in that it may be accomplished through a series of stages or progressive developmental tasks; (e) in order to grow and develop, the student must be

Source: Reprinted with permission of the authors and publisher from the *Personnel and Guidance Journal,* 1975, *53,* 672–675. Copyright 1975 The American Personnel and Guidance Association.

challenged to do so (Sanford 1966)—a large part of a career development program is need creation rather than need reduction; (f) since change is the only certainty in preparing the student to participate in a work society, planning for flexibility is essential (Super 1967).

A HIERARCHICAL PROGRAM OF CAREER GROWTH

With these assumptions, the program planners set out to construct a program of career growth during the college years. They were faced with two options: They could either create a totally new structure, or they could use existing elements and "fill in the gaps" (Parker 1974). Since their goal was to integrate career development with the total educational program, they selected the latter option. Their task thus became one of making the career development process explicit for the college. They had to outline an appropriate theoretical base for the program, link existing elements to that description, and then create new programs where there were obvious needs. (A schematic presentation of the seven stages of career development described below is available from the authors.).

Stage 1: Building Expectations

This is a preliminary stage, based on the need in decision theory to specify the problem or concern. It is important that any educational institution, especially a liberal arts college, clarify for the entering student what it can realistically offer in terms of career preparation. This stage is also the first step in need creation, since it makes students aware of the necessity of working on their own career development. To help students preassess the experiences they can expect to find at Augsburg, career action plans are available: A structured weekend trip to the city offers prospective students an educational experience in an urban setting; freshman summer orientation conducted by faculty, staff, and upperclass student advisors provides parents and students with an intensive day and a half of preregistration, orientation, and peer relationship building; preview courses in an experimental program allow high school seniors to take college courses.

Stage 2: Self-Assessment

Because the career development process is closely related to the clarification of self-concept (Super et al. 1963), the developmental task of this stage is that students be able to discover and express career-relevant characteristics about themselves. Life Planning Laboratories at Augsburg are three-hour group sessions directed toward helping students assess their needs, values, aptitudes, vocational interests, and vocational aspirations. The sessions include such exercises as lifeline, stripping of roles, preferred life style fantasy, and goal setting. A new program is the Human Development Colloquium, which focuses on personal growth themes and operates on the basis of mini-courses. A career development theme, for example, focuses on how to use the liberal arts experience to plan and implement a satisfying personal life style. Students maintain a four-year portfolio that includes self-assessment feedback, an action plan for the college experience, and work samples and references.

Stage 3: Exploration

As students become aware of the need to make career decisions, they begin the process of differentiation (Tiedeman 1963). At this time it is important that they be able to consider a number of different goals and alternatives. Their exposure to a wide range of disciplines and role models is most desirable during this time. The liberal arts curriculum should be the primary vehicle for exploring and examining personal life style. Augsburg's cooperative learning classes are one unique way in which students may confront—through the curriculum—life styles that are greatly different from their own. In this program, faculty teach courses at retirement homes, prisons, halfway houses, mental hospitals, and homes for the handicapped. Independent study, one-month interim courses, and study abroad are other examples of vehicles for exploration through the curriculum. Staff from the counseling center often serve as sponsors for such individualized courses.

Stage 4: Formation of Tentative Career Goals

After students have explored a number of potential alternatives, the first stage of crystallization occurs (Ginzberg et al. 1951). Using the decision making strategy of forecasting the consequences of various alternatives and testing them against an emerging self-concept, students begin to make a number of hypotheses about career. A seminar called the Career Exploration Encounter helps students identify possible career interests, builds career testing behaviors, and gives students a half-day exploration experience with professionals in the city. Some students change majors after seeing it "like it is"; others are more deeply motivated to pursue the field they have chosen.

Stage 5: Reality Testing

It would be easy for students to become satisfied with career plans based on unrealistic projections about the world of work. Reality testing is a crucial step in the further specification of career goals and is often best accomplished through actual involvement in the work experience (Hansen 1972). Though this element is often lacking in a liberal arts college, it is an essential one: Further career growth might be impeded until students can test themselves and their own reactions in a practical work setting. Education and social work are examples of academic majors that traditionally have included involvement in an actual work setting: in education, student teaching; in social work, field experience. For other majors, Augsburg has an internship program that offers a part-time or full-time experience for course credit and, in most cases, a stipend.

Stage 6: Access into the World of Work

This stage involves implementation of career plans and entry into the world of work. The emphasis is on helping students gain skills that would enable them to "sell" themselves to potential employers. The task is to aid students in making realistic plans to meet the various life style needs they have identified. In addition to providing regular placement services, Augsburg provides seniors with concrete assistance in preparing for exit from college. "Selling self" skills are stressed through seminars that include live interviews, mock interviews, and interaction with personnel directors. Though linkages between prospective employers and students are actively promoted, the ultimate responsibility for finding a job or a graduate position belongs to the student.

Stage 7: Reentry into College

Career development for the returning student must also be taken into account. The Augsburg program emphasizes career development as a lifelong interaction between personal growth and life style and therefore recognizes that reassessment, retraining, and continuing education may occur at any point in an individual's work life. The individual's new examination of self and career may result in a totally different integration of the preceding stages of career growth. The New Dimensions Program is designed for students who are not of traditional college age—adults whose education has been interrupted and who now wish to reenter formal education. The program helps ease their way back into the college setting by offering admissions counseling, simplified registration, and counseling for career exploration.

EVALUATION

Initial evaluations of Augsburg's career development program have focused on student response to the new activities and programs conducted by the staff. Students generally have been most excited about those programs dealing directly with the world of work. As a result of the Career Exploration Encounter, for example, approximately 75 students spent time on the job with workers in the students' potential career fields. Evaluations in the near future will be directed toward more objective measures of career maturity, sense of personal control, and satisfaction with career choices.

The Augsburg staff members themselves have become excited in dealing with career growth as a significant and integrated part of human development on the college level. They have found increasing evidence that important developmental tasks can be accomplished through a planned program of career growth within the liberal arts context.

REFERENCES

Ginzberg, E.; Ginsburg, S. W.; Axelrad, S.; & Herma, J. *Occupational choice.* New York: Columbia University Press, 1951.

Hansen, L. S. A model for career development through curriculum. *Personnel and Guidance Journal,* 1972, *51,* 243–250.

Heath, D. H. *Growing up in college.* San Francisco: Jossey-Bass, 1968.

Myers, R. A. Career development in the college years. Paper presented at the American Personnel and Guidance Association Convention, Atlantic City, New Jersey, April 1971.

Parker, C. A. Student development: What does it mean? *Journal of College Student Personnel,* 1974, *15,* 248–256.

Sanford, N. *Self and society: Social change and individual development.* New York: Atherton Press, 1966.

Super, D. E. *Floundering and trial after high school.* Horace Mann Lincoln Institute of
    School Experimentation Career Pattern Study Monograph IV. New York: Columbia
    University Teachers College, 1967.
Super, D. E.; Stareshevsky, R.; Mattin, N.; & Jordaan, T. P. *Career development: Self-
    concept theory.* Research Monograph No. 4. New York: College Entrance Examina-
    tion Board, 1963.
Tiedeman, D. V. *Career development: Choice and adjustment.* Research Monograph No. 3.
    New York: College Entrance Examination Board, 1963.

31. Counseling older persons: Career change and retirement*

Daniel Sinick

The growing proportion of older persons in the population offers counselors opportunities to exercise their expertise and to reap further rewards of professional service. To maximize the responsiveness and efficacy of such service, helping professionals must become expert regarding the counseling needs of older persons and special considerations and emphases in meeting these needs.

COUNSELING NEEDS OF OLDER PERSONS

Multiple developmental tasks continue to emerge as individuals survive the storm and stress of adolescence and move on to the not unclouded challenges of adulthood and after. Maturing and aging persons frequently face situations fraught with frustration; succumbing often seems easier than coping. Counselors knowledgeable about the developmental dilemmas of later years can help turn threats into challenges.

Hurlock [7, p. 13] enumerated 21 developmental tasks: 8 in early adulthood, 7 in middle age, and 6 in old age. The diminishing numbers are deceptive because some earlier tasks persist into later periods, the effect being cumulative and incomplete. Closure comes only with death, the final developmental task.

Earlier tasks include selecting a mate, learning to live with one, starting a family, rearing children, managing a home, getting started in an occupation, assuming civic responsibility, and finding a congenial social group. Among middle-age tasks are achieving civic and social responsibility, establishing a standard of living, helping children become adults, further relating to one's spouse, adjusting to aging parents, adjusting to physiological changes, and developing adult leisure activities. Old age brings adjusting to decreasing health, to retirement, and to death of spouse; affiliating with members of one's age group; meeting social and civic obligations; and achieving satisfactory living arrangements.

Although Hurlock's list appears extensive, it is more selective than comprehensive, making certain emphases and omitting some tasks entirely (for example, one's own death). Nor do all her tasks represent counseling needs of older persons. This article focuses on two major tasks that could profit from counseling: career change and retirement.

CAREER CHANGE

Second careers are now commonplace, and third careers are not uncommon. Sociological forces and psychological factors have combined to increase the numbers of older men and women seeking new careers. Because different combinations of these variables affect different individuals, counselors must be aware of special considerations possibly applicable to older clients.

Special Considerations   Motivations for career change are to be considered first of all, as their complexities could include avoidance vs. approach behavior, rational vs. emotional reasons, and known vs. hidden motivations. Does the client want out of a career? If so, consideration ought to be given to the satisfactions, dissatisfactions, and other factors related to that career before a new one is sought. Similar consideration may be required of rationalizations and unconscious motivations.

Career changers frequently manifest particular characteristics that need to be taken into account. Lack of self-confidence is a prominent phenomenon, together with lack of skills required for choosing a career and for finding a job. Whether such lack is related to reliance on luck as an external locus of control, it can interfere with successful career change.

Lack of self-confidence has multiple causes. Previous careers may be perceived as poor choices or as representing poor achievement. Women entering or reentering the labor force may feel unready or rusty regarding new or renewed careers. Older clients may feel incapable of competing with younger workers, sometimes adopting—in an effort to be "realistic"—generalizations based on agism and not personally applicable.

Lack of skills in career choice and jobfinding commonly arises from lack of practice. How many choose their first careers through a deliberate decision-making process? How many find jobs in other than haphazard, catch-as-catch-can ways? Effective career counseling affords older clients as well as young ones practice in the vital processes of evaluating, exploring, and choosing careers. Parallel practice in seeking and finding jobs is also a career counselor's responsibility, even if implemented by other sources, for example, the employment service.

Employment assistance for older clients is necessitated by prejudicial employer practices. Despite antidiscrimination legislation, older job applicants confront a series of hurdles that may hold little or no relationship to job performance. These include preemployment medical examinations, educational credentials, tests standardized on young persons, and interviews used for screening out instead of in.

Counseling Emphases   Although emphases appropriately overlap with pertinent considerations, added explication can assist counselors in selecting content and procedures for use with older clients. Their motivations for career change, their characteristic lack of self-confidence, and their need for jobfinding practice in the face of employment hurdles highlight important emphases.

Evaluation of motivations is essential, the client participating maximally toward the desired outcome of self-evaluation. Misperceived motivations, blurred goals, and delusive directions can yield superficial planning and unsound choices. Are the apparent motivations and aspirations the client's or spin-offs from significant others? First careers are often so motivated; career change provides a second chance for self-direction.

Delusion can come from oneself, however, as well as from others. The notion that one's higher-level needs remain unfulfilled or one's abilities unchallenged may reflect a personal Peter Principle premised on an aversion to previous job pressures. Impatience and impulsiveness may not be the best basis for a career change. Positive motivations and attributes are just as likely to emerge from a proper evaluation of proffered reasons for changing careers.

Generation of self-confidence can be accomplished in counseling by drawing on success experiences and debunking myths about older persons. The dynamics of some individuals are such that they disregard accomplishments on the job or otherwise. Excessive modesty may cause them to minimize praise received from employers, peers, or parents. A joint search by client and counselor for work or play that was well done can help to build self-confidence and suggest second careers.

Misconceptions about the aging process and about the reputed decline of mental and other capacities can be countered. Valid evidence [4, 5] regarding the functional capabilities of older workers has accrued in the burgeoning field of industrial gerontology. Real-life second career successes [12] can constitute vicarious experiences to lift the self-confidence of some clients.

Minimizing the use of tests in counseling older clients is important for two reasons: Traditional testing is less appropriate, and other approaches are more effective. Most tests used in counseling were constructed for use with younger persons. Norms may not be applicable, speed or visual acuity may be stressed, face validity may be lacking. Tests and inventories alike appear artificial and contrived to older persons.

A naturalistic approach to assessment gives credence to the lives that older persons have led. Their life histories [3] and their work histories [9] yield longitudinal information of greater value than cross-sectional test data. Interviews [23] can surpass interest inventories in tapping duration, intensity, and underlying values.

Old interests and skills can be put to work by applying the concepts of career clusters and transferability. The career clusters associated with career education and development programs can be supplemented by the worker trait groups of the *Dictionary of Occupational Titles (DOT)* [15] and other formal classifications. Informal groupings of occupations in relation to client characteristics can cover the gamut from college majors [10] to hobbies.

Transferability relates past interests, skills, and other client attributes to careers calling for them. The *DOT* facilitates the wide bridging of client characteristics and occupational characteristics, as do additional publications, some of which focus on military-civilian career shifts [2, 14].

New interests and skills may need to be developed to implement new motivations. Exploration and development of interests and skills can be addressed in part through counseling proper but in the main through education or training and trying oneself out at new jobs. Because job tryouts are hard to come by, education or training offers more realistic possibilities.

Although a full-time effort is possible for some prepared to make a dramatic switch, part-time education, training, or tryout provides both exploration and transition. The level of education or training appropriate to the new interests, the skills sought, and other client variables can be ascertained through a number of aids geared to professional preparation [6], two years beyond high school [22], and multiple levels [21].

Jobfinding assistance focuses on client skills needed and on employer hurdles to be surmounted; preparation of clients for job finding has been widely described [e.g., 11, pp. 51–60]. Employer hurdles and the stereotypes undergirding them can be overcome indirectly through successful placement of effective older employees, however, dealing with employers enhances placement efforts.

Employers can be apprised not only of the qualifications of a particular client but also of the favorable attributes of older workers [20]. Employers can be further assisted with regard to methods of matching older workers. Matching seven job relevant worker variables with the requirements of specific jobs has been done effectively in industry through use of the GULHEMP scale [8]. Redesign of jobs for workers [16] has gained increasing acceptance. Training has been improved, finally, by adopting the "discovery method" [1], which permits self-paced learner progress.

RETIREMENT

Whenever career change accompanies retirement, considerations and emphases of the kind already delineated come into play. Because retirement requires other changes and adjustments, however, counseling may call for additional considerations and emphases.

Special Considerations   *Adjustments* is the key word because of the closed minds and negative attitudes confronted by retirees. Their relatives and associates, reared in a youth-oriented society, seldom accord older persons much dignity and respect. Even less status is assigned in our work-oriented society to older persons no longer working. Role reversal often occurs, in which a parent becomes dependent on a child.

The double jeopardy imposed on older persons by the youth emphasis and work ethic makes a mockery of the so-called "free time" released by retirement. Accustomed to being paid for their time, retirees have not been acculturated to valuing leisure time. Second careers or part-time employment may be sought mainly as an escape from enforced free time. Creative use of time toward continued self-actualization is a major challenge of counseling.

Counselors may not regard as professionally challenging the many mundane matters that require attention in assisting retirees. Income and finances, housing and living arrangements, health and nutrition, consumer education and personal safety, and legal matters all call for worldly knowledgeability shunned by some counselors entranced by the intrapsychic alone. Clients live in real worlds as psychologically fascinating as their private worlds.

Counseling Emphases   Role adjustments, use of time, and mundane matters related to retirement are considerations properly paralleled by pertinent emphases in counseling. Counselors can provide retirement assistance both before and after what is generally an abrupt "event." Some adjustments could be alleviated by making retirement gradual or transitional.

Role adjustments, hampered by the attitudes of society, are not helped by retirees' introjection of these attitudes. Nor can counselors help a great deal who unconsciously accept negative stereotypes and operate on the basis of built-in biases. Troll and Schlossberg [13] concluded from their study that "counselors of adults need to take a close look at themselves with regard to their own age bias" (p. 20).

Retirees may require assistance in recognizing retirement and its adjustments as a natural phase of normal life development. Similarly, counselors must recognize that people having difficulty with retirement adjustments are not necessarily problem clients. Retirement looms large as the peak of a pile of losses of various kinds experienced in the course of life: not only losses of friends and relatives, but some loss in physical appearance, in vision and hearing, and in achievement relative to aspiration. Mourning over losses must give way to an appreciation of continued living.

Whether one should continue living actively or give up previous activities is a client decision that need not be affected by the more abstract issue raised by the concept of disengagement. A counselor's preference for maintaining active contact with young people, for example, may not be the model for a particular client. Clients may choose their own combinations of what might be called staying in and pulling out of life.

Use of time is so interactive with needed adjustments as to warrant central emphasis in counseling. It has been properly said that time is all we have. Clients have to become acquainted, first of all, with the multiple options available to them for use of time. In addition to the familiar full-time employment, other options include part-time employment, volunteer work, and what is well regarded as creative use of time.

Part-time employment serves some retirees as a transition from full-time employment and its attendant roles. Together with temporary employment, part-time work meets the needs of many older persons and of many employers as well, who gain from added scheduling flexibility and reduced fringe benefits. Part-time and temporary opportunities, reflected by increasing numbers of specialized employment agencies, are expected to keep pace with the rising interest in such use of time [19].

Unpaid volunteer work offers opportunities for full-time, part-time, or temporary use of time. The Department of Labor [18] has reported (p. 1): "(1) more volunteers, (2) different kinds of volunteers, (3) different kinds of functions, and (4) different channels for the delivery of their services." For older persons who wish (perhaps belatedly) to serve society, differential client needs and personalities might suggest whether such service should involve direct work with people or work in a community organization.

Creative use of time lacks the social sanction automatically accorded work, as well as cultural guidelines for using time freely and self-fulfillingly. Avocations are etymologically and otherwise derivative activities often distasteful to older persons advised to engage in hobbies. Pastimes just to pass time or kill time are better supplemented or supplanted by such activities, either active or passive, as playing or listening to music, growing flowers, collecting rocks or shells, crocheting or knitting, learning a language, writing letters, engaging in conversations, and simply attending to the world and being attuned to others' feelings and thoughts as well as one's own.

Mundane matters require counselor attention, in part because of their impact on role adjustments and use of time. Budgeting money is not unrelated, for example, to budgeting time. Living with relatives, in retirement communities, or in private or public housing has implications regarding dependence vs. independence, disengagement vs. participation, and other vital dimensions. Also vital are preventive as well as remedial aspects of physical and emotional well-being. Medication and nutrition overlap with such consumer education concerns as informed and cautious shopping, cost of recreational activities, and legal and illegal fees. Counselors who provide preretirement or postretirement assistance must themselves be informed regarding many matters that are more than mundane.

CONCLUSION

It seems appropriate to close with the reassuring comment that counselors can assist older persons effectively without themselves being older persons. To help others, one need not have changed careers or experienced the role adjustments of retirement; vicarious experience is the basis for most learning and understanding. Superficial similarity between client and counselor, moreover, can mask deep disparities in values, standards, and attitudes toward life and death.

REFERENCES

1 Belbin, R. M. The discovery method in training older workers. In H. L. Sheppard (Ed.), *Toward an industrial gerontology.* Cambridge, Mass.: Schenkman Publishing, 1970. Pp. 56–60.

2 Collings, K. J. *The second time around: Finding a civilian career in mid-life.* Cranston, R.I.: Carroll Press, 1971.

3 Dailey, C. A. *Assessment of lives.* San Francisco: Jossey-Bass, 1971.

4 Grace, H. A. Industrial gerontology: Behavioral science perspectives on work and aging. In *Industrial gerontology: Curriculum materials.* New York: National Council on the Aging, 1968. Pp. 1–84.

5 Green, R. F. Age, intelligence, and learning. *Industrial Gerontology,* 1972, (12), 29–41.

6 Hiestand, D. L. *Changing careers after thirty-five: New horizons through professional and graduate study.* New York: Columbia University Press, 1971.

7　Hurlock, E. B. *Developmental psychology* (4th ed.). New York: McGraw-Hill, 1975.

8　Koyl, L. F.; Hackney, M.; & Holbway, R. D. *Employing the older worker: Matching the employee to the job* (2nd ed.). Washington, D.C.: National Council on the Aging, 1974.

9　Leshner, S. S., & Snyderman, G. S. Evaluating personal characteristics from a client's work history. *Personnel and Guidance Journal,* 1963, *42,* 56–59.

10　Malnig, L. R., & Morrow, S. L. *What can I do with a major in . . . ?* Jersey City, N.J.; Saint Peter's College Press, 1975.

11　Sinick, D. *Occupational information and guidance.* Boston: Houghton Mifflin, 1970.

12　Stetson, D. *Starting over.* New York: Macmillan, 1971.

13　Troll, L., & Schlossberg, N. How "age biased" are college counselors? *Industrial Gerontology,* 1971, *(10),* 14–20.

14　U.S. Department of Defense. *Target tomorrow: Second career planning for military retirees.* Washington, D.C.: U.S. Government Printing Office, 1970.

15　U.S. Department of Labor. *Dictionary of occupational titles* (3rd ed.). Volume I, *Definitions of titles.* Vol. II, *Occupational classification.* Washington, D.C.: U.S. Government Printing Office, 1965.

16　U.S. Department of Labor. *Job redesign for older workers: Ten case studies.* Washington, D.C.: U.S. Government Printing Office, 1967.

17　U.S. Department of Labor. *Education and jobs.* Washington, D.C.: U.S. Government Printing Office, 1968.

18　U.S. Department of Labor. *Americans volunteer.* Washington, D.C.: U.S. Government Printing Office, 1969.

19　U.S. Department of Labor. *U.S. manpower in the 1970's: Opportunity and challenge.* Washington, D.C.: U.S. Government Printing Office, 1970.

20　U.S. Department of Labor. *Back to work after retirement.* Washington, D.C.: U.S. Government Printing Office, 1971.

21　U.S. Department of Labor. *Get credit for what you know.* Washington, D.C.: Author, 1971.

22　Whitfield, E. A., & Hoover, R. *Guide to careers through vocational training.* San Diego: Robert R. Knapp, 1968.

23　Whitney, D. R. Predicting from expressed vocational choice: A review. *Personnel and Guidance Journal,* 1969, *48,* 279–286.

32. Beyond Career Development—Life Career Development*

Norman C. Gysbers and Earl J. Moore

Current theories of career development began appearing in the literature during the early 1950s. At that time the occupational choice of focus of the first fifty years of career development was beginning to give way to a broader, more comprehensive view of individuals and their occupational development over the life span. Occupational choice was beginning to be seen as a developmental process. Such phrases as "life stages," "vocational tasks," "vocational maturity," and "vocational self-concept" were becoming part of the professional vocabulary.

These new perspectives represented a shift in emphasis; prior to the 1950s, theorists and practitioners had focused most of their attention on the occupational aspects of the transition from school to work. In fact, the first modern formulation of guidance, by Frank Parsons, was based on certain assumptions about occupational choice. Unfortunately, as Borow said:

> Parsons' primal version of vocational counseling, or at least the interpretation placed upon it by his followers, was lacking in several respects. It overplayed the importance of self-analysis as a means to helping the individual know his vocational potentialities, oversimplified the dissemination of occupational information as a way of shaping vocational decisions, subordinated the influence of personal values in choice making, and lent at least tacit support to the single-job-for-life hypothesis. (Borow 1973, p. 4)

CAREER DEVELOPMENT

During the 1950s, theorists began to emphasize a developmental view of occupational choice. It was during this period that the term *vocational development* became popular as a way of describing the broadened view of occupational choice and the many factors that influenced it. During the 1960s, knowledge about this aspect of human development increased dramatically. Increasingly, the terms *career* and *career development* became popular, so that today many theorists and practitioners prefer them to *vocation* and *vocational development*.

Currently many writers and researchers define career development as one aspect of human development. More specifically, it is often described as the interaction of psychological, sociological, economic, physical, and chance factors that shape the career or sequence of occupations, jobs, and positions that individuals hold during their lives (National Vocational Guidance Association 1973).

This expanded view of the career concept is more appropriate than the traditional view of career as an occupational choice. It is more appropriate because it breaks the time barrier that previously restricted the vision of career to only a cross-sectional view of an individual's life. As Super and Bohn (1970, p. 115) have pointed out, "It is well . . . to keep clear the distinction between occupation (what one does) and career (the course pursued over a period of time)." It is more appropriate too because the career concept has become the basis for organizing and interpreting the impact that the role of work has on individuals over their lifetimes. Past, present, and possible future occupational and related behaviors can be understood in the context of an individual's overall development. Thus, current conceptions of career development place emphasis on "vocational histories rather than on status at a single point in time, on career criteria rather than occupational criteria" (Jordaan 1974, p. 264).

LIFE CAREER DEVELOPMENT

Although current career development theories are more appropriate than traditional ones, most still separate individuals' work roles, settings, and events from the other roles, settings, and events in their lives. Because of the increasing complexity and interrelatedness of all aspects of society, it no longer seems possible to clearly separate one role from another, one setting from another, one event from another. We are thus proposing that the meaning of career be expanded to encompass individuals' total lives. As Jones and others (1972) have indicated, the concept of career encompasses a variety of possible patterns of personal choice related to each individual's total life style; its components are occupation, education, personal and social behavior, learning how to learn, social responsibility (i.e., citizenship), and leisure time activities.

Just as the time barrier was broken in the 1950s, it is now time to go beyond the work-oriented barrier that is inherent in some of the current definitions of career development and to focus instead on all aspects of individuals' lives—on life career development. Work roles, work settings, and work-related events are important in the lives of individuals, but they should not be seen in isolation from other important life roles, settings, and events. Nor should they be isolated and fragmented in time and space so that the focus is on only certain periods of an individual's life. Instead, work-related concerns need to be placed in the context of the total time span of human development so that they can be better understood.

Life career development is defined as self-development over the life span through the integration of the roles, settings, and events of a person's life. When defined in this manner, life career development provides a comprehensive and integrated view of human growth and development over the life span. It has the potential of helping individuals link their past and present circumstances to possible future ones. The life career development perspective provides a personal framework for individuals to help them visualize and plan for their life careers. It has the potential of creating career consciousness in individuals, allowing them to develop life competencies, attitudes, and values. In the words of Reich:

> Included within the idea of consciousness is a person's background, education, politics, insight, values, emotions, and philosophy, but consciousness is more than these or even the sum of them. It is the whole man; his "head"; his way of life. It is that by

which he creates his own life and thus creates the society in which he lives. (1971, p. 15)

CONVERGING EMPHASES

The need for an extension and expansion of the career concept from an occupational perspective to a life perspective can be traced, in part, to the many substantial changes that have taken place in society over the past seventy years. During that time, society changed from a rural, agrarian one to a highly complex industrial one. Roles, settings, and events have become more varied, fluid, and interrelated.

These and other changes represented challenges to individuals and to society. To meet these challenges, the government, public and private agencies, and the educational community sought to improve and extend their traditional programs from early childhood through the adult years. Particularly during the past few years, a common approach to meeting these challenges has been to develop specialized programs in manpower, rehabilitation, and education. While these programs have quickly brought resources and personnel to bear on problems, there has often been considerable overlap of purpose and technique. Many of these programs, for example, have focused on relevance of information and experience, involvement with individuals, the humanization of interpersonal communication, values clarification opportunities, decision making skill development, identity achievement, individual success, and positive self-worth.

A comparison of these programs' purposes and techniques reveals that they bear more than a superficial resemblance to those found in discussions of developmental guidance and counseling programs. Also, many of the processes—such as group techniques, interpersonal communication skills, and decision making procedures—used or suggested in these programs resemble guidance and counseling competencies.

DEVELOPMENTAL PROGRAMS

The emerging convergence of many of today's manpower, rehabilitation, and education program purposes, techniques, and competencies with those of guidance and counseling indicates that the government, public and private agencies, and the educational community may be ready to examine ways to develop and implement guidance and counseling in a manner commensurate with other manpower, rehabilitation, and education programs. There seems to be a readiness to develop and implement guidance and counseling goals and to see them as equal and complementary to goals in these other programs, early childhood through the adult years.

The accomplishment of this, however, will require a reconceptualization of guidance and counseling. Rather than a service-oriented, event-oriented conception focusing on only aspects and segments of human development, guidance and counseling must have a comprehensive developmental conceptualization based on individual and societal needs and must be organized programmatically around person-centered goals and activities designed to meet those needs. What is needed is a life career development perspective of human growth and development to serve as a conceptual base for guidance and counseling program development.

The program conceptualization of guidance and counseling does not deemphasize the importance of working with specific educational and occupational concerns at specific points during an individual's life. Nor is it less responsive to specific personal-social needs of individuals. Instead, this conceptualization recognizes that there are counseling-related understandings and skills that all individuals need as they grow and develop throughout their lives.

To meet current and future individual and societal needs, guidance and counseling programs must assume responsibility for assisting individuals in the development of self-knowledge and interpersonal skills; life career planning and self-placement competencies; and knowledge and understanding of their current and future life career roles, settings, and events—especially those associated with family, education, work, and leisure. Guidance and counseling programs also must assist individuals to understand and relate the meaning of instructional and training programs to their present and future life careers, whether these programs take place during the elementary and secondary school years or during the adult and continuing education years.

To reach these person-centered outcomes in a school setting, guidance and counseling programs must be seen as equal and complementary to instructional programs. The theme stressed for school settings is equally applicable to postsecondary institutions and public and private agencies, although the organizational patterns and processes in these settings may vary according to the needs of the clientele.

GUIDANCE AND COUNSELING RESPONSIBILITIES

Three major areas of responsibility emerge from a life career development perspective of guidance and counseling: curriculum-based responsibilities, individual facilitation responsibilities, and on-call responsibilities.

Curriculum-Based Responsibilities

In manpower, rehabilitation, and other public and private agency settings, curriculum-based guidance and counseling responsibilities focus on the common needs of clients in those settings. For example, some may lack self-confidence, self-understanding, or interpersonal skills. Some may not have appropriate employability skills; that is, they may not know how to find, apply for, and get along on a job. Still others may need assistance in self-assessment toward the goal of making a midlife career change. Such needs can form the basis for developmental guidance and counseling activities that, if successful, will enable the client to do something other than wait until the needs reach crisis proportions. Guidance and counseling personnel in these settings can work directly with clients to meet these needs in group or individual interactions. At other times they may provide resources and consultation to employers and other community personnel who work directly with clients.

In school settings—including elementary schools, secondary schools, post-secondary schools, vocational-technical schools, community colleges, and four-year colleges—curriculum-based guidance and counseling brings together those activities that take place primarily during regularly scheduled courses of study. These activities may be part of regular classroom instruction or may be organized around special topics in the form of units, modules, or mini-courses. They are based on the guidance-related understandings and skills that all individuals need as they grow and develop. Typical topics are: self-understanding; interpersonal relationships; decision making; values clarification; and information about roles, settings, and events in family, education, work and leisure. Counselors may be involved directly with students through classroom activities, small groups, or individual interaction, or they may work directly with teachers and instructors to provide resources and consultation.

Individual Facilitation Responsibilities

Individual facilitation responsibilities include those systematic guidance and counseling activities designed to assist all individuals in continuously monitoring and understanding their growth and development in terms of their own personal goals, values, abilities, aptitudes, and interests. In this context, counselors and others with guidance responsibilities can serve in the capacity of personal development specialists. Personalized and continuous contact and involvement with individuals is stressed rather than incidental, superficial contact.

The guidance and counseling functions in this category provide for the individual accountability needed in manpower, rehabilitation, and education to assure that the uniqueness of individuals is not lost and that resources are being used fully to facilitate people's life career development. Carrying out individual facilitation responsibilities will involve cooperative planning among personnel in elementary and secondary schools, post-secondary schools, public and private agencies, business and industry, and other interested groups and individuals.

On-Call Responsibilities

On-call guidance responsibilities focus on direct, immediate responses to individual needs, providing such assistance as information seeking, crisis counseling, and consultation. In addition, on-call activities are supportive of curriculum-based and individual facilitative guidance and counseling functions. Adjunct guidance staff—peers, paraprofessionals, volunteers, support staff—can aid counselors in carrying out on-call functions. Peers can be involved in tutorial programs, orientation activities, ombudsman functions, and—with special training—cross-age counseling and leadership in informal dialogue. Paraprofessionals and volunteers can provide meaningful assistance in such areas as placement, follow-up, and community-school-home liaison activities.

Providing direct and immediate responses to individual needs and supporting curriculum-based and individual facilitative guidance activities will require new ways of organizing activities and resources. One approach is to develop guidance and placement centers. Such centers could bring together information and resources and provide for the processing of a wide variety of guidance and counseling activities, such as career exploration groups; peer counseling; individual advisement programs; midlife and later life career counseling; community resource surveys; and educational and occupational placement, follow-up, and follow-through. Centers could be located in schools, vocational-technical centers, community colleges, four-year institutions, and public and private community agencies. There is an urgent need to develop a coordinated network of such centers in all of these settings in order to meet the life career needs of individuals.

THE PROSPECTUS

The life career development perspective of human growth and development has the potential of becoming a unifying concept around which the many and varied guidance and counseling programs in manpower, rehabilitation, and education are organized to meet the individual and societal needs of tomorrow. Here's how:

● Life career development has investment potential for everyone. It is not the property of one group. Consumers and professionals can relate equally to the basic concepts. There is common relevance for all.

● Other manpower, rehabilitation, and education programs having similar purposes and goals can be integrated around a life career development framework.

● Cultural crises and problems such as drug abuse, human sexuality, human rights, and midlife and later life career changes can be approached directly and comprehensively without creating unnecessary additional program structures.

● Linkage among and between home, school, community, and agency can be accomplished naturally. Programs for continuing and adult education are not only implied but expected.

● Guidance and counseling programs and responsibilities can become part of the total educational mainstream, early childhood through the adult years. On this basis, guidance and counseling goals and activities based on a life career development perspective become a necessary and integral part of all human development programs.

If schools, colleges, and agencies can begin to implement some of these ideas, they will have started to meet the life career needs of human beings and thus the needs of society.

REFERENCES

Borow, H. (Ed.) *Career guidance for a new age.* Boston: Houghton Mifflin, 1973.
Jones, G. B.; Hamilton, J. A.; Granchow, L. H.; Helliwell, C. B.; & Wolff, J. M. *Planning, developing, and field testing career guidance programs.* Palo Alto, Calif.: American Institutes for Research, 1972.

Jordaan, J. P. Life stages as organizing modes of career development. In E. L. Herr (Ed.), *Vocational guidance and human development.* Boston: Houghton Mifflin, 1974.

National Vocational Guidance Association. *Position paper on career development.* Washington, D. C.: National Vocational Guidance Association, 1973.

Reich, C. A. *The greening of America.* New York: Bantam Books, 1971.

Super, D. E., & Bohn, M. J., Jr. *Occupational psychology.* Belmont, Calif.: Wadsworth, 1970.

FOLLOW-UP FOR SECTION FIVE

Questions:

1 List several characteristics *and* vocational counseling needs which make each of the following groups unique:
   a Children.
   b Non-college-bound young adults
   c Young adults enrolled in college
   d The elderly

2 List several reasons why, according to Smith in "Vocational Aspects of Elementary School Guidance Programs: Objectives and Activities," vocational guidance activities are appropriate at the elementary school level.

3 According to Ginzberg in "A Critical Look at Career Guidance," the counseling professions should:

   Expand guidance resources for both young and mature adults, who are at a critical period in their lives, and retard the slow but steady trend toward bringing guidance services into the elementary school.

   Prepare a 500-word argument either agreeing or disagreeing with this premise.

4 Based upon Thoni and Olsson's article, "A Systematic Career Development Program in a Liberal Arts College," list the seven stages and several appropriate vocational behaviors for each.

5 Compare and contrast the stages outlined by Thoni and Olsson in "A Systematic Career Development Program in a Liberal Arts College" with those outlined by Super in "A Theory of Vocational Development."

6 Based on Cochran's article, "Counselors and the Noncollege-bound Student," define and give an example of each of the following types of changes:
   a Structural
   b Preparation
   c Programmatic
   d Directional

7 Morrill, Oetting, and Hurst divide the dimensions of counselor functioning into target of intervention, methods of intervention, and purposes of intervention. Using these terms, classify the recommendations presented by Sinick in "Counseling Older Persons: Career Change and Retirement."

8 What, according to Sinick in "Counseling Older Persons: Career Change and Retirement," are the appropriate counseling emphases for clients experiencing change and retirement?

9 The following questions pertain to Gysbers and Moore's article, "Beyond Career Development—Life Career Development."
   a Define life career development.
   b How does this definition differ from Super's definition of career development?
   c Give several examples of *individual facilitation responsibilities* and *on-call responsibilities.*
   d What are the similarities and differences between *curriculum-based responsibilities* and Hansen's suggestions in "A Model for Career Development through the Curriculum?"
   e To what extent does the life–career–development model overcome the criticisms expressed by Warnath in "Vocational Theories: Direction to Nowhere?"

Learn by Doing:

1 How much do elementary school children know? The purpose of this exercise is to provide counselor-trainees with an opportunity to work with elementary school children. Present a group guidance lesson featuring one of the following or similar ones:

Career Awareness Field Trips (Guidance Associates)*
Introducing Career Concepts (Science Research Associates)*
Careers (Parker Brothers)*

2 What's important? The purpose of this exercise is to provide the counselor-trainee with an opportunity to help individuals clarify their values. Use any of the materials below or similar ones with an appropriate group:
Twenty Things You Love to Do (Hart Publishing Co., Inc., page 30*)
Pie of Life (Hart Publishing Co., Inc., page 228*)
Careers and Lifestyles (Guidance Associates)*

3 What's available? Conduct a series of interviews with professionals in your community. Determine the extent to which vocational guidance services are available to various groups. Consult the Taped Interview Format in Appendix A. Consider the following groups:
   a Young adults about to enter the labor force
   b Young adults seeking or enrolled in postsecondary education
   c Individuals wishing to change career fields
   d Individuals about to retire or those who already have

4 Of what help has vocational counseling been? The purpose of this assignment is to show the counselor-trainee the extent to which vocational counseling has had an impact on individuals at various ages. Consult the Taped Interview Format, which may be found in Appendix A.

5 The past as a predictor of the future. Use the Career Logs assignment which may be found in Appendix E, Activity no. 5, with a group of high school or college students. The purpose of this assignment is to provide students with some insight into their past experiences as they may relate to their future goals.

6 What about college? The purpose of this exercise is to provide the counselor-trainee with the opportunity to work with young adults who are involved in making decisions about college. Use any of the materials below or similar ones with an appropriate group:

College? It's Up to You (Guidance Associates)*
Different Ways to Go to College (Guidance Associates)*

7 Information, please. Select one of the populations below and prepare a bibliography of both print and nonprint materials which would facilitate career awareness or career development.
   a Children
   b Noncollege-bound young adults
   c Young adults enrolled in postsecondary education
   d The elderly

8 Let's review. Based upon the bibliography prepared above, select one of the items for review. Apply the Guidelines for the Systematic Selection, Evaluation, and Use of Simulated Vocational Guidance Materials, which may be found in Appendix F.

*See Appendix H for additional information.

9 To learn more. Prepare an abstract based upon one of the articles listed below under Additional Resources. Consult Appendix G for the suggested format.

Additional Resources

American Personnel and Guidance Association. (Producer). *Career and training options for noncollege-bound students.* Washington, D.C.: American Personnel and Guidance Association Press, undated. (cassette), (order # 72911).

Antholz, M. B. Illustrative resources and programs for implementing career development curricula in the elementary grades. *Social Education,* 1975, *39,* 316–319

Ash, P. Pre-retirement counseling. *Gerontologist,* 1966, *6,* 97–99.

Bender, R. Vocational development in the elementary school: A framework for implementation. *School Counselor,* 1973, *21,* 116–120.

Bonar, J. R., & Mahler, L. R. A center for "undecided" college students. *Personnel and Guidance Journal,* 1976, *54,* 481–484.

Borow, H. *Vocational planning for college students.* Englewood Cliffs, N.J.: Prentice-Hall, Inc., 1959.

Bugg, C. A. Implications of some major theories of career choice for elementary school guidance programs. *Elementary School Guidance and Counseling,* 1969, *3,* 164–173.

Dunphy, P., Austin, S., & McEneaney, T. *Career development for the college student.* Cranston, R.I.: Carroll Press, 1968.

Heald, J. Mid-life career influence. *Vocational Guidance Quarterly,* 1977, *25,* 309–312.

Hershenson, D. B. Techniques for assisting life-stage vocational development. *Personnel and Guidance Journal,* 1969, *8,* 776–780.

Kasschau, P. L. Reevaluating the need for retirement preparation programs. *Industrial Gerontology,* 1974, *1,* 42–59.

Katz, M. *Decisions and values: A rationale for secondary school guidance.* Princeton, N.J.: College Entrance Examination Board, 1963.

Kelleher, C. H. Second careers—A growing trend. *Industrial Gerontology,* 1973, *17,* 1–8.

Lyon, R. Vocational development and the elementary school. *Elementary School Journal,* 1966, *66,* 368–376.

Matthews, E. E. (Ed.) *Counseling girls and women over the lifespan.* Washington, D.C.: American Personnel and Guidance Association, 1972.

McClelland, D. Opening job doors for mature women. *Manpower,* 1973, *5,* 8–12.

Meehan, M. L. Career exploration in middle/junior high schools. *Man/Society/Technology,* 1975, *34,* 44–116.

Parker, C., Bunch, S. & Hagberg, R. Group vocational guidance with college students. *Vocational Guidance Quarterly,* 1974, *23,* 168–172.

Roberts, N. J. Establishing a need for a vocational guidance program at the elementary and middle school level. *Elementary School Guidance and Counseling,* 1972, *6,* 252–257.

Schmidt, L. D. Issues in counseling older people. *Educational Gerontology: An International Quarterly,* 1976, *1,* 187–192.

Shapiro, M., & Asher, W. Students who seldom discuss their post high school plans. *School Counselor,* 1972, *20,* 103–108.

Super, D. E. Vocational maturity in mid-career. *Vocational Guidance Quarterly,* 1977, *25,* 294–301.

Tomita, K. Counseling middle-aged and older workers. *Industrial Gerontology,* 1975, *2,* 45–52.

Appendices

The materials in these appendices are central to the contents of this book. Appendices A through G are, for the most part, designed to assist readers in translating their cognitive knowledge into demonstratable counseling skills. Directions for their use may be found at the end of various sections. In particular, students are encouraged to use repeatedly Appendix A, the Taped Interview Format. Practice in this area, regardless of previous training, is likely to improve the student's ability to interview. Appendix H, Additional Information for Items Referred to in the Follow-Up Activities Sections, is included as a convenience for those who wish to order materials previously mentioned in this book.

Appendix A

Taped Interview Format

I Overview

Interviewing is the backbone of counseling. The interview permits the counselor to assess the client's need for counseling and readiness for change. Permitting clients to "tell their story" may perhaps be the most powerful counseling tool we know of. Without regard to philosophical orientation, work setting, or clientele, counselors need to develop good interviewing skills. The most important and basic interview technique, besides silence, is the asking of open-ended questions. Such questions permit the *interviewee* to direct the interview. Open-ended questions do not communicate the counselor's bias or imply a socially preferred response. Open-ended questions start with phrases such as: *How do you feel about . . . ?; Tell me about . . . ;* and *How have things been (on the job)?* The opposite of open-ended questions are closed-ended questions. Such questions as: *Do you like your boss?, Are you satisfied with your salary?,* and *Don't you think that people on welfare, like yourself, should go out and earn a day's pay?* communicate the counselor's bias or preferred response. Questions starting with *why* should also be avoided. Closed-ended questions and questions that start with "Why" tend to place the interviewee on the defensive.

Collecting information about a client's past experiences, present attitudes and values, and future goals are most often necessary *before* a counselor can begin helping the client to make plans for some change. Interviewing is basic to what counselors do. A thorough discussion of interview behavior may be found in A. Ivey and N. Gluckstern, *Basic attending skills* (Participant manual. North Amherst, Massachusetts: Microtraining, 1976).

II Purpose:
Because interviewing is basic to counseling, this activity has been frequently included in the *Learn by Doing* activities which follow each section. The purpose of these exercises is to provide the counselor-trainee with the opportunity to practice interviewing with a wide range of individuals.

III Materials:
Cassette tape recorder. C-40 or C-60 cassette.

IV Procedures:
Many of the assignments require interviews with individuals to whom you may not have easy access. In such circumstances, advance planning will be necessary. It is important to indicate to the interviewee *in advance* that you will tape record the interview. Also indicate that the session should not exceed an hour.

The questions supplied below are *samples* of the type of open-ended questions that are recommended. Good interviewers generate their own questions as a direct function of what the interviewee has said. In many cases you will have to expand these questions in order to obtain the information required in the particular assignment. As you become more comfortable as an interviewer, you will find asking open-ended questions easier.

V Questions:
  A *Sample questions for children and young adults still in school:*
   1 Where do you go to school?
   2 Tell me about the subjects you are taking.
   3 What do you like most about school? Least?
   4 Tell me about your classmates and teacher(s).
   5 In five, ten, or twenty years from now, what would you like to be doing?
   6 What or who has influenced your decision?
   7 What influence have your parents had on your choice?
   8 What influence have your teachers had on your choice?
   9 What influence have your classmates had on your choice?
   10 What's standing in the way of your attaining your goal?
   11 What kind of help have you ever received, or do you expect to receive, from a guidance counselor in making a career choice, or obtaining employment?

B *Sample questions for experienced workers:*
1 What is your job title?
2 Describe a typical day's work.
3 Describe your working conditions.
4 What are your coworkers and boss like?
5 What are the advantages of your present job?
6 What are the disadvantages of your present job?
7 What type of person do you think would enjoy your type of work? Who should avoid it?
8 How did you get into this sort of work?
9 How did you prepare for your present job?
10 What other ways are there for people to prepare for this job?
11 What effect did your parents have on your choice?
12 What effect did your friends have on your choice?
13 What kinds of opportunities for advancement exist for you?
14 What do you see as the employment outlook for people in this field?
15 If your son or daughter wanted to enter this field, how would you feel?
16 If you had it to do all over again, what job would you select?
17 How has a counselor ever helped you in making career decisions?
18 In what ways have you personally *experienced* discrimination on the basis of sex, age, race, national origin, or physical disability?
19 In what ways have you personally *observed* discrimination on the basis of sex, age, race, national origin, or physical disability?
20 What else would you like to add?

C *Sample questions to ask counselors, counseling psychologists, and placement officers:* These questions are intended to *supplement* those listed above.
1 How do you feel about providing vocational guidance as opposed to personal counseling?
2 When an indecisive 18-year-old comes to you for help in making a career decision, what do you do?
3 What role does career awareness have in the elementary school program?
4 What are the obstacles to helping clients make choices and secure employment?
5 If you had a personal problem, whom would you seek for help?
6 If you had a career-related problem, whom would you seek for help?
7 How does what you learned in graduate school compare with what you actually do as a counselor?
8 How does the vocational counseling which you provide differ for the following clients:
   a Children
   b College-bound young adults
   c Noncollege-bound young adults
   d Young adults enrolled in postsecondary education
   e Individuals about to retire

    f Women
    g Men
    h The disadvantaged
    i The disabled
 9 What are the advantages and disadvantages of your present job?
10 What else would you like to add?

Appendix B

What Makes You Tick?

A Purpose

To provide students with an opportunity to scrutinize critically their *values* and *attitudes* toward their present, or a very recent, job.

B Directions:

    1 State your job and write a one-paragraph description of its requirements as though it were appearing as an advertisement in a help-wanted ad. Include job requirements (entry level position), related tasks, and salary range. Identify the exact work setting (name, etc.). Limit to 150 words.

    2 Develop a comprehensive set of criteria by which you can measure or evaluate your present job. Below are several suggestions. Do not consider the suggested list as complete. There are other significant criteria that will have meaning for you.

        a Salary

        b Working conditions

        c Job satisfaction—advantages and disadvantages

        d Benefits

        e Opportunity for advancement

        f Social status

        g Job related tasks, duties, demands, expectations, and responsibilities

        h Job entry requirements

3 Once you have established the criteria you wish to use, deal with them *one at a time as follows:*

   a State the criterion

   b Label a short paragraph with the word "data," and list substantiating facts or data which describe the realities of your situation in relation to this particular criterion. If, for example, you selected "benefits" as the criterion, you would then list under "data" the various benefits your job provides. The amount of data will vary with the particular criterion under consideration.

   c Label another paragraph with the word "evaluation," and *react* on the basis of the data you supplied above. Write in the first person and describe how you *feel* about this situation. In the case of "benefits," discuss what your specific feelings are about the benefits you receive.

   d Upon completion of the discussion for the first criterion, proceed to the second and so forth. It is important to discuss the criteria one at a time.

Appendix C

Career Theory and Practice Worksheet

Read the *entire* question at least twice before beginning—especially before you commit yourself to the choice which you have to make in question 1.

    1 The theory of occupational choice/career development that I have chosen to discuss is:

    2 The name of a prominent theorist who is associated with this theory is:

    3 Which psychometric instrument would reflect or characterize the model you selected in question 1? (If none is available, so indicate and skip to question 5.)

    4 Describe briefly the type of questions asked, the format, scoring, norming characteristics, related facts, etc. of this instrument.

    5 An advantage of this model over others is:

    6 A disadvantage of this model as compared with others is:

    7 Give two facts or tenets about the theory of your choice.

    8 Discuss the practical applications of this model. Specify your intended work setting or clientele.

    9 What about this theory appeals to you?

    10 In terms of your own experience, what aspects of the theory have any applicability? Be specific.

Guidelines for a Case Study*

The Report:

The exact organization of your case study will be influenced by (1) the theory to which you relate your findings, and (2) the availability of information on the individual who serves as the subject of your investigation. The report is to be divided into three parts. It is important to focus on data relevant to the vocational development and aspirations of your subject. While the guidelines are presented in outline form, your case study report should appear in narrative or essay form. The general headings and subheadings which appear in the guidelines should be used to subdivide your presentation. Include only the information called for in each part.

Selection of Subject:

The subject should be at least eighteen years of age. The older and more experienced the subject, the greater the wealth of information available. Do not select a subject with whom there is a close emotional relationship, like a spouse, friend, or sibling. Maintaining objectivity is difficult enough without introducing other variables.

*Source: Adapted from Arthur E. Traxler, *Techniques of Guidance,* © 1957, Harper and Row, New York, and Herbert M. Burks, Jr., "Guidelines for a Case Study in Vocational Development," unpublished. Reprinted with permission.

Selection of Theory:

Select the one *best* theory that fits your *data*. Do not force the data to fit the theory. Bear in mind that theoretical models are imperfect; if they were not, they would be called *facts*.

PART ONE

Background
(Approximate length: 4–8 pages)

I Introduction
  A Identification of subject: name, address, age, sex, marital status, race, occupation
  B Sources of information: behavioral, observations, interviews with subject, interviews with others, examination of records
  C Overview of report: method of organization, salient features
II Personal and social history
  A Early childhood development
  B Body build and general health
  C Dominant values in the home (ideals, goals)
  D Educational and occupational background of parents
  E Nature of relationships with parents
  F Parental aspirations for subject
  G Nature of relationships with siblings
  H Nature of relationship with peers
  I Identification with important figures in environment
  J Other pertinent factors (identify)
III Educational history
  A Schools and colleges attended (including dates)
  B Academic performance
  C Major subjects or curricula
  D Extracurricular activities
  E Social adjustment in school
  F Changes in major field of study
  G Standing (may be estimated) on aptitude tests, interest inventories, etc. related to vocational choice
  H Vocational preferences expressed at various points in school (e.g., ninth grade, twelfth grade, first year of college)
  I Experience with counseling and guidance
  J Other pertinent factors (specify)
IV Personality variables
  A Self-concept (see Super)
  B Dominant traits (see Trait and Factor)
  C Needs (see Roe)
  D Personality type (see Holland)
  E Values (see Decision Making)
  F Other pertinent variables (specify)
V Physical, socioeconomic, and cultural environment

A Description of previous communities and neighborhoods in which subject has lived

B Description of community, neighborhood, and house in which subject now lives

C Other pertinent environmental factors (specify)

VI Vocational history

A Early occupational fantasies

B Early interests, hobbies, play activities

C Part-time jobs, in sequence, including work activities in childhood

D Full-time jobs, in sequence

Note: An attempt should be made to determine what factors led the individual to undertake each of these jobs, including part-time jobs, and why he or she left them in favor of some other activity; also, the particular likes and dislikes found in each job.

E Present interests, hobbies, leisure-time activities

F Subject's evaluation of his or her vocational development

G Present vocational plans and aspirations

VII Relationship to career counseling

A How might career counseling have helped the subject at crucial points in the past?

B In what way might it be of help to the subject now?

PART TWO

Explication of Selected Theory of Career Development/Occupational Choice

(Approximate length 2–3 pages)

A State the name of the one theory which you have chosen which best accounts for the behavior of your subject.

B Describe the major components of your selected theory.

C Discuss the theory's strengths and weaknesses.

PART THREE

The Synthesis

(Approximate length: 2–3 pages)

A Why did you select this particular theory?

B In what ways does it account for the behavior of your subject? Be specific.

C Interpretation and prognosis: On the basis of the vocational development theory to which you wish to relate your findings, what inferences can be made concerning how the individual reached his or her present state of vocational development? What do you see as the subject's prognosis for future vocational development?

D In what ways is your selected theory inadequate (or least adequate) to account for this subject's vocational development?

E In what ways does it not account for the behavior of your subject? Be specific.

F Discuss briefly how other theories might account for certain behaviors previously not accounted for.

Appendix E

Shifting Priorities and New Techniques for Guidance*

The focus of this article is to present a broad view of career guidance possibilities through a look at several proven activities which can be initiated by the career guidance counselor or, where available, the career guidance teacher. Some activities can be implemented by the classroom (or homeroom) teacher after consultation with the counselor. We shall describe the activity, discuss its applicability, and indicate its resource utilization. All the practices have three points in common—they have been tried, they involve limited costs in terms of staff time and materials, and they work!

1. AUTOBIOGRAPHIES

Through a semi-structured creative writing experience, students express their interests, attitudes, and feelings against a background of those events which they feel have made a major impact on their lives. Photographs and drawings may be included, since youngsters are often better able to express themselves visually than verbally.

*Source: Portions reprinted with permission of the publisher from Impact, 1973, 2(2), 4–11.

Purpose

Autobiographies provide constructive avenues for students to communicate with one another about themselves and to gain awareness of the similarities and differences of others.

Applicability

This activity can be used with students at all levels. It is frequently used with those entering junior and senior high school to provide helpful insights about the new student to the staff. It is very low-cost in terms of staff time and resources.

Guidelines

    1   The focus of the autobiography should be geared to the developmental level of the students.

    2   There should be enough structure to focus in on key areas suggested by the counselor, but not so much as to prohibit a high degree of self-expression.

    3   Autobiographies should not be critically evaluated but should be shared with other class members.

    4   Autobiographies should be maintained in folders, filed according to major areas of interest, and housed in the counselor's office (or adjacent materials area) after completion of use by class members. There they will be available to other students who may browse through files of those with interests similar to their own.

2. BUSINESS AND INDUSTRY VISITS

Business and industry visits provide students with the opportunity to observe workers in their functional settings and, if carefully organized, can be valuable learning experiences. Since much of the world of work is removed from public view and there is little opportunity to actually get behind the scenes, the perceptions students have about various kinds of work may have developed from limited information that might be quite unrealistic and inaccurate.

Purpose

Business and industry visits provide students with direct contact with the world of work and can motivate them to further explore their future in it.

Applicability

This activity is relevant to students at all grade levels. Elementary students can learn how different people earn their living while senior high or community college students can utilize the information gained to make tentative vocational choices. These visits are potentially very advantageous to the disadvantaged since they provide them with an opportunity to observe and interact with positive role models, and, hopefully, provide needed stimulation and encouragement. Field trips require considerable staff time and coordination and usually involve teachers, counselors and parents. However, once the trips themselves are planned, most business and industries take over with trained tour personnel, special exhibits, displays and films.

Guidelines:

1   Counselors working with students should determine what businesses or industries are available for site visits. A list of available companies should then be circulated among teachers and counselors.

2   Field visits should encompass as wide as possible a range of occupations.

3   From junior high on, students should play an active role in determining the businesses and industries to be visited so these visits are in accordance with their interests and needs.

4   The group involved and the purposes to be accomplished by the visit should be carefully considered. Elementary students would benefit most from a broad overview of those occupations most frequently encountered in the local community. For juniors in a high school vocational curriculum, tours should focus on working conditions, tools and equipment utilized, specific work processes, company organizations, entrance requirements, opportunities for advancement, pay, etc.

5   Students should understand the purposes of the visit and get as much information as possible beforehand so they can determine what they should watch for so the trip will be meaningful to them.

6   The business or industry to be visited should know ahead of time of the nature of the group and the purpose of the trip in order to make the trip meet the students' needs.

7   If possible, students should interact with and observe workers in order to obtain an understanding of their attitudes and perceptions.

8   All field visits should be followed up as soon as possible. The group should share observations, perceptions and reactions. The field trip should also be followed up with a detailed study of the occupation or industry through classroom and guidance activities.

3. COMMUNITY RESOURCE SURVEY

Through actual interviews with local people in various work settings, students develop a current, highly relevant picture of the local job market as well as an up-to-date card file of resource people in a variety of occupations. For this survey, the counselor should first compile a list of people in the community or nearby town who are willing to be interviewed by students to provide them with a first hand description of their occupations. In developing an index, counselors can start in their immediate work environment with such people as members of the faculty, the principal, maintenance and secretarial personnel. Parents and ex-graduates are also potential resources. Membership listings of local chamber of commerce and union groups are also excellent sources. At the elementary level, the work can be done by student personnel workers, while at the secondary level it can be made into a project wherein students themselves are actively involved.

Purpose

The Resource Survey provides for involvement on the part of students and members of the community in the area of career exploration. By developing a cadre of local people willing to speak to students interested in their area of employment, the activity accomplishes two objectives: (1) it personalizes and opens wide the doors of career exploration by tapping community resources, and (2) it involves students in a project *by* themselves and *for* themselves.

Applicability

This activity can be implemented at all school levels, in all types of communities. At the elementary level, it might require more staff time although even young children enjoy 'interviewing' parents, neighbors and relatives. Elementary school staff members could make contact with those community persons unavailable to the children, while at the secondary levels, students would undertake most of the contacts themselves. While the survey requires considerable initial planning on the part of the staff, the file can be developed and updated with minimum financial costs.

Guidelines:

1   A letter should first be sent to potential resource people explaining the purpose of the interview as it relates to the total career guidance program.

2   A brief questionnaire can elicit the desired information regarding type of job, where individuals can be contacted, etc. This can then be put on a 3 x 5 card for filing.

3   To maximize the effectiveness of such an approach, student knowledge of the system should be widespread.

4   The file can be placed in the materials area and thus be readily accessible for perusal by any student, or it may be utilized as a supplemental tool in career exploration wherein the counselor may suggest setting up an appointment with an individual listed in the file for a student interested in exploring a particular occupational area.

5   Periodic updating is a must to ascertain whether resource persons are still interested in continuing as consultants, and to increase the number of resource people through additional community contacts.

4. AUDIOTAPE INTERVIEWS WITH WORKERS

Going a step beyond the Resource Survey, live interviews with persons actually engaged in specific forms of work give students, at all levels, first hand knowledge not only of the job itself but of the way in which the worker perceives that job. Depending on their developmental level, the youngsters involved might: (1) plan for the interview by deciding what questions they feel are of importance to their age groups; (2) make the necessary arrangements with workers for the interviews; (3) conduct the interviews; (4) manage the equipment; and (5) edit and file the final tape for use by other students interested in the job area.

Purpose

Audiotaping interviews with workers on their jobs provides direct experiential learning for students of all ages in helping them gain understandings of specific jobs as well as of the workers' attitudes toward their jobs.

Applicability

Live interviews can be a valuable resource tool which involves students at all age levels. Younger students can familiarize themselves with broad aspects of various occupations and the settings in which they occur, while older ones can gain more specific information about particular jobs in terms of training requirements, work characteristics, job descriptions, and employment opportunities—local and otherwise. Live interviews are a particularly viable guidance resource in working with disadvantaged students—educationally, socially and physically—because they can provide positive role models with which the youngsters can interact. Unlike the other suggested activities, this approach does require a considerable degree of staff involvement in planning, coordination and taping, particularly at the lower levels. Depending on the taping equipment already available, it may also entail a modest outlay of funds.

Guidelines:

1   This activity should be coordinated by a counselor or vocational educa-tor with expertise in the area of occupational information.

2   Depending on the developmental level of the student group, the coun-selor should involve them in determining the scope of occupations to be covered given the availability of time and local resource persons.

3   The counselor should then contact, by means of a brief descriptive letter, local places of employment to determine what individuals would be willing to be interviewed.

4   The basic structure of the interview should be prepared in advance, and might include how the worker spends his day on the job, advantages and disad-vantages of the job, working conditions, etc. Students should be encouraged to input their ideas as to what they want to know about a job.

5   The content of the interviews should be geared to the developmental level of the students.

6   If possible, the interview should take place on the actual work site so a more realistic picture of the job will emerge.

7   The tapes should be readily available for the students to listen to, and opportunities should be provided for follow up discussions of reactions to them.

8   In keeping with the desire to provide the disadvantaged with positive role models, care should be taken not to present them in stereotyped work roles.

5. CAREER LOGS

Through keeping a "self-record" of abilities, values, interests, work experience, etc., over a period of time, a student can gain insights which help him develop career goals. The log also provides an opportunity for the student to hypothesize about any exploratory occupational interest he may have.

Purpose

Over a period of years a career log can provide a pattern that highlights how one has changed and grown as a result of experiences. This information can be most helpful in deciding future goals.

Applicability

This technique lends itself to use at the junior high through post high school levels. It is potentially very helpful to women as it provides a means to focus on patterns of career development. It can be initiated by either teachers or counselors and is a low-cost item in terms of human and non-human resources needed.

Guidelines:

   1   The purpose of the career log should be carefully explained so students can see its relevance to career development.

   2   The counselor or teacher should suggest basic areas to be covered in the log—e.g. what I enjoy doing most, work experience, thoughts on values etc. Enough flexibility should be left so each student can make those entries which are most meaningful to him.

   3   Students should discuss their logs with counselors during individual or group counseling sessions as they may prove to be helpful in important decision-making, such as deciding on a high school or post high school program. Career logs should be carefully evaluated at this juncture.

6. SCHOOL EMPLOYMENT SERVICE

Providing students with work experience at a relatively young age is based upon the developmental principle that a child's early experiences will influence his thinking and behavior when the same task or a similar one later presents itself. The opportunity to learn about the rules of work through simulated job experiences are, for elementary school children, vocational development opportunities of major importance which will later influence reactions to work and work-related situations.

Purpose

Establishing an "employment agency" within a school whereby students can apply for, and work at available jobs provides a variety of simulated work situations which can enlarge and broaden student's perceptions by acquainting them with the following: (1) applying for work, (2) filling out applications, (3) interviewing, and (4) performing a variety of work roles.

Applicability

This approach has been used most extensively with elementary school students but it can be adapted to use with junior high school students as well. It can be organized at a minimum cost, but does require a teacher and/or counselor time for planning, organization and implementation.

Guidelines:

   1   Prior to implementation the counselor should determine the kinds of jobs available, qualifications for specific jobs, interview and selection procedures, time limits for jobs, job transfer procedures, employment rules and regulations, etc.

   2   The counselor and the student should develop necessary materials such as job advertisements, application forms, etc.

   3   Scheduling procedures which permit students to leave classes to perform jobs must be agreed upon—cooperation by teachers, counselors and administrators.

   4   A decision must be made initially as to whether there will be a reward system to recognize student job performance.

5 Employment Service publicity must be widespread in the school so all students are aware of its existence.

6 All students should be encouraged to participate lest it be felt that only the more generally involved students are welcome in the effort.

7 The Employment Service should be supplemented by related classroom guidance activities, such as learning how to fill out applications, developing appropriate interviewing behaviors, etc.

8 This activity should be periodically evaluated by faculty and students to make improvements and necessary modifications.

REFERENCES

American Values. Social Studies. Secondary Education. Honolulu: Office of Instructional Services, Hawaii State Department of Education, 1971. ED 056 918 MF-$0.65 HC-$3.29

Barr, Robert D. (Ed.) *Values and Youth.* Washington, D.C.: National Council for the Social Studies, 1971.

Employment of High School Graduates and Dropouts, October 1971. Special Labor Force Report 145. U.S. Department of Labor, Bureau of Labor Statistics. 1972.

Erlick, A. C. *Vocational Plans and Preferences of Adolescents.* Report of Poll 94, The Purdue Opinion Panel, Purdue University, 31(2), 1972.

Furner, Beatrice A. "Creative Writing for Self-Understanding: Approaches and Outcomes." (Speech presented at Annual Convention of the National Council of Teachers of English, 1970) ED 052 184 MF-$0.65 HC-$3.29

A Guide for Teachers of a Course in Career Exploration, Grades 8-9-10. Stillwater: Oklahoma Vocational Research Coordinating Unit, 1970. ED 049 356 MF-$0.65 HC-$6.58

Hansen, Lorraine Sundal; and Others. *Career Guidance Practices in School and Community.* BR-6-2487, Ann Arbor, Mich.: ERIC Clearinghouse and Counseling and Personnel Services, 1970. ED 037 595 MF-$0.65 HC-$6.58

Kosuth, Joan, and Miltenberger, Jerry. *Teaching for Career Decision-Making.* Diversified Counseling Services, 13461 Elizabeth Way, Tustin, Cal., 1972.

Lee, Jasper S. *Occupational Orientation: An Introduction to the World of Work.* State College: Mississippi Research Coordinating Unit for Vocational-Technical Education; Jackson: Division of Vocational and Technical Education, Mississippi State Department of Education, 1971. ED 057 235 MF-$0.65 HC-$9.87

Miller, Juliet V. *Intensive High School Occupational Guidance Approaches for Initial Work and Technical School Placement.* Ann Arbor, Mich.: ERIC Clearinghouse on Counseling and Personnel Services, 1969. ED 033 254 MF-$0.65 HC-$3.29

Zimpfer Ruff, Eldon E. (Dir.) *The Indiana Career Resource Center: A Total Community Approach to Career Guidance.* South Bend: Indiana University, 1971.

Guidelines for the Systematic Selection, Evaluation, and Use of Simulated Vocational Guidance Materials*

The purpose of this article is to help counselors make better use of simulated materials. In order to do this, I will provide (1) a rationale for their use; (2) guidelines for their selection and evaluation; and (3) strategies designed to increase their impact on the counseling experience.

WHAT DOES "SIMULATED" MEAN?

Simulated refers to *any experience or activity which is designed to provide clients with an opportunity to practice, imitate, or model specified behaviors or increase clients' awareness or knowledge about specified guidance-related topics. The materials may include any kind of media, such as kits, filmstrips, cassettes, games, etc., or activities, such as role playing, structured group experiences, psychodrama, etc. The use of such materials is designed to elicit the active involvement of the user. This*

*Source: The original article, upon which this revision is based, is Stephen G. Weinrach, "Guidelines for the Systematic Selection, Evaluation and Use of Simulated Guidance Materials," *Personnel and Guidance Journal,* 1978, Vol. 56, No. 5, pp 288–292. Copyright 1978 American Personnel and Guidance Association. This article deals with guidance materials in *general.* The present article is limited to vocational guidance, and portions are reprinted with the permission of the author and publisher. Both articles are based upon the National Vocational Guidance Association's (1977) "Guidelines for the Preparation and Evaluation of Non-Print Career Media."

definition is intentionally very broad. It includes all print and nonprint devices or strategies other than the traditional verbal techniques associated with interviewing that elicit active client participation.

WHAT IS THE ROLE OF SIMULATED MATERIALS IN THE TOTAL SCOPE OF GUIDANCE SERVICES?

Simulated materials can provide the counselor with a wider range of resources. The use of simulated materials serves the following functions: First, simulated materials serve to stimulate discussion through increasing a client's awareness to a particular issue. As such, the materials can be used *prescriptively.* Counselors diagnose the client's need and select the appropriate simulated activity. A student who is unable to choose between an elective in small-appliance repair or plumbing would be given the appropriate *Job Experience Kits* (Krumboltz, 1970). Second, simulated materials can be used in the dissemination of highly specific information which would otherwise take the counselor hours to research. Computer-based occupational information programs and microfiche informational systems are two examples. Third, the use of these materials can provide clients with a nonthreatening, secure, and accurate vehicle for their exploration of sensitive topics such as human sexuality, academic requirements for admission into institutions of higher education, or personal health. By providing clients with access to information through cassettes or film loops, clients do not need to deal with their counselor's reaction to their concern. Some types of information are just better disseminated privately.

Fourth, the use of simulated materials can provide a mechanism whereby clients can practice certain new skills in a structured environment. Role playing and structured group experiences are examples. An excellent source of such exercises is *Structured Experiences* by J. William Pfeiffer and John E. Jones (1977). And fifth, the use of these materials can free the counselor to attend to other tasks which cannot be easily replaced with simulated materials. Simulated materials, besides providing a better alternative to direct counselor intervention, give the counselor additional time to work with those clients where simulation may not be indicated.

HOW DO I SELECT SIMULATED MATERIALS?

Counselors should carefully inspect the catalogues and advertisements they routinely receive, and indicate which sets of materials *might* interest them. Responsible publishers will permit counselors to either borrow materials or purchase them on approval. Unless a counselor is replacing a worn-out package with an identical item, there are probably very few situations where purchasing materials outright without first subjecting them to an extensive prepurchase evaluation would be in order. The materials of uncooperative publishers should be avoided.

With the exception of inexpensive purchases, it is unwise to rely solely on reviews in respected journals like *The School Counselor,* the *Vocational Guidance Quarterly,* or the *Personnel and Guidance Journal.* Reviewers for these journals report their experiences in the use of specific items in *their* work settings. Unless your work setting is identical, it is extremely difficult to generalize from their findings. It is crucial that the potential purchaser evaluate the materials with the specific intended audience in mind.

Common sense should prevail. It takes a considerable amount of time to apply these guidelines. It is one thing to devote five to ten hours of counselor time for the evaluation of a $5000 set of color videotape cassettes and something else to spend the same amount of time reviewing a $100 kit. As a matter of fact, for purchases under $50, purchasers should save their time, take their chances, and make intelligent predictions based upon reviews in respected journals.

The use of simulated materials is just one type of counselor intervention. As with other types of interventions, some work better than others. The counselor's job is to determine *which* interventions work with *which* clients. The effectiveness of simulated materials depends on a number of factors, such as the nature of the intended audience, its readiness for activity, and the thoroughness of its presentations and follow-up.

HOW DO I BEGIN THE EVALUATION PROCESS?

Follow these three steps: (1) using the criteria and checklist presented in this article, evaluate the materials; (2) if the materials are judged satisfactory, determine if the cost of the materials is reasonable for what is being provided (discrepancies do exist among publishers; sometimes a particular kit is disproportionately priced for its contents); and (3) experiment with the materials and determine how clients—the ultimate consumers—respond.

Since the most important consumer of the materials will be clients, they should play a major role in the review process. Counselors and clients, if they are old and mature enough, should review the evaluative criteria together. The clients should then work through the simulated materials. Counselors should observe how the clients are reacting *during* the process. When the clients are finished, there should be a debriefing session wherein the counselors seek to determine how the clients felt about and what they learned from the experience. The formal review process can then commence with the completion of the rating sheet.

THE COUNSELOR'S ROLE IN THE USE OF SIMULATED MATERIALS

Thus far I have described the role of simulated materials in the total guidance program and the process whereby such materials can be systematically evaluated prior to purchase. I will now discuss the counselor's role in the *use* of such materials.

The integration of a new simulated activity into a counselor's repertoire is no different than the integration of a new behavioral strategy or a gestalt technique. Counselors have always listened to what their clients were saying and not saying, and then asked themselves "What can I do to help this client?" The purpose of this article is to encourage counselors to consider the use of simulated materials

Name of reviewer: _____ Date: _____

This is a review of: _____

Publisher: _____ Price: _____

Our intended audience is: _____

	Appropriateness for intended audience		
	Low	**Average**	**High**
A. Content:			
1. Explicit statement of purpose	_____	_____	_____
2. Integrity of title	_____	_____	_____
3. Realistic objectives	_____	_____	_____
4. Accurate, adequate and realistic presentation of ideas, concepts or information	_____	_____	_____
5. Eliciting of user response	_____	_____	_____
B. Technical considerations:			
1. Packaging	_____	_____	_____
2. Credits	_____	_____	_____
3. Technical qualities	_____	_____	_____
4. Length	_____	_____	_____
C. User's Guide:			
1. Credits	_____	_____	_____
2. Purpose, objectives and intended audience	_____	_____	_____
3. Description	_____	_____	_____
4. Results of field testing	_____	_____	_____
5. Follow-up activities	_____	_____	_____
D. Social Orientation:			
1. Sex/age/occupational role bias	_____	x x x*	_____
2. Ethnic/race and religious bias	_____	x x x	_____
3. Value orientation, social status and self-serving purposes	_____	x x x	_____

*Either media are bias-free or they are not.

Figure 1   Reviewer's rating sheet.

E. Summary:

   1. The major strengths of this product for our population are:

   2. The major weaknesses of this product for our population are:

   3. Unusual or unique characteristics of the product:

   4. On the basis of the result of this review, I recommend that:

when answering that question. Like any counseling technique, differential diagnosis is necessary in the matching of client concern with simulated experience. It is the counselor's responsibility to be completely familiar with the various simulation experiences available. That means knowing how they work, how clients in the past have reacted, and what obstacles to completion are likely to be encountered. The counselor then needs to present the client with the option of participating. The decision should be the client's. Once a client agrees, the counselor or a paraprofessional needs to be available to supervise or oversee the client's progress. The amount of supervision is dependent both on the client's ability and on the level of difficulty of the simulated experience.

Counselors may think that counseling begins *and* ends with matching the client with a simulated guidance activity. Simulated materials serve to generate discussion, increase awareness, and help clients ask better questions. When a simulated activity is completed, counseling *continues* with such typical counselor behaviors as follow-up interviews, responding to client concerns, and helping clients integrate their previous simulated experiences into the total counseling relationship.

Developmental guidance activities are designed to meet the ongoing or anticipated needs of clients in a preventive manner. Typical developmental concerns are interpreting standardized test scores, getting ready for junior high school, and how to apply to college. The developmental approach to group vocational guidance provides many opportunities for the counselor to integrate simulated materials. Most of the commercially prepared materials are designed for group rather than individual use.

Evaluative Criteria

A Content
This section deals with the content or purpose of the simulated materials. Reviewers need to make some independent decisions about the validity of the content. Users need to ask themselves: What are our needs? What needs will the item under consideration fill? Look for:

1 *Explicit statement of purpose*
Users should know within the first few minutes what is expected of them and what is the purpose of the activity. It is important that users are provided an accurate and early mind set so as to faciliate maximal benefit from the activity. In some cases, postponing the explication of purpose of the activity is necessary and beneficial so as to increase client readiness.

2 *Integrity of title*

Publishers have been known to repackage, retitle, and reissue outdated materials. The title should reflect the purpose and content of the media. (The word "media" refers to all types of simulated materials.)

3 *Realistic objectives*
All media will not meet the needs of all clients. The activities should be consistent with the objectives. Be sure objectives are appropriate for the intended audience. It is unlikely that any media will meet the psychoeducational needs of clients whose ages range from kindergarten to postsecondary education.

4 *Accurate and complete presentation of concepts and/or information*
Ideas, information, and concepts should be presented at a vocabulary level commensurate with that of the intended audience. Technical terms should be defined in the media as well as in the user's guide. Occupational information should be up-to-date, accurate, and complete. It is essential that the occupations be presented as credible. Media which deal exclusively with conveying information about a specific occupation, as opposed to issues relating to career development in general, should include the following (National Vocational Guidance Association, 1977):
a Work performed
b Work settings
c Potential personal rewards
d Entry requirements and advancement possibilities
e Related occupations and career alternatives
f Credential requirements and union/professional affiliations
g Occupational outlook in terms of short- and long-range conditions

5 *Eliciting of user response*
It is important for the media to elicit active user participation. Unlike conventional television, which is devoted to passive entertainment,

media should make provision for involving the user. As a result of using a simulated guidance activity, clients should be able to *do* something.

B Technical Considerations
Of the four areas being evaluated, producers are usually the strongest in the technical area. This is their business. It is necessary to determine the extent to which the media live up to high technical standards for that industry. Look for:

1 *Packaging*
Have you ever dropped the contents and had to spend hours figuring out what was missing? Packaging should stand up to physical abuse. After all, that is what anything frequently used is in for. Films, film-strips, videotapes, and reel-to-reel audiotapes should have their titles clearly printed and easily read on leader tape. This will protect valuable footage in the process of threading and also make indentification easier.

2 *Credits*
Those who have contributed to the production of the media, and their educational or experiential credentials that qualify them as experts should be clearly listed. It is reasonable to expect producers to employ qualified experts to assist in the producation of media. In addition, the copyright date, name of producer, and source of funding should be stated.

3 *Technical qualities*
Whether the media be print or nonprint, it is necessary to evaluate the technical manufacturing or production quality. If it is a video product, to what extent is the picture clear and crisp? If audio, how clear is the tone? If it is a kit, how well designed are its components?

C *User's Guide*
You should be able to take a user's guide home and prepare for the use of a simulated guidance activity without having to see the entire film, play the entire game, or role-play every sequence. That is what the user's guide is for. Guides need to be complete, documented, and functional. Look for:

1 *Credits*
See entry under B (Technical Considerations) above.

2 *Purpose, objectives, and intended audience*
See entry under A (Content section) above. The user's guide is the one place where, regardless of the type of simulation, the purpose, objectives, and intended audience should be made clear. Ideally, one should be able to evaluate the user's guide so as to determine the

appropriateness of the purpose and objectives. In reality, one needs to inspect both the user's guide *and* the media. Note discrepancies.

3 *Description*
Each user's guide should include an accurate and complete synopsis or description of the simulated experience, how it works, and what the expected outcomes are.

4 *Results of field testing*
Indeally, simulated materials will have been thoroughly field-tested and the results reported in the user's guide.

5 *Follow-up activities*
This is the most important component of the user's guide. Counselors need to be provided with concrete and appropriate follow-up activities which will assist the client in integrating the simulated experience with real-life expereinces. A bibliography of related sources of information should also be included.

D Social orientation
This section is concerned with the need for bias-free materials. NVGA (1977) is to be credited with the inclusion of this criterion in the evaluation of career materials. *No matter how technically competent, well packaged, and conceptually legitimate a product is, unless it is free of bias, it is unworthy of use.* Simulated materials lacking in a high social orientation would also be deficient in their objectives and accurate presentation of information. It is the responsibility of the producers to insure their materials against bias. It is not sufficient for materials to reflect the status quo. Unfortunately, our culture is not bias-free. The materials we present should represent an ideal toward which we as a culture can strive. This means that tokenism is not to be tolerated. There are biases which will appear in simulated materials. Look for:

1 *Sex/age/occupational role bias*
This includes portrayal according to traditional sex, age, or occupational role. In addition to presenting appropriate role models, the simulated materials should not have differential expectations for male and female participants. Stereotype roles should be avoided in role-played situations unless they are being used as negative role models in assertiveness training. Furthermore, the materials should avoid the use of the male singular pronoun, "he," in a generic sense. The use of "they" or "he or she," is appropriate.

2 *Ethnic, race, and religious bias*
Our culture is multiracial and multiethnic. The materials we use and the games and activities we expose our clients to should reflect this diversity.

3 *Value orientation, social status, and self-serving purposes*

Materials should be value-free. This means that clients should be presented a wide range of alternatives and encouraged to choose for themselves. Materials produced by special interest groups which attempt to influence the decision of the participant should be avoided. This often occurs when the production of the materials has been financed by a trade association, religious organization, or special interest groups, such as the military. Materials should be devoid of any explicit or implied social status bias.

REFERENCES

Krumboltz, J., *Job experience kits,* work simulations. Chicago: Science Research Associates, 1970.

National Vocational Guidance Association, *Guidelines for the preparation and evaluation of career information media.* Washington, D.C.: American Personnel and Guidance Association Press, (mimeograph), 1971.

National Vocational Guidance Association, NVGA Guidelines for Preparation and Evaluation of Non-Print Career Media, *Vocational Guidance Quarterly,* 1977, *26*(2), 99–107.

Pfeiffer, J. W., & Jones, J. E., *Structured Experiences,* 2nd edition, 6 volumes, University Associates, 1977.

Weinrach, S. G., Guidelines of the systematic selection, evaluation and use of simulated guidance materials. *Personnel and Guidance Journal,* 1978, *56*(5), 288–292.

APPENDIX G

Format for Abstracts

1 Title
2 Author(s)
3 Source
4 Date of publication
5 List of the basic tenets or ideas presented
6 List of at least three implications for the *practice* of vocational guidance
7 Advantages, disadvantages, and possible obstacles to the implementation of the author's ideas
8 What you would do differently after becoming acquainted with the author's ideas
9 Personal reactions

Appendix H   Additional Information for Items Referred to in the Follow-up Activities

Publisher/distributor	Title	Year	Media	Ordering information
American Personnel and Guidance Association 1607 New Hampshire Ave., N.W. Washington, D.C. 20009	Back to School, Back to Work	1973	16mm color film and leader's guide leader's guide (only)	77540 72051 77568
	The Mature Woman	1977	16mm color film	
American Telephone and Telegraph, c/o any local Bell Telephone Business Office	Anything You Want to Be	1975	16mm color film	Order by title
Consulting Psychologists Press 577 College Avenue Palo Alto, CA 94306	The Self-Directed Search	1977	Interest survey	Specimen Set
The Center for Humanities Two Holland Avenue White Plains, NY 10606	Conflict in American Values: Life Style vs. Standard of Living	1973	Slides; records or cassettes; teacher's guide	0242-0750
	Man and Woman: Myths and Stereotypes	1975	Slides; records or cassettes; teacher's guide	0267-0750
Current Affairs Films 24 Danbury Road Wilton, Conn. 06897	The Work Ethic: A Victim of Progress	1974	Filmstrip; cassette; discussion guide	430
Guidance Associates 757 Third Avenue New York, NY 10017	Career Awareness Field Trips	1974 and 1975	Filmstrip; records or cassette; discussion guide	8A-302-933

Appendix H. (cont.)

Publisher/distributor	Title	Year	Media	Ordering information
Guidance Asosciates (cont.)	*Career Choices: A Lifelong Process*	1976	Filmstrip; records or cassette; discussion guide	8A-103-232
	Career Values: What Really Matters to You	1974	Filmstrip; records or cassette; discussion guide	8A-102-754
	Careers and Lifestyles	1974	Filmstrip; records or cassette; discussion guide	8A-101-350
	The Changing Work Ethic	1973	Filmstrip; records or cassette; discussion guide	8A-100-378
	College? It's Up to You	1972	Filmstrip; records or cassette; discussion guide	8A-100-139
	Different Ways to Go to College	1971	Filmstrip; records or cassette; discussion guide	8A-103-414
	Job Attitudes	1970 and 1971	Filmstrip; records or cassette; discussion guide	8A-100-295
Hart Publishing Company 15 West 4th Street New York City, NY 10012	*Values Clarification—A Handbook of Practical Strategies for Teachers and Students* by Sidney B. Simon, Leland W. Howe, and Howard Kirschenbaum	1972	Paperback book., 397 pages	Order by title

Appendix H. (cont.)

Publisher/distributor	Title	Year	Media	Ordering information
Houghton-Mifflin Company 1 Beacon Street Boston, MASS 02107	*Work Values Inventory*	1968	Values survey	**Specimen set** 974033
Parker Brothers 190 Bridge Street Salem, MASS 01970	Monopoly	1975	Board game	9
	Careers	1976	Board game	66
The Psychological Corporation 757 Third Avenue New York, NY 10017	Strong-Campbell Interest Inventory (SCII)	1974	Interest survey	**Specimen set** 9-951823
Science Research Associates (SRA) 259 East Erie Street Chicago, Ill. 60611	*Introducing Career Concepts* Series 1: (grades 5-7)	1975	Kit	Specimen set, 5-4329
	Series 2: (grades 7-9)		Kit	Specimen set, 5-4330
	Job Experience Kits	1970	Kit and discussion guide	5-4000
	KEYS—Career Exploration	1972	Filmstrip, cassettes, and discussion guide	5-3050

Appendix H. (cont.)

Publisher/distributor	Title	Year	Media	Ordering information
Science Research Associates (cont.)	*Kuder Form E General Interest Survey*	1971	Interest survey	Specimen set for consumable materials, 7-3415
	Kuder Form DD Occupational Interest Survey	1966	Interest survey	Specimen set, 7-3687
Stuart Finley, Inc. 3428 Mansfield Road Falls Church, VA 22041	*Jobs*	1976	16mm color film	Order by title

Index